Bob's Essential RV Resort Directory

A Comprehensive Directory of Over 1,000 Personally Curated RV Parks, Resorts & Campgrounds of the Continental United States

By

Robert Nichols

Copyrighted Material

Copyright © 2019 – *Valley Of Joy Publishing Press*

All Rights Reserved.

No part of this publication may be reproduced, stored in a retrieval system or transmitted in any form or by any means, electronic, mechanical, photocopying, recording or otherwise without the proper written consent of the copyright holder, except brief quotations used in a review.

Published by:

Valley Of Joy Publishing Press

Cover & Interior designed

By

Jessica Simms

First Edition

Table of Contents

INTRODUCTION 4

ALABAMA 7

Northern Alabama 8

Central Alabama 12

Southern Alabama 14

ARIZONA 22

Northwest Arizona 23

Northeast Arizona 30

Southeast Arizona 31

Southwest Arizona 36

ARKANSAS 50

Arkansas – The Ozarks 51

Arkansas – River Valley 53

Arkansas – Central and Delta 54

Arkansas - Ouachitas and Timberlands 55

CALIFORNIA 57

California – North Coast 57

California – Shasta Cascade 62

California – San Francisco Bay Area 66

California – Central Valley 69

California – Gold Country 75

California – High Sierra 77

California – Central Coast 79

California – Los Angeles and Orange County 83

California – Inland Empire 85

California – San Diego County 91

COLORADO 94

Northern Colorado 94

Southern Colorado 98

CONNECTICUT 104

DELAWARE 107

FLORIDA 110

Florida – Northwest 111

Florida – Northeast 117

Florida – Central West 123

Florida – Central 138

Florida – Central East 149

Florida – Southwest 154

Florida – Southeast 163

GEORGIA 167

Northern Georgia 168

Southern Georgia 172

IDAHO 178

Idaho – Western 179

Eastern Idaho 184

ILLINOIS 188

INDIANA 192

Northern Indiana 193

Southern Indiana 196

IOWA 198

KANSAS 201

KENTUCKY 205

LOUISIANA 209

MAINE 215

Maine – Northern 216

Maine - Southern 219

MARYLAND 226

MASSACHUSETTS 228

MICHIGAN 233

Michigan – Upper Peninsula 234

Michigan – North 236

Michigan – Central 239

Michigan – South 241

MINNESOTA ... 244
Minnesota – North ... 245
Minnesota – South ... 248

MISSISSIPPI ... 250
Mississippi – East ... 251
Mississippi – West ... 256

MISSOURI ... 258
Missouri – North ... 259
Missouri – Central ... 262
Missouri – Southwest ... 264
Missouri – Southeast ... 267

MONTANA ... 268
Montana - Glacier Country ... 268
Montana – Eastern ... 272

NEBRASKA ... 277

NEVADA ... 280
Nevada – Reno/Tahoe Area ... 281
Nevada – North ... 284
Nevada – South ... 286

NEW HAMPSHIRE ... 290
New Hampshire – North ... 291
New Hampshire - South ... 295

NEW JERSEY 297

NEW MEXICO 303
New Mexico – North 304
New Mexico – Central 308
New Mexico – South 310

NEW YORK 314
New York – West 314
New York – North 319
New York – Central 322
New York – South 325

NORTH CAROLINA 327
North Carolina – West 327
North Carolina – Central 332
North Carolina – East 335

NORTH DAKOTA 338

OHIO 340
Ohio – North 341
Ohio – South 346

OKLAHOMA 349
Oklahoma – North 349
Oklahoma – South 354

OREGON 356

Oregon – Coast 356

Oregon – North 364

Oregon – Willamette Valley 366

Oregon – Central 369

Oregon – South 371

Oregon – East 375

PENNSYLVANIA 376

Pennsylvania – North 376

Pennsylvania – South 380

RHODE ISLAND 386

SOUTH CAROLINA 388

SOUTH DAKOTA 394

South Dakota – East 394

South Dakota – West 397

TENNESSEE 401

Tennessee – West 401

Tennessee – East 404

TEXAS 408

Texas – Panhandle 408

Texas – Big Bend 411

Texas – Hill Country 412

Texas – Prairies and Lakes 415

Texas – Piney Woods 418

Texas – Southern Plains 420

Texas – Gulf Coast 424

UTAH 430

VERMONT 433

VIRGINIA 435

WASHINGTON 438

WEST VIRGINIA 441

WISCONSIN 442

WYOMING 444

SPECIAL THANKS 446

CONCLUSION 447

Introduction

This guidebook is a definitive listing for nearly every private RV park and campground in the lower 48 states.

I say "nearly" because I have only included RV parks and resorts that either I have personally stayed at or those that my friends and others in the RV community have recommended to me. I have mostly included parks that allow pets, as many RV enthusiasts travel with their fur babies.

I have been living out of my RV full time since about 2012. At that time, I determined that it was more economical to set out on the road full time after I was laid off from my corporate job.

I am an accountant by trade, and I don't consider myself to be a great writer, but I do like to keep records. This book is a compilation of the cream of the crop of RV parks and resorts.

It just made sense for me to catalog the notes that I have kept in order to share them with other RV enthusiasts and with the world at large

One important note for you to consider: I have not sold any space in this compilation of listings. None of these businesses have paid for their spot in this book. This is not a listing of advertisements. It is not a contest of who could pay the most money to be a part of my catalog of campgrounds.

The businesses I have listed here have been hand-picked and personally curated by my colleagues, who are also a part of the RV lifestyle, and me.

I felt that the campground listing books that are currently on the market are just too commercial and too corporate. What I mean to say is, why not rely upon those who actually enjoy the RV life - those who have personally stayed at these locations, and not just those businesses who can pay to be in a catalog.

Here is how you use this guide:

Each campground, RV park or RV resort is listed in its own table. The tables are organized by geographic area. Most states I have broken the listings into separate areas, so you can more easily find the park you where you want to stay.

The tables are separated into different information that I feel is most important for an RV'er to know when deciding on a park to stay.
In each listing, you'll find:

- Street address
- Phone number
- Website (It will be clickable if you're reading the eBook version.)
- Operating days
- Price
- Discounts
- Maximum width and length of the sites
- The total number of spaces offered
- Road conditions (paved, gravel, dirt)
- Any restrictions (for example, if they have any conditions concerning pets)
- A list of a few of the amenities the site offers

Of course, most campgrounds require advanced reservations, so you should contact them ahead of time to double-check rates and availability.

This information is current as of October 2019. We make no guarantees as to whether or not the establishments are still in business. Due diligence has been performed to the best of our ability to ensure that the info is accurate and correct. As always, if you have questions, you should contact the RV Park or Campground directly.

This is just a guidebook, to attempt to steer you in the right direction.

You may also want to use a map app like Apple Maps, Google Maps, or a Garmin to help you navigate to the correct location. I would assume that most modern RV'ers would have a maps app or GPS device to assist with directions.

Here is an introduction for the way the tables are organized for each listing:

As you can see in this example table, the sections of each table correspond to a specific category.

If any information is blank in the table, that just means that the particular listing does not have that information available (such as a business not having a website).

RV Park or Campground Name

A brief description.

Street Address City, State	Phone Website	Operating Days
Price	Discounts Offered	Restrictions
Spaces	Road Conditions	Width/Length
Amenities	Amenities	Amenities
Amenities	Amenities	Amenities

I hope this listing of RV parks, resorts, and campgrounds is helpful to you. I have been keeping meticulous notes over the years. As I said, I'm an accountant by trade, and keeping records comes as second nature to me.

Enjoy this book, and please don't forget to leave feedback for me – a comment, a review – wherever you purchased this book. I will take those comments to heart to hopefully improve my writing with whatever book I can think of to write next.

Alabama

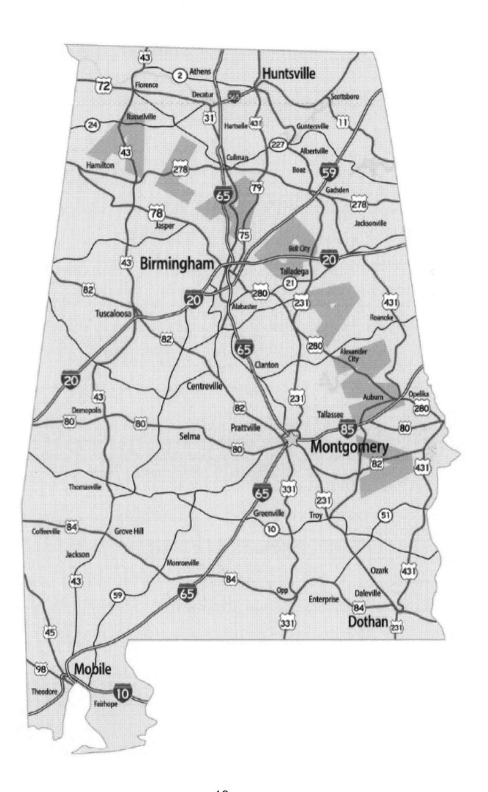

Northern Alabama

Northern Alabama is home to a variety of city sights to see as well as a range of outdoor activities.

Hidden Cove Outdoor Resort

This small but beautiful outdoor park is a wonder of nature. There is plenty of activities in and around the park, so you are sure to find something to keep you busy, or you can just lounge and enjoy nature.

687 County Rd 3919, Arley, AL 35541	(205) 221-7042	All Year
$47	Military Discount	No Pets
63 spaces/16 hookups	Paved/gravel	30W/70L
Internet, Laundry Restrooms, Showers	Ice, Playground, Pool Cabin/Cottage Rentals	Pool, Mini-golf, Pavilion Tables, BBQ, Fire Rings

Cullman Campground

This park is a peaceful place to stay away from traffic and noise.

220 County Road 1185, Cullman, AL 35057	256-734-5853 https://cullman-campground.business.site/	All Year
$32	Military/Good Sam	Pet Breed Restrictions
80 spaces/26 hookups	Paved/Gravel	25W/75L
Internet Showers	Firewood Metered LP Gas	Playground Pavilion

Point Mallard Campground

Larger campground close to the city. It offers long-term stays and plenty of nearby activities in both nature and the city.

2600C Point Mallard Dr. SE, Decatur, AL 35601	256-341-4826 http://www.pointmallardpark.com/	All Year
$33	No Discounts	No Restrictions
233 spaces /119 hookups	Paved/Gravel	25W/60L
Internet, Laundry Restrooms, Showers	Pools, RV Wash Playground, Golf	Horseshoes Recreation Hall

Wills Creek RV Park

Small park with excellent service and standard amenities. A great place to stay for those who love a variety of outdoor activities.

1310 Airport Rd W, Fort Payne, AL 35968	256-845-6703 http://willscreekrvpark.com/	All Year
$28-30	Military/Good Sam	No Restrictions

43 Spaces	Gravel	30W/70L
Internet, Laundry Restrooms, Showers	Firewood, RV Wash Cabin/Cottage/Lodge	Outdoor Games Pavilion, Rec. Hall

Little River RV Park

Small park with your standard amenities and nearby outdoor activities. The perfect place to stay if you want to relax and enjoy a quiet time in nature.

1357 County Road 261, Fort Payne, AL 35967	256-619-2267 http://www.littleriverrvpark.com/	All Year
$27-30	No Discounts	No Restrictions
30 Sites	Gravel	30W/60L
Internet, Laundry Restrooms, Showers	RV Wash Playground	Fire Rings

Seibold Campground

Medium-sized campground with plenty of amenities and even more outdoor activities to enjoy in the surrounding area.

54 Seibold Creek Rd, Guntersville, AL 35976	256-582-0040 http://southsautyresort.com/	March 1 - October 31
$22-27	No Discounts	No Tents
136 Sites	Paved	34W/95L
Restrooms, Showers Gated Access	Pool, Playground Recreation Hall	Tables and BBQ Grills at sites

Quail Creek RV Resort

This park may be small, but it offers beautiful views and plenty of recreational activities.

233 Quail Creek Drive, Hartselle, AL 35640	256-784-5033	All Year
$35	Military/Good Sam	No Restrictions
17 Sites	Gravel	34W/95L
Internet, Laundry, Ice Snack Bar, Golf Carts	Religious Services Pool, Rec. Hall, Pavilion	Game Room, Playground Golf, Fire Rings, Gym

Decatur Wheeler Lake KOA

Smaller KOA campground featuring the standard amenities with lots of activities for people of all ages and interests.

44 CR 443, Hillsboro, AL 35643	256-280-4390 https://koa.com/campgrounds/decatur/	March 1 - November 30
$37-52	No Discounts	No Restrictions
52 Sites	Paved	20W/60L
Internet, Laundry Restrooms, Showers	Cabin/Cottage Rentals Firewood, RV Supplies	Playground, Pavilion Outdoor Games

US Space and Rocket Center Campground

A small campground that puts you near to the US Space and Rocket Center. Great place to visit for families who want a cheap place to visit while taking their kids to see the nearby sites.

1 Tranquility Base, Huntsville, AL 35805	256-837-3400 https://rocketcenter.com/RVPark	All Year
$20-25	No Discounts	No Restrictions
27 Sites	Paved	26W/80L
Internet	Restrooms, Showers	Laundry

Windemere Cove RV Resort

This park has the best of nature to enjoy all around you. Located along the shores of Lake Guntersville, this is a great place for water enthusiasts. Plus there are plenty of places of interest nearby so you'll never be short on activities.

10174 County Road 67, Langston, AL 35755	256-228-3010 https://www.windemerecove.com/	All Year
$35-45	Good Sam Discount	RV Age, Pet Quantity
106 Sites	Paved	40W/80L
Internet, Laundry, Ice Restrooms, Showers	Gated Access, Pool Rec. Hall, RV Wash	Pavilion, Gym Patios at Sites

South Sauty Creek Resort

A smaller sized resort with above-average amenities. There are lots of outdoor activities to enjoy while staying at this resort.

6845 S Sauty Rd, Langston, AL 35755	256-582-6157	All Year
$22	No Discounts	No Restrictions
86 Sites	Paved/Gravel	24W/60L
Restrooms, Showers, Ice Groceries, Restaurant	Cabin/Cottage/Lodge Rentals, Pool	Fire Rings Picnic Tables

Heritage Acres RV Park

An easy to access park, designed to handle the larger rigs. With plenty of activities to do in and around the area, this is the most convenient and enjoyable park to stay at in the area.

1770 Neil Morris Rd, Tuscumbia, AL 35674	256-383-7368 http://www.heritageacresrvpark.com/	All Year
$30-35	Military/Good Sam	Pet Quantity, Pet Breed
61 Sites	Gravel	30W/90L
Internet, Laundry Restrooms, Showers	RV Supplies Ice, Cable	RV Wash Metered LP Gas

Parnell Creek RV Park

This green RV park offers eco-friendly accommodations with plenty of activities for the whole family to enjoy.

115 Parnell Cir, Woodville, AL 35776	256-508-7308	All Year
$27-32	Good Sam Discount	No Restrictions
46 Sites	Gravel	24W/50L
Internet, Ice, Laundry RV Supplies, Firewood	Groceries, Pool, Games Playground, Pavilion	Mini Golf, RV Wash Gym, Fire Rings, Rec. Hall

Central Alabama

Central Alabama is home to smaller towns and plenty of outdoor adventures.

Scenic Drive

This small park isn't big on amenities, but it is close to the NASCAR races at Talladega.

24 Cheaha State Park Drive, Anniston, AL 36207	256-201-8012 http://scenicdrivervpark.com/	All Year
$36-$38	Military Discounts	No Restrictions
24 Sites	Gravel	30W/65L
Internet, Laundry, Restrooms	Fire Rings, Firewood	Picnic Tables, Showers

Campground of Oxford (aka Oxford / Talladega / Dandy RV KOA)

Close to the NASCAR races at Talladega.

20 Garrett Circle, Anniston, AL 36207	256-241-2295	All Year
$35-$48	Military Discounts	No Restrictions
59 Sites	Gravel	30W/72L
Internet, Laundry, Fire Rings	Playground, Horseshoes	Restrooms, Showers

Country Court

This small and simple park doesn't have much to offer.

3459 US Highway 78 E, Anniston, AL 36207	256-835-2045	All Year
$30-$33	No Discounts	No Restrictions
69 Sites	Gravel	24W/60L
	Internet, RV Wash	

Noccalula Falls Campground

A location that is easy to access and offers beautiful views.

1500 Noccalula Rd, Gadsden, AL 35904	256-549-4663 noccalulafallspark.com/campground/	All Year
$25	Military/Good Sam	Pet Breed/ 28 Days Max
127 Sites	Paved/Gravel	25W/70L
Internet, Laundry, Ice Firewood, RV Supplies	Restrooms, Showers, Cable Pool, Rec. Hall	Playground, Pavilion Fire Rings, Tables

The Cove Lakeside

Located near a private lake, this RV park allows you to sit back and enjoy nature.

4122 Old Pump Station Rd, Gadsden, AL 35904	256-467-3157	All Year

$34-$42	Military/Good Sam	Pet Breed/Pet Quantity
60 Sites	Gravel	30W/70L
Internet, Restroom, Showers	Gated Access, Cable	Game Room, Playground
Laundry, RV Supplies	RV Wash & Service, Pools	Rec. Hall, Pavilion

River Country

This large campground offers plenty of activity for those who don't want to travel too far for fun.

1 River Rd. Gadsden, AL 35901	256-543-7111 rivercountrycampground.com	All Year
$38-$42	No Discounts	Pet Quantity
185 Sites	Gravel	24W/60L
Internet, Laundry, Pools	Restrooms, Showers	Rec. Hall, Game Room

Sleepy Holler Campground

This large campground offers basic amenities with plenty to do in the surrounding area.

174 Sleepy Holler Cir, Cordova, AL 35550	205-483-7947	All Year
$39	Military/Good Sam	No Restrictions
130 Sites	Gravel	18W/60L
Restrooms, Showers	Laundry, Pavilion, Rec. Hall	RV Supplies, RV Wash

Peach Queen Campground

This simple park offers affordable rates and convenient amenities. This park makes RV living a fun experience.

12986 County Road 42, Jemison, AL 35085	205-688-2573 peachqueenrvpark.com/	All Year
$35	Military/Good Sam	No Restrictions
54 Sites	Gravel	24W/60L
Internet, Laundry, Ice	Pools, Firewood, LP Gas	Restrooms, Showers

Birmingham South RV Park

This park is perfectly located for either an overnight stay or a long-term stay.

222 County Road 33, Pelham, AL 35124	205-664-8832	All Year
$38-$41	Military/Good Sam	No Restrictions
99 Sites	Paved/Gravel	30W/60L
Internet, Laundry, Ice	Restrooms, Showers	Pool, Playground, Pavilion

Southern Alabama

Point A Park
This small park offers basic amenities in a great place to stay.

25882 Sailboat Rd, Andalusia, AL 36421	334-388-0342 http://www.pointalake.com/	All Year
$30-$40	No Discounts	No Restrictions
30 Sites	Gravel	45W/60L
Restrooms, Showers	Laundry, Playground	Fire Rings

Wind Creek Atmore Casino
Small and simple park near a casino.

303 Poarch Rd, Atmore, AL 36502	866-946-3360 https://windcreekatmore.com/	All Year
$38	Good Sam Discount	No Restrictions
28 Sites	Paved	25W/70L
Internet, Laundry, Showers	ATM, Restaurant, Lounge	Pool, Gym, Casino

Magnolia Branch Wildlife Reserve
This park is a great place to visit if you are into watersports.

24 Big Creek Rd, Atmore, AL 36502	251-446-3423 http://www.magnoliabranch.com/	All Year
$25-$35	No Discounts	No Restrictions
82 Sites	Gravel	36W/100L
Restrooms, Showers	Laundry, Playground	Horseshoes, Fire Rings

Eagles Landing RV Park
A small but luxurious RV park.

1900 Wire Road, Auburn, AL 36832	334-821-8805 http://eagleslandingrv.com/	All Year
$35-$85	Military/Good Sam	No Restrictions
60 Sites	Gravel	30W/60L
Internet, Firewood, Supplies	LP Gas, Ice, RV Wash	Rec. Hall, Pavilion, Rentals

Auburn RV Park At Leisure Time
This medium-sized park is a great place to go if you want to have leisure time.

2670 S College St Auburn, AL 36832	334-821-2267	All Year
$29-$45	Military/Good Sam	Pet Breed
100 Sites	Paved/Gravel	24W/70L
Internet, Laundry, Cable	Ice, Rentals, RV Wash	Showers, BBQ's, Tables

Dothan Cherry Blossom RV Park

A conveniently located park near the major roadways.

4100 S Oates St, Dothan, AL 36301	334-792-3313 http://www.cherryblossomrv.com/	All Year
$44	Military/Good Sam	RV Age
98 Sites	Paved	25W/70L
Internet, Laundry, Cable	Showers, RV Wash, Games	Playground, Pavilion

Lake Osprey RV Park

Staying at Lake Osprey RV Park puts you just 19½ miles North of beautiful beaches.

12096 County Road 95, Elberta, AL 36530	251-986-3800	All Year
$70-$85	Military/Good Sam	Pet Breed & Quantity, RV Age
98 Sites	Paved	45W/85L
Internet, Laundry, Cable, Ice	Restrooms, Showers, Pool	Rec. Hall, Rentals, Gym

Lake Eufaula Campground

Perfect for the quiet overnight stay or a full weekend getaway.

151 W Chewalla Creek Dr, Eufaula, AL 36027	334-687-4425 https://lakeeufaulacampground.com/	All Year
$27-$30	Military/Good Sam	Pet Breed
50 Sites	Gravel	25W/45L
Internet, Laundry, Cable	Showers, Firewood, Pool	RV Wash, Games, Mini Golf

Coastal Haven RV Park

This smaller park is a great place to stay for water-based vacations.

10151 County Road 32, Fairhope, AL 36532	251-990-9011	All Year
$42	No Discounts	Pet Breed
65 Sites	Gravel	30W/80L
Internet, Laundry, Rec. Hall	Restrooms, Showers	RV Wash

Ahoy RV Resort

This park is clean and comfortable with a personable atmosphere.

13000 Springsteen Ln. Foley, AL 36535	251-233-7250 https://www.ahoyrvresort.com/	All Year
$35-$75	Military Discounts	Pet Breed
71 Sites	Paved	30W/70L

| Ice, Cable, Groceries | Supplies, Laundry, LP Gas | Internet, Restrooms, Shower |

Bella Terra of Gulf Shores
Here you'll experience luxury RV living, offering best-in-class amenities.

101 Viabella Terra, Foley, AL 36535	866-417-2416	All Year
$52-$105	Military/Good Sam	Pet Breed, RV Age, Class B/C
120 Sites	Paved	50W/70L
Internet, Cable, Ice, Gated	Restrooms, Showers, Sauna	Putting Green, Pool, Gym

Alabama Coast Campground
This park features large spaces for nearly any size RV.

11959 Barin Field Rd, Foley, AL 36535	(251) 752-0474 https://www.alabamacoastrv.com/	All Year
$30-$35	Good Sam	No Restrictions
45 Sites	Paved	30W/90L
Horseshoes	Outdoor Games, Frisbee Golf	Pavilion

RV Hideaway Campground
A well-maintained park that is close to conveniences. This park has the best of both worlds.

10723 Magnolia Springs Hwy, Foley, AL 36535	(251) 965-6777 http://magnoliaspringsgolf.com	All Year
$32	Good Sam	Pet Breed&Quantity, RV Age
103 Sites	Paved/Gravel	35W/62L
Internet, Laundry, Ice	Playground, Waterslide	Rec. Hall, Pavilion, Patios

Anchors Aweigh RV Resort
The amenities are few at this park, but it has a lot to offer in the way of recreation.

19814 County Road 20, Foley, AL 36535	(251) 971-6644 http://anchorsaweighrvresort.com/	All Year
$50-$55	Military Discounts	Pet Breed, Pet Quantity
110 Sites	Gravel	30W/85L
Internet, RV Wash, Pool	Rec. Hall, Game Room, Laundry	Restrooms, Showers

Bluegrass RV Park
The is a basic, small RV park.

21403 US Highway 98, Foley, AL 36535	(251) 971-1874	All Year

$40	No Discounts	Pet Size&Quantity, RV Age
51 Sites	Gravel	25W/75L
Internet, Laundry, Rec. Hall	Restrooms, Showers	RV Wash

Beach Express RV Park

This is a basic RV park offers you the standard amenities and a few recreational options.

22225 US Highway 98, Foley, AL 36535	(251) 970-7277	All Year
$39	Military Discounts	Pet Breed
41 Sites	Gravel	30W/50L
Internet, Restrooms, Shower	Laundry, RV Wash	Horseshoes, Playground

Island Retreat RV Park

Located right along the beautiful white sand beaches and emerald waters.

18201 State Highway 180, Gulf Shores, AL 36542	(251) 967-1666 islandretreatrvpark.com/	All Year
$50-$90	Military/Good Sam	Pet Breed, RV Age
173 Sites	Paved	30W/100L
Internet, Laundry, LP Gas	Ice, Showers, Cable	Playground, Fire Rings, Patio

Bay Breeze RV on the Bay

Located very close to the Gulf of Mexico, this is the place to go if you want to relax.

1901 Bay Breeze Pkwy, Gulf Shores, AL 36542	(251) 540-2362 https://baybreezerv.com	All Year
$47-$62	No Discounts	Pet Breed & Quantity
25 Sites	Gravel	20W/50L
Internet, Laundry, Ice	Rentals, Games, Showers	Horseshoes, Patios

Lazy Lake RV Park

This small park is your basic RV park to spend the night while visiting the surrounding area.

18950 Old Plash Island Rd, Gulf Shores, AL 36542	(251) 968-7875 http://www.lazylakervpark.com/	All Year
$33	No Discounts	No Restrictions
40 Sites	Gravel	30W/90L
Internet, Laundry	Restrooms, Showers	Horseshoes, Playground

Gulf Breeze RV Resort

This large RV park doesn't have a lot in the way of amenities.

19800 Oak Rd W, Gulf Shores, AL 36542	(251) 968-8462	All Year

$40	No Discounts	Pet Breed
250 Sites	Gravel	30W/80L
Internet, Laundry, Pools	RV Wash, Showers	Rec. Hall, Playground

Sun-Runners RV Park
A basic RV park with access to plenty of local activities.

19480 County Road 8, Gulf Shores, AL 36542	(251) 955-5257 sunrunnersrvparkgulfshores.com/	All Year
$35	No Discounts	Pet Breed
65 Sites	Gravel	25W/65L
Internet	Restrooms, Shower	Laundry

Montgomery South RV Park
Offering a quiet and secure park with all the basic amenities.

731 Venable Rd, Hope Hull, AL 36043	(334) 284-7006 http://www.montgomerysouthrvpark.com/	All Year
$31-$40	Military/Good Sam	Pet Breed
43 Sites	Gravel	40W70L
Internet, Laundry, Ice	LP Gas, Firewood, RV Wash, Rentals	Firewood, Showers

Lost Bay KOA
A standard KOA campground with basic amenities and plenty of recreational opportunities.

11650 County Road 99, Lillian, AL 36549	(251) 961-1717 https://koa.com/campgrounds/gulf-shores/	All Year
$43-$68	No Discounts	Pet Breed
115 Sites	Gravel	24W/65L
Internet, Restrooms	Showers, Pool, RV Wash	Rec. Hall, Playground

Shady Acres Campground
The perfect park to stay at if you want to spend time exploring Mobile.

2500 Old Military Rd, Mobile, AL 36605	(251) 478-0013 http://shadyacresmobile.com/	All Year
$35	Military/Good Sam	Pet Breed, RV Age
92 Sites	Paved	25W/85L
Internet, Laundry, Pavilion	Restrooms, Showers, Cable	RV Wash, Rec. Hall, LP Gas

I-10 Kampground
Close enough to enjoy Mobile, but far enough away from the hustle and bustle of the city.

6430 Theodore Dawes Rd, Theodore, AL 36582	(251) 653-9816	All Year

$30	Good Sam Discount	No Restrictions
100 Sites	Paved/Gravel	20W/60L
Internet, Laundry, Cable	Restrooms, Showers, Pool	RV Wash, Pavilion

All About Relaxing RV Park

This park is well kept with several amenities and is centrally located.

8950 Three Notch Rd, Theodore, AL 36582	(251) 375-0661 http://www.allaboutrelaxingrv.com/	All Year
$38-$80	Discounts	No Restrictions
41 Sites	Paved/Gravel	28W/74L
Internet, Pool, RV Wash	Restrooms, Showers, Ice, LP Gas	Supplies, Gated Access

I-65 RV Campground

This medium-sized park is a place to park while exploring the surrounding area.

730 Jackson Rd, Creola, AL 36525	(800) 287-3208 http://i65rvcampground.com/	All Year
$33	Military/Good Sam	Pet Breed, Pet Size
87 Sites	Paved/Gravel	30W/90L
Internet, Laundry, LP Gas	Restrooms, Showers, Patios	RV Service, Horseshoes

The Woods RV Park

It is the closest you can get to Montgomery with plenty of activities to enjoy.

4350 Sassafras Cir, Montgomery, AL 36105	(334) 356-1887 http://woodsrvpark.com/	All Year
$30	Military/Good Sam	RV Age
105 Sites	Gravel	30W/80L
Internet, Laundry, Supplies	LP Gas, Restrooms, Showers	Firewood, Cable, Fire Rings

Capital City RV Park

If you're in the Montgomery area, be sure to check out this RV park.

4655 Old Wetumpka Hwy, Montgomery, AL 36110	(334) 271-8063 http://capitalcityrvpark.net/	All Year
$30-$35	Military/Good Sam	Pet Breed, RV Age
89 Sites	Paved/Gravel	35W/65L
Internet, Laundry, Ice, Cable	Restrooms, Showers	Rec. Hall, Playground, Patios

Lakeside RV Park

Large sites with all the modern amenities are the feature of this park.

5664 US Highway 280 E, Opelika, AL 36804	(334) 705-0701 http://www.lakesidervparkopelikaal.com/	All Year
$45	Military/Good Sam	Pet Breed, Quantity&Size
54 Sites	Gravel	40W/80L
Internet/Cable, Laundry	RV Wash, Restrooms, Showers	Playground, Firewood

Heritage Motorcoach Resort Marina

This is the premier park to stay at when you're in Orange Beach.

28888 Canal Rd, Orange Beach, AL 36561	(251) 923-3400 https://heritageorangebeach.com/	All Year
$70-$165	Military Discounts	Pet Breed, RV Age, Class B/C
79 Sites	Paved/Gravel	30W/70L
Internet, Laundry, Pool	Restrooms, Showers	RV Wash, Hot Tub

Buena Vista Coastal RV Resort

There isn't much in the way of amenities, but there is plenty of recreational activities.

23601 Perd Bch Blvd, Orange Beach, AL 36561	(251) 980-1855 http://www.buenavistarvresort.com/	All Year
$95-$420	Military Discounts	Pet Breed, RV Age, Class B/C
41 Sites	Paved/Gravel	45W/70L
Internet, Restrooms, Pool	Laundry, Rec. Hall	Showers, Hot Tub

Pandion Ridge Luxury RV Resort

This is one of the largest parks you can stay at in Orange Beach.

22800 Canal Rd, Orange Beach, AL 36561	(844) 707-4343 http://pandionridge.com/	All Year
$59-$109	Military Discounts	Pet Breed, RV Age
142 Sites	Paved/Gravel	40W/90L
Internet, Laundry	Restrooms, Showers	Pool, Rec. Hall, RV Wash

Kountry Air RV Park

A little out of the way, but well worth the drive, this quiet park is well kept in a country setting.

2133 Highway 82 W, Prattville, AL 36067	(334) 365-6861 https://www.kountryairrv.com/	All Year
$38-$45	Military/Good Sam	Pet Breed, RV Age
39 Sites	Gravel	30W/75L
Internet, Restrooms, Shower	Laundry, RV Supplies/Wash	LP Gas, Firewood, Ice, Pool

Azalea Acres RV Park

This park is in a peaceful country setting with plenty of room for the larger RVs.

27450 Glass Rd, Robertsdale, AL 36567	(251) 947-9530 http://www.azaleaacresrvpark.com/	All Year
$30-$36	Military/Good Sam	Pet Breed & Quantity
70 Sites	Gravel	43W/92L
Internet, Laundry, LP Gas	RV Wash, Rec. Hall, Pavilion	Restrooms, Showers

Hilltop RV Park

Easy access off the Interstate makes this a great overnight destination.

23420 County Road 64, Robertsdale, AL 36567	(251) 942-3531 http://www.hilltoprvpark.com/	All Year
$40-$45	Military/Good Sam	Pet Breed & Quantity
86 Sites	Paved/Gravel	28W/85L
Internet, Laundry, Showers	RV Wash, Rec. Hall, Activity	Pavilion, LP Gas, Rentals

Wilderness RV Park

This park provides quick access to Mobile, AL and Pensacola, FL.

24280 Patterson Rd, Robertsdale, AL 36567	(251) 960-1195 https://wildernessrvpark.com/	All Year
$31-$36	No Discounts	Pet Breed & Quantity
74 Sites	Dirt	25W/65L
Internet, Laundry, Ice	Rec. Hall, Activities, Pool	RV Wash, LP Gas, Pavilion

Wales West RV Resort and Light Railway

This park is a great place to visit if you have kids.

13670 Smiley St, Silverhill, AL 36576	(888) 569-5337 http://www.waleswest.com/	All Year
$36-$60	Military/Good Sam	Pet Breed&Quantity, RV Age
100 Sites	Gravel	30W/70L
Internet, Laundry, Cable	Ice, Pool, Snack Bar, LP Gas	Activities, Playground, Gym

Deer Run RV Park

A beautiful park where you can sit back and relax for a few days.

25629 US Highway 231, Troy, AL 36081	(334) 566-6517 https://deerrunrvpark.com/	All Year
$38	Military/Good Sam	RV Age
102 Sites	Gravel	30W/65L
Internet, Cable, Laundry	Restrooms, Showers, Pool	Activities, Rec. Hall, RVwash

Arizona

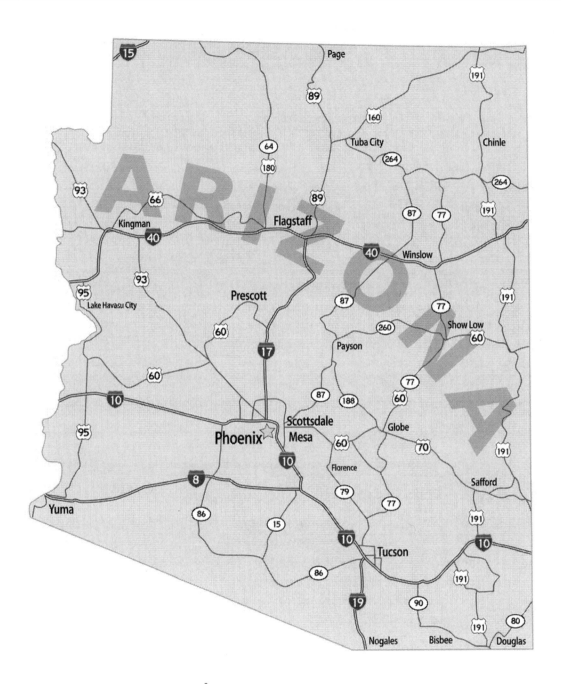

Northwest Arizona

Northwest Arizona is home to the famous Grand Canyon. However, there is still plenty more to see and do in the Northwest part of Arizona.

Vista Del Sol RV Resort
A 55+ gated retirement community within easy distance to both outdoor and city activities.

3249 Felipe Dr, Bullhead City, AZ 86442	(928) 754-0182 https://robertsresorts.com	All Year
$33-$47	Military/Good Sam	Age 55+, PetQty, RVAge, ClassB
89 Sites	Paved	40W/80L
Internet, Laundry, Gated	Restrooms, Shower, Gym	Pool, Activities, Rec. Hall

Silver View RV Resort
This park is located right along the Colorado River.

1501 Goldrush Rd, Bullhead City, AZ 86442	(928) 763-5500 http://www.silverviewrvresort.com/	All Year
$40-$55	Good Sam Discounts	Pet Quantity, RV Age
350 Sites	Paved	30W/60L
Internet, Laundry, Supplies	Ice, Showers, Groceries, Food	Pool, Game Room, Gym

Colorado River Oasis Resort
Although small, this park is the perfect destination along the Colorado River.

1641 Highway 95, Bullhead City, AZ 86442	(928) 763-4385	All Year
$40-$60	Military/Good Sam	Pet Breed&Quantity, RV Age
27 Sites	Gravel	30W/45L
Internet, Laundry, Cable	Pool, Rentals, RV Wash	Rec. Hall, Activities, BBQ's

Fiesta RV Resort
This large RV park offers standard amenities with quite a few recreational options.

3190 Highway 95, Bullhead City, AZ 86442	(928) 758-7671 http://fiestarvresort.com/	All Year
$25-$30	No Discounts	Pet Breed, RV Age
368 Sites	Gravel	30W/50L
Restrooms, Showers, Pool	RV Wash, Laundry, Rec. Hall	Game Room, Games

Verde River RV Resort

The amenities and recreation facilities are the things to stay for here.

1472 W Horseshoe Bend Dr, Camp Verde, AZ 86322	(928) 202-3409 https://verderiverrvresort.com/	All Year
$29-$52	Military/Good Sam	RV Age
130 Sites	Paved/Gravel	30W/110L
Internet, Laundry, Gated, Ice	Groceries, Cable, RV Wash	Rentals, Pool, Rec. Hall

Distant Drums RV Resort

This park puts you close to the activities in Sedona while also enjoying views of the mountains.

583 W Middle Verde Rd, Camp Verde, AZ 86322	(877) 577-5507 https://ddrvresort.com/	All Year
$38-$46	Military/Good Sam	No Restrictions
156 Sites	Paved	22W/77L
Internet, Laundry, Supplies	Ice, Pool, Cable, Rec. Hall	Game Room, Gym, Patios

Zane Grey RV Village

This rural and quiet park is actually centrally located to many nearby activities.

4500 E Hwy 260, Camp Verde, AZ 86322	(928) 567-4320 https://www.zanegreyrv.com/	All Year
$42-$44	Military/Good Sam	Pet Breed, Quantity, Size
69 Sites	Gravel	30W/65L
Internet, Laundry, Supplies	Restrooms, Showers, LP Gas	Rec. Hall, Activities, Supplies

Cordes Junction Motel and RV Park

Step back in time at this '50s themed destination.

19780 E Hitching Post Way, Cordes Lakes, AZ 86333	(928) 632-5186 https://motelrvpark.com/	All Year
$44	Military/Good Sam	Pet Breed
22 Sites	Gravel	25W/40L
Internet, Laundry, Restaurant	Ice, Rentals, Lounge, LP Gas	Putting Green, Showers

Verde Valley RV Camping Resort

This park is a 300-acre oasis in the high desert of Arizona surrounded by mountains.

6400 E Thousand Trails Rd, Cottonwood, AZ 86326	(888) 460-2975	All Year
$40	Good Sam	Pet Quantity
309 Sites	Paved/Gravel	15W65L
Internet, Laundry, Gated, Ice	Groceries, Cable, RV Wash	Rentals, Pool, Rec. Hall

Rio Verde RV Park

Unique amenities and recreation are what sets this park apart from others.

3420 E State Rte 89A, Cottonwood, AZ 86326	(928) 634-5990 http://www.rioverdervpark.com/	All Year
$36	Good Sam	No Restrictions
63 Sites	Gravel	30W/45L
Internet, Laundry, Rentals	Restrooms, Shower, Cable	LP Gas, Pavilion, Patios

Turquoise Triangle RV Park

This park is a comfortable year-round destination.

2501 E State Rte 89A, Cottonwood, AZ 86326	(928) 634-5294	All Year
$35-$40	Good Sam	Pet Breed, Pet Quantity
63 Sites	Gravel	27W/50L
Internet	Laundry, Ice, Cable	Rec. Hall, Showers

Orchard Ranch RV Resort

Located in the shadow of majestic mountains; this 55+ community features nice weather.

11250 E State Route 69, Dewey, AZ 86327	(928) 772-8266 https://www.orchardranchrvpark.com/	All Year
$44	Good Sam	Age (55+), Pet Breed&Qty
430 Sites	Paved	31W/50L
Internet, Laundry, Ice	RV Services, Games, Rec. Hall	Golf Carts, Pool, Cable

Greer's Pine Shadows RV Park

Located in a beautiful pine forest, there is plenty of activities within the park.

7101 N US Highway 89, Flagstaff, AZ 86004	(928) 526-4977 greerspineshadowsrvpark.com/	All Year
$37-$44	Military/Good Sam	No Restrictions
76 Sites	Paved/Gravel	20W/70L
Internet, Pit Toilets, Laundry	Supplies, RV Wash, Rec. Hall	Games, Activities, Tables

Black Barts RV Park

A park that offers the standard amenities at a reasonable rate.

2760 E Butler Ave, Flagstaff, AZ 86004	(928) 774-1912 blackbartssteakhouse.com/	All Year
$44	Military/Good Sam	Pet-Friendly
174 Sites	Paved/Gravel	25W/50L
Restrooms, Showers	Laundry, Ice, Supplies	Restaurant, Lounge, Games

J & H RV Park

A clean, safe, and friendly RV park located in the mountains near Flagstaff.

7901 North Highway 89, Flagstaff, AZ 86004	(928) 526-1829 https://flagstaffrvparks.com/	May 1 to October 15
$57	Military/Good Sam	Age (55+), Pet Breed
50 Sites	Gravel	30W/55L
Internet, Laundry, Supplies	Ice, Cable, Activities	Games, Showers, Pavilion

Flagstaff KOA

Your standard KOA park with basic amenities in a convenient location.

5803 North US Highway 89, Flagstaff, AZ 86004	(928) 526-9926 koa.com/campgrounds/flagstaff/	All Year
$39-$83	Military Discounts	No Restrictions
194 Sites	Gravel	20W/50L
Internet, Laundry	Restrooms, Showers, Rec. Hall	Horseshoes, Playground

Adobe RV Park

A 55+ park surrounded by mountains.

4950 W Apache Way, Golden Valley, AZ 86413	(928) 565-3010 http://adobervpark.com/	All Year
$27	Good Sam Discount	Pet Size, Quantity, Breed
75 Sites	Paved	32W/58L
Internet, Laundry, Ice	Supplies, Showers, Rec. Hall	Activities, Horseshoes

Tradewinds RV Park

A great place to stay that is close to several sites and cities.

152 S Emery Park Rd, Golden Valley, AZ 86413	(928) 565-5115 http://tradewindsrvpark.com/	All Year
$35-$38	Military/Good Sam	Pet Quantity
113 Sites	Gravel	32W/60L
Internet, Firewood, Ice	Restroom, Shower, Laundry	Supplies, Games, Rec. Hall

Blake Ranch RV Park

It offers great amenities for those who need a place to stay with horses.

9315 E Blake Ranch Rd, Kingman, AZ 86401	(800) 270-1332 http://blakeranchrv.com/	All Year
$33-$45	Military/Good Sam	No Restrictions
55 Sites	Paved	30W/65L
Horse Motel, Internet, Ice	LP Gas, Showers, Laundry	Rec. Hall, Pavilion

Zuni Village RV Park

Located close to historic Route 66 and the many sites in Kingman.

2840 Airway Ave, Kingman, AZ 86409	(928) 692-6202 https://zunirvpark.com/	All Year
$44	Military/Good Sam	Pet Quantity, Pet Breed
130 Sites	Paved	30W/60L
Internet, Showers, Laundry	Supplies, LP Gas, Pool	Pavilion, Tables

Campbell Cove RV Resort

If you want to relax with scenic views, then this is the park for you.

1523 Industrial Blvd, Lake Havasu City, AZ 86403	(928) 854-7200 campbellcovervresort.com/	All Year
$39-$47	Military/Good Sam	Pet Quantity, Pet Breed
122 Sites	Paved	22W/60L
Restrooms, Showers, Cable	Pool, Laundry, Rec. Hall	Hot Tub, Gym, Tables

Islander Resort

This large park gets you right on the water.

751 Beachcomber Blvd, Lake Havasu City, AZ 86403	(928) 680-2000 http://islanderlakehavasu.com/	All Year
$59-$95	No Discounts	Pet Quantity, Pet Breed
500 Sites	Gravel	36W/50L
Internet, Laundry, RV Wash	Pool, Showers, Rec. Hall	Game Room

Meadview RV Park

The closest park to the Grand Canyon and also conveniently located near Lake Mead.

28100 N Pierce Ferry Rd, Meadview, AZ 86444	(928) 564-2662 https://www.rv-park.com/	All Year
$30-$33	Military/Good Sam	No Restrictions
32 Sites	Gravel	39W/75L
Internet, showers, Laundry	ATM, Supplies, Groceries	Rentals, Games, LP gas

Moon River RV Resort

Closely located near Nevada and plenty of casino opportunities.

1325 E Boundary Cone Rd, Mohave Valley, AZ 86440	(928) 788-6666 https://www.moonriverresort.com/	All Year
$36-$39	Military/Good Sam	Pet Size, Breed, Qty
89 Sites	Gravel	22W/76L
Internet, Showers, Laundry	Supplies, Groceries, Ice	Rentals, Pool, Rec. Hall

Crossroads RV Park
A tranquil park that provides all the amenities of a resort without the cost.

3299 Boundary Cone Rd, Mohave Valley, AZ 86440	(928) 768-3303 http://crossroadsrvspace.com/	All Year
$35-$45	Good Sam Discount	Pet Size, Breed, Quantity
136 Sites	Paved	30W/50L
Internet, Showers	Laundry, Rec. Hall	Planned Activities

Page Lake Powell Campground
Conveniently located near Lake Powell, this park offers you plenty of recreational activities.

849 Coppermine Rd, Page, AZ 86040	(928) 645-3374 pagelakepowellcampground.com/	All Year
$39-$48	Military/Good Sam	No Restrictions
120 Sites	Paved/Gravel	28W/40L
Internet, Showers, Laundry	Supplies, LP Gas, Ice, Cable	Groceries, Pool, Gym

Fairgrounds RV Park
With basic amenities, this park is conveniently located close to many activities.

10443 Highway 89A, Prescott Valley, AZ 86315	(928) 227-3310 fairgroundsrvpark.com/	All Year
$38	Good Sam Discount	Pet Quantity, Pet Breed
153 Sites	Paved	45W/70L
Internet, Laundry, LP Gas	Cable, Rec. Hall	Patios, Horseshoes

Rancho Sedona RV Park
Although in the heart of Sedona, this park offers a very tranquil setting.

135 Bear Wallow Ln, Sedona, AZ 86336	(928) 282-7255 https://ranchosedona.com	All Year
$37-$77	Military/Good Sam	No Restrictions
84 Sites	Gravel	30W/40L
Internet, Shower, Laundry	Supplies, Ice, Cable	Games, Patios, Tables

Grand Canyon Railway RV Park
Staying at this park puts you close to Route 66, and lets you take a unique train ride.

601 W Franklin Ave, Williams, AZ 86046	(800) 843-8724 https://www.thetrain.com	All Year
$43-$48	Military/Good Sam	Max Stay 28 Days
124 Sites	Paved	30W/65L
Internet, Shower, Laundry	ATM, Supplies, Ice, Cable	Groceries, Games, Pavilion

Canyon Gateway RV Park

In a tranquil hilltop area, this park gives you the best views of the surrounding area.

1060 N. Grand Canyon Blvd. Williams, AZ 86046	(888) 635-0329 grandcanyonrvparks.com/	All Year
$30-$45	Military/Good Sam	No Restrictions
98 Sites	Gravel	25W/60L
Internet, Showers, Laundry	Rentals, Rec. Hall	Game Room, Horseshoes

Canyon Motel and RV Park

Located in Williams, this park offers excellent views of the mountains.

1900 E Rodeo Rd, Williams, AZ 86046	(928) 635-9371 http://thecanyonmotel.com/	All Year
$39-$47	Military/Good Sam	No Restrictions
47 Sites	Gravel	30W/70L
Internet, Shower, Laundry	Supplies, Firewood, Grocery	Cable, Ice, Pool, Games

Northeast Arizona

There aren't a lot of options when it comes to places to stay in Northeast Arizona, but there are still plenty of activities to enjoy.

OK RV Park
Conveniently located along historic Route 66, this is your premier stop.

1576 Roadrunner Rd, Holbrook, AZ 86025	(928) 524-3226	All Year
$35-$40	Military/Good Sam	Pet Quantity, Breed
89 Sites	Paved/Gravel	18W/108L
Internet, Showers	Laundry, Supplies, Ice	Cable, Rec. Hall, Tables

Overgaard RV Resort
This is the place to go if you want to escape the summer heat.

2750 Yates Rd, Overgaard, AZ 85933	(928) 535-4430	All Year
	overgaardrvresortaz.com/	
$46	Good Sam Discount	Pet Quantity, Breed
71 Sites	Gravel	24W/50L
Internet	Shower, Laundry	Pavilion

Meteor Crater RV Park
Conveniently located off the Interstate, this is your place to stay when visiting nearby Winslow.

Interstate 40 Exit 233, Winslow, AZ 86047	(800) 289-5898	All Year
	https://www.meteorcrater.com	
$37-$42	Military/Good Sam	Pet Quantity
71 Sites	Gravel	30W/60L
Internet	Restrooms, Showers	Laundry, Gated Access

Southeast Arizona

Southeast Arizona is home to Tucson, as well as a number of small picturesque towns and plenty of enjoyable outdoor activities. The following are just a few of the outdoor activities you can enjoy while staying at RV parks in Southeast Arizona.

De Anza RV Resort

This is one of the most unique RV parks in Arizona that you can choose to stay at.

2869 W Frontage Rd, Amado, AZ 85645	(520) 398-8628 http://www.deanzarvresort.com/	All Year
$36-$48	Good Sam Discounts	Pet Quantity
130 Sites	Paved	30W/70L
Internet, Showers, Laundry	Gated, ATM, Ice, Restaurant	RV Wash, Games, Pool

Butterfield RV Resort Observatory

Centrally located so you can visit some of the areas top attractions with reasonable rates.

251 S Ocotillo Ave, Benson, AZ 85602	(520) 586-4400 butterfieldrvresort.com	All Year
$40	Military/Good Sam	RV Age, Pet Breed
173 Spaces	Paved	30Width/55Length
Internet, Showers, Laundry	Supplies, LP Gas, Ice, Pool	RV Wash, Rentals, Pavilion

Valley Vista RV Resort

This is a 55+ park that offers you plenty of activities or a nice place to sit back and relax.

1060 S Highway 80, Benson, AZ 85602	(520) 586-1343	All Year
$40	Good Sam Discount	Pet Quantity, Age 55+
123 Spaces	Gravel	30Width/60Length
Internet, Showers, Laundry	Cable, Pool, RV Wash	Rec. Hall, Activities

Pato Blanco Lakes RV Resort

A peaceful and relaxing oasis of an RV park.

635 E Pearl St, Benson, AZ 85602	(520) 586-8966 http://patoblancolakes.com/	All Year
$43	Military/Good Sam	RV Age
105 Spaces	Gravel	35Width/80Length)
Internet, Showers, Laundry	Gated, LP Gas, Pool, Cable	Rentals, Rec. Hall, Gym

San Pedro Resort Community

This park is ideal for a relaxing stay or a long-term retirement living option.

1110 S Highway 80,	(520) 586-9546	All Year

Benson, AZ 85602	http://sanpedrorv.com/	
$42	Good Sam	RV Age, Pet Quantity, Breed
270 Spaces	Paved	30Width/50Length
Internet, Showers, Laundry	Cable, RV Wash, Pool	Rec. Hall, Games, Patios

Mountain View RV Park
Surrounded by five mountain ranges with plenty of interesting things to explore.

99 W Vista Ln, Huachuca City, AZ 85616	(520) 456-2860 http://mountainviewrvpark.com/	All Year
$30-$37	Good Sam	Pet Breed
81 Spaces	Paved	25Width/60Length
Internet, Showers, Laundry	RV Wash, Rec. Hall, Gym	Activities, Tables, Patios

Payson Campground and RV Resort
This park is the best place to camp among the ponderosa pines.

808 East Hwy 260, Payson, AZ 85541	(928) 472-2267 https://www.paysoncampground.com/	All Year
$41	Good Sam	No Restrictions
109 Spaces	Paved/Gravel	25Width/65Length)
Internet, Laundry	Showers, Supplies, Game Room	Pool, Firewood, Rentals

Picacho Peak RV Resort
This 55+ park offers beautiful views, along with plenty of outdoor sites to enjoy.

17065 E Peak Ln, Picacho, AZ 85141	(520) 466-7841 picachopeakrvpark.com/	All Year
$40-$45	Military/Good Sam	Pet Breed&Qty,RV Age,Age 55+
311 Spaces	Paved	31Width/65Length)
Internet, Showers, LP Gas	Rentals, Pool, Rec. Hall	Activities, Gym, Patios

Venture In RV Resort
This park is ideal for those who want to be close to excellent fishing destinations.

270 N. Clark Rd, Show Low, AZ 85901	(800) 576-8568	May 1st to October 31st
$42	Military/Good Sam	Pet Quantity, Pet Size
378 Spaces	Gravel	34Width/50Length)
Internet, Showers, Laundry	Ice, Cable, RV Wash, Games	Activities, Gym, Patios

Springerville RV Park

This park is your base of operations for exploring the White Mountains of Arizona.

1630 E Main Street, Springerville, Arizona	505-215-0712 http://springervillervpark.com/	All Year
$20-$40	Good Sam	No Restrictions
44 Spaces	Gravel	25Width/45Length)
Internet	Horse Friendly	Electric Vehicle Charging

Tombstone Territories RV Resort

This park has views and plenty of trails to explore the outdoors however you like.

2111 E Highway 82, Huachuca City, AZ 85616	(520) 457-2584 http://tombstoneterritories.com	All Year
$23-$38	Military/Good Sam	Pet Quantity, Pet Breed
102 Spaces	Paved	40Width/80Length)
Internet, Ice, Cable, Pool	Showers, Laundry, LP Gas	RV Wash, Games, Patios

Tombstone RV Park

An excellent family-friendly destination.

1475 N Highway 80, Tombstone, AZ 85638	(520) 457-3829 tombstonervparkandcampground.com/	All Year
$45	Military/Good Sam	Pet Quantity
83 Spaces	Road Conditions	30Width/50Length)
Internet, Showers, Ice	LP Gas, Rentals, Pool, Firewood	Rec. hall, Playground

Far Horizons RV Resort

Staying here allows you to explore historic Tucson while enjoying views of the mountains.

555 N Pantano Rd, Tucson, AZ 85710	(520) 296-1234	All Year
$35-$55	Good Sam	Age 55+, Pet Quantity
514 Spaces	Paved	36Width/47Length)
Internet, Showers, Ice	Laundry, Gated, Pool	Games, Rec. Hall, Sauna

Sentinel Peak RV Park

Due to the light rail at this park, you can explore all that Tucson has to offer within 3 minutes.

450 N Grande Ave, Tucson, AZ 85745	(520) 495-0175 http://sentinelpeakrv.com/	All Year
$30-$49	Good Sam	No Restrictions
23 Spaces	Paved	30Width/70Length
Internet, Restrooms, Ice	Laundry, Firewood, Pool	Supplies, Games, Tables

Rincon Country West
This 55+ park is like staying at a high-end resort.

4555 S Mission Rd, Tucson, AZ 85746	(520) 294-5608 https://www.rinconcountry.com	All Year
$55-$61	Good Sam	RV Age, Pet Breed&Quantity
1083 Spaces	Paved	22Width/57Length
Internet, Showers, Ice	Laundry, Cable, RV Wash	Pool, Games, Rec. Hall

Mission View RV Resort
Located on an Indian Reservation, this park offers plenty of amenities.

31 W Los Reales Rd, Tucson, AZ 85756	(520) 741-1965 http://www.missionviewrv.com/	All Year
$43	Good Sam	RV Age, Pet Breed&Quantity
342 Spaces	Paved	36Width/50Length
Internet, Showers, RV wash	Pool, Game Room, Gym	Rec. hall, Patios, Activities

Crazy Horse RV Campgrounds
A family and pet-friendly park in a convenient location designed for comfort and relaxation.

6660 S Craycroft Rd, Tucson, AZ 85756	(520) 574-0157 crazyhorservcampgrounds.com/	All Year
$39-$46	Military/Good Sam	RV Age, Pet Breed&Qty
176 Spaces	Gravel	20Width/55Length)
Internet, Showers, Laundry	LP Gas, Rentals, Pool, Rec.Hall	Activities, Patios, Games

Rincon Country East RV Resort
A quaint 55+ community in a serene desert setting.

8989 E Escalante Rd, Tucson, AZ 85730	(520) 886-8431 rinconcountry.com	All Year
$49-$53	Good Sam	RV Age, Pet Quantity, 55+
456 Spaces	Paved	30Width/45Length)
Internet, Showers, Ice, Gated	Pool, Rentals, Games, Patios	Cable, RV Wash, Tennis

Pima County Fairgrounds RV Park
Pet and horse-friendly with plenty of opportunities to do things within the park.

11300 S Houghton Rd, Tucson, AZ 85747	(520) 762-8579 https://www.the-rvpark.com/	All Year
$30	Good Sam	No Restrictions
350 Spaces	Paved/Gravel	20Width/45Length

| Internet, Gated, Supplies | Restaurant, Ice, Rec. Hall | Horse Friendly, LP Gas |

Prince of Tucson RV Park
Affordable rates for resort-style amenities.

3501 N Freeway, Tucson, AZ 85705	(520) 887-3501 princeoftucsonrvpark.com/	All Year
$40	Good Sam	RV Age, Pet Qty&Breed
176 Spaces	Gravel	24Width/70Length
Internet, Showers, Laundry	Supplies, Ice, RV Wash	Pool, Pavilion, Activities

Voyager RV Resort
A 55+ park that gives you the best of desert living.

8701 S. Kolb Rd, Tucson, AZ 85756	(800) 424-9191	All Year
$42-$54	Military/Good Sam	RV Age, 55+
1576 Spaces	Paved	17Width/100Length)
Showers, Laundry, SnackBar	Gated, Grocery, Restaurant	Tennis, Sauna, Games, Rec.

South Forty RV Ranch
Offering basic amenities, this is a relaxing park for those who want to have a laid back vacation.

3600 W Orange Grove Rd, Tucson, AZ 85741	(520) 297-2503 http://southfortyrvranch.com/	All Year
$41-$48	Military/Good Sam	RV Age,Pet Size,Qty,Breed
230 Spaces	Paved	30Width/50Length)
Showers, Laundry, Rentals	Pool, Games	Gym, Patios, Tables

Grande Vista RV Park
A brief description.

711 N Prescott Ave, Willcox, AZ 85643	(520) 384-4002 https://grandevistarvparkaz.com/	All Year
$36-$38	Military/Good Sam	Pet Breed
57 Spaces	Gravel	23Width/55Length)
Internet, Showers, Laundry	Supplies, Rentals, Games	Rec. Hall, Tables

Southwest Arizona

Southwest Arizona is where the majority of your travel options exist. There are lots of major towns and small quaint historical areas as well. In addition, there are more RV parks to consider in this corner of Arizona than the rest of Arizona.

Superstition Sunrise RV Resort

With so many amenities to do at this park, you may not want to leave.

702 S Meridian Rd, Apache Junction, AZ 85120	(480) 986-4524 https://superstitionsunrise.com/	All Year
$50	Good Sam	55+, RV Age, Pet Qty
1119 Spaces	Paved	33Width/48Length
Internet, Showers, Laundry	Gated, Ice, Snack Bar	Cable, Pool, Game Room

Weaver's Needle RV Resort

This 55+ park offers some of the best views of the area and is conveniently located.

250 S Tomahawk Road Apache Junction, AZ 85119	(480) 982-3683 http://www.weaversneedle.com/	All Year
$44	Good Sam	55+, Pet Qty, Breed
400 Spaces	Paved	30Width/40Length
Internet, Showers, Laundry	Pool, Ice, Rec. Hall, Games	Pavilion, Gym, Patios

Sunrise RV Resort

A 55+ resort that offers first-class amenities. Staying here is like staying in paradise.

1403 West Broadway Ave., Apache Junction, AZ 85120	(480) 983-2500	All Year
$38-$59	Good Sam	RV Age/Pet Qty/Breed/ClassB
501 Spaces	Paved	35Width/55Length
Internet, Showers, Laundry	Gated, Ice, Cable, Pool	RV Wash, Rentals

Blue Star at Lost Dutchman

Enjoy the beauty and desert at this park located conveniently near Mesa and Phoenix.

10936 E Apache Trl Lot 33, Apache Junction, AZ 85120	(866) 471-0761	All Year
$41-$55	Good Sam	55+, Pet Size, Qty, Breed
200 Spaces	Paved	25Width/55Length
Internet, Showers, Laundry	RV Wash, Pool, Game Room	Activities, Pavilion, Patios

Countryside RV Resort

This 55+ park offers spectacular views of the mountains.

2701 S. Idaho Rd, Apache Junction, AZ 85119	(866) 226-6090	All Year
$54	Military/Good Sam	55+, Pet Breed
560 Spaces	Paved	26Width/38Length
Showers, Laundry, Gated	Ice, RV Wash, Pool, Hot Tub	Rec. Hall, Game Room, Gym

Golden Sun RV Resort

This 55+ park offers plenty of activities to keep you busy.

999 W. Broadway Avenue, Apache Junction, AZ 85120	(866) 226-6180	All Year
$41-$44	Good Sam	55+, Pet Qty, Breed
329 Spaces	Paved	30Width/40Length
Internet, Showers, Laundry	Ice, RV Wash, Pool, Rec.Hall	Library, Game Room, Gym

VIP RV Resort

Located at the foothills of the mountains, this 55+ park is the best value for your money.

401 S Ironwood Dr, Apache Junction, AZ 85120	(480) 983-0847 https://viprvresort.com/	All Year
$39	Good Sam	55+, Pet Size, Qty, Breed
128 Spaces	Paved	30Width/45Length
Internet, Showers, Laundry	RV Wash, Rentals, Rec. Hall	Activities, Putting Green

Black Canyon Campground

Conveniently located between Phoenix and Prescott, you won't have to travel far for fun!

19600 E St Josephs Rd, Black Canyon City, AZ 85324	(623) 374-5318 blackcanyoncampground.com/	All Year
$40-$50	Military/Good Sam	No Restrictions
46 Spaces	Gravel	24Width/50Length
Internet, Showers, Laundry	Ice, Firewood, Rentals, Pool	Playground, Tables, BBQ

Black Canyon Ranch RV Resort

Located close to the Interstate in a quaint mining town, this place offers a quiet park-like setting.

33900 S Old Black Canyon Hwy, Black Canyon City, AZ 85324	(623) 374-9800 blackcanyonranchrv.com	All Year
$50	Military/Good Sam	Pet Qty
107 Spaces	Paved	30Width/50Length

| Internet, Showers, Laundry | Ice, Cable, Restaurant, Pool | Games, Rec. Hall, Fire Pits |

Black Rock RV Village

Located in the outback of Arizona, this is the place to go for a peaceful setting.

46751 Highway 60, Salome, AZ 85348	(928) 927-4206 https://www.blackrockrv.com/	All Year
$32-$39	Good Sam	Pet Breed
408 Spaces	Gravel	30Width/100Length
Showers, Firewood, Rentals	Laundry, ATM, LP Gas	Game Room, Rec. Hall, Gym

Desert Gold RV Resort

Surround yourself with wildlife and plenty of rugged outdoor experiences.

46628 Highway 60, Salome, AZ 85348	(928) 927-7800 https://www.g7rvresorts.com	All Year
$33-$39	Military/Good Sam	Pet Breed
550 Spaces	Paved	30Width/70Length
Internet, Showers, Laundry	Ice, RV Wash, Rec. Hall	Kitchen, Pool, Rec. Hall

Leaf Verde RV Resort

Located just outside Phoenix, you'll get away from the bustle of the city.

1500 S Apache Rd, Buckeye, AZ 85326	(623) 386-3132	All Year
$39-$49	Military/Good Sam	No Restrictions
377 Spaces	Paved	24Width/75Length
Internet, Showers, Laundry	LP Gas, Ice, RV Wash, Pool	Rec. Hall, Game Room, Gym

Casa Grande RV Resort

Located between Phoenix and Tucson, this park offers plenty of amenities.

195 W Rodeo Rd, Casa Grande, AZ 85122	(520) 421-0401 https://casagrandervresort.com	All Year
$32-$49	Military/Good Sam	No Restrictions
340 Spaces	Paved	20Width/60Length
Internet, Showers, Laundry	Ice, RV Wash, Rentals, Pool	Games, Rec. hall, Gym

Palm Creek Golf and RV Resort

A 55+ park for the active individual.

1110 N Henness Rd, Casa Grande, AZ 85122	(520) 421-7000 https://palmcreekgolf.com/	All Year
$41-$77	Good Sam	55+, RV Age, Pet Qty, Breed
2047 Spaces	Paved	16Width/100Length
Internet, Showers, Laundry	Rentals, RV Wash, Pool	Tennis, Games, Patios

Sundance 1 RV Resort

This 55+ park gives you the best of resort living.

1703 N Thornton Rd, Casa Grande, AZ 85122	(520) 426-9662 http://sundance1rv.com/	All Year
$37-$50	Good Sam	55+, RV Age, Pet Breed&Qty
707 Spaces	Paved	39Width/55Length
Internet, Showers, Laundry	Gated, Ice, Cable, Pool	Game Room, Activities

Fiesta Grande RV Resort

A conveniently located 55+ park.

1511 East Florence Blvd, Casa Grande, AZ 85122	(888) 934-3782	All Year
$41-$47	Military/Good Sam	55+, RV Age, Pet Breed
766 Spaces	Paved	36Width/60Length
Shower, Laundry, Pool, Ice	Hot Tub, Game Room, Gym	Activities, Driving Range

Casita Verde RV Resort

This park offers you a relaxed atmosphere at a reasonable price.

2200 N. Trekell Rd, Casa Grande, AZ 85122	(877) 697-8737 Website	All Year
$44-$54	Military/Good Sam	55+, Pet Breed
192 Spaces	Paved	30Width/50Length
Internet, Showers, Laundry	RV Wash, Pool, Rec. Hall	Games, Pavilion, Hot Tub

Foothills West RV Resort

This 55+ park is pet-friendly. It is the perfect place to stay if you want a relaxing atmosphere.

10167 N. Encore Dr., Casa Grande, AZ 85122	(800) 576-8567	All Year
$44-$54	Military/Good Sam	55+, Pet Size, Breed
186 Spaces	Gravel	24Width/60Length
Internet, Showers, Laundry	Ice, Pool, Hot Tub, Rec. Hall	Games, Activities, Putting

Sunscape Estates RV Park

This conveniently located 55+ park offers lots of amenities.

1083 East Sunscape Way, Casa Grande, AZ 85294	(520) 723-9533 sunscapervresort.com/	All Year
$25-$35	No Discounts Offered	55+
504 Spaces	Paved	30Width/60Length
Showers, Laundry, Gated	LP Gas, Pool, Hot Tub, Gym	Games, Activities

Ho Ho Kam RV Park

Located in the Central part of Arizona and a short freeway drive to Phoenix and Tucson.

1925 S Arizona Blvd, Coolidge, AZ 85128	(520) 723-3697 http://hohokammobilevillage.com/	All Year
$35	Good Sam	Pet Size, Breed
202 Spaces	Paved	25Width/45Length
Internet, Showers, Laundry	RV Wash, Pool, Rec. hall	Games, Gym, Activities

River Breeze RV Resort

This clean park is the ideal place for a family vacation.

50202 Ehrenberg Rd, Ehrenberg, AZ 85334	(928) 923-7483 http://www.riverbreezerv.com/	All Year
$42-$63	Military/Good Sam	No Restrictions
94 Spaces	Paved	40Width/65Length
Internet, Showers, Laundry	Supplies, LP Gas, Ice, Cable	Pool, Hot Tub, Playground

Pueblo El Mirage RV Golf Resort

This 55+ park offers a lush, resort lifestyle at an affordable price.

11201 North El Mirage Road, # 2, El Mirage, AZ 85335	(623) 583-0425 puebloelmiragegolf.com/	All Year
$54-$84	Good Sam	55+, RV Age, Pet Breed
1075 Spaces	Paved	40Width/100Length
Internet, Showers, Laundry	Gated, Ice, Restaurant, Golf	Tennis, Sauna, Games

Silverado RV Resort

There are many places close to this 55+ park that you'll never run out of things to see and do.

4555 W Tonto Rd, Eloy, AZ 85131	(520) 466-4500 http://www.silveradorvresort.com/	All Year
$42	Military/Good Sam	55+, Pet Size, Breed
350 Spaces	Paved	30Width/60Length
Internet, Showers, Laundry	Gated, Pool, Rec. Hall	Games, Activities, Putting

Las Colinas RV Resort

This park feels like a small community at an affordable price.

7136 S Sunland Gin Rd, Eloy, AZ 85131	(520) 836-5050 http://lascolinasrvresort.com/	All Year
$39	Military/Good Sam	55+, Pet Breed
150 Spaces	Paved	32Width/70Length

| Internet, Showers, Laundry | Supplies, Ice, Pool, Gym | Games, Rec. Hall, Putting |

Eagle View RV Resort

This resort offers serenity and solitude.

9605 N Fort Mcdowell Rd, Fort Mcdowell, AZ 85264	(480) 789-5310 eagleviewrvresort.com/	All Year
$36-$58	Military/Good Sam	RV Age, Pet Breed
150 Spaces	Paved	30Width/69Length
Internet, Showers, Laundry	Gated, Ice, Snack Bar, Pool	Cable, Golf, Gym, Games

Cotton Lane RV Resort

You'll be comfortable with the amenities offered at this park.

17506 W Van Buren St, Goodyear, AZ 85338	(623) 853-4000 http://www.cottonlanervresort.com/	All Year
$34	Military/Good Sam	55+, RV Age, Pet Breed
438 Spaces	Paved	24Width/70Length
Internet, Shower, Laundry	Ice, Pool, Hot Tub, Game Room	Rec. Hall, Games, Golf

Destiny RV Resort

This park puts you within a short distance to all the Phoenix area has to offer.

416 N Citrus Rd, Goodyear, AZ 85338	(623) 853-0537 http://www.destinyrvresort.com	All Year
$38-$46	Military/Good Sam	RV Age, Pet Breed&Qty.
284 Spaces	Paved	30Width/48Length
Internet, Showers, Laundry	Gated, Pool, Gym, Games	Putting, Tables, Hot Tub

Western Acres

Near mountains and lakes for plenty of outdoor activities.

9913 E Apache Trl, Mesa, AZ 85207	(480) 986-1158 http://western-acres.com/	All Year
$38	Good Sam	Pet Breed, Quantity
180 Spaces	Paved	25Width/35Length
Internet, Showers, Laundry	Rec. Hall, Horseshoes	Patios, Shuffleboard

Good Life RV Resort

This 55+ community is great for active guests.

3403 E Main St, Mesa, AZ 85213	(480) 832-4990	All Year
$49	Military/Good Sam	55+, RV Age, Pet Breed&Qty.
1156 Spaces	Paved	30Width/42Length

| Internet, Showers, Laundry | Gated, Ice, Restaurant | RV Wash, Pool, Gym |

Val Vista Village RV Resort
This 55+ community is your destination for fun.

233 N Val Vista Dr, Mesa, AZ 85213	(480) 981-4822	All Year
$55-$97	Good Sam	55+, Pet Size, Breed
1498 Spaces	Paved	32Width/82Length
Showers, Laundry, SnackBar	ATM, Pool, Hot Tub, Games	Rec. Hall, Activities

Mesa Regal RV Resort
One of the largest RV resorts, offering state of the art amenities.

4700 E Main St, Mesa, AZ 85205	(480) 830-2821	All Year
$70	Good Sam	Pet Breed, Qty.
2005 Spaces	Paved	35Width/45Length
Internet, Showers, Laundry	ATM, Ice, Snack Bar, Sauna	Tennis, Massage, Patios

Towerpoint Resort
This active, yet relaxed 55+ community is the perfect destination.

4860 E Main St, Mesa, AZ 85205	(480) 924-0433	All Year
$52	Good Sam	55+, RV Age, Pet Size/Breed
1112 Spaces	Paved	30Width/50Length
Internet, Showers, Laundry	Pool, ATM, Restaurant	Game Room, Gym, Pool

Sun Life RV Resort
If you want to be centrally located to all that Mesa has to offer, then this is your best option.

5055 E University Dr, Mesa, AZ 85205	(480) 981-9500	All Year
$62	Good Sam	55+, Pet Size, Qty.
761 Spaces	Paved	32Width/45Length
Internet, Showers, Laundry	Gated, ATM, Ice, Pool	Restaurant, RV Wash, gym

Apache Wells RV Resort
With so much to do within the park, you may never have time to explore the surrounding area.

2656 N 56th St, Mesa, AZ 85215	(480) 832-4324	All Year
$46	Good Sam	55+, RV Age, Pet Breed
320 Spaces	Paved	32Width/45Length

| Internet, Showers, Laundry | Ice, Pool, Rec. Hall | Game Room, Activities |

Valle Del Oro RV Resort

This 55+ park gives new meaning to the term "luxury." Stay here, and you'll have it all.

1452 S Ellsworth Rd, Mesa, AZ 85209	(480) 984-1146	All Year
$35-$69	Good Sam	55+, Pet Breed, Qty.
1761 Spaces	Paved	35Width/50Length
Internet, Showers, Laundry	Gated, ATM, Snack Bar	Pool, Game Room, Sauna

Mesa Spirit RV Resort

Here you'll find yourself to the west of the Superstition Mountains.

3020 E Main St, Mesa, AZ 85213	(855) 388-9419	All Year
$33-$82	Military/Good Sam	55+, RV Age, Pet Breed
1678 Spaces	Paved	24Width/80Length
Internet, Showers, Laundry	Gated, Ice, Cable, Pool	Rec. Hall, Activities, Patios

Viewpoint RV Resort

Located at the base of the Superstition Mountains, this park lives up to its name.

8700 E University Dr, Mesa, AZ 85207	(800) 822-4404	All Year
$60-$77	Good Sam	55+, Pet Breed
2500 Spaces	Paved	15Width/50Length
Internet, Showers, Laundry	Gated, Ice, Restaurant	Rec. Hall, Sauna, Tennis

Monte Vista Village RV Resort

There aren't a lot of amenities and services, but you're close enough to get what you need.

8865 E. Baseline Road, Mesa, AZ 85209	(888) 509-1694 Website	All Year
$64-$67	Military/Good Sam	55+, Pet Breed
1184 Spaces	Paved	30Width/70Length
Showers, Laundry, Gated	Rentals, Pool, Rec. Hall	Sauna, Tennis, Games

Palm Gardens RV Park

A beautiful gated 55+ community in Mesa, close to lots of activities and services.

2929 E Main St, Mesa, AZ 85213	(480) 832-0290 https://palmgardensonline.com/	All Year
$45	Good Sam	55+, Pet Breed
439 Spaces	Paved	30Width/50Length
Showers, Laundry, Gated	Pool, Rec. Hall, Activities	Gym, Games, Patios

Arizona Cowboy RV Park

A small park that provides a quaint atmosphere with beautiful landscaping.

139 S Crismon Rd 35, Mesa, AZ 85208	(480) 354-3700	All Year
$40	Good Sam	No Restrictions
38 Spaces	Paved	24Width/50Length
Restrooms, Showers	Laundry, Gated	Patios, Trash Pickup

Pleasant Harbor Marina RV Resort

A brief Located along the shores of Lake Pleasant.

8708 W Harbor Blvd, Peoria, AZ 85383	(602) 269-0077 https://pleasantharbor.com/	All Year
$45-$59	Good Sam	Pet Quantity
253 Spaces	Paved	31Width/70Length
Internet, Showers, Laundry	Gated, Restaurant, Grocery	Rec. Hall, Game Room, Pool

Desert Shadows RV Resort

Located in North Phoenix, this is a tranquil park with plenty of amenities.

19203 N 29th Ave, Phoenix, AZ 85027	(623) 869-8178 https://www.phoenixrvresorts.com/	All Year
$52-$64	Good Sam	Pet Breed
638 Spaces	Paved	30Width/75Length
Internet, Shower, Laundry	Ice, Pool, Games, Rec. Hall	Pavilion, Putting, Gym

Phoenix Metro RV Park

Nestled in Northwest Phoenix, this park is a mountain community.

22701 N Black Canyon Hwy, Phoenix, AZ 85027	(623) 582-0390 phoenixmetrorvpark.com/	All Year
$50	Military/Good Sam	55+, RV Age, Pet Breed
310 Spaces	Paved	30Width/43Length
Internet, Showers, Laundry	Pool, Rec. Hall, Game Room	Activities, Gym, Putting

Pioneer RV Resort

This 55+ community offers affordable rates for luxury amenities.

36408 N Black Canyon Hwy, Phoenix, AZ 85086	(623) 465-7465 http://www.arizonarvresorts.com	All Year
$40	Good Sam	55+, RV Age, Pet Breed
583 Spaces	Paved	28Width/98Length
Internet, Showers, Laundry	Ice, Snack Bar, Pool, Rec. Hall	Gym, Pavilion, Games

Quail Run RV Park

This is the park to visit if you want to enjoy rugged outdoor activities.

918 N Central Blvd, Quartzsite, AZ 85346	(928) 927-8810 http://www.quailrv.com/	All Year
$25-$36	Good Sam	Pet Size, Breed
168 Spaces	Paved	30Width/70Length
Internet, Showers, Laundry	Supplies, Rec. Hall, Games	Activities, Patios

Holiday Palms Resort

Easy access from the freeway and yet in the heart of town.

355 W. Main St., Quartzsite, AZ 85359	(928) 927-5666 http://holidaypalmsrv.com/	All Year
$32-$36	Military/Good Sam	Pet Breed
243 Spaces	Paved	27Width/75Length
Internet, Showers, Laundry	Firewood, RV Wash, Hot Tub	Rec. Hall, Activities, Tables

88 Shades RV Park

This is your best value for amenities in the area.

575 W Main St, Quartzsite, AZ	(928) 927-6336 88shadesquartzsitervpark.com/	All Year
$29	Military/Good Sam	Pet Breed
230 Spaces	Gravel	25Width/70Length
Internet, Showers, Laundry	Supplies, Hot Tub, Rec. Hall	Game Room, Activities

The Scenic Road RV Park

Located in downtown Quartzsite, this is the ideal desert getaway.

480 N Central Blvd, Quartzsite, AZ 85346	(928) 927-6443 http://thescenicroad.com/	All Year
$34-$44	Good Sam	No Restrictions
97 Spaces	Gravel	30Width/60Length
Internet, Showers, Laundry	Rentals, Rec. Hall, Games	Patios, Pavilion, Horseshoes

Desert Vista KOA Campground

If you like off-roading, then this park has direct access to plenty of trails for you.

64812 Harcuvar Drive, Salome, AZ 85348	(928) 859-4639	All Year
$39-$44	Military/Good Sam	No Restrictions
125 Spaces	Gravel	45Width/60Length
Internet, Showers, Laundry	Ice, Grocery, Pool	Rec. Hall, Game Room

Paradise RV Resort

This 55+ community offers you the extras you want in an RV park.

10950 W. Union Hills Dr., Sun City, AZ 85373	(888) 408-5048 Website	All Year
$32-$48	Good Sam	55+, Pet Quantity
950 Spaces	Paved	38Width/55Length
Showers, Laundry, Gated	Restaurant, Pool, Rec. Hall	Gym, Games, Patios, Tennis

Sunflower RV Resort

This park offers a small community feel while offering plenty of amenities and services.

16501 N El Mirage Rd, Surprise, AZ 85378	(623) 583-0100	All Year
$35-$69	Good Sam	55+, RV Age, Pet Breed
1139 Spaces	Paved	30Width/60Length
Internet, Showers, Laundry	Gated, Ice, Snack Bar, Lounge	Sauna, Tennis, Putting Green

Apache Palms RV Park

This central location makes it easy for you to visit Tempe, Phoenix, and Scottsdale.

1836 E Apache Blvd, Tempe, AZ 85281	(480) 966-7399	All Year
$50-$55	Military/Good Sam	Pet Breed
80 Spaces	Paved	24Width/70Length
Internet, Showers, Laundry	Cable, RV Wash, Pool	Hot Tub, Pavilion, Patios

Saddle Mountain RV Park

Located just a half-mile from the Interstate, this offers a quiet desert getaway.

40902 W Osborn Rd, Tonopah, AZ 85354	(623) 386-3892 saddlemountainrvpark.com/	All Year
$32	Military/Good Sam	Pet Breed
344 Spaces	Paved	30Width/60Length
Internet, Showers, Laundry	Rentals, LP Gas, Pool, Tennis	Gym, Games, Activities

Coach Stop RV Park

This park gives you a unique western feel.

30333 E Wellton Mohawk Dr, Wellton, AZ 85356	(928) 785-9798 https://www.coachstoprvpark.com	All Year
$30	Good Sam	No Restrictions
190 Spaces	Paved	30Width/75Length
Showers, Laundry, Pool	Rec. Hall, Activities, Gym	RV Wash, Horseshoes

Horspitality RV Resort

You don't need to own a horse to stay here, but it is a very horse-friendly park.

51802 Us Highway 60 89 89, Wickenburg, AZ 85390	(928) 684-2519 https://horspitality.com/	All Year
$47-$54	Military/Good Sam	Pet Breed
100 Spaces	Paved	30Width/65Length
Internet, Showers, Laundry	Supplies, LP Gas, Firewood	Ice, Rec. Hall, Activities

Fortuna de Oro RV Resort

You won't have to leave the park to enjoy a variety of activities.

13650 N Frontage Rd, Yuma, AZ 85367	(928) 342-5051	All Year
$42-$52	Good Sam	55+, RV Age, Pet Breed
1294 Spaces	Paved	30Width/50Length
Internet, Showers, Laundry	ATM, Ice, Pool, Golf, Games	Activities, Patios, Gym

Villa Alameda RV Resort

This 55+ community offers you whatever you want.

3547 S Avenue 5 E, Yuma, AZ 85365	(928) 344-8081 https://villaalamedarvresort.com/	All Year
$40	Good Sam	Pet Breed
302 Spaces	Paved	33Width/52Length
Internet, Showers, Laundry	Ice, Cable, RV Wash, Pool	Game Room, Patios

Del Pueblo RV Park

This 55+ park is among the top-rated in Arizona. It is clean, friendly, and full of activities.

14794 S AVE 3E, Yuma, AZ 85365	(928) 341-2100 http://www.delpueblorv.com/	All Year
$49-$59	Good Sam	55+, Pet Quantity
478 Spaces	Paved	40Width/90Length
Internet, Showers, Laundry	Restaurant, Cable, Rentals	Pavilion, Tennis, Gym

Sun Vista RV Resort

This park is full of amenities, including indoor and outdoor pools.

7201 E 32nd St, Yuma, AZ 85365	(928) 726-8920 https://sunvistarvresort.com	All Year
$50	Good Sam	Pet Size
1226 Spaces	Paved	30Width/60Length
Internet, Showers, Laundry	Gated, ATM, LP Gas, Ice	SnackBar, Restaurant, Games

Westwind RV Resort

This resort features a golf course that runs through it.

9797 East 32nd St, Yuma, AZ 85365	(928) 342-2992	All Year
$30-$50	Good Sam	RV Age, Pet Breed
1075 Spaces	Paved	32Width/84Length
Internet, Showers, Laundry	Gated, ATM, Ice, Pool, Golf	Pavilion, Gym, Patios

Sundance RV Resort

You can enjoy the beauty of the desert from the foothills of the mountains at this resort.

13502 N Frontage Rd, Yuma, AZ 85367	(928) 342-9333	All Year
$37	Good Sam	RV Age, Pet Quantity
460 Spaces	Paved	30Width/40Length
Internet, Showers, Laundry	Ice, Pool, Rec. Hall, Games	Gym, Patios, Activities

Desert Paradise RV Resort

Located in the foothills, this park is far enough away from town to give you peace and quiet.

10537 S Ave 9 E, Yuma, AZ 85365	(928) 342-9313	All Year
$52-$59	Military/Good Sam	55+, Pet Breed
252 Spaces	Paved	30Width/48Length
Showers, Laundry, Pool, Ice	Rec. Hall, Activities, Games	Gym, Patios

Shangri-La RV Resort

There is plenty of shade so you can stay cool while relaxing at this RV resort.

10498 N Frontage Rd, Yuma, AZ 85365	(928) 342-9123 http://www.shangrilarv.com/	All Year
$38-$51	Military/Good Sam	55+, Pet Breed
300 Spaces	Paved	30Width/90Length
Internet, Showers, Laundry	Cable, LP Gas, Pavilion	Rec. Hall, Gym, Mini Golf

Desert Holiday RV Resort

This 55+ community is in downtown Yuma so you can walk to nearly anything.

3601 S 4th Ave, Yuma, AZ 85365	(928) 344-4680 https://www.rvdesertholiday.com/	All Year
$30-$40	Military/Good Sam	55+, Pet Size
225 Spaces	Paved	25Width/70Length
Internet, Showers, Laundry	Pool, Rentals, Rec. Hall	Game Room, Gym, Patios

Blue Sky RV Ranch
A quaint park with the amenities of a larger resort.

5510 E 32nd St, Yuma, AZ 85365	(928) 726-0160 https://www.blueskyranchyuma.com/	All Year
$40-$50	Military/Good Sam	55+, Pet Breed
200 Spaces	Paved	30Width/65Length
Internet, Showers, Pool	Laundry, Rec. Hall, Games	Patios, Pavilion

Caravan Oasis RV Resort
Conveniently located in town, you have plenty of amenities to keep you busy

10500 N Frontage Rd, Yuma, AZ 85365	(928) 342-1480 http://www.caravanoasisresort.com	All Year
$48	Military/Good Sam	55+, Pet Breed
510 Spaces	Paved	28Width/60Length
Internet, Shower, Laundry	Ice, Rentals, Pool, Rec. Hall, Gym	Putting, Activities, Patios

Bonita Mesa RV Resort
This park is in the beautiful foothills of Yuma.

9400 N Frontage Rd, Yuma, AZ 85365	(928) 342-2999 https://bonitamesa.com/	All Year
$46	Military/Good Sam	Pet Quantity, Breed
470 Spaces	Paved	30Width/50Length
Internet, Showers, Laundry	Rentals, Pool, Game Room	Activities, Gym, Patios

Arkansas

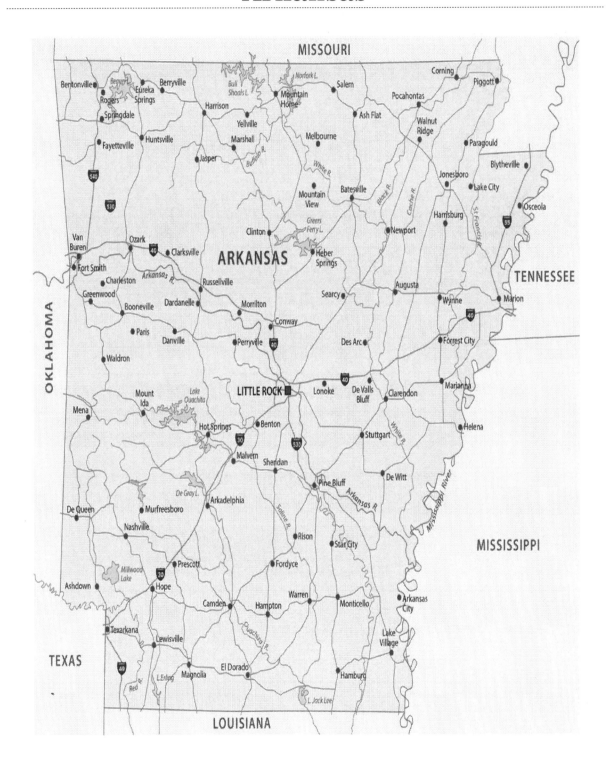

Arkansas – The Ozarks

The Ozarks in the Northern portion of Arkansas is full of mountains and natural beauty. When RVing here, you'll be staying at smaller towns and quaint RV parks. However, that doesn't mean you'll be sacrificing amenities and activities.

The Creeks Golf RV Resort

Located in the Osage Valley, this RV park offers plenty of amenities and services.

1499 S Main St., Cave Springs, AR 72718	(479) 248-1000	All Year
$50	Good Sam	RV Age
113 Spaces	Paved	30Width/77Length
Internet, Showers, Laundry	ATM, LP Gas, Ice, Cable	Restaurant, Rec. Hall, Golf

Denton Ferry RV Park Resort

This park is located in a historic town along the White River in the Ozark Mountains.

740 Denton Ferry Rd, Cotter, AR 72626	1 (800) 275-5611	All Year
$30-$42	Military/Good Sam	No Restrictions
44 Spaces	Gravel	30Width/65Length
Internet, Showers, Laundry	LP Gas, Firewood, Ice	Rentals, Rec. Hall, Tables

Wanderlust RV Park

Located on a ridge in the Ozark Mountains, this park offers exceptional views.

468 Passion Play Rd, Eureka Springs, AR 72632	(479) 253-7385 http://www.wanderlustrvpark.com/	All Year
$37-$47	Military/Good Sam	No Restrictions
93 Spaces	Gravel	27Width/84Length
Internet, Showers, Laundry	Supplies, Firewood, Rentals	Ice, Pool, Rec. Hall

Kettle Campground, Cabins & RV Park

Located in the heart of the Ozark Mountains, this is a true wilderness experience.

4119 E Van Buren, Eureka Springs, AR 72632	(479) 253-9100 https://kettlecampground.net/	All Year
$30-$36	Military/Good Sam	No Restrictions
57 Spaces	Gravel	26Width/70Length
Internet, Showers, Laundry	Supplies, LP Gas, Firewood	Ice, Rentals, RV Wash

Southgate RV Park

This is the only place to park overnight within the city of Fayetteville.

2331 S School Ave, Fayetteville, AR 72701	(479) 442-2021 http://www.southgatervpark.com/	All Year
$38	Military/Good Sam	RV Age, Pet Size
50 Spaces	Gravel	30Width/70Length
Internet, Showers, Laundry	RV Wash, Games	Pavilion

Parkers RV Park

This park is a great option for those who want to be out on the water.

3629 Highway 65 N, Harrison, AR 72601	(870) 743-2267 http://www.parkersrvpark.com/	All Year
$29-$33	Military/Good Sam	RV Age
41 Spaces	Paved	30Width/65Length
Internet, Showers, Laundry	LP Gas, Supplies, Ice	RV Service, Rec.Hall, Games

Arkansas – River Valley

Below the Ozark Mountain region of Arkansas is the beautiful River Valley region. This small area of the state features some small towns and beautiful RV parks

Fort Smith-Alma RV Park
Located just off the highway, this park offers convenience and beauty.

3539 N Highway 71, Alma, AR 72921	(479) 632-2704 https://fortsmithalmarvpark.com/	All Year
$36-$46	Military/Good Sam	Pet Breed
58 Spaces	Paved	18Width/70Length
Internet, Showers, Laundry	Supplies, LP Gas, Ice, Cable	RV Service, Rentals, Pool

Eagle Crest RV Park
This RV park is located at one of the premier golf courses in Arkansas.

3926 Golf Course Dr, Alma, AR 72921	479-632-8857 golfeaglecrest.com/rv-park/	All Year
$35	Good Sam	Pet Quantity
19 Spaces	Gravel	25Width/80Length
Golf, Ice, Golf Carts, Snacks	Games, Driving Range	Putting Green, Pavilion

Morrilton I40/107 RV Park
This park provides easy access to a number of activities in the surrounding area.

30 Kamper Ln, Morrilton, AR 72110	(501) 354-8262 http://morriltonrvpark.com/	All Year
$35	Military/Good Sam	No Restrictions
54 Spaces	Gravel	30Width/75Length
Internet, Showers, Laundry	Supplies, Ice, Grocery	Rentals, Playground, Pavilion

Outdoor Living Center RV Park
Conveniently located off the highway and a short distance to a variety of attractions and towns.

Highway 7 N, Russellville, AR 72801	(479) 968-7705	All Year
$37-$40	Military/Good Sam	Pet Breed
50 Spaces	Paved/Gravel	20Width/60Length
Internet, Showers, Laundry	Ice, Cable, RV Wash	Rec. Hall, Pavilion, Tables

Arkansas – Central and Delta

Central Arkansas is a small area and doesn't require a lot of places to stay. In fact, you can stay near the state capital and be able to visit most areas in this region of Arkansas. The Delta region covers the eastern side of the state and offers some nice quaint parks.

Downtown Riverside RV Park

The name says it all! This park is located in downtown Little Rock and is right along the river.

250 S Locust St, North Little Rock, AR 72114	(501) 340-5312 downtownriversidervpark.com/	All Year
$24-$33	Military/Good Sam	Pet Breed
61 Spaces	Paved	40Width/100Length
Internet, Showers, Laundry	Gated, Ice	Pavilion, RV Wash

Pecan Grove RV Park

Located on the banks of Lake Chicot, this park takes you back in time.

3764 S Highway 65, Lake Village, AR 71653	(870) 265-3005 http://www.pecangrove.net/	All Year
$25-$40	Military/Good Sam	Pet Breed
104 Spaces	Gravel	35Width/90Length
Internet, Shower, Laundry	Firewood, Snack Bar, Food	Cable, Rentals, Rec. Hall

Tom Sawyer's RV Park

Located right along the river, this is a great RV park.

1286 S 8th St, West Memphis, AR 72301	(870) 735-9770 http://tomsawyerrvpark.com/	All Year
$27-$49	Good Sam	Pet Breed
121 Spaces	Paved/Gravel	30Width/130Length
Internet, Showers, Laundry	Firewood, Ice, RV Wash	Games, Tables, Gated

Arkansas - Ouachitas and Timberlands

The Ouachitas region in the Southwest of the state features an impressive mountain range for those who want adventurous outdoor activities. The Timberlands region in the south portion of the state has a few RV parks that provide a relaxed outdoor experience.

Cloud Nine RV Park
This park offers only the basic amenities and services, but that is fine.

136 Cloud Nine Trl, Hot Springs, AR 71901	(501) 262-1996 https://cloudninerv.com/	All Year
$33	Good Sam	No Restrictions
45 Spaces	Paved	38Width/70Length
Internet, Showers, Laundry	RV Wash, Rec. Hall, Games	Gym, Fire Ring, Tables

Hot Springs National Park KOA
Stay within the National Park and spend your time exploring the Ouachita Mountains.

838 McClendon Road, Hot Springs, AR 71901	(501) 624-5912 koa.com/campgrounds/hot-springs-national-park/	All Year
$44-$92	Military	No Restrictions
81 Spaces	Paved	25Width/70Length
Internet, Showers, Laundry	Supplies, Firewood, Ice	Grocery, Playground, Tables

J & J RV Park
This park provides a scenic setting for either a relaxing adventure or a base of operations.

2000 E Grand Ave, Hot Springs, AR 71901	(501) 321-9852 http://www.jjrvpark.com/	All Year
$37	Military/Good Sam	No Restrictions
46 Spaces	Paved	30Width/70Length
Internet, Showers, Laundry	Ice, Rec. Hall, Playground	Pavilion, Tables

Young's Lakeshore RV Resort
This is your best destination to stay while doing everything you want in Hot Springs.

1601 Lakeshore Dr, Hot Springs, AR 71913	(501) 767-7946 http://www.rvhotsprings.com/	All Year
$37	Military/Good Sam	Pet Size, Quantity, Breed
44 Spaces	Paved/Gravel	30Width/60Length
Internet, Showers, Laundry	LP Gas, Firewood, Ice	RV wash, Rentals, Games

Treasure Isle RV Park

There are plenty of outdoor activities and historical sites to visit in the surrounding area.

205 Treasure Isle Rd, Hot Springs, AR 71913	(501) 767-6852 https://www.treasureislerv.com/	All Year
$33-$48	Military/Good Sam	Pet Breed
65 Spaces	Paved/Gravel	24Width/55Length
Internet, Showers, Laundry	Firewood, Ice, Cable	Rentals, Pool, Playground

Catherine's Landing At Hot Springs

This park is only minutes away from Hot Springs but seems to be a different world.

1700 Shady Grove Road, Hot Springs, AR 71901	(501) 262-2550 https://catherineslanding.com	All Year
$50-$75	Military/Good Sam	No Restrictions
211 Spaces	Paved	32Width/62Length
Internet, Showers, Laundry	Rentals, Fishing, Pool	Rec. Hall, Games, Fire Rings

Shadow Mountain RV Park

Conveniently located off the highway, but yet far enough into the mountains.

3708 Highway 71 S, Mena, AR 71953	(479) 394-6099 shadowmountaincampground.com/	All Year
$20-$45	Military/Good Sam	Pet Size
64 Spaces	Paved/Gravel	20Width/40Length
Internet, Shower, Laundry	Ice, Cable, Rentals, Pool	Rec. Hall, Fire Ring, Tables

California

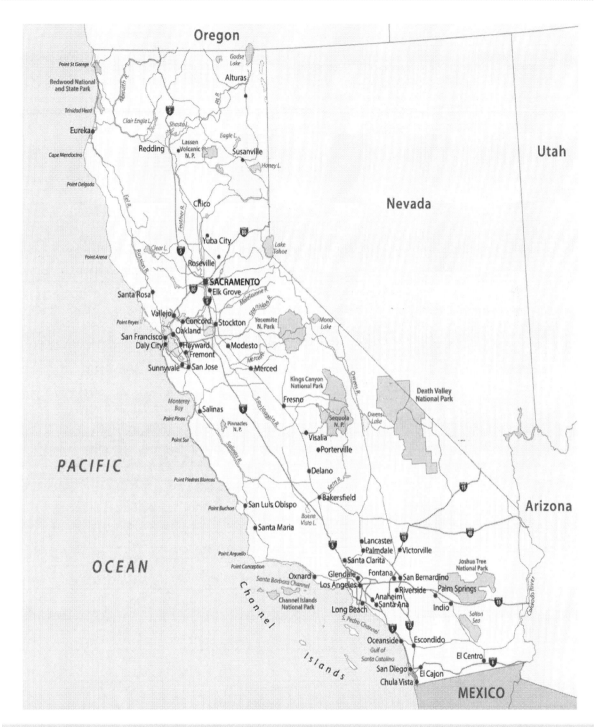

California – North Coast

Mad River Rapids RV Park

Conveniently located near the freeway and several cities, this park is the perfect place to stay.

3501 Janes Rd, Arcata, CA 95521	(707) 822-7275 https://www.madriverrv.com/	All Year
$50	Military/Good Sam	No Restrictions
92 Spaces	Paved	28Width/63Length
Internet, Showers, Laundry	Grocery, Snack Bar, Ice	Pool, Rec. Hall, Playground

Russian River RV Campground

Located right along the Russian River and surrounded by the natural beauty of the redwoods.

33655 Geysers Rd, Cloverdale, CA 95425	(888) 399-8976	All Year
$40-$45	Good Sam	No Restrictions
120 Spaces	Paved	30Width/55Length
Showers, Laundry, Gated	LP Gas, Firewood, Ice	Rec. Hall, Games, Playground

Village Camper Inn RV Park

This is your best summer destination for sightseeing and doing all things nature.

1543 Parkway Dr, Crescent City, CA 95531	(707) 464-3544 villagecamperinn.com/	All Year
$46	Military/Good Sam	No Restrictions
135 Spaces	Paved	25Width/50Length
Internet, Showers, Laundry	Firewood, Cable, Rentals	Games, Tennis, Tables

Redwood Harbor Village

This is the perfect base of operations for exploring the North Coast of California.

159 Starfish Way, Crescent City, CA 95531	(707) 388-0159 redwoodharborvillage.com/	All Year
$45-$50	Good Sam	No Restrictions
117 Spaces	Paved	18Width/40Length
Internet, Showers, Laundry	Cable, Patios	Tables

Redwood Meadows RV Resort

Located next to the Redwood National Park so you can explore it at your leisure.

2000 US Highway 199, Crescent City, CA 95531	(707) 458-3321 redwoodcoastrv.com/redwood-meadows/	All Year
$43-$51	Good Sam	Pet Quantity
120 Spaces	Paved	35Width/60Length

| Internet, Showers, Laundry | Rentals, RV Wash, Games | Rec. Hall, Horseshoes |

Shoreline RV Park
This RV park is close to the harbor.

2600 6th St, Eureka, CA 95501	(707) 443-2222 redwoodcoastrv.com/shoreline/	All Year
$41-$53	Good Sam	Pet Breed
59 Spaces	Paved	26Width/74Length
Internet	Showers, Laundry	Cable, RV Service

Redwood Coast RV Resort
Perfectly situated in the town of Eureka.

4050 N US Highway 101, Eureka, CA 95503	(707) 822-4243 https://www.redwoodcoastrv.com/	All Year
$46-$49	Military/Good Sam	Pet Breed
83 Spaces	Paved	25Width/40Length
Internet, Showers, Laundry	Firewood, LP Gas, Ice	Groceries, Game Room

Pomo RV Park Campground
This park provides large secluded lots so you can enjoy your vacation.

17999 Tregoning Ln, Fort Bragg, CA 95437		All Year
$51	Good Sam	No Restrictions
96 Spaces	Paved	30Width/60Length
Internet, Showers, Laundry	Firewood, Supplies, Cable	Fishing, Fire Rings, Games

Riverwalk RV Park Campground
Considered one of the best RV parks on the North Coast.

2189 Riverwalk Dr, Fortuna, CA 95540	(707) 725-3359 http://riverwalkrvpark.com/	All Year
$42-$52	Military/Good Sam	Pet Breed
89 Spaces	Paved	25Width/60Length
Internet, Showers, Laundry	Ice, Firewood, Grocery	Pool, Rec. Hall, Games

Ramblin' Redwoods Campground & RV Park
This RV park is close in proximity to many different outdoor activities to enjoy.

6701 Highway US-101 North Crescent City, California 95531	(707) 487-7404 https://ramblinredwoodsrv.com/	All Year
$35	Good Sam	No Restrictions

30 Spaces	Paved/Gravel	15Width/40Length
Restrooms, Showers	Firewood, Groceries	Rentals, Games

Kamp Klamath RV Park Campground
This is the perfect base camp for an adventurous redwood experience.

1661 W Klamath Beach Rd, Klamath, CA 95548	(707) 482-0227	All Year
$40	Military/Good Sam	No Restrictions
49 Spaces	Gravel	25Width/70Length
Internet, Showers, Laundry	Supplies, Firewood, Cable	Grocery, Fishing, Fire Rings

Konocti Vista RV Park
Stay near the casino and take part in some of the best entertainment.

2755 Mission Rancheria Rd, Lakeport, CA 95453	(707) 262-1900 konocti-vista-casino.com/	All Year
$40-$45	Good Sam	28 Day Stay Max
74 Spaces	Paved	15Width/42Length
Casino, Internet, Showers	Laundry, ATM, Ice, Cable	Restaurant, Pool, Gym

Giant Redwoods RV Park and Camp
The perfect place to have a relaxing redwood area vacation.

455 Boy Scout Road, Myers Flat, CA 95554	(707) 943-9999	All Year
$43-$50	Good Sam	Pet Breed
53 Spaces	Gravel	18Width/50Length
Internet, Showers, Laundry	Firewood, Ice, Grocery, Pool	Cable, Games, Fire Rings

Ancient Redwoods RV Park
Located within the Avenue of the Giants, this is your place to stay in the redwoods.

28101 Avenue Of The Giants, Redcrest, CA 95569	(707) 722-4396 http://ancientredwoods.net	May 1st to October 31st
$50	Good Sam	Pet Breed
49 Spaces	Paved	30Width/60Length
Internet, Showers, Laundry	Supplies, Firewood, Ice	Pavilion, Snack Bar, Tables

Dean Creek Resort
Located along the banks of the Eel River, this park gives you all the comforts of home.

4112 Redwood Dr, Redway, CA 95560	(707) 923-2555 stayhereandplay.com/dean-creek-resort/	All Year
$39-$55	Good Sam	No Restrictions

40 Spaces	Paved	20Width/80Length
Internet, Showers, Laundry	Playground, Sauna, Games	Rec. Hall, Rentals, Pool

Emerald Forest
Stay where the redwoods meet the sea.

753 Patricks Point Dr, Trinidad, CA 95570	(707) 677-3554 https://www.emeraldforestcabins.com/	All Year
$38-$50	Military	Pet Breed
47 Spaces	Gravel	18Width/40Length
Internet, Showers, Ice	Firewood, Grocery, Supplies, LP Gas	Rec. Hall, Game Room

Golden Rule RV Park
A very peaceful park. Perfect for birdwatchers and nature lovers.

16100 N Highway 101, Willits, CA 95490	(707) 459-2958 http://goldenrulervpark.com/	All Year
$37	Good Sam	No Restrictions
33 Spaces	Paved	18Width/55Length
Restrooms, Showers, Ice	Laundry, RV Service, Pool	Horseshoes

California – Shasta Cascade

This is the farthest north of California just before the Oregon border. A truly rugged outdoor experience. Come to relax in beautiful nature or enjoy plenty of outdoor adventures.

Almond Tree RV Park
There is a lot more to see in the Chico area than people may think.

3124 Esplanade, Chico, CA 95973	(530) 899-1271 almondtreervandstorage.com/	All Year
$47	Military/Good Sam	No Restrictions
42 Spaces	Paved	25Width/65Length
Internet, Showers, Laundry	Supplies, Grocery, Cable	Pavilion, Pool, Rec. Hall

Heritage RV Park
This smaller RV park is hidden, but it is a gem well worth finding.

975 Highway 99 W, Corning, CA 96021	(530) 824-6130 http://heritagervcorning.com/	All Year
$44-$50	Good Sam	Pet Quantity, Breed
87 Spaces	Paved	22Width/70Length
Internet, Showers, Laundry	RV Service, Ice, Pool	RV Wash, Rec. Hall, Tables

Rancheria RV Park
This is the number one fishing destination in California.

15565 Black Angus Ln, Hat Creek, CA 96040	(530) 335-7418	All Year
$47	Good Sam	No Restrictions
65 Spaces	Paved	25Width/75Length
Internet, Showers, Laundry	Supplies, Firewood, Rentals	Rec. Hall, Activities, Tables

Berry Creek Rancheria RV Park
This park puts you at the gateway to the Feather River recreational area.

3900 Olive Hwy, Oroville, CA 95966	(866) 991-5061 http://www.goldcountrycasino.com	All Year
$40-$50	Good Sam	No Restrictions
79 Spaces	Paved	30Width/50Length
Internet, Showers, Cable	Grocery, Supplies, Pool, Games	Rec. Hall, LP Gas, Ice

River Reflections RV Park

These shaded RV spots are located right along the Feather River.

4360 Pacific Heights Rd, Oroville, CA 95965	(530) 533-1995 http://riverreflectionsrvpark.com/	All Year
$50	Good Sam	Pet Breed
91 Spaces	Paved	30Width/70Length
Internet, Showers, Ice	Firewood, Supplies, Fishing	Fire Rings, Game Room

Pioneer RV Park

This is a peaceful year-round park with plenty of outdoor activities.

1326 Pioneer Rd, Quincy, CA 95971	(530) 283-0769 http://pioneerrvpark.com/	All Year
$37	Military/Good Sam	Pet Breed
62 Spaces	Paved	30Width/70Length
Internet, Showers, Laundry	Supplies, LP Gas, Ice	RV Service, Rec. Hall, Tables

Durango RV Resort

This is a luxury RV park along the Sacramento River.

100 Lake Ave, Red Bluff, CA 96080	(530) 527-5300 http://www.durangorvresorts.com/	All Year
$56-$65	Military/Good Sam	Pet Breed
174 Spaces	Paved	35Width/85Length
Internet, Showers, Laundry	Gated, Supplies, LP Gas	Grocery, Cable, Games

Redding Premier RV Resort

A wonderful park for relaxing and enjoying nature.

280 N Boulder Dr, Redding, CA 96003	(530) 246-0101 premierrvresorts.com/redding-ca.html	All Year
$45-$55	Good Sam	Pet Breed
104 Spaces	Paved	25Width/70Length
Internet, Showers, Laundry	Rentals, Supplies, Pool	Rec. Hall, Activities, Gym

Mountain Gate RV Park

This your best place to stay if you want to boat and fish on Lake Shasta.

14161 Holiday Rd, Redding, CA 96003	(530) 275-4600 http://mt-gatervpark.com/	All Year
$33-$41	Good Sam	Pet Breed
108 Spaces	Paved	27Width/60Length

| Internet, Showers, Laundry | LP Gas, Ice, Supplies | Rec. Hall, Playground, Pool |

Marina RV Park
This RV park has amenities and services only seen at resorts.

2615 Park Marina Dr, Redding, CA 96001	(530) 241-4396 https://www.marinarvpark.com/	All Year
$35-$38	Good Sam	Pet Breed
75 Spaces	Paved	20Width/45Length
Internet, Showers, Laundry	Ice, Pool, Hot Tub	Rec. Hall, Patios, Tables

Redding RV Park
Located in Redding with easy access off the Interstate.

11075 Campers Court Redding, CA 96003	(530) 241-0707 https://reddingrvpark.com	All Year
$42	Military/Good Sam	No Restrictions
107 Spaces	Paved	22Width/67Length
Internet, Showers, Laundry	Supplies, LP Gas, Cable	Grocery, Rec. Hall, Games

JGW RV Park
This park is located within the native black oak trees.

6612 Riverland Dr, Redding, CA 96002	(530) 365-7965 https://jgwrvpark.com/	All Year
$40-$55	Military/Good Sam	No Restrictions
75 Spaces	Paved	26Width/60Length
Internet, Shower, Laundry	Cable, LP Gas, Ice, Pool	Rec. Hall, Tables, Games

Days End RV Park
Enjoy beautiful views of the Standish and Cascade Mountains from your site.

718-755 US Highway 395 E, Standish, CA 96128	(530) 254-1094 http://daysendrv.com/	All Year
$33	Military/Good Sam	No Restrictions
27 Spaces	Gravel	23Width/75Length
Internet, Showers	Laundry, Supplies	Tables, Restrooms

Susanville RV Park
A quiet and serene park, just like the nearby town of Susanville.

3075 Johnstonville Rd, Susanville, CA 96130	(877) 686-7878 http://susanvillervpark.com/	All Year
$40-$44	Military/Good Sam	Pet Breed
101 Spaces	Paved	25Width/60Length
Internet, Showers, Laundry	Ice, Cable, Rec. Hall	Games, Gym, Patios

Waiiaka RV Park

Relax at the park or enjoy the great outdoors.

240 Sharps Rd, Yreka, CA 96097	(530) 842-4500 https://www.yrekarvparkca.com/	All Year
$40	Military/Good Sam	No Restrictions
60 Spaces	Paved	22Width/60Length
Internet, Showers, Laundry	RV Service, Game Room, Ice	Playground, Games, Tables

California – San Francisco Bay Area

There are plenty of RV parks to visit and sites to see.

Bodega Bay RV Park
This is the ideal park for nature lovers and outdoor enthusiasts

2001 N Hwy 1, Bodega Bay, CA 94923	(707) 875-3701 http://www.bodegabayrvpark.com/	All Year
$64-$66	Military	No Restrictions
68 Spaces	Paved	29Width/62Length
Internet, Shower, Laundry	Restaurant, Ice, Cable, Supplies	Rec. Hall, Games, Tables

Calistoga RV Park
This park is a perfect base of operations while exploring beautiful Wine Country.

1601 N Oak St, Calistoga, CA 94515	(707) 942-5221 https://www.calistogarvpark.org/	All Year
$37-$60	No Discounts Offered	14 Day Stay Max69
69 Spaces	Paved	30Width/Length
Internet, Showers, Golf	Snack Bar, Driving Range	Pavilion, RV Service

River Bend Resort
Located in the Russian River Valley, this is a great place to stay while exploring Sonoma County.

11820 River Rd, Forestville, CA 95436	(707) 887-7662 http://riverbendresort.net/	All Year
$85-$105	Military/Good Sam	Pet Breed
98 Spaces	Paved	17Width/50Length
Internet, Showers, Laundry	Grocery, Ice, Fishing	Rentals, Fire Rings, Games

Marin Park
This is the closest RV park to San Francisco.

2140 Redwood Hwy, Greenbrae, CA 94904	(415) 461-5199 Website	All Year
$99	Good Sam	Pet Quantity
89 Spaces	Paved	17Width/50Length
Internet, Showers, Laundry	Supplies, RV Service	Cable, Pool

Napa Valley Expo RV Park
The perfect place to stay while exploring Wine Country.

575 3rd St, Napa, CA 94559	(707) 253-4900	All Year

$60	Military/Good Sam	Pet Quantity, 28 Day Max
28 Spaces	Paved	30Width/75Length
Internet, Showers, Laundry	RV Service, Rec. Hall, Games	Pavilion, Tables

Novato RV Park

This puts you at the center of everything there is to do in the San Francisco Bay Area.

1530 Armstrong Ave, Novato, CA 94945	(800) 733-6787 http://www.novatorvpark.com/	All Year
$99	Military/Good Sam	No Restrictions
69 Spaces	Paved	30Width/45Length
Internet, Showers, Laundry	Supplies, Grocery, Restaurant	Pool, Games, Patios

Olema Campground

Whether you want an outdoor adventure or a leisure spot to hang out, you'll get it here.

10155 Highway 1, Olema, CA 94950	(800) 655-2267 olemacampground.net/	All Year
$47-$65	Good Sam	Pet Breed&Qty., 14 Day Max
80 Spaces	Paved/Gravel	20Width/50Length
Internet, Showers, Laundry	Firewood, Games, Rec. Hall	ATM, LP Gas, BBQ's

San Francisco RV Resort

This park is set on a bluff overlooking the ocean, so you get spectacular views from your site.

700 Palmetto Ave., Pacifica, CA 94044	(888) 416-8094	All Year
$77-$128	Good Sam	Pet Quantity
122 Spaces	Paved	15Width/66Length
Internet, Showers, Laundry	LP Gas, Cable, Pool, Ice	Playground, Game Room

The Fair Park RV

Although located in a Fairgrounds, this place is park-like.

4501 Pleasanton Ave, Pleasanton, CA 94566	(925) 426-7600	All Year
$30-$50	No Discounts Offered	21 Day Max
176 Spaces	Paved	20Width/80Length
Internet, Showers, Laundry	Restaurant, Golf	Pavilion, Driving Range

Coyote Valley RV Resort

It provides easy access to a number of bay area tourist attractions.

9750 Monterey Rd, San Jose, CA 95037	(408) 463-8400 https://coyotevalleyresort.com/	All Year

$70-$80	Good Sam	RV Age, Pet Qty.&Breed
127 Spaces	Paved	30Width/60Length
Internet, Showers, Laundry	Grocery, Snack Bar, Pool	Games, Pavilion, Patios

California – Central Valley

Stretching from the Shasta Cascade to the Los Angeles area, the Central Valley takes in the central belt of California. It is a place of farmland and history. There are some great RV parks to stay at while exploring what the area has to offer.

Bakersfield River Run RV Park
Centrally located so you can easily walk to most of the attractions and activities.

3715 Burr St, Bakersfield, CA 93308	(661) 377-3600 https://www.riverrunrvpark.com/	All Year
$40-$83	Good Sam	Pet Size, Qty, Breed/28DayMax
121 Spaces	Paved	24Width/60Length
Internet, Showers, Laundry	Grocery, RV Service, Cable	Pool, Game Room, Gym

Bakersfield RV Resort
This park has it all: comfort, luxury, and style.

5025 Wible Rd, Bakersfield, CA 93313	(661) 833-9998 https://www.bakrv.com/	All Year
$55	Military/Good Sam	Pet Qty, Breed/28 Day Max
215 Spaces	Paved	30Width/65Length
Internet, Showers, Laundry	Gated, Supplies, Ice, Cable	Grocery, RV Wash, Gym

A Country RV Park
Easy access off the freeway and surrounding by National Parks, this is the perfect place to stay.

622 S Fairfax Rd, Bakersfield, CA 93307	(661) 363-6412	All Year
$40	Military/Good Sam	No Restrictions
120 Spaces	Paved	25Width/65Length
Internet, Showers, Laundry	Grocery, Cable, Ice, Pool	Pavilion, Rec. Hall, Gym

Bakersfield RV Travel Park
A brief description.

8633 E Brundage Ln, Bakersfield, CA 93307	(661) 366-3550 http://bakersfieldrvtravelpark.com/	All Year
$35	Military/Good Sam	Pet Size, Breed
100 Spaces	Paved	18Width/72Length
Internet, Showers, Laundry	Grocery, Ice, Supplies, Cable	Game Room, Patios

Castaic Lake RV Park

This park puts you within walking distance to Hollywood and Universal Studios.

31540 Ridge Route Rd, Castaic, CA 91384	(661) 257-3340 https://castaiclakervpark.com/	All Year
$40-$65	Military/Good Sam	Pet Size, Quantity, Breed
103 Spaces	Paved	27Width/60Length
Internet, Showers, Laundry	Grocery, Ice, Cable, Pool	RV Wash, Playground, Patios

The Lakes RV Golf Resort

This park offers plenty of amenities and services so you can enjoy your stay.

5001 East Robertson Blvd, Chowchilla, CA 93610	1 (866) 665-6980	All Year
$42-$60	Good Sam	No Restrictions
87 Spaces	Paved	30Width/77Length
Internet, Showers, Laundry	Golf Carts, Pool, Rec. Hall	Golf, Tennis, Hot Tub, Ice

Arena RV Park

A pet and family-friendly park located right by the highway.

203 Chowchilla Blvd, Chowchilla, CA 93610	(559) 981-0131 http://www.arenarvpark.net/	All Year
$42-$48	Military/Good Sam	Pet Quantity
38 Spaces	Paved/Gravel	18Width/55Length
Internet, Showers	Laundry	Dog Run, Pavilion

Blackstone North RV Park

Offering oversized sites, you are sure to enjoy your stay at this park.

6494 N Blackstone Ave, Fresno, CA 93710	(559) 785-9020	All Year
$43-$50	Military/Good Sam/Senior	RV Age, Pet Breed
94 Spaces	Paved	55Width/65Length
Internet, Showers, Laundry	RV Service, Cable, RV Wash	Patios, Tables

Fresno Mobile Home and RV Park

Offering short and long term stays so you can enjoy all the area has to offer.

1362 N Hughes Ave, Fresno, CA 93728	(559) 264-3122 fresnomobilehomeandrv.com/	All Year
$54	Military/Good Sam	Pet Size, Quantity, Breed
61 Spaces	Paved	16Width/80Length
Internet, Showers	Laundry, RV Service	RV Wash, Pool

Casa de Fruta RV Park

Located among the hills and trees, this is a great place to stay and relax.

10021 Pacheco Pass Hwy, Hollister, CA 95023	(408) 842-9316 http://www.casadefruta.com/	All Year
$50-$60	Good Sam	Pet Quantity
250 Spaces	Paved	22Width/46Length
Internet, Showers, Laundry	ATM, Grocery, Snack Bar	Rec. Hall, Playground, Pool

Club Royal Oak RV Resort

A serene park located along the Kings River.

39700 Road 28, Kingsburg, CA 93631	(559) 897-0351	All Year
$45-$95	Military/Good Sam	Pet Quantity, Breed
100 Spaces	Paved	32Width/100Length
Internet, Showers, Laundry	Gated, LP Gas, Firewood	Ice, RV Wash, Gym, Sauna

Jellystone Park Camp-Resort

This is your ideal family destination.

14900 W Highway 12, Lodi, CA 95242	(209) 369-1041 https://towerparkresort.com/	All Year
$97-$154	No Discounts Offered	Pet Quantity, Breed
210 Spaces	Paved	30Width/78Length
Internet, Showers, Laundry	Gated, Ice, Firewood, Pool	Waterslide, Playground

Flag City RV Resort

This is a large and modern RV resort.

6120 W Banner Rd, Lodi, CA 95242	(866) 371-4855 https://www.flagcityrvresort.com/	All Year
$65	Military/Good Sam	Pet Quantity, Breed
180 Spaces	Paved	28Width/60Length
Internet, Showers, Laundry	Grocery, Pool, Cable, Ice	Rec. Hall, Games, Patios

Ponderosa RV Resort

This small park is located at the foothills of the Sierra mountains and along the American River.

7291 Hwy 49, Lotus, CA 95651	(888) 397-4183	All Year
$42-$62	Good Sam	No Restrictions
10 Spaces	Paved/Gravel	25Width/65Length
Internet, Showers, Laundry	Snack Bar, Fishing, Rec. Hall	Game Room, Rentals, Tables

Turtle Beach

A laid back park along the San Joaquin River.

703 E. Williamson Rd., Manteca, CA 95337	(209) 239-0991	All Year
$42-$54	Good Sam	Pet Quantity
60 Spaces	Gravel	30Width/45Length
Internet, Showers, Gated	Firewood, Rec. Hall, Games	RV Wash, Tables

The Parkway RV Resort

The natural area of this park makes it a paradise.

6330 County Road 200, Orland, CA 95963	(530) 865-9188 https://theparkwayrv.com/	All Year
$55-$64	Good Sam	No Restrictions
40 Spaces	Gravel	46Width/74Length
Internet, Showers, Laundry	Ice, Grocery, Playground	Games, Tables, Pool

Kit Fox RV Park

This park and the nearby town of Patterson offer a unique and beautiful vacation experience.

240 Rogers Rd, Patterson, CA 95363	(209) 892-2638 https://www.kitfoxrvpark.com/	All Year
$45-$48	Military/Good Sam	Pet Size, Quantity, Breed
151 Spaces	Paved	20Width/70Length
Internet, Showers, Laundry	Ice, Game Room, Patios	Games, Rec. Hall, LP Gas

Duck Island RV Park

Surrounded by historic sites and visitor attractions, you're sure to be busy while staying here.

16814 Hwy 160, Rio Vista, CA 94571	(916) 777-6663	All Year
$45	Military/Good Sam	Pet Size, Breed
50 Spaces	Paved	30Width36/Length
Internet, Laundry, Gated	LP Gas, Ice, RV Wash	Fishing, Rec. Hall, Patios

Santa Nella RV Park

Located in a quiet and comfortable section of town.

13023 California 33, Santa Nella, CA 95322	(209) 826-3105 https://www.santanellarvpark.com/	All Year
$40-$42	Military/Good Sam	No Restrictions
57 Spaces	Paved	30Width/65Length
Internet, Shower, Laundry	LP Gas, Ice	Outdoor Games, Patios

Sequoia RV Ranch

Located close to Sequoia National Park, you won't be short of outdoor activities here.

43490 N Fork Dr, Three Rivers, CA 93271	(559) 561-4333 http://www.sequoiarvranch.com/	All Year
$31-$66	Military/Good Sam	14 Day Max
47 Spaces	Paved/Gravel	22Width/60Length
Internet, Showers, Firewood	Ice, Laundry, Game Room	Fire Ring, Rec. Hall, Tables

Vineyard RV Park

This beautiful park puts you close to San Francisco and the Napa Valley.

4985 Midway Rd, Vacaville, CA 95688	(707) 693-8797 https://www.vineyardrvpark.com/	All Year
$69-$79	Good Sam	No Restrictions
256 Spaces	Paved	30Width/64Length
Internet, Showers, Laundry	Supplies, LP Gas, Ice, Pool	Game Room, Playground

Midway RV Park

A clean and quiet park. Enjoy the many amenities while you relax at your site.

4933 Midway Rd, Vacaville, CA 95688	(707) 446-7679 http://midwayrvpark.com/	All Year
$65	Good Sam	Pet Breed
64 Spaces	Paved	32Width/55Length
Internet, Showers, Laundry	Cable, RV Wash, Pool	Playground, Frisbee Golf

Visalia Sequoia National Park KOA

This is your perfect base of operations for visiting Sequoia or Kings National Park.

7480 Avenue 308, Visalia, CA 93291	(559) 651-0544 koa.com/campgrounds/visalia/	All Year
$45-$59	Military	Pet Breed
75 Spaces	Paved/Gravel	25Width/60Length
Internet, Grocery, Laundry	Rentals, Pool, Rec. Hall	Playground, Game Room

Country Manor RV Community

This is a fine 55+ community for a short-term or long-term stay.

820 S Chinowth St, Visalia, CA 93277	(559) 732-8144 http://countrymanormhc.com/	All Year
$50	Good Sam	55+, Pet Qty&Breed, RV Age
118 Spaces	Paved	20Width/75Length
Internet, Showers, Laundry	RV Service, Pool, Rec. Hall	Patios, Tables

Sac-West RV Park and Campground

This park offers fun for everyone with plenty of amenities and fun activities.

3951 Lake Rd, West Sacramento, CA 95691	(916) 371-6771	All Year
$54-$76	Good Sam	Pet Breed
70 Spaces	Paved	20Width/42Length
Internet, Showers, Laundry	Cable, Fishing, Rentals, Pool	Paddle Boats, Patios, Games

California – Gold Country

This little area of California is steep in history, as well as plenty of outdoor experiences. Located between the mountains of the High Sierras and the plains of the Central Valley, this beautiful area is a great place to spend some time exploring all there is to see and do.

Angels Camp RV & Camping Resort
Located conveniently in Gold Country with a short drive to Yosemite.

3069 Highway 49, Angels Camp, CA 95222	(209) 736-0404 https://angelscamprv.com/	All Year
$57-$66	Military/Good Sam	Pet Quantity, Breed
102 Spaces	Gravel	24Width/70Length
Internet, Showers, Laundry	Rentals, Pavilion, Games	Frisbee Golf, Fire Rings

Yosemite RV Resort
You won't even have to leave your site to enjoy nature.

34094 Hwy 41, Coarsegold, CA 93614	(559) 683-7855 https://yosemitervresort.com/	All Year
$53-$83	Military/Good Sam	RV Age, 28 Day Max
84 Spaces	Paved/Gravel	20Width/45Length
Internet, Showers, Laundry	Supplies, LP Gas, Pool	Firewood, Ice, Fire Rings

49er RV Ranch
Stay at one of the oldest campgrounds in California, dating back to 1852.

23223 Italian Bar Rd, Columbia, CA 95310	(209) 532-4978 https://49rv.com/	All Year
$40-$49	Military/Good Sam	Pet Quantity
55 Spaces	Paved	20Width/60Length
Internet, Showers, Laundry	Firewood, Ice, Cable, Rentals	LP Gas, Rec. Hall, Games

Jackson Rancheria RV Park
Perhaps one of the best parks in Northern California, you can stay in a forested setting.

12222 New York Ranch Rd, Jackson, CA 95642	(209) 223-1677 https://www.jacksoncasino.com/	All Year
$60-$70	Good Sam	Pet Quantity, 14 Day Max
100 Spaces	Paved	35Width/60Length
Internet, Showers, Laundry	LP Gas, Ice, Snack Bar, Cable	Rec. Hall, Gym, Tables

49er Village RV Resort

Located at the foothills of the Sierras, this park puts you close to all the attractions.

18265 Golden Chain Highway, Plymouth, CA 95669	(209) 245-6981	All Year
$54-$92	Good Sam	No Restrictions
325 Spaces	Paved	27Width/50Length
Internet, Showers, Laundry	Grocery, Rentals, Cable	Games, Pool, Rec. Hall

Cal Expo RV Park

Conveniently located in Sacramento and offering all the luxuries of a high-end RV park.

1600 Exposition Blvd, Sacramento, CA 95815	(916) 263-3187 https://calexpo.com/	All Year
$45	No Discounts Offered	14 Day Max
177 Spaces	Paved/Gravel	22Width/50Length
Internet, Shower, Restrooms	Laundry, Ice	Rec. Hall, Patios

California – High Sierra

Located in the mountains, this is the place to go when you want to enjoy the rugged wilderness and picturesque beauty.

Highlands RV Park

The rivers and lakes around here are prime locations for fishing.

2275 N Sierra Hwy, Bishop, CA 93514	(760) 873-7616 https://www.bishopvisitor.com/	All Year
$45	Good Sam	No Restrictions
103 Spaces	Paved	20Width/55Length
Internet, Showers, Laundry	LP Gas, Cable, Rec. Hall	Patios, Tables, Ice

Brown's Town Campground

This rugged RV park offers the basic amenities and allows you a place to stay.

395 & Schober Ln, Bishop, CA 93514	(760) 873-8522 https://brownscampgrounds.com/	March 1 to November 30
$32	No Discounts Offered	14 Day Max
47 Spaces	Gravel/Dirt	22Width/40Length
Showers, Firewood, Ice	Laundry, Snack Bar, Cable	RV Wash, Fishing Supplies

Yosemite Lakes RV Resort

The Tuolumne River flows through the park so you can find plenty of water-based activities.

31191 Hardin Flat Rd., Groveland, CA 95321	(877) 570-2267 http://stayatyosemite.com/	All Year
$58-$90	Good Sam	Pet Quantity
254 Spaces	Paved	25Width/55Length
Internet, Showers, Laundry	Grocery, ATM, Ice, Firewood	Pavilion, Activities, Tables

Boulder Creek RV Resort

Within range of this wonderful park, there is an endless supply of activities.

2550 S Highway 395, Lone Pine, CA 93545	(760) 876-4243 bouldercreekrvresort.com/	All Year
$45	Military/Good Sam	28 Day Max
109 Spaces	Paved	33Width/60Length
Internet, Showers, Laundry	RV Service, RV Wash, Pool	Tables, Playground, Games

Tahoe Valley Campground

Located in the beauty of the mountains, this park allows you to relax and enjoy nature.

1175 Melba Dr, South Lake Tahoe, CA 96150	(888) 408-8079	All Year

$59-$90	Military/Good Sam	Pet Quantity, Breed
338 Spaces	Paved	18Width/50Length
Internet, Showers, Laundry	Grocery, Ice, Game Room	Activities, Playground, Tennis

The RV Park at Black Oak Casino

This park is your perfect base camp for outdoor activities.

19400 Tuolumne Rd N, Tuolumne, CA 95379	(209) 928-9553 blackoakcasino.com/lodging/the-rv-park/	All Year
$37-$42	Good Sam	No Restrictions
85 Spaces	Paved	30Width/45Length
Internet, Showers, Laundry	Grocery, Restaurant, Casino	Pool, Game Room, Patios

Truckee River RV Park

Conveniently located along the Interstate and along the Truckee River.

10068 Hirschdale Rd, Truckee, CA 96161	(530) 448-4650 http://www.truckeeriverrv.com/	All Year
$47	Good Sam	No Restrictions
50 Spaces	Paved	25Width/45Length
Internet, Showers, Laundry	Snack Bar, Ice, Grocery	Playground, Fishing, Patios

California – Central Coast

This beautiful area of California is bordered by the San Francisco Bay Area to the north, the Central Valley to the east, and Los Angeles County to the south. From parks in this area, you can sit back and relax while enjoying the beautiful scenery, or you can plan an outdoor adventure.

Flying Flags RV Resort
A variety of onsite amenities make this a unique place to stay.

180 Avenue of Flags, Buellton, CA 93427	(805) 688-3716 highwaywestvacations.com	All Year
$68-$350	Good Sam	Pet Quantity, 21 Day Max
260 Spaces	Paved	30Width/60Length
Internet, Showers, Laundry	Rentals, Pool, Splash Pad	Activities, Games, Gym

Marina Dunes RV Resort
This park is as close to the ocean as you can get.

3330 Dunes Drive, Marina, CA 93933	(831) 384-6914 http://marinadunesrv.com/	All Year
$65-$85	Military/Good Sam	No Restrictions
63 Spaces	Paved	28Width/45Length
Internet, Showers, Laundry	Ice, Cable, Rentals, Rec. Hall	Gym, Fire Rings, Tables

Morgan Hill RV Resort
This park puts you in the middle of the Central Coast area.

12895 Uvas Rd, Morgan Hill, CA 95037	(888) 397-0278	All Year
$60-$63	Good Sam	No Restrictions
320 Spaces	Paved/Gravel	20Width/60Length
Shower, Laundry, Rentals	Playground, Tennis, Games	Pavilion, Mini Golf, Rec. Hall

Morro Dunes RV Park
Whether you want adventure or relaxation, you can find it here.

1700 Embarcadero, Morro Bay, CA 93442	(805) 772-2722 https://morrodunes.com/	All Year
$37-$45	No Discounts Offered	Pet Quantity, 14 Day Max
152 Spaces	Paved	20Width/48Length
Internet, Showers, Laundry	Supplies, RV Service, Ice	Grocery, Rec. Hall, Fire Ring

Pismo Sands RV Park

Beautiful ocean views and luxury amenities, you can have it all at a park like this.

2220 Cienaga St, Oceano, CA 93445	(805) 481-3225 https://www.pismosands.com/	All Year
$63-$65	Military/Good Sam	Pet Quantity
133 Spaces	Paved	24Width/70Length
Internet, Shower, Laundry	Grocery, Snack Bar, Games	Rec. Hall, Rentals, Pool

Pacific Dunes Ranch RV Resort

Located near Pismo Beach, this is the place to go for ocean-based activities.

1205 Silver Spur Place, Oceano, CA 93445	(888) 416-4376	All Year
$61-$74	Military/Good Sam	No Restrictions
215 Spaces	Paved	20Width/66Length
Internet, Showers, Laundry	Ice, RV Wash	Game Room, Tables

Cava Robles RV Resort

This park offers more than just great views, it offers an experience.

3800 Golden Hill Rd, Paso Robles, CA 93446	(805) 242-4700	All Year
$69-$150	Good Sam	Pet Quantity, 28 Day Max
312 Spaces	Paved	35Width/65Length
Internet, Showers, Laundry	Restaurant, Pavilion, Pool	Gym, Activities, Games

Wine Country RV Resort

Paso Robles is a wine region, and from this park, you can visit over 170 tasting rooms.

2500 Airport Rd, Paso Robles, CA 93446	(866) 550-2117	All Year
$69-$111	Military/Good Sam	Pet Quantity
180 Spaces	Paved	24Width/80Length
Internet, Showers, Laundry	Lounge, Pool, Rentals	Activities, Playground, Tables

Vines RV Resort

Here you'll find luxury living in a comfortable setting.

88 Wellsona Rd, Paso Robles, CA 93446	(805) 467-2100	All Year
$56-$111	Military/Good Sam	RV Age, Pet Quantity
125 Spaces	Paved	30Width/72Length
Internet, Shower, Laundry	Grocery, Lounge, Pool, Rentals	Rec. Hall, Pavilion, Gym

Pismo Coast Village RV Resort

Relax at your site while enjoying the coast.

165 South Dolliver St, Pismo Beach, CA 93449	(805) 773-1811	All Year
$54-$73	No Discounts Offered	Pet Qty, Breed/28 Day Max
400 Spaces	Paved	26Width/45Length
Internet, Showers, Laundry	Snack Bar, Restaurant, Pool	Rec. Hall, Game Room

Betabel RV Park

A quiet and pristine park that is conveniently located in the Central Coast area.

9664 Betabel Rd, San Juan Bautista, CA 95045	(831) 623-2202 http://betabel.com/	All Year
$52	Military/Good Sam	RV Age, Pet Qty, Breed
164 Spaces	Paved	24Width/60Length
Internet, Showers, Laundry	Playground, Gym, Patios	Pool, LP Gas, Ice, Tables

Ocean Mesa at El Capitan

This luxurious park sits overlooking the El Capitan State Beach.

100 El Capitan Terrace Lane, Santa Barbara, CA 93117	(805) 685-3887 http://www.oceanmesa.com/	All Year
$95-$125	Military	14 Day Max
80 Spaces	Paved	33Width/50Length
Internet, Showers, Laundry	Pool, Snack Bar, Ice	Playground, Rentals, Tables

Rancho Oso RV Campground

Bordered by the Santa Ynez River and the Los Padres National Forest, this is a beautiful place.

3750 Paradise Rd, Santa Barbara, CA 93105	(805) 683-5686	All Year
$60-$80	Military/Good Sam	Pet Quantity, 21 Day Max
99 Spaces	Paved	30Width/40Length
Showers, Laundry, Rentals	Pool, Snack Bar, Restaurant	Activities, Playground, Tennis

Cachuma Lake Campground

Located in a beautiful area bordered by a river and mountains, this is a great base camp.

2225 Highway 154, Santa Barbara, CA 93105	(805) 686-5055	All Year
$25-$50	No Discounts Offered	14 Day Max
157 Spaces	Paved	23Width/56Length

| Laundry, ATM, LP Gas, Ice | Firewood, Fishing, Rec. Hall | Playground, Pavilion, Rentals |

Santa Cruz Ranch RV Resort

Within minutes of Santa Cruz, this RV park is a great spot for a relaxing ocean getaway.

917 Disc Drive, Scotts Valley, CA 95066	(800) 546-1288	All Year
$78-$95	Military/Good Sam	Pet Quantity
101 Spaces	Paved	21Width/45Length
Internet, Shower, Laundry	Ice, Cable, Pool, LP Gas	Game Room, Tables, HotTub

California – Los Angeles and Orange County

Most people think if Los Angeles and Orange County as a major city with tourist attractions. However, if you stay at an RV park in the county, you can spend your days at any number of tourist attractions while also enjoying a few outdoor activities.

Soledad Canyon RV Camping Resort
Take a walk among pleasant tree-filled trails or swim in the large pool.

4700 Crown Valley Road, Acton, CA 93510	(888) 408-4713	All Year
$60-$64	Good Sam	No Restrictions
900 Spaces	Paved/Gravel	24Width/65Length
Showers, Rentals, Ice	Grocery, Tennis, Pool	Rec. Hall, Playground

The Californian RV Resort
This resort-style RV park offers plenty of amenities.

1535 Sierra Hwy, Acton, CA 93510	(661) 269-0919 http://www.calrv.com	All Year
$47	Military/Good Sam	Pet Quantity, Breed
193 Spaces	Paved	25Width/60Length
Internet, Showers, Laundry	Supplies, Ice, LP Gas	Rec. Hall, Gym, Game Room

Anaheim RV Park
The only RV park that puts you close to Disneyland.

200 W. Midway Drive, Anaheim, CA 92805	(714) 774-3860 anaheimrvpark.com/	All Year
$62-$105	Military/Good Sam	RV Age, Pet Breed, 14 Day Max
115 Spaces	Paved	20Width/70Length
Internet, Showers, Laundry	Supplies, Ice, Cable, Pool	Rec. Hall, Pavilion, Patios

Antelope Valley Fairgrounds RV Park
A general park with basic amenities.

2551 W Avenue H, Lancaster, CA 93536	(661) 206-0427 https://avfair.com/	All Year
$25-$30	No Discounts Offered	21 Day Max
62 Spaces	Paved	22Width/60Length
Internet	Showers	Restrooms

Newport Dunes Waterfront Resort Marina

Located at a private lagoon and beach connected to the Pacific Ocean.

1131 Back Bay Dr, Newport Beach, CA 92660	(949) 729-3863 https://www.newportdunes.com/	All Year
$64-$500	Military/Good Sam	RV Age, Pet Qty, Breed
411 Spaces	Paved	24Width/40Length
Boat Launch, Internet, Ice	Grocery, Rentals, Cable, Pool	Paddle Boats, Rec. Hall

Walnut RV Park

Conveniently located near everything Los Angeles has to offer.

19130 Nordhoff St, Northridge, CA 91324	(818) 775-0704 http://www.walnutrvpark.com	All Year
$70	Military/Good Sam	Pet Size, Qty, Breed
114 Spaces	Paved	26Width/42Length
Showers, Laundry, Supplies	Ice, RV Wash	Pool, Rec. Hall

Orangeland RV Park

Located in the heart of Orange County and nearby to a number of local attractions.

1600 West Stuck Avenue, Orange, CA 92867	(714) 633-0414 https://www.orangeland.com	All Year
$70-$85	Military/Good Sam	RV Age, Pet Qty, Breed
195 Spaces	Paved	26Width/50Length
Internet, Showers, Laundry	ATM, Ice, Cable, Pool	RV Wash, Rec. Hall, Gym

Bonelli Bluffs RV Resort

A brief description.

1440 Camper View Rd, San Dimas, CA 91773	(909) 599-8355 https://www.bonellibluffsrv.com	All Year
$65-$75	Good Sam	RV Age, Pet Size
518 Spaces	Paved	33Width/45Length
Showers, Laundry, Ice	Grocery, Rec. Hall, Pool	Fishing Supplies, Fire Rings

California – Inland Empire

Just inland from the city of Los Angeles and Orange Counties, you'll find the Inland Empire.

Big River RV Park
Located along the Colorado River, this park gets you close to many water-based activities.

1 Marina St, Big River, CA 92242	(760) 665-9359 bigriverrvpark.com	All Year
$50-$60	Good Sam	Pet Quantity
183 Spaces	Gravel	30Width/40Length
Internet, Showers, Laundry	Cable, Gated, Ice, Rec. Hall	Activities, Pavilion, Gym

Hidden Beaches River Resort
For a reasonable price, you can stay right on the Colorado River.

6951 6th Ave, Blythe, CA 92225	(760) 922-7276 hiddenbeachesresort.com/	All Year
$32-$39	Good Sam	No Restrictions
144 Spaces	Paved/Gravel	37Width/60Length
Internet, Shower, Laundry	Supplies, Firewood, Ice	Rentals, Pavilion, Tables

Destiny RV Resorts
A brief description.

8750 Peter D Mcintyre Ave, Blythe, CA 92225	(760) 922-8205 https://www.destinyrv.com/	All Year
$35-$37	No Discounts Offered	Pet Breed, 14 Day Max
222 Spaces	Paved/Dirt	20Width/40Length
Internet, Showers, Supplies	LP Gas, Firewood, Ice	Grocery, Tables

Leapin' Lizard RV Ranch
The best place to stay in the desert for off-road activities.

5929 Kunkler Ln, Borrego Springs, CA 92004	(760) 767-4526 leapinlizardrvranch.com	October 1st to June 1st
$35-$45	Good Sam	No Restrictions
60 Spaces	Gravel/Dirt	30Width/50Length
Internets, Showers, Laundry	Gated, Ice, RV Wash, Pool	Playground, Tables

Palm Canyon Hotel and RV Resort
Relax at this unique and amenity-filled park, or take in the many surrounding activities.

221 Palm Canyon Drive, Borrego Springs, CA 92004	(760) 767-5341	August 31st to May 31st
$48-$86	Good Sam	RV Age, Pet Qty, Breed

80 Spaces	Paved	22Width/40Length
Internet, Showers, Laundry	Restaurant, Lounge, Cable	Rec. Hall, Pavilion, Gym

Outdoor Resort Palm Springs

There is no shortage of ways to enjoy the outdoors or relax around this area.

69411 Ramon Rd, Cathedral City, CA 92234	(760) 321-0301 http://orps.com/	All Year
$40-$84	No Discounts Offered	RV Age, Pet Qty, No Class B
1213 Spaces	Paved	36Width/65Length
Internet, Showers, Laundry	Snack Bar, Gated, Cable	Pool, Rec. Hall, Golf

Cathedral Palms RV Resort

This relaxed and quiet RV park offers you private sites with the basic amenities.

35901 Cathedral Canyon Dr, Cathedral City, CA 92234	(760) 324-8244 https://aarvparks.com	All Year
$49-$52	Military/Good Sam	No Restrictions
110 Spaces	Paved/Gravel	33Width/55Length
Internet, Laundry, Showers	Snack Bar, Pool, Rentals	Games, Pavilion, Patios

Palm Springs Oasis RV Resort

Located at the base of the mountains and close to several entertainment options.

36100 Date Palm Drive, Cathedral City, CA 92234	(888) 520-7990	All Year
$67-$74	Military/Good Sam	Pet Qty, Breed
140 Spaces	Paved	22Width/40Length
Internet, Showers, Laundry	Ice, Cable, RV Wash, Pool	Tennis, Golf, Gym

Catalina Spa and RV Resort

A great RV park with a number of resort-style amenities.

18800 Corkill Rd, Desert Hot Springs, CA 92241	(760) 329-4431 catalinasparvresort.com/	All Year
$45-$79	Military/Good Sam	Pet Quantity
466 Spaces	Paved	24Width/50Length
Internet, Shower, Laundry	Gated, Supplies, Snack Bar	Rec. Hall, Activities, Mini Golf

The Sands Golf and RV Resort

Your best place to stay in the Palm Springs area.

16400 Bubbling Wells Rd, Desert Hot Springs, CA 92240	(760) 251-1030	All Year

$26-$62	Military/Good Sam	RV Age, Pet Quantity, Breed
507 Spaces	Paved	30Width/80Length
Internet, Shower, Laundry	Gated, Ice, Golf Carts, Pool	Rentals, Golf, Sauna, Gym

Rio Bend RV Golf Resort

A pleasant climate and relaxing atmosphere give you plenty to enjoy at this amenity-filled park.

1589 Drew Rd, El Centro, CA 92243	(800) 545-6481 http://www.riobendrvgolfresort.com/	All Year
$38-$50	Good Sam	RV Age, Pet Quantity, Breed
500 Spaces	Paved	28Width/50Length
Internet, Shower, Laundry	ATM, Ice, Snack Bar, Pool	Golf, Gym, Pavilion

Golden Village Palms RV Resort

This is the largest luxury resort in California, and you'll enjoy your stay here.

3600 W Florida Ave, Hemet, CA 92545	(951) 474-1821 goldenvillagepalms.com/	All Year
$50-$90	Military/Good Sam	Pet Quantity, Breed
1000 Spaces	Paved	30Width/90Length
Internet, Showers, Laundry	Gated, Ice, Cable, Rentals	Game Room, Rec. Hall

Desert Willow RV Resort

Offering RV sites designed for long term stays.

12624 Main St, Hesperia, CA 92345	(760) 949-0377 https://www.desertwillowrv.com/	All Year
$20-$30	No Discounts Offered	Pet Size, Qty, Breed
173 Spaces	Paved	35Width/87Length
Internet, Showers	Laundry, Gated, Pool	Hot Tub, Rec. Hall

Idyllwild RV Resort

Located in the refreshing pine mountains, this is a great place to enjoy the outdoors.

24400 Canyon Trail, Idyllwild, CA 92549	(888) 395-1958	All Year
$49-$56	Military/Good Sam	Pet Quantity
287 Spaces	Paved	25Width/45Length
Shower, Laundry, Gated	Supplies, LP Gas, Ice	Grocery, Rentals, Playground

Indian Waters RV Resort & Cottages

A great place to stay long term.

47202 Jackson St,	(760) 342-8100	All Year

Indio, CA 92201		
$25-$78	Military/Good Sam	No Restrictions
265 Spaces	Paved	30Width/60Length
Internet, Showers, Laundry	Ice, RV Wash	Gated Access

Indian Wells RV Resort
Offering beautiful views of the Santa Rosa Mountains.

47340 Jefferson St, Indio, CA 92201	(760) 347-0895	All Year
$26-$120	Military/Good Sam	RV Age
349 Spaces	Paved	20Width/70Length
Internet, Showers, Laundry	Ice, Cable, RV Wash	Rentals, Pool, Gym

Shadow Hills RV Resort
Putting you close to all the activities that the Palm Springs area has to offer.

40655 Jefferson St, Indio, CA 92203	(760) 360-4040 shadowhillsrvresort.com	All Year
$45-$75	Military/Good Sam	RV Age, Pet Quantity
121 Spaces	Paved	25Width/96Length
Internet, Showers, Laundry	RV Wash, Rentals, Pool	Games, Rec. Hall, Cable

Lake Park RV Resort & Motel
Here you can enjoy lakefront living at its best.

32000 Riverside Dr, Lake Elsinore, CA 92530	(951) 674-7911 lakeparkrvresort.com/	All Year
$40	Good Sam	RV Age, Pet Size, Quantity
200 Spaces	Paved	28Width/32Length
Internet, Showers, Laundry	Ice, Cable, Rvwash, Rentals	Pool, Rec. Hall, Pavilion

Sierra Trails RV Park
Stay long term in this great environment or come to get away from the winter weather.

21282 State Highway 14, Mojave, CA 93501	(760) 373-4950 https://sierratrailsrvpark.com/	All Year
$40	Military/Good Sam	No Restrictions
70 Spaces	Gravel/Dirt	25Width/70Length
Internet, Showers, Laundry	Ice, Pool, Rec. Hall	Patios, Tables, BBQ's

Needles Marina Resort
This quiet, 55+ park offers plenty of activities to keep people busy.

100 Marina Dr, Needles, CA 92363	(760) 326-2197 https://needlesmarinaresort.com/needles-	All Year

	marina-mobile-home-park.html	
$48-$55	Military/Good Sam	55+, RV Age, Pet Qty.
157 Spaces	Paved/Gravel	20Width/45Length
Internet, Showers, Ice	Grocery, Fishing, Pool, Rec. Hall, Patios	Activities, Tables

Pirate Cove Resort

A secluded waterfront park with plenty of amenities to offer a great vacation.

100 Park Moabi Rd, Needles, CA 92363	(760) 326-9000 http://www.piratecoveresort.com/	All Year
$60-$80	Good Sam	Pet Quantity, Breed
157 Spaces	Gravel	24Width/60Length
Internet, Showers, Laundry	Firewood, Ice, Restaurant, Ice	Rec. Hall, Playground

Desert View RV Resort

A tranquil oasis in the desert, this is your home away from home.

5300 Old National Trl, Needles, CA 92363	(760) 326-4000 https://www.desertviewrv.com/	All Year
$48	Military/Good Sam	RV Age, Pet Qty, Breed
66 Spaces	Paved/Gravel	30Width/60Length
Internet, Showers, Laundry	Ice, Pool, Rec. Hall, Patios	Pavilion, Games

Palm Springs RV Resort

A popular winter destination or a long term place to stay.

77500 Varner Rd, Palm Desert, CA 92211	(760) 345-1682	September 15 to May 15
$71	Good Sam	Pet Quantity
359 Spaces	Paved	27Width/75Length
Internet, Showers, Laundry	Ice, Rentals, Pool, Rec. Hall	Activities, Playground

Emerald Desert RV Resort

A vibrant community with plenty of amenities and a great place to stay.

76000 Frank Sinatra Dr, Palm Desert, CA 92211	(760) 289-3568 https://www.emeralddesert.com/	All Year
$50-$139	Military/Good Sam	RV Age, Pet Qty, Breed
261 Spaces	Paved	30Width/100Length
Internet, Showers, Laundry	Ice, Cable, RV Wash	Pool, Rentals, Games, Tennis

Pechanga RV Resort

Located in the hills of wine country, this park offers you endless opportunities for fun.

45000 Pechanga Pkwy, Temecula, CA 92592	(877) 997-8386 pechanga.com/rvresort	All Year
$60-$145	Military/Good Sam	RV Age, Pet Qty, 29DayMax
210 Spaces	Paved	28Width/55Length
Casino, Internet, Showers	Laundry, ATM, Ice, Cable	Restaurant, Sauna, Gym

TwentyNine Palms Resort RV Park

A resort-style RV park within minutes of plenty of activities.

4949 Desert Knoll Ave, Twentynine Palms, CA 92277	(760) 367-3320 twentyninepalmsresort.com	All Year
$42-$45	Good Sam	Pet Size, Qty, Breed
173 Spaces	Paved	27Width/52Length
Internet, Showers, Laundry	Rentals, Pool, Rec. Hall	Tennis, Sauna, Gym

California – San Diego County

Located at the southern end of the state, this California county offers plenty of outdoor experiences and sites among cities. There are also plenty of good RV parks to consider.

Chula Vista RV Resort
Located on the San Diego Bay with its own marina, this park boasts a number of amenities.

460 Sandpiper Way, Chula Vista, CA 91910	(619) 422-0111	All Year
$79-$123	Good Sam	RV Age, Pet Qty, Breed
237 Spaces	Paved	20Width/62Length
Internet, Showers, Laundry	ATM, LP Gas, Grocery	Cable, Pool, Rec. Hall

Vacationer RV Park
Located near San Diego, this gated park is a great place for a vacation or a long term stay.

1581 E Main St, El Cajon, CA 92021	(619) 442-0904 https://www.vacationerrv.com/	All Year
$50-$80	Military/Good Sam	RV Age, Pet Qty, Breed
146 Spaces	Paved	27Width/67Length
Internet, Showers, Laundry	Cable, Ice, Pool, Hot Tub	Rec. Hall, Activities, Patios

Circle RV Resort
This is a great place to call home, close to all the activities that San Diego has to offer.

1835 E Main St, El Cajon, CA 92021	(866) 460-1589 https://www.circlerv.com/	All Year
$70-$95	Military/Good Sam	RV Age, Pet Qty, Breed
165 Spaces	Paved	18Width/65Length
Internet, Showers, Laundry	Cable, Pool, Rec. Hall	Game Room, Gym, Patios

Oak Creek RV Resort
This peaceful park is close to the heart of San Diego.

15379 Oak Creek Rd, El Cajon, CA 92021	(866) 916-1318 https://www.oakcreekrv.com/	All Year
$60-$90	Military/Good Sam	RV Age, Pet Qty, Breed
120 Spaces	Paved	18Width/70Length
Internet, Showers, Laundry	Ice, Cable, Pool, Rec. Hall	Activities, Games, Patios

Escondido RV Resort
This pet-friendly park offers plenty of amenities.

1740 Seven Oakes Rd, Escondido, CA 92026	(858) 206-8476 https://www.escondidorv.com/	All Year

$65-$101	Military/Good Sam	RV Age, Pet Qty, Breed
125 Spaces	Paved	24Width/50Length
Internet, Showers, Laundry	LP Gas, Cable, Pool	Rec. Hall, Activities, Patios

San Diego RV Resort
Centrally located, this park allows you to get anywhere in San Diego.

7407 Alvarado Rd, La Mesa, CA 91942	(619) 775-3567 https://www.sdrvresort.com/	All Year
$70-$125	Military/Good Sam	RV Age, Pet Qty, Breed
172 Spaces	Paved	25Width/70Length
Internet, Showers, Laundry	Cable, Ice, Pool, Rec. Hall	Game Room, Gym, Patios

Rancho Los Coches RV Park
This park is close to the freeway but is also a quiet location to stay.

13468 Highway 8 Business, Lakeside, CA 92040	(619) 443-2025 https://rancholoscochesrv.com/	All Year
$60-$85	Military/Good Sam	Pet Breed
135 Spaces	Paved	22Width/55Length
Internet, Showers, Laundry	Pool, Rec. Hall, Activities	Gym, Games, Patios

Oceanside RV Park
The beautiful weather here and close proximity means you can enjoy the beaches year-round.

1510 S Coast Hwy, Oceanside, CA 92054	(760) 722-4404 https://www.traveloceanside.com/	All Year
$75-$110	Military/Good Sam	RV Age, Pet Qty, Breed
139 Spaces	Paved	20Width/50Length
Internet, Showers	Supplies, Cable, Pool, Ice	Rec. Hall, Game Room

Pala Casino RV Resort
Located in the shade of the mountains, this is the park to come to if you want to have fun.

11042 Highway 76, Pala, CA 92059	(844) 472-5278 https://www.palacasino.com	All Year
$55-$110	Military/Good Sam	Pet Qty, 29 Day Max
100 Spaces	Paved	30Width/70Length
Internet, Showers, Laundry	ATM, Supplies, LP Gas, Ice	Grocery, Snack Bar, Rec.Hall

Mission Bay RV Resort
A quiet, clean, and secure park for a long term stay or a brief vacation.

2727 De Anza Rd, San Diego, CA 92109	(877) 219-6900 https://missionbayrvresort.com/	All Year

$70-$125	Military/Good Sam	RV Age, Pet Qty, 31 Day Max
260 Spaces	Paved	24Width/48Length
Gated, Internet, Showers	Firewood, Supplies, Cable	Snack Bar, Games, Patios

Campland on the Bay
Located on a private beach overlooking the bay.

2211 Pacific Beach Dr, San Diego, CA 92109	(858) 581-4260 https://www.campland.com/	All Year
$67-$443	Good Sam	Pet Qty, Breed
568 Spaces	Paved	20Width/45Length
Internet, Showers, Laundry	Restaurant, Lounge	Pavilion, Tennis, Gym

Santee Lakes Recreation Preserve
Here you can explore the beach, mountains, and deserts.

9310 Fanita Parkway, Santee CA 92071	(619) 596-3141 https://www.santeelakes.com/	All Year
$45-$67	Good Sam	RV Age, Pet Quantity
300 Spaces	Paved	30Width/62Length
Internet, Showers, Laundry	Gated, Supplies, Firewood	Pool, Splash Pad, Games

Colorado

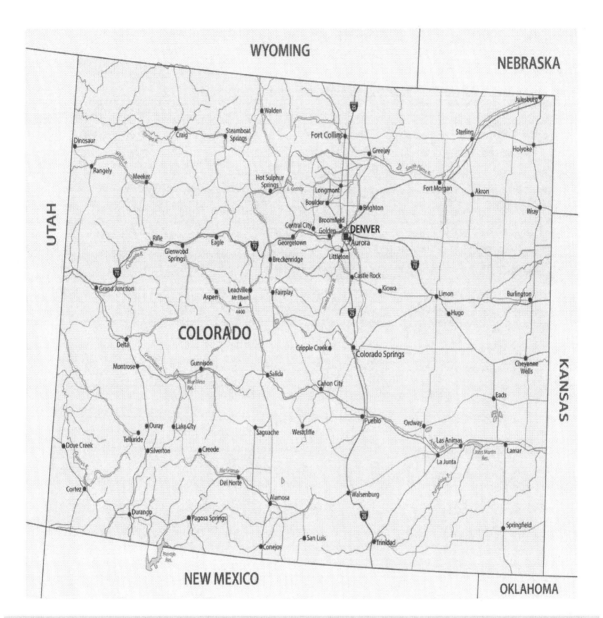

Northern Colorado

Colorado is still a place of untouched wilderness and beauty. No place lets you explore this more than the Northern half of Colorado. Here you can stay at many different RV parks while enjoying the great outdoors.

South Park Mobile Home & RV Community

This 55+ park is conveniently located south of Denver.

3650 S Federal Blvd Ste 97, Englewood, CO 80110	(303) 761-0121 https://www.southparkmhc.com/	All Year
$50	Military/Good Sam	55+, **NO PETS**, RV Age
230 Spaces	Paved	24Width/60Length
Internet, Showers, Laundry	Pool, Rec. Hall, Patios	RV Service, Activities

Elk Meadow Lodge and RV Resort

Located near Rocky Mountain National Park, this place is the ideal vacation destination.

1665 State Highway 66, Estes Park, CO 80517	(970) 586-5342 https://elkmeadowrv.com/	May 1st to October 3rd
$65	Military/Good Sam	Pet Qty, Breed
169 Spaces	Gravel	30Width/60Length
Internet, Showers, Laundry	LP Gas, Supplies, Cable	Rentals, Pool, Rec. Hall

Spruce Lake RV Resort

Close to the Rocky Mountain National Park, where you have spectacular views.

1050 Marys Lake Rd, Estes Park, CO 80517	(970) 586-2889 https://sprucelakerv.com/	May 1st to October 8th
$62	Military/Good Sam	Pet Qty, Breed
110 Spaces	Gravel	40Width/40Length
Internet, Showers, Laundry	Cable, RV Wash, Fishing	Activities, Rec. Hall, Rentals

Monument RV Resort

Conveniently located off the freeway and the closest RV park to Colorado National Monument.

607 Highway 340, Fruita, CO 81521	(970) 858-4405 http://monumentrvresort.com/	All Year
$33-$44	Good Sam	No Restrictions
77 Spaces	Paved	30Width/95Length
Internet, Showers, Laundry	Rentals, Playground, Pavilion	Games, Gym, Playground

Glenwood Canyon Resort

Located along the Colorado River with plenty of good biking trails nearby to enjoy.

1308 County Road 129, Glenwood Springs, CO 81601	(800) 958-6737 Website	All Year
$44-$69	Military/Good Sam	Pet Qty, Breed, 7 Day Max
64 Spaces	Paved/Gravel	30Width/70Length
Shower, Restaurant, Lounge	Fishing, Pavilion, Rentals	Tables, Rec. Hall, Grocery

Dakota Ridge RV Resort

A blend of outdoor adventure and big city life await you at this RV park.

17800 W Colfax Ave, Golden, CO 80401	(303) 279-1625 https://dakotaridgerv.com/	All Year
$50-$65	Military/Good Sam	Pet Qty, Breed
141 Spaces	Paved	28Width/70Length
Internet, Shower, Laundry	RV service, Pool, Gym	Playground, Putting, Tables

Junction West RV Park

Explore the natural and cultural wonders of the Grand Junction area.

793 22 Rd, Grand Junction, CO 81505	(970) 245-8531 https://junctionwestrvpark.com/	All Year
$39-$52	Military/Good Sam	Pet Qty, Breed
63 Spaces	Gravel	35Width/65Length
Internet, Showers, Laundry	Grocery, Cable, Rentals	Splash Pad, Playground

Grand Junction KOA

This pet and the family-friendly park is a great place to stay in the Grand Junction area.

2819 Highway 50, Grand Junction, CO 81503	(970) 242-2527 koa.com/campgrounds/grand-junction/	All Year
$39-$61	Military	Pet Breed
66 Spaces	Gravel	30Width/75Length
Internet, Showers, Laundry	Cable, Rentals, Pool	Game Room, Activities

Winding River Resort

This is your perfect vacation destination.

1447 County Road 491, Grand Lake, CO 80447	(970) 627-3215 https://windingriverresort.com/	May 25 to September 30
$49-$57	Military/Good Sam	No Restrictions
116 Spaces	Gravel	40Width/60Length
Internet, Showers, Laundry	Rentals, Fire Rings, Ice	Grocery, Games, Snack Bar

Greeley RV Park

This is a smaller park, offering general amenities.

501 E 27th St, Greeley, CO 80631	(970) 353-6476 http://greeleyrvpark.com/	All Year
$36	Military/Good Sam	Pet Breed
178 Spaces	Paved/Gravel	27Width/60Length
Internet, Showers, Laundry	Supplies, LP Gas, Ice	Grocery, Game Room, Gym

Aunt Sara's River Dance RV Resort

A small and quaint RV park offering the standard amenities.

6700 Highway 6, Gypsum, CO 81637	(720) 933-9212	All Year
$42	Military/Good Sam	No Restrictions
34 Spaces	Paved/Gravel	40Width/65Length
Internet, Showers, LP Gas	Firewood, RVservice, Games	Fire Ring, Tables, BBQ's

Pepper Pod Campground

Located off the freeway and close to Denver, this is a basic amenities campground.

450 5th Ave, Hudson, CO 80642	(303) 536-4763 http://pepperpodcamp.com/	All Year
$25-$35	Military	Pet Quantity
36 Spaces	Gravel	30Width/60Length
Showers, Laundry	Ice, RV service, LP Gas	Rec. Hall, Tables

Loveland RV Resort

This park is your gateway to outdoor adventures.

4421 E US Highway 34, Loveland, CO 80537	(970) 667-1204 https://www.lovelandrvresort.com/	All Year
$50-$62	Military/Good Sam	Pet Quantity, Pet Breed
160 Spaces	Paved	25Width/60Length
Internet, Shower, Laundry	Ice, Grocery, LP Gas, Pool	Playground,Games,Pavilion

Riverview RV Park

Set in the rolling foothills of the Rocky Mountains, this is a great base camp.

2444 River Rim Rd, Loveland, CO 80537	(970) 667-9910 https://riverviewrv.com/	All Year
$40-$54	Military/Good Sam	Pet Quantity, Pet Breed
165 Spaces	Gravel	25Width/70Length
Internet, Showers, Laundry	Grocery, Rentals, Games	Activities, Fire Rings

Southern Colorado

Southern Colorado is home to some larger cities to explore, but it still has plenty of wilderness to explore. Consider some of the RV parks you can stay at while exploring this beautiful part of the state.

Bayfield Riverside RV Park

Located near the larger town of Durango, this park is the best place to visit.

41743 US Highway 160, Bayfield, CO 81122	(970) 884-2475 https://bayfieldriversidervpark.com/	All Year
$46-$70	Military/Good Sam	Pet Breed
119 Spaces	Gravel	28Width/65Length
Internet, Shower, Laundry	Rec.Hall, Activities, Games	Pavilion, Fire Rings

Vallecito Resort

Located on a beautiful mountain lake, this resort is a great place for a leisurely vacation.

13030 County Road 501, Bayfield, CO 81122	(970) 884-9458 http://vallecitoresort.com/	May 1st to October 1st
$44	Good Sam	Pet Qty, Breed
150 Spaces	Paved/Gravel	26Width/80Length
Shower, Laundry, Firewood	Fishing, Rentals, Hot Tub	Games, Playground

Arrowhead Point Campground

A brief description.

33975 US Highway 24 N, Buena Vista, CO 81211	(719) 395-2323 https://arrowheadpointresort.com/	April 15 to October 15
$39-$69	Military/Good Sam	Pet Qty.
66 Spaces	Gravel	30Width/60Length
Internet, Showers, Laundry	Grocery, Rentals, Activities	Playground, Snack Bar

Royal View Campground

At this RV park, you can enjoy the natural beauty around you.

227 County Road 61, Canon City, CO 81212	(719) 275-1900 https://royalviewcampground.com/	May 1 to September 21
$45-$70	Good Sam	Pet Qty, Breed
57 Spaces	Gravel	30Width/65Length
Internet, Shower, Laundry	Rentals, Pool, Game Room, Ice	Firewood, Pavilion

Goldfield RV Park

A quaint and friendly park that puts you close to all the activities Colorado Springs has to offer.

411 S 26th St, Colorado Springs, CO 80904	(719) 471-0495 http://goldfieldrvpark.com/	All Year
$32-$43	Military/Good Sam	RV Age
52 Spaces	Gravel	19Width/75Length
Internet, Showers, Laundry	RV Supplies, Ice, Cable	Rentals, RV Services

Garden of the Gods RV Resort

Wonderful views of Pikes Peak are found from this park.

3704 West Colorado Avenue, Colorado Springs, CO 80904	(719) 475-9450 gardenofthegodsrvresort.com/	All Year
$36-$71	Good Sam	RV Age, Pet Breed
154 Spaces	Paved	24Width/60Length
Internet, Showers, Laundry	Snack Bar, Ice, Restaurant	Rentals, Pool, Game Room

Sleeping Ute RV Park

In the historic Four Corners region, here you can explore a number of archeological sites.

3 Weeminuche Dr, Towaoc, CO 81334	(970) 565-6544 http://www.utemountaincasino.com/	April 1 to November 1
$39	Military/Good Sam	No Restrictions
61 Spaces	Gravel	35Width/62Length
Casino, Internet, Showers	Grocery, Playground, Pavilion	Sauna, Tables, Gym

Sundance RV Park

This park puts you close to the enjoyment of the Mesa Verde National Park.

815 E Main St, Cortez, CO 81321	(970) 565-0997 http://sundancervpark.com/	All Year
$44	Military/Good Sam	No Restrictions
64 Spaces	Paved	30Width/65Length
Internet, Showers, Laundry	Supplies, Ice, Cable, RVWash	Pavilion, Games

La Mesa RV Park

This small and basic park is the perfect place to spend the night.

2430 E Main St, Cortez, CO 81321	(970) 759-1305 http://lamesarvpark.com/	All Year
$30-$42	Military/Good Sam	Pet Breed
33 Spaces	Paved	30Width/70Length

| Restrooms, Showers | Laundry | Cable, Internet |

Alpen Rose RV Park

This park is close to all the main attractions so you are sure to find something that interests you.

27847 Highway 550, Durango, CO 81301	(970) 247-5540 https://alpenroservpark.com/	April 1 – October 31
$50-$62	Military	Pet Quantity
100 Spaces	Gravel	27Width/70Length
Internet, Laundry, Showers	Supplies, Ice Snack Bar	Grocery, Pool, Playground

Middlefork RV Resort

Located along the river in a historic Colorado town, this is your place to stay.

295 US HWY 285, Fairplay, CO 80440	(719) 836-4857 https://www.middleforkrvpark.com/	All Year
$47-$62	Military/Good Sam	Pet Breed
46 Spaces	Paved	20Width/45Length
Internet, Shower, Laundry	Firewood, Game Room	Tables

Falcon Meadow RV Campground

This small, rural campground offers you a chance to stay within view of Pikes Peak.

11150 E US Highway 24, Peyton, CO 80831	(719) 495-2694 falconmeadowrvcampground.com/	All Year
$37-$39	No Discounts Offered	No Restrictions
55 Spaces	Gravel	28Width/60Length
Internet, Shower, Laundry	Playground, Games, Ice	SnackBar,Tables, Firewood

Gunnison Lakeside RV Park & Cabins

A brief description.

28357 US Highway 50, Gunnison, CO 81230	(970) 641-0477 https://gunnisonlakeside.com/	May 1 to October 15
$40-$45	Military/Good Sam	No Restrictions
67 Spaces	Gravel	35Width/100Length
Internet, Showers, Laundry	Supplies, Grocery, Fishing	Games, Rentals, Pavilion

Sky Ute Fairgrounds RV Park

This park offers the basic amenities and puts you in town, close to all of the activities.

| 200 Co-151, Ignacio, CO 81137 | (970) 563-5541 www.skyutefairgrounds.com/ | All Year |

$30	No Discounts Offered	Pet Breed
64 Spaces	Gravel	25Width/60Length
Internet	Laundry	Showers, RV Wash

Circle the Wagons RV Park

Located at the base of the Spanish Mountains, this park provides you a perfect base camp.

126 W 2nd St, La Veta, CO 81055	(719) 742-3233 http://www.circlethewagonsrvpark.com/	May 1 to October 31
$38-$45	No Discounts Offered	No Restrictions
43 Spaces	Gravel	30Width/60Length
Internet, Showers, Ice	Laundry, Rec. Hall, Game Room	Supplies, Pavilion

Mesa Verde RV Resort

The perfect base camp while you explore the cliff dwellings of Mesa Verde National Park.

35303 Highway 160, Mancos, CO 81328	(970) 533-7421 http://www.mesaverdervresort.com/	March 1 to November 1
$37-$47	Military/Good Sam	Pet Breed
48 Spaces	Gravel	35Width/60Length
Internet, Shower, Laundry	Grocery, RV Wash, Rentals	Pool, Hot Tub, Playground

Ancient Cedars Mesa Verde RV Park

A family-friendly destination that allows you to visit all the attractions in the Four Corners region.

34979 Hwy160, Mancos, CO 81328-8742	(970) 565-3517 ancientcedarsmesaverde.com/	March 15 to November 1
$36-$47	Military/Good Sam	No Restrictions
61 Spaces	Gravel	25Width/65Length
Internet, Showers, Laundry	Firewood, Grocery, Ice, Pool	Rec. Hall, Game Room

Pikes Peak RV Park

This peaceful and tranquil park puts you close to all of the attractions in the area.

320 Manitou Ave, Manitou Springs, CO 80829	(719) 685-9459 https://www.pprvpk.com/	All Year
$38-$42	Good Sam	Pet Size, Quantity, Breed
48 Spaces	Gravel	20Width/40Length
Internet, Showers, Laundry	Snack Bar, Rec. Hall, Games	Tables, RV Service, Supplies

Cedar Creek RV Park

A tranquil setting beside the creek, this park puts you close to all the main outdoor activities.

126 Rose Lane,	(970) 249-3884	All Year

Montrose, CO 81401	https://cedarcreekrv.com/	
$30-$51	Military/Good Sam	No Restrictions
45 Spaces	Gravel	24Width/80Length
Internet, Showers, Laundry	Supplies, LP Gas, Ice	Firewood, Fire Rings, Tables

Pagosa Riverside Campground

Relax at your site or enjoy nearby fishing in the river, among other outdoor adventures.

2270 E Highway 160, Pagosa Springs, CO 81147	(970) 264-5874 www.pagosariverside.com/	April 15 to November 15
$49-$55	Military/Good Sam	No Restrictions
60 Spaces	Paved/Gravel	35Width/60Length
Internet, Showers, Laundry	Grocery, Cable, Fishing	Playground, Games, Tables

Silver Summit RV Park

You're close to the railroad that takes you to Durango.

640 Mineral St, Silverton, CO 81433	(970) 387-0240 http://www.silversummitrvpark.com/	May 15 to October 15
$40	Military/Good Sam	No Restrictions
39 Spaces	Gravel	25Width/60Length
Internet, Shower, Laundry	Supplies, Ice	Fishing Supplies, Tables

Peacock Meadows Riverside RV Park

This modern, pet-friendly park offers plenty of amenities.

29059 US Highway160, South Fork, CO 81154	(719) 657-1129 peacock-meadows.com/	All Year
$36-$49	Good Sam	No Restrictions
56 Spaces	Gravel	40Width/70Length
Internet, Showers, Laundry	Grocery, Playground, Ice	Firewood, Fire Wings, BBQ's

South Fork Campground

Stay close to the Rio Grande River and away from the noise of the highway.

26359 US Highway 160, South Fork, CO 81154	(719) 873-5500 southforkcampground.com/	May 1 to October 1
$36-$42	Good Sam	Pet Breed
51 Spaces	Gravel	40Width/60Length
Internet, Laundry, Showers	Rentals, Firewood, Ice	Rec. Hall, Games, Tables

Alpine Trails RV Park

There is plenty of activities in the surrounding area for the entire family.

0111 Wharton Rd,	(719) 873-0261	May 15 to September 22

South Fork, CO 81154	https://alpinetrailsrvpark.com/	
$33-$38	Good Sam	RV Age
42 Spaces	Gravel	24Width/60Length
Internet, Showers, Laundry	Supplies, Firewood, Rentals	Pavilion, Fire Rings, Tables

Grape Creek RV Park

Located in a beautiful valley with wonderful views of the mountains.

56491 US Highway 69, Westcliffe, CO 81252	(719) 783-2588 https://grapecreekrv.net/	All Year
$40-$50	Good Sam	Pet Quantity
34 Spaces	Gravel	30Width/60Length
Internet, Showers, Laundry	Supplies, Snack Bar, Rentals	Rec. Hall, Games, Pavilion

Connecticut

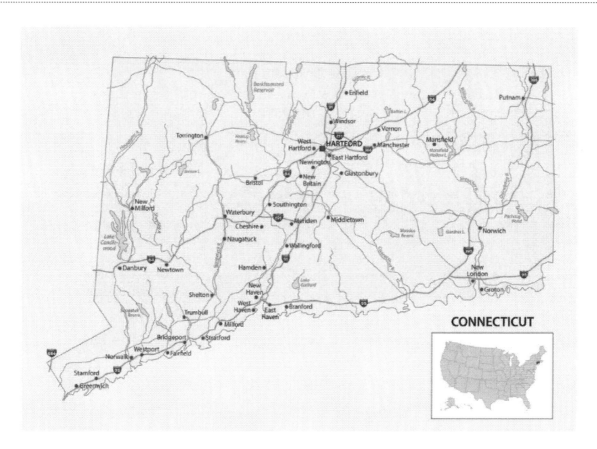

The small state of Connecticut has a lot of offer in the way of outdoor enjoyment.

Cozy Hills Campground
A family-friendly park with several amenities and activities to keep everyone busy.

1311 Bantam Rd, Bantam, CT 06750	(860) 567-2119 https://www.cozyhills.com/	April 15 to October 15
$62-$72	Good Sam	Pet Quantity
167 Spaces	Gravel	25Width/45Length
Internet, Showers, Snack Bar	Grocery, Restaurant, Rentals	Pool, Playground, Archery

Bear Creek Campground
A family-friendly place to stay with plenty of activities to keep the kids busy.

186 Enterprise Dr, Bristol, CT 06010	(860) 583-3300 campbearcreek.com	May 4 to October 29
$45-$60	Military/Good Sam	No Restrictions
56 Spaces	Gravel	25Width/60Length

| Amusement Park Shuttle | Ice, Grocery, Playground | Games, Rentals, Fire Rings |

Riverdale Farm Campsites

Located in the beautiful countryside, this park offers a wonderful vacation experience.

111 River Rd, Clinton, CT 06413	(860) 669-5388 riverdalefarmcampsites.com/	April 15 to October 13
$45-$50	Good Sam	No Restrictions
230 Spaces	Paved/Gravel	34Width/60Length
Internet, Showers, Laundry	Gated, Firewood, Rentals	Rec. Hall, Game Room, Patio

Stateline Campresort

Centrally located so you can visit sites in both Connecticut and Rhode Island.

1639 Hartford Pike, East Killingly, CT 06243	(860) 774-3016 statelinecampresort.com/	April 15 to October 15
$38-$76	Military/Good Sam	Pet Quantity, Breed
241 Spaces	Paved/Gravel	32Width/43Length
Internet, Showers, Laundry	LP Gas, Firewood, Snack Bar	Rentals, Pool, Cable

Seaport RV Resort

Stay at a luxury RV park while exploring the charm of a 19th-century seaport town.

45 Camp Ground Rd, Mystic, CT 06355	(860) 245-0271 seaportcampground.com	April 15 to October 15
$46-$88	Military/Good Sam	Pet Quantity
141 Spaces	Gravel	53Width/110Length
Internet, Cable, Laundry	Gated, Fishing, Game Room	Rec. Hall, Gym, Games

Gentile's Campground

A great place to relax and enjoy nature while getting away from busy city life.

262 Mount Tobe Rd, Plymouth, CT 06782	(860) 283-8437 gentilescampground.com/	All Year
$50-$53	Military/Good Sam	Pet Quantity, Breed
110 Spaces	Gravel	30Width/80Length
Internet, Showers, Pool, Ice	Gated, ATM, LP Gas	Playground, Games, Tables

Hidden Acres Family Campground

This campground isn't short on activities both in the park and in the surrounding area.

47 River Rd, Preston, CT 06365	(860) 887-9633 hiddenacrescamp.com/	May 1 to October 10
$53-$72	Military/Good Sam	Pet Breed

200 Spaces	Paved/Gravel	45Width/65Length
Internet, Showers, Laundry	Firewood, Supplies, Ice	Firewood, Rentals, Pool

Witch Meadow Lake Family Campground

A pristine lake with a number of resort-style amenities, this park is the perfect place.

139 Witch Meadow Rd, Salem, CT 06420	(860) 859-1542 witchmeadowcampground.com/	May 1 to October 13
$53-$63	Good Sam	Pet Quantity, Breed
280 Spaces	Gravel	40Width/65Length
Internet, Showers, Laundry	Grocery, Restaurant, Pool	Games, Activities, Tennis

Salem Farms Campground

A family and pet-friendly campground offering a pleasant vacation experience.

39 Alexander Rd, Salem, CT 06420	(860) 859-2320 salemfarmscampground.com/	May 1 to October 14
$47-$55	Military/Good Sam	No Restrictions
189 Spaces	Gravel	30Width/60Length
Internet, Showers, Laundry	Gated, ATM, Snack Bar	Game Room, Playground

Branch Brook Campground

An enjoyable place to stay that is close to town.

435 Watertown Rd, Thomaston, CT 06787	(860) 283-8144 branchbrookcampgroundct.com/	April 1 to November 1
$48-$53	Good Sam	Pet Breed
71 Spaces	Gravel	28Width/60Length
Internet, Showers, Laundry	Supplies, Cable, Pool	Games, Pavilion, Ice

Delaware

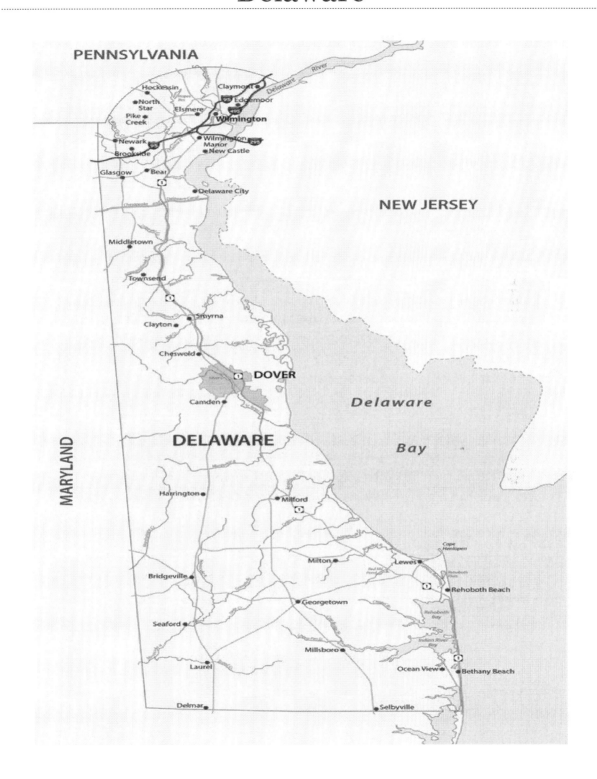

Homestead Campground

Located in a quiet rural setting, this park gives you close access to all the beach attractions.

25165 Prettyman Rd, Georgetown, DE 19947	(302) 684-4278 https://www.homesteadde.com/	May 1 to September 30
$65-$80	No Discounts Offered	No Restrictions
358 Spaces	Paved/Gravel	40Width/80Length
Internet, Showers, Laundry	RV Wash, Fishing, Pool	Rec. Hall, Game Room

Tall Pines Campground Resort

A family-friendly campground with plenty to do in the area and in the park as well.

29551 Persimmon Rd, Lewes, DE 19958	(302) 684-0300 tallpines-del.com/	All Year
$50-$70	Military	No Restrictions
535 Spaces	Paved	26Width/40Length
Internet, Showers, Laundry	Gated, Snack Bar, Cable	Activities, Games, Rentals

Holly Lake Campsites

This campground is close to the Delaware beaches and outlet shopping.

32087 Holly Lake Rd, Millsboro, DE 19966	(302) 945-3410 hollylakecampsites.com/	All Year
$60-$70	Good Sam	No Restrictions
1000 Spaces	Gravel/Dirt	40Width/80Length
Internet, Showers, Laundry	Firewood, LP Gas, Rentals	Fishing, Pool, Rec. Hall

Lighthouse Beach RV Resort

A laid back campground offering you a great chance to relax for your vacation.

26162 Bay Blvd, Millsboro, DE 19966	(302) 549-1232	April 1 to October 31
$70-$90	No Discounts Offered	RV Age
167 Spaces	Paved	40Width/50Length
Internet, Gated, Firewood	RV Wash, Rentals, Mini Golf	Fire Rings, Playground

The Resort at Massey's Landing

This luxury RV resort is located in the heart of Delaware's seashore area.

20628 Long Beach Dr, Millsboro, DE 19966	(302) 947-2600 masseyslanding.com/	March 30 to October 31
$59-$209	Military/Good Sam	No Restrictions
254 Spaces	Paved	40Width/90Length
Internet, Showers, Laundry	Gated, Firewood, Snack Bar	Rentals, Pool, Games

Big Oaks Family Campground

Located close to the beach and boardwalk as well as several historic towns.

35567 Big Oaks Ln, Rehoboth Beach, DE 19971	(302) 645-6838 https://bigoakscamping.com	May 1 to October 1
$56-$72	No Discounts Offered	Pet Breed
120 Spaces	Paved/Gravel	25Width/50Length
Showers, Laundry, Supplies	Firewood, Grocery, Cable	Rentals, Playground

Florida

Florida – Northwest

The Florida panhandle is a great destination if you want to vacation on a beach with crystal clear gulf waters. It can also be a great place to go for fishing and water activities.

Ho Hum RV Park
This park is near undeveloped beaches so you can really enjoy your time on the gulf.

2132 Scenic Hwy 98 E, Carrabelle, FL 32322	(850) 697-3926 https://hohumrvpark.com/	All Year
$37-$43	Military/Good Sam	No Restrictions
60 Spaces	Gravel	30Width/70Length
Internet, Showers, Laundry	LP Gas, Ice, Cable	Pavilion, Games, Tables

Carrabelle Beach RV Resort
Located along Florida's Forgotten Coast, this park gives you plenty of amenities.

1843 Hwy 98 W, Carrabelle, FL 32322	(850) 697-2638 carrabellebeachrv.com/	All Year
$50-$70	Good Sam	Pet Quantity
81 Spaces	Paved	30Width/65Length
Internet, Laundry, Rentals	Fishing, Pool, Playground	Rec. Hall, Cable, Ice, Games

Triple C's Campground
At this park, you can get back to nature while being near many attractions.

2309 Flat Creek Rd, Chattahoochee, FL 32324	(850) 442-3333 http://cccscampground.com/	All Year
$44	Military/Good Sam	No Restrictions
59 Spaces	Gravel	25Width/60Length
Internet, Showers, Laundry	Rec. Hall, Grocery, RV Wash	Playground, Pavilion

Twin Lakes Camp Resort
Situated between two lakes, this is your park for a relaxing vacation away from it all.

580 Holley King Rd, Defuniak Springs, FL 32433	(850) 892-5914 twinlakescampresort.com/	All Year
$47-$56	Military/Good Sam	No Restrictions
66 Spaces	Gravel	30Width/60Length
Internet, Showers, Laundry	Fishing, Cable, Rentals	Pool, Games, Playground

Sunset King Lake RV Resort
Great amenities and proximity to several activities means you have it all at this RV resort.

366 Paradise Island Dr, Defuniak Springs, FL 32433	(850) 892-7229 https://www.sunsetking.com/	All Year

$43	Military/Good Sam	No Restrictions
280 Spaces	Paved	30Width/60Length
Internet, Showers, Laundry	Pavilion, Games, Pool	Hot Tub, Gym, Patios

Geronimo RV Park

Located just two blocks from the gulf, this park offers breathtaking views of the beach.

75 Arnett Ln, Miramar Beach, FL 32550	(850) 424-6801 https://geronimorvresort.com/	All Year
$64-$84	Military/Good Sam	No Restrictions
34 Spaces	Paved	30Width/60Length
Internet, Showers	Laundry, Cable	Patios

Camp Gulf

Beachfront camping with amenities and plenty of nearby activities

10005 Emerald Coast Pkwy W, Miramar Beach, FL 32550	(877) 226-7485 https://campgulf.com/	All Year
$90-$219	Military/Good Sam	No Restrictions
190 Spaces	Paved	36Width/55Length
Internet, Showers, Laundry	Gated, Supplies, LP Gas, Ice	Cable, Golf Carts, Rentals

Calypso Cove RV Park

Located along the bay, this park offers you a relaxing tropical setting.

18655 US-331, Freeport, FL 32439	(850) 835-4606 http://www.calypsorv.com/	All Year
$52-$65	Military/Good Sam	No Restrictions
70 Spaces	Gravel	25Width/60Length
Internet, Showers	Laundry, LP Gas, Cable	Rentals

Live Oak Landing

This park offers easy access and convenience.

229 Pitts Avenue, Freeport, FL 32439	(877) 436-5063 liveoaklandingrvresort.com/	All Year
$50-$70	Military/Good Sam	Pet Quantity, Breed
71 Spaces	Paved	30Width/70Length
Internet, Showers, Laundry	Rentals, Pool, Pavilion	Games, Patios, Tables

Rivers Edge RV Campground

Located in a secluded wooded area along the Yellow River.

4001 Log Lake Rd, Holt, FL 32564	(850) 537-2267 https://riversedgerv.co/	All Year

$30	Military/Good Sam	Pet Breed
98 Spaces	Gravel	40Width/85Length
Internet, Showers, Laundry	Firewood, Ice, LP Gas	Rec.Hall,Activities,Playground

Florida Caverns RV Resort
A brief description.

4820 Highway 90, Marianna, FL 32446	(850) 482-5583 floridacavernsrvresort.com/	All Year
$50	Military/Good Sam	No Restrictions
105 Spaces	Paved/Gravel	30Width/60Length
Internet, Showers, Laundry	LP Gas, Ice, Restaurant	Rec.Hall, Games, Playground

Alliance Hill RV Resort
A brief description.

639 Plymouth Loop, Marianna, FL 32448	(850) 545-4928 https://www.alliancehillrv.com/	All Year
$43	Good Sam	RV Age
30 Spaces	Paved	30Width/80Length
Internet, Showers, Laundry	Gated, Pool, Games	Pavilion, Patios, Tables

Stay N Go RV
A brief description.

4951 Malloy Plaza East, Marianna, FL. 32448	(850) 372-4198 http://stayngorv.com/	All Year
$40	Good Sam	Pet Breed
52 Spaces	Paved	30Width/80Length
Internet, Laundry	LP Gas, Ice	Horseshoes, Pavilion

Avalon Landing RV Park
Located only 5 minutes from some of the most beautiful beaches in the world.

2444 Avalon Blvd, Milton, FL 32583	(850) 995-5898 https://avalonlandingrvpark.com/	All Year
$39-$49	Good Sam	Pet Quantity, Breed
79 Spaces	Paved	30Width/60Length
Internet, Showers, Laundry	Cable, Ice, RV Wash	Rec. Hall, Rentals, Fishing

Pelican Palms RV Park

Located in the panhandle of Florida just off the interstate.

3700 Garcon Point Rd, Milton, FL 32583	(850) 623-0576	All Year
$39	Military/Good Sam	No Restrictions
49 Spaces	Dirt/Gravel	25Width/50Length
Internet, Showers, Laundry	LP Gas, Ice, Pool, Rec. Hall	Game Room, Pavilion

Sunburst RV Resort

Offering long and short term sites, this resort is a great place to go when you want to relax.

2375 Horn Rd, Milton, FL 32570	(850) 889-3391 https://sunburstrvresort.com/	All Year
$45-$59	Good Sam	No Restrictions
50 Spaces	Gravel	30Width/50Length
Internet, Showers, Laundry	Rentals, Pool, Rec. Hall	Game Room, Pavilion

Santa Rosa Waterfront RV Resort

Waterfront views and plenty of amenities are what you get when you stay here.

8315 Navarre Pkwy, Navarre, FL 32566	(850) 936-4791 santarosarvresort.com/	All Year
$69-$130	Good Sam	Pet Breed
88 Spaces	Paved	30Width/80Length
Internet, Showers, Laundry	Ice, Cable, Fishing	Pool, Rec. Hall, Playground

Emerald Beach RV Park

Private beach access and water views make this a great place to stay.

8885 Navarre Pkwy, Navarre, FL 32566	(850) 939-3431 emeraldbeachrvpark.com/	All Year
$49-$75	Good Sam	Pet Quantity, Breed
76 Spaces	Paved	37Width/60Length
Internet, Showers, Laundry	Cable, RV Wash, Pool	Activities, Games, Patios

Navarre Beach Camping Resort

Close access from the interstate gets you to crystal blue waters and beautiful beaches.

9201 Navarre Pkwy, Navarre, FL 32566	(850) 939-2188 https://navbeach.com/	All Year
$64-$90	Military/Good Sam	No Restrictions
116 Spaces	Paved/Gravel	30Width/60Length
Internet, Showers, Laundry	Cable, Rentals, Pool	Rec. Hall, Games, Patios

Heritage Oaks RV Park
There are plenty of hiking and biking options in this area.

407 Maple Ave, Panama City, FL 32401	(850) 215-2188 watsonbayoumarina.net/	All Year
$40	Good Sam	Pet Quantity
10 Spaces	Paved	30Width/60Length
Internet, Showers	Fishing Guides	Pavilion, Lawn Bowling

Camper's Inn
Clean and easy access sites along with a number of amenities to give you a great vacation.

8800 Thomas Dr, Panama City, FL 32408	(850) 234-5731 https://campersinn.net/	All Year
$55-$65	Good Sam	No Restrictions
115 Spaces	Paved	20Width/65Length
Internet, Showers, Laundry	Grocery, Ice, Pool	Supplies, Game Room

Panama City Beach RV Resort
Considered one of the best RV destinations in North Florida.

4702 Thomas Dr, Panama City Beach, FL 32408	(850) 249-7352 https://panamacityrvresort.com/	All Year
$75-$225	No Discounts Offered	No Restrictions
68 Spaces	Paved	30Width/60Length
Gated, Pool	Laundry	Restrooms

Pensacola RV Park
Located in town, but still close to the beaches.

3117 Wilde Lake Blvd, Pensacola, FL 32526	(850) 944-1734 https://www.pensacolarvpark.net/	All Year
$44	Military/Good Sam	Pet Quantity, Breed
87 Spaces	Gravel	34Width/80Length
Internet, Showers, Laundry	LP Gas, Cable, Ice	Rec. Hall, Games, Patios

Pensacola Beach RV Resort
Located on a barrier island, this resort gives you all there is to offer on the island.

17 Via De Luna Dr, Pensacola Beach, FL 32561	(850) 932-4670 pensacolabeachrvresort.com	All Year
$70-$130	Military/Good Sam	No Restrictions
72 Spaces	Paved	30Width/60Length
Internet, Showers, Laundry	Supplies, Ice, Cable, Rentals	Games, Pavilion, Patios

Perdido Key RV Resort

Here you'll experience the full Florida lifestyle and community experience.

13770 River Rd, Pensacola, FL 32507	(850) 492-7304 http://perdidokeyrv.com/	All Year
$79-$120	Military/Good Sam	RV Age
56 Spaces	Paved	29Width/80Length
Internet, Showers, Laundry	Fishing, Rentals, Pool	Rec. Hall, Activities, Games

Presnell's Bayside Marina & RV Resort

A wonderful RV park on the Gulf Coast.

2115 Highway C30, Port Saint Joe, FL 32456	(850) 229-9229 https://presnells.com/	All Year
$50-$60	Good Sam	Pet Quantity
66 Spaces	Gravel	30Width/65Length
Internet, Showers, Laundry	Grocery, Cable, Fishing	Pavilion, Game Room, Gym

Florida – Northeast

Northeast Florida offers some excellent beaches as well as some of the oldest towns in America. There is plenty of water activities to enjoy as well as land-based activities.

Travelers Campground
Located close to Gainesville and the University of Florida in the rolling hills.

17701 April Blvd, Alachua, FL 32615	(386) 462-2505 travelerscampground.com/	All Year
$55-$89	Military/Good Sam	No Restrictions
148 Spaces	Paved	30Width/70Length
Internet, Showers, Laundry	LP Gas, Grocery, Cable, Pool	Rec. Hall, Activities

Kelly's Countryside RV Park
The park puts you in unspoiled nature with the amenities needed to enjoy your stay.

36065 Kelly Ln, Callahan, FL 32011	(904) 845-4252 http://kellyscountrysidervpark.com/	All Year
$38	Good Sam	Pet Breed
70 Spaces	Gravel	25Width/50Length
Internet, Shower, Laundry	Ice, Firewood, Horseshoes	Rec. Hall, Pavilion, Tables

Sunset Isle RV Resort
Located on Cedar Key Bay, you can enjoy a range of water activities.

11850 State Road 24, Cedar Key, FL 32625	(352) 543-5375 http://www.cedarkeyrv.com/	All Year
$43-$50	Good Sam	No Restrictions
66 Spaces	Gravel	20Width/60Length
Internet, Showers, Laundry	Restaurant, Ice, Cable	Rec. Hall, Game Room

Cedar Key RV Resort
At this pet-friendly park, you have a chance to get away from it all and get back to nature.

11980 SW Shiloh Rd, Cedar Key, FL 32625	(352) 543-5097 http://www.cedarkeyrvresort.com/	All Year
$43-$60	Good Sam	Pet Breed
98 Spaces	Paved	45Width/80Length
Internet, Showers, Laundry	Ice, Pool, Rec. Hall	Activities, Patios

Anglers RV Campground

At this park, you can experience the leisurely pace known as "island time."

11951 SW Shiloh Rd, Cedar Key, FL 32625	(352) 543-6268 http://anglersrv.com/	All Year
$32-$35	Good Sam	Pet Quantity
66 Spaces	Gravel	25Width/60Length
Internet, Showers, Laundry	Gated, Supplies, Firewood	Pavilion, Activities

Breezy Acres RV Park

This is a quiet RV park that allows you to relax in a rural environment.

10050 NE 20th Ave, Chiefland, FL 32626	(352) 493-7602 https://www.breezyacresrv.com/	All Year
$35-$38	Good Sam	Pet Quantity
60 Spaces	Paved/Dirt	25Width/90Length
Internet, Showers, Laundry	Ice, Rec. Hall, Games	Pavilion, Patios, Tables

Southern Leisure RV Resort

This park is upscale and affordable at the same time.

505 NW 21st Ave. Chiefland, Florida 32626	(352) 284-9900 southernleisurervresort.com/	All Year
$62-$72	Good Sam	55+
260 Spaces	Paved	30Width/65Length
Internet, Showers, Laundry	Ice, Cable, Pool, Rec. Hall	Activities, Games, Gym

Beverly Beach Camptown RV Resort

This park has a large amount of beachfront area.

2815 N Ocean Shore Blvd, Flagler Beach, FL 32136	(386) 439-3111 beverlybeachcamptown.com/	All Year
$65-$185	Military/Good Sam	No Restrictions
205 Spaces	Paved	30Width/60Length
Internet, Showers, Laundry	Supplies, Grocery, Fishing	Game Room, Pavilion

Bulow RV Resort

The best park if you want access to outdoor activities.

3345 Old Kings Road South, Flagler Beach, FL 32136	(888) 472-0752	All Year
$44-$64	Military/Good Sam	No Restrictions
303 Spaces	Paved/Gravel	50Width/75Length
Internet, Showers, Laundry	Cable, Firewood, Pool, Ice	Game Room, Pavilion, Tables

Rivers Edge RV Park

A quiet and relaxing park located in nature.

1393 County Road 309, Georgetown, FL 32139	(386) 467-7147 riversedge-rvpark.com/	All Year
$45-$50	Good Sam	No Restrictions
43 Spaces	Gravel	30Width/60Length
Internet, Showers, Laundry	Rentals, Ice, Rec. Hall	Horseshoes, BBQ's

Flamingo Lake RV Resort

A beautiful park located around a lake. You are close to local attractions but still secluded.

3640 Newcomb Rd, Jacksonville, FL 32218	(904) 766-0672 https://www.flamingolake.com/	All Year
$56-$94	Military/Good Sam	RV Age, Pet Breed
433 Spaces	Paved	35Width/60Length
Internet, Showers, Laundry	Gated, ATM, Supplies	Rentals, Pool, Games

Pecan Park RV Resort

Located near the airport, this is the newest and finest park in Jacksonville.

650 Pecan Park Rd, Jacksonville, FL 32218	(904) 751-6770	All Year
$60-$75	Military/Good Sam	No Restrictions
183 Spaces	Paved	40Width/70Length
Internet, Laundry, Showers	Pool, Cable, Rec. Hall	Game Room, Pavilion

Lake City RV Resort

Easy access from the Interstate and near the old and new downtown portions of Lake City.

3864 N U.S. Hwy. 441, Lake City, FL 32055	(386) 752-0830 http://lakecityrvresort.com/	All Year
$45	Good Sam	Pet Quantity, Breed
67 Spaces	Gravel	30Width/66Length
Internet, Showers, Laundry	Cable, Rentals, Rec. Hall	Games, Pavilion, Patios

Lake City Campground

A family-oriented park with plenty of activities for the whole family to enjoy.

4743 N US Highway 441, Lake City, FL 32055	(386) 752-9131 https://lakecitycampground.com/	All Year
$34-$36	Good Sam	No Restrictions
40 Spaces	Paved	25Width/70Length
Internet, Showers, Laundry	Supplies, Firewood	Rec. Hall, Playground

Yogi Bear's Jellystone Park
This park offers family fun for everyone.

1051 SW Old Saint Augustine Rd, Madison, FL 32340	(850) 973-8269 http://jellystonefla.com/	All Year
$56-$96	Good Sam	No Restrictions
175 Spaces	Gravel	35Width/60Length
Internet, Splash Pad, Pool	Gated, Laundry, Supplies	Playground, Fire Rings

Rocky's Campground
A small campground with basic amenities.

5175 W US Highway 98, Perry, FL 32347	(850) 584-6600 http://www.rockyscampground.com/	All Year
$33	Good Sam	No Restrictions
47 Spaces	Paved	30Width/80Length
Internet, Showers	Laundry, Supplies, Ice	Grocery, Tables

Perry KOA
A standard KOA with the basic amenities.

3641 S Byron Butler Pkwy Lot 400, Perry, FL 32348	(850) 584-3221 koa.com/campgrounds/perry/	All Year
$32-$49	No Discounts Offered	No Restrictions
115 Spaces	Paved/Gravel	30Width/60Length
Internet, Shower, Laundry	Grocery, Cable, Rentals	Rec. Hall, Playground

North Beach Camp Resort
Here you can see the sunrise over the ocean and set on the river.

4125 Coastal Hwy, Saint Augustine, FL 32084	(904) 824-1806 https://northbeachcamp.com/	All Year
$68-$88	Military/Good Sam	Pet Size, Quantity, Breed
150 Spaces	Gravel	40Width/90Length
Internet, Showers, Laundry	Grocery, Ice, Cable, Fishing	Rentals, Pool, Rec. Hall

Stagecoach RV Park
Visit one of the oldest cities in America and check out some award-winning beaches.

2711 County Rd 208, Saint Augustine, FL 32092	(877) 824-2319 https://www.stagecoachrv.net/	All Year
$50-$52	Military/Good Sam	Pet Size, Breed
80 Spaces	Gravel	40Width/60Length
Internet, Showers, Laundry	LP Gas, Cable, Ice	Rec. Hall, Game Room

Compass RV Park

A quaint park that puts you within minutes of downtown and beautiful beaches.

1505 State Road 207, Saint Augustine, FL 32086	(904) 824-3574	All Year
$43-$80	Military/Good Sam	RV Age
175 Spaces	Paved	30Width/75Length
Internet, Showers, Laundry	Ice, Cable, RV Wash	Rentals, Pool, Playground

St Johns RV Park

Pet-friendly with your standard amenities.

2495 State Road 207, Saint Augustine, FL 32086	(904) 824-9840	All Year
$54	Military/Good Sam	Pet Breed
60 Spaces	Paved/Gravel	30Width/70Length
Laundry, Cable	Showers, Internet	Horseshoes, Tables

Tallahassee RV Park

A quaint and smaller park with basic amenities.

6504 Mahan Dr, Tallahassee, FL 32308	(850) 878-7641 http://tallahasseervpark.com/	All Year
$50	Good Sam	Pet Breed
66 Spaces	Paved	20Width/60Length
Internet, Showers, Laundry	Cable, Pool, Horseshoes	Rec. Hall, Activities, Tables

Big Oak RV Park

Located just minutes from Florida's state capital.

4024 N Monroe St, Tallahassee, FL 32303	(850) 562-4660 https://bigoakrv.com/	All Year
$60	Military/Good Sam	No Restrictions
156 Spaces	Paved/Gravel	30Width/65Length
Internet, Showers, Laundry	LP Gas, Cable, Games	Pavilion, Patios

Dixieland Music & RV Park

A quiet and peaceful park located close to attractions and activities.

17500 NE US Highway 301, Waldo, FL 32694	(352) 468-3988 https://www.dixielandrvparkfl.com/	All Year
$36-$55	Good Sam	RV Age, Pet Quantity
150 Spaces	Gravel	30Width/70Length
Internet, Shower, Laundry	Lounge, Restaurant, Rec. Hall	Activities, Games, Tables

Williston Crossings RV Resort

This park is nothing short of paradise, you'll want to turn your vacation into a long-term stay.

410 NE 5th St, Williston, FL 32696	(352) 528-7100 http://willistoncrossingrv.com/	All Year
$65-$75	Good Sam	Pet Quantity
455 Spaces	Paved	35Width/100Length
Internet, Showers, Laundry	Cable, RV Wash, Pool, Ice	Playground, Pavilion

Florida – Central West

Sandy Oaks RV Resort
This park offers you plenty of amenities to keep you busy.

6760 N Lecanto Hwy, Beverly Hills, FL 34465	(352) 465-7233 http://www.sandyoaksrvresort.com/	All Year
$47-$57	Good Sam	Pet Breed
185 Spaces	Paved	30Width/75Length
Internet, Shower, Laundry	Cable, RV Wash, Pool	Rec. Hall, Putting, Patios

Pleasant Lake RV Resort
This park features a freshwater lake for fishing or wildlife viewing.

6633 53rd Ave E, Bradenton, FL 34203	(941) 756-5076 Website	All Year
$49-$75	Military/Good Sam	Pet Quantity, Breed
341 Spaces	Paved	40Width/50Length
Internet, Showers, Laundry	Cable, Rentals, Pool	Gym, Patios, Tables

Horseshoe Cove RV Resort
Located along the Braden River, this luxury RV resort features its own private island.

5100 60th St E, Bradenton, FL 34203	(941) 758-5335	All Year
$45-$93	Military/Good Sam	Pet Quantity, Breed
476 Spaces	Paved	30Width/60Length
Internet, Showers, Laundry	Gated, Ice, RVWash, Rentals	Pavilion, Gym, Patios

Arbor Terrace RV Resort
Close to some of the best beaches on the Gulf and a number of local attractions.

405 57th Ave W, Bradenton, FL 34207	(941) 755-6494	All Year
$43-$72	Military/Good Sam	Pet Quantity, Breed
361 Spaces	Paved	20Width/60Length
Internet, Showers, Laundry	Rec. Hall, Gym, Pavilion	Patios, Tables, Games

Winter Quarters Manatee RV Resort
A great central location to all you may want to see and do.

800 Kay Road NE, Bradenton, FL 34212	(800) 678-2131	All Year
$35-$94	Military/Good Sam	No Restrictions

415 Spaces	Paved	30Width/80Length
Internet, Showers, Laundry	Ice, RV Service, Pool	HotTub, GameRoom, Rec.Hal

Sarasota Bay RV Park

A 55+ park located on Sarasota Bay.

10777 Cortez Rd W, Bradenton, FL 34210	(941) 794-1200 https://www.sarabayrvpark.com	All Year
$55-$85	No Discounts Offered	**NO PETS** 55+
240 Spaces	Paved	25Width/55Length
Internet, Showers, Laundry	Pool, Rec. Hall, Hot Tub	Gym, Patios

Belle Parc RV Resort

A park that is close to all the sites and attractions.

11050 Elliots Way, Brooksville, FL 34601	(352)593-5852 http://www.belleparcrvresorts.com/	All Year
$60-$87	Military/Good Sam	55+, Pet Quantity
280 Spaces	Paved	35Width/60Length
Internet, Shower, Laundry	Hot Tub, Rec. Hall, Game Room	Pavilion, Gym, Patios

Clover Leaf Forest RV Resort

Located in a tranquil county setting, here you can enjoy a number of amenities.

910 North Broad Street, Brooksville, FL 34601	(352) 796-8016	All Year
$58-$71	Good Sam	Pet Quantity, Breed
285 Spaces	Paved	18Width/80Length
Internet, Showers, Laundry	Pool, Hot Tub, Gym	Patios, Shuffleboard

Avalon RV Resort

This RV park is located in the heart of Florida, with affordable rates for any length of stay.

16860 US Highway 19 N, Clearwater, FL 33764	(727) 531-6124 bayshorehomesales.com	All Year
$45	Good Sam	Pet Breed
258 Spaces	Paved	30Width/60Length
Showers, Laundry	Pool, LP Gas	Patios, Tables

Buttonwood Inlet RV Resort

This is your destination for relaxing and anything water-related.

12316 Cortez Rd W, Cortez, FL 34215	(941) 798-3090 http://buttonwoodinletrvresort.com/	All Year

$50-$95	Military/Good Sam	Pet Size, Quantity, Breed
80 Spaces	Paved	28Width/60Length
Internet, Shower, Laundry	Cable, Rentals, Rec. Hall	Activities, Games, Patios

Holiday Cove RV Resort

Located in the historic fishing village of Cortez and within minutes of beautiful beaches.

11900 Cortez Rd W, Cortez, FL 34215	(941) 251-7809 http://holidaycovervinc.com/	All Year
$75-$130	Military/Good Sam	Pet Quantity
97 Spaces	Paved	30Width/60Length
Internet, Showers, Laundry	Ice, Cable, Pool, Rec. Hall	Patios, Tables, Games

Rock Crusher Canyon RV Resort

This park feels as if you are staying at a state park. The atmosphere is fun and relaxing.

237 S Rock Crusher Rd, Crystal River, FL 34429	(888) 726-7805	All Year
$40-$47	Good Sam	Pet Quantity, Breed
391 Spaces	Paved	35Width/80Length
Internet, Showers, Laundry	Gated, Ice, Cable, RV Wash	Activities, Playground

Crystal Isles RV Park

Located on the scenic West Coast of Florida.

11419 W. Fort Island Trail, Crystal River, FL 34429	(888) 783-6763	All Year
$69-$74	Military/Good Sam	Pet Quantity
436 Spaces	Paved	25Width/60Length
Internet, Shower, Laundry	LP Gas, Firewood, Cable	Snack Bar, Pool, Playground

Lake Rousseau RV Fishing Resort

Stay at the waters' edge and under the trees.

10811 North Coveview Ter, Crystal River, FL 34428	(352) 795-6336	All Year
$40-$50	Good Sam	Pet Quantity, Breed
120 Spaces	Paved	30Width/50Length
Internet, Showers, Laundry	RV Wash, Fishing, Games	Rec. Hall, Activities

Blue Jay RV Resort

This 55+ park puts you close to both Orlando and Tampa.

38511 Wilds Rd, Dade City, FL 33525	(352) 567-9678	All Year

$42	Good Sam	55+, Pet Size, Qty, Breed
263 Spaces	Paved/Gravel	26Width/40Length
Restrooms, Laundry, Ice	RV Wash, Rentals, Pool	Rec. Hall, Patios

Grove Ridge RV Resort
This 55+ park is located in the beautiful countryside.

10721 US Highway 98, Dade City, FL 33525	(352) 523-2277	All Year
$37-$49	Military/Good Sam	55+, Pet Breed
247 Spaces	Paved	35Width/50Length
Internet, Laundry, RV Wash	Rentals, Rec. Hall, Pool	Pavilion, Patios

Citrus Hill RV Resort
This 55+ park is located close to historic downtown.

9267 US Highway 98, Dade City, FL 33525	(352) 567-6045	All Year
$38-$42	Good Sam	55+, Pet Qty, Size, Breed
182 Spaces	Paved	35Width/50Length
Showers, Laundry, Gated	RV Wash, Rentals	Rec. Hall, Activities

Many Mansions RV Resort
This 55+ park is located near all the popular destinations and outdoor activities.

40703 Stewart Rd, Dade City, FL 33525	(352) 567-8667 manymansionsrvpark.com/	All Year
$40	Military/Good Sam	55+
235 Spaces	Paved	30Width/60Length
Internet, Showers, Laundry	LP Gas, RV Wash, Rec. Hall	Activities, Games, Patios

Town and Country RV Resort
This 55+ community offers you a great option for a short-term or long-term stay.

18005 US Highway 301, Dade City, FL 33523	(352) 567-7707 townandcountryrvresortfl.com/	All Year
$33-$44	Good Sam	55+, Pet Size, Qty, Breed
200 Spaces	Paved	40Width/60Length
Internet, Showers, Laundry	Rentals, Games, Playground	Pavilion, Patios, Tables

Tampa East RV Resort
This park puts you at a great location near all the popular attractions of Central Florida.

4630 Mcintosh Rd, Dover, FL 33527	(813) 659-2504	All Year
$32-$57	Military/Good Sam	Pet Quantity, Breed

700 Spaces	Paved	30Width/70Length
Internet, Showers, Laundry	LP Gas, Rentals, Pool	Pavilion, Gym, Patios

Dunedin RV Resort
Enjoy exploring beaches and islands.

2920 Alternate 19, Dunedin, FL 34698	(727) 784-3719	All Year
$56-$100	Military/Good Sam	Pet Breed
239 Spaces	Paved	30Width/60Length
Internet, Showers, Laundry	LP Gas, RV Wash, Pool	Rentals, Gym, Patios

Ellenton Gardens RV Resort
This grassy RV park is located along the Manatee River.

7310 US Highway 301 N, Ellenton, FL 34222	(941) 722-0341	All Year
$42-$52	Military/Good Sam	Pet Size, Qty, Breed
190 Spaces	Paved	24Width/50Length
Rentals, Internet, Showers	Pool, Rec. Hall, Pavilion	Gym, Patios, Games

Nature's Resort
Affordable rates mean you can enjoy the scenery as long as you want.

10359 W Halls River Rd, Homosassa, FL 34448	(352) 628-9544 http://naturesresortfla.com/	All Year
$50-$55	Good Sam	No Restrictions
400 Spaces	Paved	30Width/60Length
Internet, Showers, Laundry	Lounge, Cable, Fishing	Rentals, Pavilion, Pool

Homosassa River RV Resort
Stay along a peaceful river and enjoy nature at its best.

10200 W Fishbowl Dr, Homosassa Springs, FL 34448	(352) 628-2928	All Year
$38-$60	Military/Good Sam	Pet Quantity, Breed
222 Spaces	Paved	25Width/50Length
Internet, Showers, Laundry	LP Gas, Ice, Cable, RV Wash	Pavilion, Patios, Pool

Chassahowitzka River Campground
This park is your gateway to scenery, water activities, and wildlife viewing.

8600 W Miss Maggie Dr, Homosassa, FL 34448	(352) 382-2200 http://chassahowitzkaflorida.com/	All Year
$46	Good Sam	Pet Quantity

| 52 Spaces | Gravel | 35Width/50Length |
| Internet, Showers, Laundry | Grocery, Firewood, Ice | Horseshoes, Rec. Hall |

Winter Paradise RV Resort
This is the premier RV resort in Hudson.

16108 US Highway 19, Hudson, FL 34667	(727) 868-2285	All Year
$30	Good Sam	Pet Breed
290 Spaces	Paved	25Width/45Length
Showers, Laundry, Pool	LP Gas, Rec. Hall, Pavilion	Patios, Activities

Three Lakes RV Resort
Here you can have all the amenities of home while staying on the Florida coast.

10354 Smooth Water Dr, Hudson, FL 34667	(727) 869-8511	All Year
$40-$54	Good Sam	Pet Quantity, Breed
308 Spaces	Paved	40Width/65Length
Internet, Showers, Laundry	Rentals, Pool, Rec. Hall	Activities, Gym, Patios

Barrington Hills RV Resort
This 55+ park is located near plenty of local attractions to keep you busy.

9412 New York Avenue, Hudson, FL 34667	(727) 868-3586	All Year
$44-$50	Good Sam	55+, Pet Size, Qty, Breed
390 Spaces	Paved	30Width/50Length
Internet, Showers, Laundry	RV Wash, Pool, Rec. Hall	Game Room, Activities, Patio

Gulf Coast RV Resort
This peaceful and tranquil park allows you to enjoy the Nature Coast of Florida.

13790 W Foss Groves Path, Inglis, FL 34449	(352) 447-2900 http://www.gulfcoastrvfl.com/	All Year
$30	Good Sam	Pet Breed
158 Spaces	Paved	50Width/65Length
Internet, Showers, Laundry	Cable, Pool, Playground	Games, Pavilion, Patios

Yankee Traveler RV Park
Centrally located to three larger towns and just minutes from the beach.

8500 Ulmerton Rd, Largo, FL 33771	(727) 531-7998 https://yankeetraveler.net/	All Year
$44-$51	Good Sam	55+, Pet Size, Quantity

222 Spaces	Paved	25Width/60Length
Internet, Showers, Laundry	Pool, RV Wash, LP Gas	Game Room, Activities, Patio

Rainbow Village of Largo RV Resort

This 55+ park offers quick access from the freeway and puts you close to the Gulf Coast.

11911 66th St, Largo, FL 33773	(727) 536-3545	All Year
$45-$68	Military/Good Sam	RV age, Pet Qty, Breed
308 Spaces	Paved	20Width/70Length
Showers, Laundry, Gated	RV Wash, Rentals, Gym	Games, Pool, Patios

Vacation Village RV Resort

This park is designed for extended stays and offers you all you need to feel at home.

6900 Ulmerton Road, Largo, FL 33771	(877) 297-2757	All Year
$43-$54	Military/Good Sam	No Restrictions
275 Spaces	Paved	25Width/48Length
Internet, Showers, Laundry	RV Service, Rentals, Pool	Rec. Hall, Activities, Tables

Winter Quarters Pasco RV Resort

This is your destination for an exciting family vacation.

21632 State Road 54, Lutz, FL 33549	(800) 879-2131	All Year
$48-$64	Military/Good Sam	No Restrictions
253 Spaces	Paved	50Width/80Length
Showers, Laundry, Pool	Hot Tub, Rec. Hall, Activities	Games, Gym, Patios

Seven Springs Travel Park

This quiet, gated RV park offers you a relaxing vacation opportunity.

8039 Old County Road 54, New Port Richey, FL 34653	(727) 376-0000 http://sevenspringsrvpark.com/	All Year
$45	Good Sam	**NO PETS**
220 Spaces	Paved	30Width/65Length
Internet, Showers, Laundry	RV Service, Rec. Hall, Patios	Pool, Activities, Tables

Silver Dollar RV Resort

This is your destination for golf with three courses to choose from.

12515 Silver Dollar Drive, Odessa, FL 33556	(877) 657-8737	All Year
$24-$72	Military/Good Sam	Pet Quantity

483 Spaces	Paved	20Width/30Length
Internet, Showers, Laundry	ATM, Ice, Snack Bar, Pool	Game Room, Golf

Fiesta Grove RV Resort
This 55+ park puts you close to many cities and their attractions.

8615 Bayshore Rd, Palmetto, FL 34221	(941) 722-7661 http://www.fiestagroverv.com/	All Year
$35-$50	Military/Good Sam	55+, RV Age, PetQty,Size,Breed
221 Spaces	Paved	30Width/60Length
Internet, Showers, Laundry	RV Wash, Pool, Rec. Hall	Activities, Patios, Tables

Terra Ceia RV Resort
You'll want to turn your vacation into a long-term stay to get everything done.

9303 Bayshore Road, Palmetto, FL 34221	(866) 315-9337	All Year
$36-$74	Military/Good Sam	Pet Quantity, Breed
206 Spaces	Paved	30Width/58Length
Internet, Showers, Laundry	RV Wash, Pool, Rec. Hall	Activities, Frisbee Golf

Fisherman's Cove RV Resort
Stay for a short time or stay for a long time, you'll enjoy this quiet and peaceful park.

100 61st St E, Palmetto, FL 34221	(941) 729-3685 https://myfishermanscove.com/	All Year
$49-$65	Good Sam	Pet Breed
82 Spaces	Paved	24Width/50Length
Internet, Showers, Laundry	Pool, Hot Tub, Tennis	Pavilion, Gym, Game Room

Sundance Lakes RV Resort
The unhurried pace here will make you want to extend your vacation.

6848 Hachem Dr, Port Richey, FL 34668	(727) 862-3565 rvresorts.com/sundancelakes.html	All Year
$49	Good Sam	Pet Size, Qty, Breed
523 Spaces	Paved	30Width/50Length
Showers, Laundry, LPGas	RV Wash, Pool, Rec. Hall	Activities, Tennis, Patios

Ja-Mar North Travel Park
Here you can enjoy a clean and friendly park with the amenities you need.

6650 San Marco Dr, Port Richey, FL 34668	(727) 862-8882 ja-mar-travelpark.com/	All Year
$40	Good Sam	Pet Breed

353 Spaces	Paved	35Width/57Length
Showers, Laundry, Rentals	Pool, Rec. Hall, Activities	Games, Pavilion, Patios

Oak Springs RV Resort

This park puts you close to all the main attractions of Central Florida.

10521 Scenic Dr, Port Richey, FL 34668	(727) 863-5888 rvresorts.com/oak-springs.html	All Year
$49	Good Sam	Pet Breed
528 Spaces	Paved	22Width/38Length
Showers, Laundry, Ice	Pool, Rec. Hall, LP Gas	Activities, Horseshoes

Rice Creek RV Resort

Close to all the main tourist attractions if you want to see them.

10719 Rice Creek Dr, Riverview, FL 33578	(813) 677-6640 rvresorts.com/rice-creek.html	All Year
$50	Military/Good Sam	Pet Size, Qty, Breed
573 Spaces	Paved	30Width/50Length
Internet, Laundry, Showers	RV Wash, Pool, Rentals	Ice, Rec. Hall, Gym, Patios

Hidden River Resort

With this park, you are in the middle of it all.

12500 Mcmullen Loop, Riverview, FL 33569	(813) 677-1515	All Year
$42-$53	Military/Good Sam	55+, Pet Qty, Breed
313 Spaces	Paved	30Width/45Length
Internet, Showers, Laundry	LP Gas, RV Wash, Pool	Rec. Hall, Activities, Games

Tampa South RV Resort

This is your place to stay when you want to explore the Tampa area.

2900 S US Highway 41, Ruskin, FL 33570	(813) 645-1202 http://tampasouthrvresort.com/	All Year
$45-$65	Military/Good Sam	**NO PETS**, RV Age
121 Spaces	Paved	30Width/50Length
Internet, Showers, Laundry	Pool, Rec. Hall, RV Wash	Activities, Pavilion, Patios

Hawaiian Isles RV Resort

A central location on the Gulf Coast, this is a great place to soak up the sun.

4054 Aloha Blvd, Ruskin, FL 33570	(813) 645-9517 rvresorts.com/hawaiian-isles.html	All Year

$56	Good Sam	Pet Qty, Breed
939 Spaces	Paved	35Width/60Length
Showers, Laundry, Pool	Horseshoes, Rec. Hall	Gym, Patios, Activities

River Vista RV Village
This 55+ park offers a variety of experiences no matter what your interest is.

2206 Chaney Dr. Ruskin, FL 33570	(813) 645-6037	All Year
$39-$64	Military/Good Sam	55+, Pet Breed
400 Spaces	Paved	30Width/60Length
Internet, Showers, Laundry	LP Gas, RV Wash, Pool	Rec. Hall, Game Room

Lazydays RV Resort
Relax and enjoy your vacation or take the time to plan an activity.

6210 County Road 579, Seffner, FL 33584	(800) 350-6731 lazydays.com/locations/florida/tampa-florida/rv-resort	All Year
$30-$70	Military	Pet Quantity
300 Spaces	Paved	30Width/45Length
Internet, Shower, Laundry	Restaurant, Cable, Lounge, Pool	Rec. Hall, Game Room

Topics RV Resort
Easy access from the highway and close to the gulf.

13063 County Line Rd, Spring Hill, FL 34609	(866) 315-9338	All Year
$42-$49	Good Sam	Pet Quantity
233 Spaces	Paved	40Width/100Length
Showers, Laundry	Pool, Rec. Hall	Activities, Tables

Big Oaks RV
Offering the basic comforts at a laid back park.

16654 US Highway 41, Spring Hill, FL 34610	(352) 799-5533 http://www.bigoakspark.com/	All Year
$40	Good Sam	Pet Breed
115 Spaces	Paved	30Width/60Length
Internet, Showers, Laundry	LP Gas, Rec. Hall, Pool	Patios, Gym, Tables

Bay Bayou RV Resort

Located in nature along the banks of a creek.

8492 Manatee Bay Dr, Tampa, FL 33635	(813) 855-1000 https://www.baybayou.com/	All Year
$48-$90	Military/Good Sam	RV Age, Pet Quantity, Breed
300 Spaces	Paved	35Width/60Length
Internet, Showers, Laundry	Firewood, Ice, Pool, Cable	Activities, Games, Patios

Tampa RV Park

Conveniently located off the highway, this park puts you in the center of all the city action.

10314 N Nebraska Ave, Tampa, FL 33612	(813) 971-3460 tampa-rv-park-camp-nebraska.com/	All Year
$31-$37	Military/Good Sam	Pet Size, Quantity, Breed
86 Spaces	Paved/Gravel	20Width/50Length
Internet, Showers, Laundry	RV Wash, Restrooms	Patios, Tables

Southern Aire RV Resort

Located on the Gulf Coast where you can enjoy all the sun you want.

10511 Florence Ave, Thonotosassa, FL 33592	(813) 986-1596 rvresorts.com/southern-aire.html	All Year
$50	Good Sam	RV Age, Pet Size, Qty, Breed
450 Spaces	Paved	30Width/60Length
Showers, Restroom, Laundry	RV Wash, Rentals, Pool	Rec. Hall, Activities, Gym

Spanish Main RV Resort

Set in the wooded countryside for a break from the sun.

12110 Spanish Main Resort Trl, Thonotosassa, FL 33592	(813) 986-2415 Website	All Year
$41-$56	Military/Good Sam	Pet Qty, Breed
331 Spaces	Paved	30Width/60Length
Showers, Laundry, Rentals	Pool, Rec. Hall, Playground	Patios, Tables, Gated

Happy Traveler RV Resort

This 55+ park gives you the option to relax and enjoy your vacation.

9401 E Fowler Ave, Thonotosassa, FL 33592	(813) 986-3094 https://happytravelerrvpark.com/	All Year
$55-$60	Military/Good Sam	55+, RV Age, Pet Qty, Breed

216 Spaces	Paved	25Width/60Length
Internet, Showers, Laundry	Cable, RV Wash, Rentals	Pool, Rec. Hall, Tables

Florida Pines Mobile Home Court
This park has everything you want if you are staying for the winter or longer.

150 Satulah Cir, Venice, FL 34293	(941) 493-0019	All Year
$38-$56	Good Sam	**NO PETS**
130 Spaces	Paved	45Width/65Length
Internet, Showers, Laundry	Cable, Rec. Hall, Patios	RV Wash, Activities

Ramblers Rest RV Campground
Located in a tranquil wooded setting on the river, you are also close to the city life of Sarasota.

1300 N River Rd, Venice, FL 34293	(877) 570-2267	All Year
$40-$101	Military/Good Sam	Pet Quantity, Breed
650 Spaces	Paved	25Width/60Length
Internet, Showers, Laundry	Gated, Ice, RVWash, Rentals	Playground, Games, Tennis

Quail Run RV Resort
A friendly park in the country. Plenty of fun activities to keep you busy.

6946 Old Pasco Rd, Wesley Chapel, FL 33544	(813) 973-0999 http://www.quailrunrv.com/	All Year
$50-$70	Good Sam	RV Age, Pet Size, Qty, Breed
292 Spaces	Paved	35Width/70Length
Internet, Showers, Laundry	Gated, Supplies, LP Gas	Cable, Grocery, Pool, Gym

Beginning Point RV Park
Get away from it all and reconnect with nature at this RV park.

4205 Lado Dr, Wesley Chapel, FL 33543	(813) 788-2415 beginning-point-rv-park.com/	All Year
$38	Good Sam	No Class B, Pet Size, Breed
47 Spaces	Gravel	35Width/60Length
Internet, Showers	Laundry, RV Wash	Pool, Pavilion, Patios

Happy Days RV Park
This 55+ park offers excellent planned activities to fill your vacation days

4603 Allen Rd, Zephyrhills, FL 33541	(813) 788-4858 happy-days-rv-park.com/	All Year

$33-$38	Military/Good Sam	55+, Pet Quantity, Breed
292 Spaces	Paved	30Width/60Length
Internet, Showers, Laundry	Rentals, Pool, Rec. Hall	Shuffleboard, Tables

Baker Acres RV Resort
This 55+ park offers plenty of options for those who want to relax.

7820 Wire Rd, Zephyrhills, FL 33540	(813) 782-3950	All Year
$41-$48	Military/Good Sam	55+, Pet Breed
353 Spaces	Paved	25Width/45Length
Internet, Laundry, Rentals	Pool, Rec. Hall, Game Room	Games, Pavilion, Gym

Rainbow Village RV Resort
Each site at this park is like a private home site.

4150 Lane Rd, Zephyrhills, FL 33541	(813) 782-5075	All Year
$37-$46	Military/Good Sam	55+, Pet Breed
382 Spaces	Paved	30Width/55Length
Showers, Laundry, Cable	RV Wash, Rentals, Pool	Rec. Hall, Games, Patios

Waters Edge RV Resort
This 55+ park offers down to earth fun in a country setting.

39146 Otis Allen Rd, Zephyrhills, FL 33540	(813) 783-2708	All Year
$35-$70	Military/Good Sam	55+, Pet Breed
217 Spaces	Paved	30Width/45Length
Internet, Showers, Laundry	Rentals, Pool, Rec. Hall	Activities, Patios, Tables

Southern Charm RV Resort
This 55+ is located in a historic part of Florida and features southern charm.

37811 Chancey Rd, Zephyrhills, FL 33541	(813) 783-3477	All Year
$35	Military/Good Sam	55+, Pet Breed
497 Spaces	Paved	35Width/50Length
Internet, Showers, Laundry	Pool, Rec. Hall, Activities	Games, Patios, Tables

Sweetwater RV Resort
This 55+ park gives you a quiet getaway.

37647 Chancey Rd, Zephyrhills, FL 33541	(813) 788-7513	All Year
$38-$44	Military/Good Sam	55+, Pet Breed

289 Spaces	Paved	30Width/50Length
Internet, Showers, Laundry	Pool, Rec. Hall, Games	Pavilion, Patios, Tables

Settlers Rest RV Resort
This 55+ park allows you to enjoy your vacation in a peaceful setting.

37549 Chancey Rd, Zephyrhills, FL 33541	(813) 782-2003	All Year
$38-$44	Military/Good Sam	55+, Pet Breed
379 Spaces	Paved	30Width/50Length
Internet, Showers, Laundry	Rentals, Rec. Hall, Pavilion	Shuffleboard

Glen Haven RV Resort
This is a great place to stay when you want to explore nature.

37251 Chancey Rd, Zephyrhills, FL 33541	(813) 782-1856	All Year
$32-$44	Military/Good Sam	55+, Pet Breed
218 Spaces	Paved	35Width/50Length
Internet, Showers, Laundry	RV Wash, Rentals, Pool	Rec. Hall, Activities, Patios

Palm View Gardens RV Resort
At this park, you get a new and exciting experience on the sunny California coast.

3331 Gall Blvd, Zephyrhills, FL 33541	(813) 782-8685 rvresorts.com/palm-view-gardens.html	All Year
$49	Good Sam	Pet Size, Quantity, Breed
497 Spaces	Paved	30Width/60Length
Showers, Laundry, LP Gas	Rentals, Pool, Rec. Hall	Activities, Pavilion, Patios

Majestic Oaks RV Resort
This 55+ park is the perfect place to spend your retirement days.

3751 Laurel Valley Blvd, Zephyrhills, FL 33542	(813) 783-7518	All Year
$48	Military/Good Sam	55+, RV Age, Pet Qty, Breed
252 Spaces	Paved	40Width/70Length
Internet, Showers, Laundry	Pool, Rec. Hall, Activities	Gym, Patios, PickleBall, Tennis

The Oaks at Zephyrhills
This 55+ park is a relaxing place to spend your days in Florida.

39442 Co Rd 54, Zephyrhills, FL 33542	(866) 499-9026 http://oakszephyrhills.com/	All Year
$35	Military/Good Sam	55+, Pet Size

75 Spaces	Paved	30Width/75Length
Internet, Showers, Laundry	Pool, Ice, Rec. hall	Games, Tables

Hillcrest RV Resort

This 55+ park focuses on those who want an active lifestyle.

4421 Lane Rd, Zephyrhills, FL 33541	(813) 782-1947 https://hillcrestrvresortfl.com/	All Year
$39	Good Sam	55+, Pet Size, Qty, Breed
502 Spaces	Paved	35Width/65Length
Showers, Laundry, Pool	Rec. Hall, Activities	Pavilion, Shuffleboard

Zephyr Palms RV Resort

This is a beautiful 55+ park, located within minutes of some of the best attractions in the area.

35120 SR 54 W, Zephyrhills, FL 33541	(813) 782-5610	All Year
$42	Military/Good Sam	RV Age, Breed
153 Spaces	Paved	30Width/60Length
Internet, Showers, Laundry	Pool, Rec. Hall, Game Room	Pavilion, Games

Florida – Central

Lost Lake RV Park
Offering an affordable and quiet park to stay while exploring Central Florida.

3400 Clarcona Rd, Apopka, FL 32703	(407) 886-1996 lostlakervpark.com/	All Year
$34	Good Sam	Pet Size, Breed
81 Spaces	Gravel	25Width/45Length
Internet, Showers, Laundry	Supplies, Ice, Grocery	Pool, Games, Tables

Little Willies RV Resort
You'll feel right at home at this RV resort.

5905 NE Cubitis Ave, Arcadia, FL 34266	(863) 494-2717 littlewilliesrvresort.com/	All Year
$52	Good Sam	Pet Size, Breed
331 Spaces	Paved	30Width/60Length
Internet, Showers, Laundry	Firewood, Ice, RV Wash	Rec. Hall, Game Room, Patio

Craig's RV Park
Located near plenty of attractions, this park also offers tons of planned activities.

7895 NE Cubitis Ave, Arcadia, FL 34266	(863) 494-1820 https://www.craigsrvpark.com/	All Year
$25-$60	Military/Good Sam	Pet Quantity, Breed
333 Spaces	Paved	30Width/45Length
Internet, Showers, Laundry	Cable, Pool, Rec. Hall	Game Room, Pavilion

Big Tree RV Resort
This 55+ park is located among large oak trees.

2626 NE Highway 70, Arcadia, FL 34266	(863) 494-7247	All Year
$40-$61	Military/Good Sam	55+, Pet Breed
392 Spaces	Paved	30Width/55Length
Internet, Showers, Laundry	Ice, RV Wash, Pool, Hot Tub	Game Room, Pavilion, Patios

Cross Creek RV Resort
This 55+ park is gated with pristine landscaping.

6837 NE Cubitis Ave, Arcadia, FL 34266	(863) 494-7300 https://crosscreekrv.com/	All Year
$50-$75	Military/Good Sam	Pet Breed

625 Spaces	Paved	40Width/75Length
Internet, Showers, Gated	Ice, Cable, Pool, Hot Tub	Tennis, Gym, Games, Patios

Toby's RV Resort

This park is conveniently located near everything.

3550 NE Highway 70, Arcadia, FL 34266	(800) 307-0768	All Year
$28-$59	Military/Good Sam	Pet Quantity
406 Spaces	Paved	25Width/75Length
Internet, Showers, Rec. Hall	Activities, Gym, Tennis	Pavilion, Patios

Pioneer Creek RV Resort

Close enough to take part in tourist attractions, but far enough away to avoid congestion.

138 E Broward St, Bowling Green, FL 33834	(863) 375-4343 rvresorts.com/pioneer-creek.html	All Year
$50	Military/Good Sam	Pet Size
377 Spaces	Paved	30Width/50Length
Internet, Showers, Rentals	Laundry, Rec. Hall, Gym	Activities, Pavilion

Breezy Oaks RV Resort

An easily accessible park located among majestic oak trees.

9683 Cr 671, Bushnell, FL 33513	(352) 569-0300 https://breezyoaksrvpark.com/	All Year
$49	Military/Good Sam	No Restrictions
161 Spaces	Paved	35Width/75Length
Internet, Showers, Laundry	Ice, Cable, Pool, Rec. Hall	Game Room, Pavilion

Paradise Oaks RV Resort

This pet-friendly park offers first-class accommodations.

4628 Cr 475, Bushnell, FL 33513	(352) 251-2004 paradiseoaksrv.com/	All Year
$45-$70	Military/Good Sam	Pet Quantity, Breed
440 Spaces	Paved	30Width/110Length
Internet, Showers, Laundry	Cable, Golf Carts, Pool	Game Room, Gym, Patios

Blueberry Hill RV Resort

This one of a kind resort offers you a range of amenities. This is the best luxury RV living.

6233 Lowery St, Bushnell, FL 33513	(352) 793-4112	All Year
$43-$53	Military/Good Sam	55+, Pet Quantity

405 Spaces	Paved	21Width/60Length
Internet, Showers, Laundry	Rentals, Pool, Game Room	Pavilion, Gym, Shuffleboard

Red Oaks RV Resort
This park offers a variety of fun activities, so you are sure to enjoy your stay.

5551 SW 18th Ter, Bushnell, FL 33513	(352) 793-7117	All Year
$42-$56	Military/Good Sam	55+, Pet Quantity, Breed
910 Spaces	Paved	25Width/60Length
Internet, Showers, Laundry	Cable, Pool, Hot Tub, Gym	Rec. Hall, Activities

Clerbrook RV Resort
Located in a beautiful lake area, this park offers a golf course and plenty of other activities.

20005 US Hwy 27N, Clermont, FL 34715	(800) 440-3801	All Year
$35-$67	Good Sam	Pet Size, Qty, Breed
1251 Spaces	Paved/Gravel	40Width/60Length
Internet, Showers, Laundry	Gated, LP Gas, Ice, Pool	Golf, Games, Pavilion

Orlando RV Resort
Located in the orange groves and nature, this is your perfect spot for recreation and relaxation.

2110 Thousand Trails Blvd, Clermont, FL 34714	(352) 394-5531	All Year
$48-$57	Good Sam	No Restrictions
840 Spaces	Paved	40Width/60Length
Showers, Laundry, Supplies	LP Gas, Ice, Snack Bar, Pool	Restaurant, Fishing, Games

Lake Magic RV Resort
This park puts you a short drive from all the main attractions of Central Florida.

9600 Hwy 192 West, Clermont, FL 34714	(888) 558-5777	All Year
$46-$88	Good Sam	No Restrictions
505 Spaces	Paved	35Width/60Length
Internet, Showers, Laundry	Tennis, Pool, Hot Tub, Patios	Rec. Hall, Activities, Games

Kissimmee South RV Resort
This park gives you the best of everything.

3700 US Highway 17 92 N, Davenport, FL 33837	(863) 424-1286	All Year

$41-$59	Good Sam	55+, Pet Breed
347 Spaces	Paved/Gravel	20Width/45Length
Internet, Showers, Laundry	Gated, Supplies, Rentals	Rec. Hall, Activities, Patios

Rainbow Chase RV Resort

A quiet, clean, and well-maintained park that puts you close to all the main tourist attractions.

6300 Lake Wilson Rd, Davenport, FL 33896	(863) 424-2688 http://www.rainbowchaserv.com/	All Year
$47	Good Sam	RV Age, Pet Size, Breed
162 Spaces	Paved	30Width/60Length
Internet, Showers, Laundry	Horseshoes, Rec. Hall	Patios, Fire Rings

Mouse Mountain Travel Resort

This park puts you a convenient six miles from Disney World.

7500 Osceola Polk Line Rd, Davenport, FL 33896	(863) 424-2791	All Year
$40-$50	Good Sam	Pet Size, Qty, Breed
302 Spaces	Paved	28Width/55Length
Internet, Showers, Laundry	RV Wash, Pool, Rec. Hall	Activities, Games, Patios

Southern Palms RV Resort

This RV park is full of fun and offers different activities each day.

One Avocado Lane, Eustis, FL 32726	(800) 277-9131	All Year
$43-$46	Good Sam	Pet Quantity
1200 Spaces	Paved	30Width/50Length
Showers, Laundry	Cable, Pool, Rec. Hall	Game Room, Activities

Rainbow RV Resort

Here you'll find yourself at an amenity-packed resort in a relaxed atmosphere.

700 County Road 630A, Frostproof, FL 33843	(863) 635-7541	All Year
$66	Military/Good Sam	55+, RV Age, Pet Size, Qty, Breed
499 Spaces	Paved	40Width/90Length
Internet, Showers, Laundry	Gated, RV Wash, Pool	Gym, Pavilion, Activities

Camp Inn RV Resort

Centrally located to the main tourist attractions and both beaches.

10400 U S 27, Frostproof, FL 33843	(863) 635-2500 bayshorehomesales.com/	All Year
$34	Good Sam	Pet Breed

| 796 Spaces | Paved | 25Width/60Length |
| Internet, Showers | Laundry, Pool, Rec. Hall | Activities, LP Gas |

Central Park RV Resort
Here you'll find the best form of RV living.

1501 W Commerce Ave, Haines City, FL 33844	(863) 422-5322	All Year
$44-$74	Military/Good Sam	Pet Qty, Breed
354 Spaces	Paved	32Width/60Length
Internet, Showers, Laundry	RV Wash, Rentals, Pool	Rec. Hall, Patios, Gym

Tropical Palms RV Resort
The perfect family getaway.

2650 Holiday Trail, Kissimmee, FL 34746	(407) 396-4595 equitylifestyleproperties.com/	All Year
$58-$94	Good Sam	No Restrictions
556 Spaces	Paved	30Width/62Length
Internet, Showers, Laundry	Gated, Supplies, Snack Bar	Grocery, Cable, Fishing

Mill Creek RV Resort
Located along wooded creek banks, this family-friendly park puts you close to Disney World.

2775 Michigan Ave, Kissimmee, FL 34744	(407) 847-6288	All Year
$57-$78	Good Sam	No Restrictions
156 Spaces	Paved	30Width/50Length
Internet, Showers, Laundry	LP Gas, Pool, Rec. Hall	Activities, Shuffleboard, Patio

Sherwood Forest RV Resort
There are many amenities to enjoy at this park in addition to local attractions.

5300 W. Irlo Bronson Memorial Hwy, Kissimmee, FL 34746	(800) 548-9981	All Year
$68-$101	Good Sam	Pet Breed
512 Spaces	Paved	26Width/45Length
Internet, Showers, Laundry	Cable, Pool, Rec. Hall	Playground, Pavilion

Merry D RV Sanctuary
Peaceful camping in natural surroundings.

4261 Pleasant Hill Rd, Kissimmee, FL 34746	(407) 870-0719 http://www.merryd.com/	All Year
$41	Good Sam	Pet Breed

| 121 Spaces | Paved | 50Width/100Length |
| Internet, Showers, Laundry | Cable, Rec. Hall, Gated | Patios, Pavilion, Shuffleboard |

Grand Oaks Resort
Offering you all the services you need to be at home.

3000 Marion County Rd, Weirsdale, FL 32195	(352) 750-5500 https://home.thegrandoaks.com/	All Year
$65-$70	Good Sam	No Restrictions
60 Spaces	Paved	40Width/85Length
Internet, Showers, Laundry	Rentals, Snack Bar, Lounge	Rec. Hall, Games, Patios

Blue Parrot RV Resort
A peaceful park within minutes of all the main tourist attractions in Central Florida.

40840 County Road 25, Lady Lake, FL 32159	(352) 753-2026 rvresorts.com/blue-parrot.html	All Year
$50	Good Sam	No Restrictions
448 Spaces	Paved	30Width/60Length
Showers, Laundry, Pool, Ice	Rec. Hall, Game Room	Activities, Golf, Shuffleboard

Lake Pan RV Village
Located on Lake Panasoffkee with a convenient dock and boat ramp.

190 NW 4th Dr, Lake Panasoffkee, FL 33538	(352) 793-2051 lakepanrvvillage.com/	All Year
$40-$68	Good Sam	No Restrictions
130 Spaces	Paved/Gravel	30Width/60Length
Internet, Showers, Laundry	Cable, Rentals, Pool	Rec. Hall, Game Room,

Countryside RV Park
Enjoy onsite activities, leisurely hikes, or the lively city atmosphere of Orlando.

741 County Road 489, Lake Panasoffkee, FL 33538	(352) 793-8103 https://countrysidervparkfl.com/	All Year
$32-$36	Good Sam	Pet Breed
72 Spaces	Paved	45Width/56Length
Internet, Showers, Laundry	Rec. Hall, Activities, Patios	Horseshoes, Shuffleboard

Sunshine RV Resort
This park community is friendly and active.

| 303 State Road 70 E, | (863) 465-4815 | All Year |

Lake Placid, FL 33852	http://www.sunshinervresort.com/	
$36-$47	Good Sam	Pet Breed
328 Spaces	Paved	30Width/52Length
Internet, Showers,	Cable, Pool, Game Room	Activities, Tennis, Gym

Lake Placid Campground
At this park, you can enjoy private lake access for your favorite water activities.

1801 US 27 S, Lake Placid, FL 33852	(863) 465-2934	All Year
$40	Military/Good Sam	Pet Breed
145 Spaces	Paved	25Width/55Length
Showers, Laundry, RV Wash	Rentals, Rec. Hall, Patios	Shuffleboard, Horseshoes

Sanlan RV Resort
You'll be close to attractions and beaches from this resort.

3929 US 98 S, Lakeland, FL 33812	(863) 665-1726 https://www.sanlan.com/	All Year
$25-$60	Military/Good Sam	Pet Quantity
531 Spaces	Paved/Dirt	35Width/60Length
Internet, Showers, Laundry	Gated, Ice, Cable, Golf	Gym, Rec. Hall, Golf Carts

Lakeland RV Resort
This getaway park offers you all the extras.

900 Old Combee Rd, Lakeland, FL 33805	(863) 687-6146	All Year
$40-$55	Military/Good Sam	RV Age, Pet Qty, Breed
230 Spaces	Paved	35Width/80Length
Showers, Laundry, Gated	Ice, RV Wash, Rentals	Pool, Rec. Hall, Pavilion

Holiday RV Village
A tranquil RV community with plenty of activities to keep you busy.

28229 County Road 33, Leesburg, FL 34748	(800) 428-5334	All Year
$61	Military/Good Sam	No Restrictions
935 Spaces	Paved	35Width/65Length
Internet, Showers, Laundry	Gated, Ice, Snack Bar, Cable	RV Wash, Game Room

Ocala Sun RV Resort
Located in the middle of all the destinations you could want to visit in Central Florida.

2559 SW Highway 484, Ocala, FL 34473	(352) 307-1100 http://www.ocalasunrvresort.com	All Year

$42-$52	Military/Good Sam	RV Age, Pet Quantity
387 Spaces	Paved	30Width/60Length
Internet, Showers, Laundry	Gated, Pavilion, Cable, Ice, Pool	Rec. Hall, Pavilion

Oak Tree Village Campground
Conveniently located within town, so you can be close to shopping and restaurants.

4039 NW Blitchton Rd, Ocala, FL 34475	(352) 629-1569 http://www.oaktreevillagerv.com/	All Year
$40	Good Sam	Pet Breed
187 Spaces	Paved/Gravel	25Width/60Length
Internet, Showers, Laundry	Ice, Pool, Rec. Hall	Playground, Tennis

Wild Frontier RV Resort
Here you can enjoy a quiet visit far from city noise.

3101 NW 16th Ave, Ocala, FL 34475	(352) 629-3540 wildfrontiercampground.com/	All Year
$52-$68	Military/Good Sam	RV Age, Pet Breed
333 Spaces	Paved	30Width/60Length
Internet, Showers, Laundry	Cable, Pool, Rec. Hall	Activities, Mini Golf, Patios

Cliftwood RV Park
This 55+ park is located in the rolling hills of horse country.

7101 W Anthony Rd, Ocala, FL 34479	(352) 368-3887	All Year
$40	Good Sam	55+, Pet Quantity
104 Spaces	Paved	30Width/60Length
Internet, Laundry, Cable	Games, Horseshoes	Activities, Shuffleboard

Ocala RV Camp Resort
Surround yourself with beauty at this pet-friendly RV park.

3200 SW 38th Ave, Ocala, FL 34474	(352) 237-2138 http://rvcampocala.com/	All Year
$44	Good Sam	Pet Breed
291 Spaces	Paved/Dirt	25Width/50Length
Showers, Laundry, Cable	Dog Run, Pool, Rec. Hall	Horseshoes, Game Room

Ocala North RV Park
This park is a short distance to shopping and entertainment.

16905 NW Highway 225, Reddick, FL 32686	(352) 591-1723 http://ocalanorthrv.com/	All Year
$35-$47	Good Sam	Pet Breed

126 Spaces	Paved	30Width/80Length
Internet, Showers, Laundry	Cable, Pool, Rec. Hall	Game Room, Games, Patios

Wekiva Falls RV Resort
Here you'll enjoy modern amenities while getting close to nature.

30700 Wekiva River Rd, Sorrento, FL 32776	(352) 254-5123 https://wekivafalls.com/	All Year
$39-$60	Military/Good Sam	RV Age
817 Spaces	Paved/Gravel	40Width/60Length
Internet, Showers, Laundry	Supplies, Gated, Snack Bar	Cable, Grocery, Pool

Lake Josephine RV Resort
This beautiful resort offers a comfortable and relaxing stay.

10809 US Highway 27 S, Sebring, FL 33876	(863) 655-0925	All Year
$46-$68	Military/Good Sam	Pet Breed
178 Spaces	Paved	26Width/60Length
Showers, Laundry, Pool, Ice	Rec. Hall, Activities, Patios	Horseshoes, Pickle Ball

Outback RV Resort at Tanglewood
This 40+ park is located in a gated community.

3000 Tanglewood Pkwy, Sebring, FL 33872	(863) 402-1500 http://www.outbackrvresort.com/	All Year
$39-$89	Good Sam	40+, Pet Breed
151 Spaces	Paved	50Width/85Length
Internet, Showers, Laundry	Rec. Hall, Rentals, Pool	Tennis, Pavilion, Gym

Buttonwood Bay RV Resort
A premier vacation destination with a friendly atmosphere and an amenity package.

10001 US 27 S, Sebring, FL 33876	(863) 655-1122	All Year
$34-$71	Military/Good Sam	55+, Pet Breed
533 Spaces	Paved	30Width/60Length
Showers, Laundry, Pool	Rentals, Rec. Hall, Tennis	Gym, Patios, Pavilion

The Springs RV Resort
Here you can visit one of the largest artesian springs in the world.

2950 NE 52nd Ct, Silver Springs, FL 34488	(352) 236-5250 rvresorts.com/the-springs.html	All Year
$49	Good Sam	Pet Breed

618 Spaces	Paved	30Width/60Length
Showers, Laundry, Pool	Rec. Hall, Game Room	Activities, Tennis, Tables

Lake Waldena Resort

Feels like you're staying in the country, but putting you close to everything.

13582 E Highway 40 Ste 300, Silver Springs, FL 34488	(352) 625-2851 http://lakewaldena.com/	All Year
$39-$45	Military/Good Sam	Pet Breed
190 Spaces	Paved	30Width/50Length
Internet, Showers, Laundry	Grocery, Rentals, Rec. Hall	Activities, Pavilion, Patios

Fisherman's Cove RV Resort

Fishing and golf are two popular vacation activities you can do here.

100 61st St E, Palmetto, FL 34221	(941) 729-3685 https://myfishermanscove.com/	All Year
$55-$85	Good Sam	Pet Breed
300 Spaces	Paved	30Width/60Length
Internet, Showers, Laundry	Gated, Supplies, Cable, Ice	Pool, Rec. Hall, Game Room

Crystal Lake Village

Get away from traffic, crowds, and noise at this RV park.

237 Maxwell Dr, Wauchula, FL 33873	(863) 773-3582 crystallake-village.com/	All Year
$30-$40	Good Sam	55+, Pet Breed
404 Spaces	Paved	25Width/50Length
Internet, Showers, Laundry	Gated, RV Wash, Rentals	Pool, Rec. Hall, Patios

Peace River RV Resort

A nearby river gives you a chance for plenty of water-based activities.

2555 River Road, Wauchula, FL 33873	(863) 735-8888	All Year
$26-$49	Military/Good Sam	Pet Breed
400 Spaces	Paved/Gravel	30Width/50Length
Internet, Showers, Laundry	Gated, Rentals, Pool, Games	Playground, Mini Golf

Sunshine Village RV Resort

This 55+ community offers plenty of activities and unique amenities.

2236 SE 100th Ln,	(352) 793-8626	All Year

Webster, FL 33597	https://sunshinevillageflorida.com	
$42-$52	Military/Good Sam	55+, Pet Quantity
134 Spaces	Paved	50Width/100Length
Internet, Showers, Laundry	Rentals, Pool, Rec. Hall	Activities, Pavilion

Three Flags RV Campground

Here you can be less than an hour from major attractions.

1755 East State Road 44, Wildwood, FL 34785	(877) 357-1728	November 1 to May 1
$42-$52	Good Sam	No Restrictions
220 Spaces	Paved	30Width/70Length
Internet, Showers, Laundry	Pool, RV Wash, Rec. Hall	Activities, Shuffleboard

The Oasis at Zolfo Springs

A simple yet beautiful park where you can spend a short or long term vacation.

937 Sabal Palm Dr, Zolfo Springs, FL 33890	(863) 735-0030	All Year
$40	Military	Pet Breed
72 Spaces	Gravel	27Width/70Length
Internet, Showers, Laundry	Supplies, Rec. Hall, Games	Patios, Tables, LP Gas

Florida – Central East

Sonrise Palms RV Park
Spend your time in the park lounging or strolling the trail for wildlife.

660 Tucker Ln, Cocoa, FL 32926	(321) 633-4335 http://www.sonrisepalmsrv.com/	All Year
$50-$54	Military/Good Sam	Pet Breed
96 Spaces	Paved	30Width/60Length
Internet, Showers, Laundry	Cable, Rentals, RV Wash	Rec. Hall, Patios, Tables

J.O.Y. RV Park
This RV park gives you an excellent vacation experience.

245 Flamingo Dr, Cocoa, FL 32926	(321) 631-0305 https://www.joyrvpark.com/	All Year
$41-$51	Good Sam	Pet Breed
75 Spaces	Paved	26Width/65Length
Internet, Showers, Laundry	Rentals, Pool, Rec. Hall	Patios, Tables, Games

Nova Family Campground
This is your home away from home. Located near the world's most famous beach.

1190 Herbert St, Port Orange, FL 32129	(386) 767-0095 https://www.novacamp.com/	All Year
$39-$93	Good Sam	Pet Breed
371 Spaces	Paved/Gravel	21Width/55Length
Internet, Showers, Laundry	Firewood, Grocery, Ice	Cable, Rentals, Pool

Highbanks Marina and Campresort
Located along the shaded banks of St. John River, this is a wonderful place to enjoy nature.

488 West Highbanks Rd, DeBary, FL 32713	(386) 668-4491	All Year
$48-$75	Good Sam	Pet Breed
235 Spaces	Paved	30Width/60Length
Internet, Showers, Laundry	Restaurant, Cable, Fishing	Pool, Rental, Rec. Hall

Road Runner Travel Resort
Located in the natural Florida Hammock, this full-service resort gives you all you want.

5500 St Lucie Blvd, Fort Pierce, FL 34946	(772) 464-0969 roadrunnertravelresort.com/	All Year
$43-$63	Military/Good Sam	Pet Breed
452 Spaces	Paved	30Width/70Length
Internet, Showers, Laundry	Gated, Supplies, Firewood	Ice, Grocery, Restaurant,

		Golf

Causeway Cove RV Park
From your site, enjoy views of the Intercoastal Waterway.

601 Seaway Dr, Fort Pierce, FL 34949	(772) 242-3552 https://causewaycove.com/	All Year
$80-$130	Good Sam	No Restrictions
10 Spaces	Paved	50Width/75Length
Internet, Showers, Gated	Cable, Ice, Rentals	Patios, Activities

Ocean Breeze Resort
Here you can truly enjoy the vacation lifestyle and create any memories you want.

3000 NE Indian River Dr, Jensen Beach, FL 34957	(772) 334-2494	All Year
$59-$78	Military/Good Sam	Pet Breed
489 Spaces	Paved	35Width/65Length
Internet, Showers, Laundry	Lounge, Rentals, Pool	Activities, Sauna, GameRoom

Camelot RV Park
You can either relax on the beach, at your site or take part in many fun activities.

1600 S US Highway 1, Malabar, FL 32950	(321) 724-5396 http://camelotrvpark.com/	All Year
$46-$48	Good Sam	Pet Breed, 55+
160 Spaces	Paved	20Width/60Length
Internet, Showers, Laundry	Gated, Ice, Cable, Pool	Activities, Shuffleboard

Sugar Mill Ruins Travel Park
Located near a quaint beachfront town.

1050 Old Mission Rd, New Smyrna Beach, FL 32168	(386) 427-2284	All Year
$37-$43	Good Sam	Pet Breed
225 Spaces	Gravel	25Width/60Length
Internet, Showers, Laundry	Gated, Supplies, Grocery	Cable, Ice, Pool, Rec. Hall

New Smyrna Beach RV Park
Gets you close to Daytona Beach without having to deal with the crowds.

1300 Old Mission Rd, New Smyrna Beach, FL 32168	(386) 427-3581 http://beachcamp.net/	All Year
$50-$57	Good Sam	RV Age
291 Spaces	Paved/Dirt	25Width/65Length

| Internet, Showers, Laundry | Cable, Pool, Rec. Hall | Playground, Gym, Tables |

Orange City RV Resort

This park puts you close to everything from Daytona Beach to Disney World.

2300 E Graves Ave, Orange City, FL 32763	(386) 775-2545	All Year
$52-$60	Military/Good Sam	Pet Breed
344 Spaces	Paved/Gravel	25Width/55Length
Internet, Laundry, Showers	Ice, Cable, Guest Services	Rec. Hall, Pavilion, Pool

Coral Sands Oceanfront RV Resort

Centrally located to many city attractions as well as popular outdoor destinations.

1047 Ocean Shore Blvd, Ormond Beach, FL 32176	(386) 441-1831 https://coralsandsrvresort.com/	All Year
$55-$162	Military/Good Sam	No Restrictions
31 Spaces	Gravel	20Width/50Length
Internet, Showers, Laundry	Ice, Pool, Rentals	Games, Pavilion, Gym

Harris Village RV Park

Easy access to the freeway means you can access many of the local attractions.

1080 N US Highway 1, Ormond Beach, FL 32174	(386) 673-0494 https://harrisvillage.com/	All Year
$54-$58	Military/Good Sam	Pet Breed
32 Spaces	Paved	30Width/60Length
Internet, Showers, Laundry	Cable, Ice, Game Room	Games, Pavilion, Patios

Sunshine Holiday Daytona RV Resort

This is your perfect destination for relaxation or activity, depending on your vacation goals.

1701 North US Hwy 1, Ormond Beach, FL 32174	(877) 277-8737	All Year
$40-$66	Good Sam	No Restrictions
258 Spaces	Paved/Gravel	35Width/60Length
Internet, Showers, Laundry	Pool, Rec. Hall, Playground	Tennis, Games, Patios

Daytona Beach RV Resort

Stay at the world-famous Daytona Beach area.

4601 Clyde Morris Blvd, Port Orange, FL 32129	(386) 761-2663	All Year
$50-$55	Good Sam	Pet Breed
176 Spaces	Paved	28Width/70Length
Internet, Showers, Laundry	Cable, Supplies, Rentals	Pool, Pavilion, Gym

Rose Bay Travel Park

Relax at the park or enjoy the many attractions the area has to offer.

5200 S Nova Rd, Port Orange, FL 32127	(386) 767-4308	All Year
$41-$58	Good Sam	Pet Breed
308 Spaces	Paved	25Width/50Length
Showers, Fishing, Laundry	Pool, RV Wash, Rec. Hall	Activities, Tables

Port St. Lucie RV Resort

This park offers amenities and seasonal discount rates so you can extend your vacation.

3703 SE Jennings Rd, Port Saint Lucie, FL 34952	(772) 337-3340 http://portstluciervresort.com	All Year
$53-$58	Good Sam	Pet Quantity
117 Spaces	Paved	24Width/66Length
Internet, Showers, Laundry	Pool, Rec. Hall, Activities	Games, Pavilion, Patios

Space Coast RV Resort

Close to all the sites and attractions of the Space Coast.

820 Barnes Blvd, Rockledge, FL 32955	(800) 982-4288	All Year
$55-$65	Good Sam	Pet Size
267 Spaces	Paved	28Width/50Length
Internet, Showers, Laundry	Pool. Game Room, Rec. Hall	Activities, Pavilion

Vero Beach Kamp

Stay just 2 miles from the ocean.

8850 US 1, Sebastian, FL 32958	(772) 589-5665 http://www.verobeachkamp.com/	All Year
$37-$69	Military/Good Sam	Pet Breed
130 Spaces	Paved	30Width/70Length
Internet, Showers, Laundry	Supplies, Cable, Rentals	Activities, Playground, Patio

The Great Outdoors RV Resort

It places you near all the major attractions on the east coast of Florida.

125 Plantation Dr, Titusville, FL 32780	(321) 269-5004 https://www.tgoresort.com/	All Year
$60-$75	Good Sam	Pet Quantity
600 Spaces	Paved	40Width/80Length
Internet, Showers, Laundry	Supplies, Snack Bar, Gated	Lounge, Golf, Tennis

Whispering Pines

This 55+ park offers plenty to keep you entertained and to meet any vacation needs.

359 Cheney Hwy, Titusville, FL 32780	(321) 267-2081 http://www.mywhisperingpines.com/	All Year
$44	Good Sam	55+, Pet Size
200 Spaces	Paved	26Width/50Length
Showers, Laundry	Rec. Hall, Activities	Shuffleboard, Patios

Sunshine Travel RV Resort

Located among the unspoiled beauty of the Treasure Coast.

9455 108th Ave, Vero Beach, FL 32967	(800) 628-7081	All Year
$25-$67	Military/Good Sam	RV Age
301 Spaces	Paved	29Width/80Length
Showers, Laundry, Gated	Rentals, Rec. Hall, Pool	Game Room, Activities, Golf

Florida – Southwest

Gulf Coast Camping Resort
Located only 6 miles from the Gulf of Mexico.

24020 Production Circle, Bonita Springs, FL 34135	(239) 992-3808 gulfcoastcampingresort.com	October 1 to June 1
$55-$70	Good Sam	55+, RV Age
260 Spaces	Paved	40Width/50Length
Internet, Showers, Laundry	RV Wash, Guest Services	Game Room, Pool. Rec. Hall

Sanctuary RV Resort
Conveniently located between Naples and Fort Myers.

13660 Bonita Beach Rd SE, Bonita Springs, FL 34135	(239) 495-9700 https://sanctuaryrvresort.com/	All Year
$60-$80	Good Sam	Pet Breed, RV Age
185 Spaces	Paved	35Width/85Length
Internet, Showers, Laundry	Gated, Restaurant, Pool	Golf Carts, Patios

Imperial Bonita Estates RV Resort
Located on the Imperial River, this park offers access to beaches, golf, fishing, and shopping.

27700 Bourbonniere Dr, Bonita Springs, FL 34135	(239) 992-0511 imperialbonitaestates.com/	All Year
$40-$65	Military/Good Sam	55+
307 Spaces	Paved	30Width/60Length
Internet, Showers, Laundry	Pool, Ice, Tennis, Pavilion	Shuffleboard, Patios

Bonita Lake RV Resort
This all age and pet-friendly park is just 6 miles from the beach.

26325 Old 41 Road, Bonita Springs, FL 34135	(239) 992-2481 http://www.bonitalake.com/	All Year
$55-$80	Good Sam	Pet Breed
181 Spaces	Paved	30Width/45Length
Internet, Showers, Laundry	Pool, Rec. Hall, Activities	Gym, RV Wash, Patios

Big Cypress RV Resort
Here is your best place to enjoy the Florida Everglades.

30290 Josie Billie Hwy PMB 1002, Clewiston, FL 33440	(800) 437-4102 bigcypressrvresort.com/	All Year
$50-$60	Good Sam	Pet Breed
110 Spaces	Paved	25Width/60Length
Internet, Showers, Laundry	Rentals, Pool, Rec. Hall	Activities, Games, Pavilion

Okeechobee Landings RV Resort

A calm and serene environment is found at this park.

420 Holiday Blvd, Clewiston, FL 33440	(863) 983-4144 https://www.olrv.net/	All Year
$29-$42	Good Sam	Pet Breed
370 Spaces	Paved	25Width/55Length
Showers, Laundry, Rentals	Pool, Rec. Hall, Tennis	Activities, Games, Patios

Everglades Isle Motorcoach Resort

A resort for Class A motorcoaches. Featuring luxury amenities and a great place to stay.

803 Collier Ave, Everglades City, FL 34139	(239) 695-2600 http://www.evergladesisle.com/	November 1 to April 30 No Class B or C
$115-$150	Military/Good Sam	RV Age, Pet Qty, Breed
61 Spaces	Paved	40Width/60Length
Internet, Showers, Laundry	Gated, Ice, Cable, Lounge	Movie Theater, Rec. Hall

Woodsmoke Camping Resort

A beautiful RV resort with many top amenities.

19551 S Tamiami Trl, Fort Myers, FL 33908	(239) 267-3456 woodsmokecampingresort.com/	All Year
$55-$92	Military/Good Sam	Pet Breed
300 Spaces	Paved	35Width/75Length
Internet, Showers, Laundry	Supplies, Pool, Rec. Hall	Pavilion, Gym, Patios

Seminole Campground

Stay in a natural setting among the oak trees.

8991 Triplett Rd, North Fort Myers, FL 33917	(239) 543-2919 seminolecampground.com/	All Year
$55-$75	Good Sam	RV Age
129 Spaces	Gravel	30Width/70Length
Internet, Showers, Laundry	RV Wash, Rec. Hall, Games	Activities, Fire Rings, Gym

Upriver RV Resort

This 55+ park offers fun activities for the active adult.

17021 Upriver Drive, Fort Myers, FL 33917	(239) 543-3330 https://www.upriver.com/	All Year
$39-$90	Military/Good Sam	55+, RV Age, Pet Breed
391 Spaces	Paved	35Width/100Length
Internet, Showers, Laundry	Golf Carts, Rentals, Pool	Tennis, Gym, Patios

Sunseekers RV Park
Events and activities here focus on making memories and friendships.

19701 N. Tamiami Trail, North Ft. Meyers, FL 33903	(239) 731-1303 equitylifestyleproperties.com/	All Year
$50-$74	Good Sam	Pet Breed
240 Spaces	Paved	25Width/80Length
Showers, Laundry, Pool	Rec. Hall, Game Room	Activities, Tables, Games

Orange Grove RV Park
This pet-friendly and gated community is located minutes from downtown Fort Myers.

647 Nuna Ave, Fort Myers, FL 33905	(239) 694-5534 http://orangegroverv.com/	All Year
$60	Good Sam	Pet Breed
126 Spaces	Paved	30Width/50Length
Internet, Showers, Laundry	Gated, Pool, Gym, Rec. Hall	Tables, Patios, Game Room

Fort Myers RV Resort
Offering great year-round weather near the Gulf of Mexico.

16800 S Tamiami Trl, Fort Myers, FL 33908	(239) 267-2141 rvresorts.com/fortmyers.html	All Year
$59	Good Sam	Pet Breed
345 Spaces	Paved	30Width/75Length
Internet, Showers, Laundry	Ice, Pool, Boat Rentals	Mini Golf, Patios

Orange Harbor RV Resort
This 55+ park is gated and pet-friendly.

5749 Palm Beach Blvd, Fort Myers, FL 33905	(239) 672-2994 http://orangeharborcoop.com/	All Year
$34-$79	Military/Good Sam	55+, Pet Size
504 Spaces	Paved	35Width/50Length
Internet, Showers, Laundry	Gated, Ice, Pool, Rec. Hall	Pavilion, Shuffleboard

Tamiami Village RV Park
This is the perfect place to spend time and have fun.

16555 North Cleveland Ave, Fort Myers, FL 33903	(866) 573-2041 tamiamicommunity.com/	All Year
$32-$36	Good Sam	Pet Breed
242 Spaces	Paved	28Width/47Length
Internet, Showers, Laundry	Pool, Rec. Hall, Game Room	Activities, Patios, Tables

Groves RV Resort

Just minutes from this charming resort, you can find a variety of water-related activities.

16175 John Morris Rd, Fort Myers, FL 33908	(239) 466-4300	All Year
$38-$65	Military/Good Sam	Pet Breed
268 Spaces	Paved	30Width/50Length
Showers, Laundry, Rentals	Pool, Rec. Hall, Games	Pavilion, Gym, Patios

Siesta Bay RV Resort

Here you'll find resort-style living with great service.

19333 Summerlin Rd, Fort Myers, FL 33908	(239) 466-8988	All Year
$44-$70	Military/Good Sam	55+, **NO PETS**
836 Spaces	Paved	37Width/55Length
Internet, Showers, Laundry	Snack Bar, Ice, Cable, Pool	GameRoom, Tennis, Pavilion

Pioneer Village RV Resort

This pet-friendly RV park has plenty of activities, so you'll always have something fun to do.

7974 Samville Road, North Fort Myers, FL 33917	(877) 897-2757	All Year
$42-$74	Military/Good Sam	Pet Quantity
734 Spaces	Paved	27Width/60Length
Internet, Showers, Laundry	Pool, Rec. Hall, Games	Pavilion, Tennis, Gym

Fort Myers Beach RV Resort

When you stay here, it will be like staying in a tropical paradise.

16299 San Carlos Blvd, Fort Myers, FL 33908	(800) 553-7484	All Year
$58-$84	Military/Good Sam	Pet Quantity
296 Spaces	Paved	25Width/55Length
Internet, Showers, Laundry	Rentals, Pool, Cable, Ice	Activities, Shuffleboard, Gym

Lazy J RV Park

Stay at a tranquil location that puts you close to anything.

1263 Golden Lake Rd, Fort Myers, FL 33905	(239) 694-5038 http://lazyjpark.com	All Year
$35-$65	Military/Good Sam	Adults Only
127 Spaces	Paved	25Width/50Length
Restrooms, Shower, Laundry	RV Wash, Rec. Hall	Activities, Patios

Tice Courts & RV Park
A simple park with good rates.

541 New York Dr, Fort Myers, FL 33905	(239) 694-3545 ticemobilehomecourt.com/	All Year
$55	Military/Good Sam	Pet Size
100 Spaces	Paved	25Width/50Length
Showers, Laundry, Ice	RV Wash, Pool, Horseshoes	Rec. Hall, Activities, Patios

Raintree RV Resort
This 55+ park is a very active community.

19250 N Tamiami Trl, North Fort Myers, FL 33903	(239) 731-1441 http://www.raintreerv.com/	All Year
$75-$85	Good Sam	55+, Pet Breed
340 Spaces	Paved	34Width/70Length
Internet, Showers, Laundry	Gated, Ice, Cable, Pool	Rec. Hall, Game Room, Gym

Gulf Waters RV Resort
Located next to Fort Myers Beach with a trolley service to take you there.

11201 Summerlin Sq Dr, Fort Myers Beach, FL 33931	(239) 437-5888 http://www.gulfwatersrv.com/	All Year
$48-$96	Military/Good Sam	RV Age
319 Spaces	Paved	30Width/100Length
Internet, Showers, Laundry	Gated, ATM, Cable	Lounge, Tennis, Games

Indian Creek RV Resort
This RV park is a true gem in Southwest Florida.

17340 San Carlos Blvd, Fort Myers Beach, FL 33931	(239) 466-6060	All Year
$38-$66	Military/Good Sam	55+, Pet Breed
1430 Spaces	Paved	30Width/60Length
Internet, Showers, Laundry	Rentals, Cable, Ice, Pool	Tennis, Rec. Hall, Games

Gulf Air RV Resort
Just 2 miles from the pier of the beach, this is your destination to enjoy the beaches.

17279 San Carlos Blvd., Fort Myers Beach, FL 33931	(877) 937-2757	All Year
$52-$82	Military/Good Sam	No Restrictions
246 Spaces	Paved	30Width/50Length
Internet, Showers, Laundry	Cable, Rentals, Pool	Rec. Hall, Activities

Whisper Creek RV Resort

Stay just 1 mile from the historic town of La Belle.

1887 N State Road 29, Labelle, FL 33935	(863) 675-6888 http://whispercreekrvresort.com/	All Year
$50-$60	Military/Good Sam	Pet Breed, Qty.
462 Spaces	Road Conditions	Width/Length
Internet, Showers, Laundry	Ice, Golf Carts, Pool	Rec. Hall, Activities, Gym

The Glades RV Resort

Centrally located between La Belle and Clewiston.

1679 Indian Hills Dr, Moore Haven, FL 33471	(863) 983-8464 https://www.thegladesresort.com/	All Year
$50-$60	Military/Good Sam	No Restrictions
360 Spaces	Paved	30Width/70Length
Internet, Showers, Laundry	Supplies, Ice, Snack Bar	Pool, Rentals, Patios, Golf

Grandma's Grove RV Park

A simple park offering basic amenities while you explore the surrounding areas.

2250 US Highway 80 W, LaBelle, FL 33935	(863) 675-2567	All Year
$30-$35	Good Sam	Pet Breed
205 Spaces	Paved	35Width/60Length
Showers, Laundry, RV Wash	Pool, Rec. Hall, Pavilion	Shuffleboard, Patios

North Lake Estates RV Resort

This RV resort offers the perfect getaway.

12044 E State Road 78, Moore Haven, FL 33471	(863) 946-0700	All Year
$45-$54	Military/Good Sam	55+, RV Age, Pet Breed
272 Spaces	Paved	34Width/50Length
Internet, Showers, Laundry	Ice, RV Wash, Rentals	Pool, Horseshoes

Club Naples RV Resort

Surround yourself with nature reserves while being within minutes of city activities in Naples.

3180 Beck Blvd, Naples, FL 34114	(239) 455-7275	All Year
$51-$85	Military/Good Sam	RV Age, Pet Breed
305 Spaces	Paved	20Width/60Length
Internet, Showers, Laundry	Ice, Cable, Rentals, Games	Gym, Activities, Rec. Hall

Naples RV Resort
Located in the trees, this resort is like staying in the tropics.

8230 Collier Blvd, Naples, FL 34114	(239) 775-4340	All Year
$53-$74	Military/Good Sam	Pet Breed
167 Spaces	Paved	25Width/60Length
Internet, Showers, Laundry	Rentals, Pool, Rec. Hall	Activities, Gym, Patios

Marco-Naples RV Resort
This is your destination if you want fun in the sun.

100 Barefoot Williams Rd, Naples, FL 34113	(239) 774-1259	All Year
$49-$64	Military/Good Sam	55+, Pet Breed
298 Spaces	Paved	26Width/63Length
Internet, Showers, Rentals	Games, Pavilion, Patios	Rec. Hall, Shuffleboard

Lake San Marino RV Resort
A relaxed atmosphere and a great location make for a wonderful vacation.

1000 Wiggins Pass Rd, Naples, FL 34110	(239) 597-4202 Website	All Year
$46-$78	Military/Good Sam	55+, Pet Breed
407 Spaces	Paved	25Width/50Length
Internet, Showers, Laundry	Rentals, Pool, Rec. Hall	Gym, Patios, Tables

Silver Lakes RV Resort
This park offers a full range of amenities as well as a golf course.

1001 Silver Lakes Blvd, Naples, FL 34114	(239) 775-2575 http://www.silverlakesrvresort.com/	All Year
$55-$110	No Discounts Offered	Pet Breed
560 Spaces	Paved	50Width/100Length
Showers, Laundry, Gated	Pool, Hot Tub, Golf, Cable, Ice	Tennis, Shuffleboard, Gym

Pelican Lake Motorcoach Resort
Enjoy an island climate and location. Offering the amenities of a country club.

4555 Southern Breeze Dr, Naples, FL 34114	(239) 775-3005 pelicanlakemotorcoachresort.com/	All Year
(239) 775-3005	No Discounts Offered	No Class B or C
289 Spaces	Paved	55Width/95Length
Showers, Laundry, Gated	Ice, Cable, RV Wash, Pool	Tennis, Pavilion, Patios

Naples Motorcoach Resort – Sunland

Whether you want a quick getaway or a winter vacation, this is a great location.

13300 Tamiami Trl E, Naples, FL 34114	(888) 323-4985 naplesmotorcoachresort.com/	All Year No Class B or C
$90-$175	Military/Good Sam	RV Age, Pet Breed
184 Spaces	Paved	38Width/90Length
Internet, Showers, Laundry	Gated, Cable, Breakfast	Rec. Hall, Sauna, Pavilion

Royal Coachman RV Resort

This is one of the highest-rated RV resorts in the world.

1070 Laurel Road East, Nokomis, FL 34275	(941) 488-9674	All Year
$56-$96	Military/Good Sam	No Restrictions
561 Spaces	Paved	35Width/60Length
Internet, Showers, Laundry	Pool, BoatRental, GameRoom	Mini Golf, Tennis, Playground

Harbor Lakes RV Resort

At this park, you can enjoy a peaceful and relaxing experience.

3737 El Jobean Road, Port Charlotte, FL 33953	(800) 468-5022	All Year
$47-$90	Military/Good Sam	No Restrictions
528 Spaces	Paved	30Width/80Length
Internet, Showers, Laundry	Ice, RV Wash, Rentals, Pool	Rec. Hall, Game Room, Gym

Riverside RV Resort

The relaxing atmosphere at this park is like visiting an untouched paradise.

9770 SW County Road 769, Arcadia, FL 34269	(863) 993-2111 equitylifestyleproperties.com/	All Year
$53-$75	Military/Good Sam	No Restrictions
499 Spaces	Paved	35Width/80Length
Internet, Showers, Laundry	Gated, Supplies, Firewood	Pavilion, Game Room, Cable

Sun N Shade RV Resort

A peaceful place to stay while enjoying all that Southern Florida has to offer.

14880 Tamiami Trl, Punta Gorda, FL 33955	(941) 639-5388 http://sunnshade.com/	All Year
$36-$48	Military/Good Sam	Pet Breed
191 Spaces	Paved	30Width/60Length
Internet, Showers, Laundry	Supplies, Pool, Rec. Hall	Games, Patios, RV Wash

Shell Creek RV Resort

Located along the banks of Shell Creek, this 55+ park is a wonderful relaxing retreat.

35711 Washington Loop Rd, Punta Gorda, FL 33982	(941) 639-4234	All Year
$43-$54	Military/Good Sam	55+, Pet Breed
239 Spaces	Paved	30Width/60Length
Internet, Showers, Laundry	Rentals, Pool, Ice, Rec. Hall	Game Room, Activities

Gulf View RV Resort

This quaint park is just 4 miles from downtown Punta Gorda.

10205 Burnt Store Rd., Punta Gorda, FL 33950	(877) 237-2757	All Year
$40-$72	Military/Good Sam	Pet Quantity
204 Spaces	Paved	30Width/60Length
Internet, Showers, Laundry	Rentals, Pool, RV Wash	Gym, Activities, Patios

Sun N Fun RV Resort

Here you can camp with amenity and endless fun. There is plenty to enjoy at this resort.

7125 Fruitville Rd, Sarasota, FL 34240	(941) 371-2505	All Year
$64-$102	Military/Good Sam	Pet Quantity
1519 Spaces	Paved	30Width/60Length
Internet, Showers, Laundry	Gated, ATM, Snack Bar, Ice	Rentals, Sauna, Tennis

Pine Island RV Resort

Stay within 30 minutes of some of the most popular beaches in Florida.

5120 Stringfellow Rd, Saint James City, FL 33956	(239) 283-2415 https://rvonthego.com/	All Year
$74	Military/Good Sam	Pet Breed
360 Spaces	Paved	30Width/40Length
Internet, Showers, Laundry	Rentals, Pool, Rec. Hall	Games, Tennis, Gym

Florida – Southeast

Southeast Florida is a land of fun in the sun. There is no shortage of beautiful beaches to enjoy. Plus a wide range of other fun outdoor activities. All can be enjoyed from some wonderful RV parks.

Sunshine Key RV Resort
This unique resort is located right beside a marina.

38801 Overseas Highway, Big Pine Key, FL 33043	(888) 408-5018	All Year
$93-$195	Military/Good Sam	Pet Size, Qty, Breed
400 Spaces	Paved/Gravel	25Width/53Length
Internet, Showers, Laundry	Grocery, Cable, Ice, ATM	Tennis, Pavilion, GameRoom

Paradise Island RV Resort
Located near beaches and city activities.

2121 NW 29th Ct, Fort Lauderdale, FL 33311	(800) 487-7395 http://paradiserv.com/	All Year
$45-$57	Military/Good Sam	Pet Size, Qty, Breed
232 Spaces	Paved	30Width/61Length
Internet, Showers, Laundry	Pool, Rec. Hall, Game Room	Gym, Shuffleboard, Patios

Yacht Haven Park
This park is surrounded by deep canals with boardwalks.

2323 W State Road 84, Fort Lauderdale, FL 33312	(954) 583-2322 http://www.yachthavenpark.com/	All Year
$43-$105	Military/Good Sam	Pet Size, Qty, Breed
250 Spaces	Paved	25Width/45Length
Internet, Shower, Laundry	Ice, Gated, Pool, Rec. Hall	Shuffleboard, Patios

Sunshine Holiday Fort Lauderdale
This fun and active resort is close to beaches and attractions.

2802 W Oakland Park Blvd, Fort Lauderdale, FL 33311	(855) 826-2336	All Year
$41-$65	Military/Good Sam	Pet Size, Qty, Breed
400 Spaces	Paved	22Width/60Length
Internet, Showers, Laundry	Gated, Pool, Rec. Hall	Playground, Patios

Boardwalk RV Resort
A brief description.

100 NE 6th Ave,	(305) 248-2487	All Year

Homestead, FL 33030	http://boardwalkrv.com/	
$57-$69	Military/Good Sam	Pet Size, Qty, Breed
311 Spaces	Paved	30Width/60Length
Showers, Laundry, Gated	Grocery, Supplies, Activities	Games, Gym, Patios

Palm Beach Motorcoach Resort

Offering resort-style amenities while still being close to beaches and other attractions.

11075 Indiantown Rd, Jupiter, FL 33478	(561) 741-1555 https://www.pbrvresort.com/	All Year
$75-$135	Military/Good Sam	No Class B or C, Pet Qty.
100 Spaces	Paved	38Width/90Length
Internet, Showers, Laundry	Cable, Pool, Patios	Activities, Rec. Hall, Games

West Jupiter RV Resort

This tropical resort is in a rustic setting.

17801 130th Ave N, Jupiter, FL 33478	(561) 746-6073	All Year
$40-$65	Military/Good Sam	RV Age, Pet Breed
101 Spaces	Paved	28Width/50Length
Internet, Showers, Laundry	Pool, Rec. Hall, Game Room	Playground, Pavilion

Riptide RV Resort

This park offers a marina for boats and a private beach.

97680 Overseas Hwy, Key Largo, FL 33037	(305) 852-8481	All Year
$75-$85	Military/Good Sam	Pet Breed
38 Spaces	Paved	25Width/40Length
Beach Access, Ice	Laundry, Showers, Cable	Rentals, Games, Patios

Boyd's Key West Campground

This is the southernmost campground in the United States.

6401 Maloney Ave, Key West, FL 33040	(305) 294-1465 boydscampground.com/	All Year
$61-$143	No Discounts Offered	Pet Breed
203 Spaces	Paved	24Width/44Length
Internet, Showers, Laundry	ATM, Cable, Grocery	Paddle Boats, Pavilion

Pelican RV Resort

This park is a paradise for the fishing enthusiast, but also offers a range of other activities.

59151 Overseas Hwy, Marathon, FL 33050	(844) 728-1737	All Year

$64-$95	Military/Good Sam	Pet Breed
85 Spaces	Paved	25Width/38Length
Fishing, Showers, Internet	Cable, Laundry, Rentals	Pool, Games, Pavilion

Jolly Roger RV Resort

A beautiful location in the Florida keys offering basic amenities and plenty of outdoor activities.

59275 Overseas Hwy, Marathon, FL 33050	(305) 289-0404 https://www.jrtp.com/	All Year
$73-$105	Good Sam	Pet Breed
162 Spaces	Paved	25Width/60Length
Internet, Showers, Laundry	Supplies, Ice, Cable, Pool	Pavilion, Patios, Games

Grassy Key RV Park

Located in the heart of the Florida Keys, here you can access all the area has to offer.

58671 Overseas Hwy, Marathon, FL 33050	(305) 289-1606 grassykeyrvpark.com/	All Year
$69-$198	Military/Good Sam	Pet Breed
38 Spaces	Paved	30Width/62Length
Internet, Laundry, Cable	Pool, Guest Services, Tables	Activities, Games, Rec. Hall

Miami Everglades Resort

Located in paradise among the trees with easy access to many local attractions.

20675 SW 162nd Ave, Miami, FL 33187	(305) 233-5300	All Year
$41-$69	Military/Good Sam	Pet Breed
300 Spaces	Paved	38Width/65Length
Internet, Showers, Laundry	Supplies, Cable, Rentals	Pool, Game Room, Tennis

Brighton RV Resort

A newly renovated resort with enough amenities to make you feel at home.

14695 Reservation Rd NE, Okeechobee, FL 34974	(863) 467-0474 brightonrvresort.com/	All Year
$50	Military/Good Sam	No Restrictions
56 Spaces	Paved	40Width/75Length
Internet, Showers, Laundry	Restaurant, Grocery, Rentals	Pool, Games, Patios

Silver Palms RV Resort - Sunland

There is everything to choose from, including lakefront and wildlife viewing.

4143 US Highway 441 S, Okeechobee, FL 34974	(888) 323-4967 Website	All Year
$61-$127	Military/Good Sam	RV Age, Pet Qty

364 Spaces	Paved	40Width/90Length
Internet, Showers, Laundry	Gated, Lounge, Hunting	Rec. Hall, Game Room, Gym

Water's Edge RV Resort

Relax in a beautiful and friendly environment.

12766 US Highway 441 SE, Okeechobee, FL 34974	(863) 357-5757 http://okeervpark.com/	All Year
$45-$90	Military/Good Sam	RV Age
30 Spaces	Paved	35Width/65Length
Internet, Gated, Pool	Rec. Hal, Activities, Patios	Horseshoes, Shuffleboard

Breezy Hill RV Resort

There are many events to enjoy in the nearby areas around this resort.

800 NE 48th St., Pompano Beach, FL 33064	(888) 472-0727	All Year
$44-$84	Military/Good Sam	Pet Breed
763 Spaces	Paved	16Width/66Length
Internet, Showers, Laundry	Pool, Rec. Hall, Activities	Games, Pavilion, Gym

Highland Woods RV Resort

Located in the heart of southeast Florida with easy access to Atlantic beaches.

900 NE 48th Street, Pompano Beach, FL 33064	(866) 340-0649	All Year
$44-$81	Military/Good Sam	Pet Size
147 Spaces	Paved	18Width/58Length
Internet, Showers, Laundry	Pool, Activities, Games	Pavilion, Patios, Gym

Lion Country Safari KOA

Here you'll find unique attractions like a drive-thru safari and an amusement park.

2000 Lion Country Safari Rd, Loxahatchee, FL 33470	(561) 793-9797 lioncountrysafari.com/	All Year
$84-$87	No Discounts Offered	Pet Breed
211 Spaces	Paved	30Width/50Length
Internet, Showers, Laundry	Grocery, Rentals, Pool	Safari, Amusement Park

Georgia

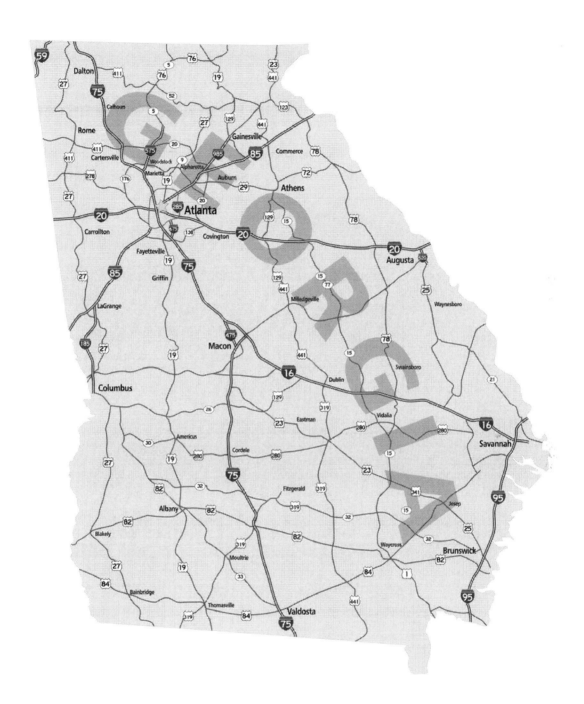

Northern Georgia

Northern Georgia is a place of rugged beauty in the mountains and bustling cities like Atlanta. There are several outdoor activities and attractions to enjoy. Plenty of wonderful RV parks allow you to enjoy your time in Northern Georgia.

Harvest Moon RV Park
Offering daily, weekly, and monthly rates to meet any vacation time frame.

1001 Poplar Springs Rd, Adairsville, GA 30103	(770) 773-7320 https://harvestmoonrvpark.net/	All Year
$41-$45	Military/Good Sam/AAA/AARP	Pet Breed
77 Spaces	Paved/Gravel	35Width/90Length
Showers, Laundry, Supplies	Ice, Cable, Horseshoes	Rec. Hall, Games, Tables

Yogi Bears Jellystone Park
This park offers inclusive camping with wonderful amenities and fun for all interests.

106 King St, Bremen, GA 30110	(404) 855-2778 https://www.gajellystone.com/	All Year
$45-$70	Military/Good Sam	Pet Breed
89 Spaces	Paved	25Width/80Length
Internet, Showers, Laundry	Gated, ATM, Snack Bar	Activities, GameRoom, Tables

Calhoun A-OK Campground
Enjoy the beautiful setting while peacocks roam the grounds.

2523 Red Bud Rd NE, Calhoun, GA 30701	(706) 629-7511 calhounaokcampground.com/	All Year
$36-$49	Good Sam	No Restrictions
69 Spaces	Paved/Gravel	25Width/60Length
Food Delivery, Petting Zoo	Rentals, Pavilion, GameRoom	Mini Golf, Games, Pool

Allatoona Landing Marine Resort
A beautiful lakeside resort where you can relax.

24 Allatoona Landing Rd SE, Cartersville, GA 30121	(770) 974-6089 http://allatoonalandingmarina.com/	All Year
$36-$50	Military/Good Sam	No Restrictions
99 Spaces	Paved	30Width/70Length
Internet, Showers, Laundry	Gated, Supplies, Firewood	Rec. Hall, Playground, Pool

Cedar Creek RV

Located along Big Cedar Creek, this park gives you a chance to explore.

6770 Cave Spring Rd SW, Cave Spring, GA 30124	(706) 777-3030 http://www.bigcedarcreek.com/	All Year
$39	Good Sam	No Restrictions
62 Spaces	Gravel	30Width/65Length
Internet, Showers, Laundry	Supplies, Firewood, Ice	Supplies, Rentals, Games

Leisure Acres Campground

Located at the entrance to the beautiful North Georgia Mountains.

3840 Westmoreland Rd, Cleveland, GA 30528	(706) 865-6466 http://leisureacrescampground.com/	All Year
$45-$50	Military/Good Sam	Pet Breed
116 Spaces	Gravel	25Width/60Length
Internet, Shower, Laundry	Firewood, Pool, Playground	Games, Rec. Hall, FireRing

Yonah Mountain Campground

A brief description.

3678 Helen Hwy, Cleveland, GA 30528	(706) 865-6546 http://yonahgocamping.com	All Year
$43-$55	Military/Good Sam	Pet Breed
110 Spaces	Paved/Gravel	35Width/60Length
Internet, Showers, Laundry	Firewood, Supplies, Pool	Rec. Hall, Ice, RV Wash

Jenny's Creek Family Campground

Situated along Jenny's Creek with access to a private pond.

4542 Highway 129 N, Cleveland, GA 30528	(706) 865-6955 https://www.jennyscreek.com/	All Year
$33-$37	Military/Good Sam	No Restrictions
24 Spaces	Gravel	30Width/35Length
Internet, Showers, Laundry	Grocery, Firewood, Supplies	Rec. Hall, Playground

Twin Lakes RV Park

Enjoy relaxing, or take your time to explore the area.

3300 Shore Dr, Cumming, GA 30040	(770) 887-4400 https://twinlakes-rvpark.com/	All Year
$45-$50	No Discounts	No Restrictions
130 Spaces	Paved/Gravel	25Width/60Length
Internet, LP Gas, Ice	RV Wash, Horseshoes	Tables

River Vista RV Resort
Find yourself surrounded by resort-style amenities that help you enjoy your stay.

20 River Vista Dr, Dillard, GA 30537	(706) 746-2722 https://rvmountainvillage.com/	All Year
$30-$80	Good Sam	RV Age, Pet Breed
110 Spaces	Paved	35Width/75Length
Internet, Showers, Laundry	Cable, Firewood, Ice, Pool	Rec. Hall, Activities, Sauna

Plum Nelly Campground
This park is nestled in the North Georgia Mountains but still has easy access to the highway.

15828 Highway 515 S, Ellijay, GA 30536	(706) 698-7586 plumnellycampground.com/	All Year
$40	Military/Good Sam	Pet Breed
47 Spaces	Gravel	. 29Width/60Length
Internet, Showers, Laundry	Ice, Rentals, Rec. Hall	Playground, Pavilion

Creekwood Resort
This 55+ park is located in the beautiful mountains.

5730 Highway 356, Sautee Nacoochee, GA 30571	(706) 878-2164 https://creekwoodresort.com/	All Year
$45-$76	Good Sam	55+, Pet Breed
17 Spaces	Paved	30Width/60Length
Internet, Showers, Laundry	Firewood, Cable, Rentals	Horseshoes, Games, Tables

Atlanta-Marietta RV Resort
On your vacation, you can relax in a peaceful, wooded site surrounded by nature.

1031 Wylie Rd SE, Marietta, GA 30067	(770) 427-6853 http://amrvresort.com/	All Year
$54	Military/Good Sam	Pet Breed
62 Spaces	Paved	26Width/40Length
Internet, Showers, Laundry	Supplies, Cable, Ice, Pool	Patios, Tables, LP Gas

Atlanta South RV Resort
Easy access on and off the interstate allows you to enjoy any local attractions.

281 Mount Olive Rd, McDonough, GA 30253	(770) 957-2610 http://atlantasouthrvresort.com	All Year
$40-$55	Military/Good Sam	Pet Breed
170 Spaces	Paved/Gravel	20Width/50Length
Internet, Showers, Laundry	Firewood, Cable, Rentals	Pool, Playground, Pavilion

Stone Mountain Park Campground
This popular attraction in Georgia offers fun for the whole family.

1000 Robert E. Lee Blvd, Stone Mountain, GA 30083	(770) 498-5690 https://www.stonemountainpark.com/	All Year
$31-$70	Good Sam	No Restrictions
385 Spaces	Paved	25Width/55Length
Internet, Shower, Laundry	Restaurant, Grocery, ATM, Gated	Cable, Rentals, Pavilion

Southern Georgia

Southern Georgia is a place with beautiful white sand beaches that rival Florida. There is a lot of history and outdoor sites to explore. Consider the activities you can enjoy from the great parks in the area.

Coastal Georgia RV Resort
Fun and amenities for the whole family.

287 S Port Pkwy, Brunswick, GA 31523	(912) 264-3869 coastalgarvresort.com/	All Year
$47	Military/Good Sam	Pet Breed
157 Spaces	Paved	35Width/75Length
Internet, Showers, Laundry	Ice, Cable, Pool, Boats	Game Room, Rec. Hall

Cecil Bay RV Park
Easy access from the interstate, offering the basic amenities

1787 Old Coffee Rd, Cecil, GA 31627	(229) 794-1484 http://cecilbayrv.com/	All Year
$31	Military/Good Sam	No Restrictions
104 Spaces	Gravel	40Width/62Length
Internet, Showers, Laundry	Horseshoes	Restrooms, Rec. Hall

Lake Pines RV Park
Located close to historic sites, museums, shopping, and outdoor activities.

6404 Garrett Road Midland (Columbus), GA 31820	706-561-9675 https://lakepines.net/	All Year
$42-$45	Military/Good Sam	Pet Breed
112 Spaces	Gravel	30Width/60Length
Internet, Showers, Laundry	Firewood, Ice, Pool	Rec. Hall, Playground

Cathead Creek RV Park
Located close to several major cities in Georgia.

1334 Cox Rd SW, Townsend, GA 31331	(912) 437-2441 https://www.catheadcreek.com/	All Year
$36-$39	Military/Good Sam	Pet Breed
24 Spaces	Gravel	25Width/90Length
Internet, Showers, Laundry	Firewood, Cable, Pavilion	Games, RV Wash, Tables

Twin Oaks RV Park
This park is easily and centrally located in historical central Georgia.

305 Georgia 26 E, Elko, GA 31025	(478) 987-9361 http://twinoaksrvpark.com/	All Year
$40-$45	Good Sam	Pet Breed
64 Spaces	Gravel	30Width/90Length
Internet, Showers, Laundry	Rentals, Playground, Pool	Games, Patios, Firewood

Jenny Ridge RV Park
A centralized location with a small-town atmosphere is what you get at this RV park.

2790 Second St S, Folkston, GA 31537	(912) 496-1172 jennyridgervpark.com/	All Year
$39	Good Sam	Pet Breed
55 Spaces	Gravel	34Width/100Length
Internet, Showers, Laundry	Firewood, Ice, LP Gas	Rec. Hall, Games, Fire Rings

Okefenokee RV Park
A small, pet-friendly RV park offering the basic amenities.

252 Bowery Ln, Homeland, GA 31537	(912) 496-2220 http://okefenokeervpark.com/	All Year
$29-$32	Military/Good Sam	No Restrictions
50 Spaces	Gravel	30Width/65Length
Internet, Showers, Laundry	Restaurant, Rec. Hall	Games, Patios

L & D RV Park
This luxury park offers affordable rates so you can stay as long as you like.

1655 Dames Ferry Rd, Forsyth, GA 31029	(478) 994-8977 Website	All Year
$27-$30	Military/Good Sam	Pet Size
30 Spaces	Paved	22Width/60Length
Internet, Showers, Laundry	Firewood, Pool	Guest Services, Pavilion

Jekyll Island Campground
Hike miles of beaches, salt marshes, and oak tree-lined trails.

1197 Riverview Dr, Jekyll Island, GA 31527	(912) 635-3021 https://www.jekyllisland.com	All Year
$43-$65	No Discounts	No Restrictions
175 Spaces	Gravel	25Width/50Length
Internet, Showers, Laundry	Firewood, Grocery, Cable	Rec. Hall, Rentals

Country Oaks RV Park

Come to this park and make it your home for an extended stay.

2456 Scrubby Bluff Road, Kingsland, GA 31548	(912) 729-6212 http://www.countryoaksrv.com/	All Year
$38-$42	Good Sam	Pet Breed
43 Spaces	Paved	28Width/60Length
Internet, Showers, Laundry	Firewood, LP Gas, Ice	Rec. Hall, Games

Jacksonville North/St Mary's KOA

Get your day started with a complimentary breakfast.

2970 Scrubby Bluff Road, Kingsland, GA 31548	(912) 729-3232 koa.com/campgrounds/jacksonville/	All Year
$46-$72	Military	No Restrictions
111 Spaces	Paved/Gravel	30Width/60Length
Internet, Shower, Laundry	Breakfast, Rentals, Restaurant	Game Room, Sauna, Gym

Eagles Roost RV Resort

Easily accessible from the interstate, located among moss-draped oak trees.

5465 Mill Store Rd, Lake Park, GA 31636	(229) 559-5192 https://www.eaglesroostresort.com/	All Year
$40-$47	Military/Good Sam	No Restrictions
111 Spaces	Paved/Gravel	26Width/60Length
Internet, Shower, Laundry	Supplies, Rentals, Pool	Playground, Pavilion

Beaver Run RV Park

A peaceful campground just off the interstate.

22321 Excelsior Church Rd, Metter, GA 30439	(912) 362-4737 http://beaverrunrvpark.com/	All Year
$34-$38	Military/Good Sam	Pet Breed
71 Spaces	Gravel	31Width/100Length
Internet, Shower, Laundry	Firewood, Rentals, Rec. Hall	Game Room, Pavilion

Scenic Mountain RV Park

A quiet and pet-friendly park.

2686 Irwinton Rd, Milledgeville, GA 31061	(478) 454-1013	All Year
$44-$48	Military/Good Sam	No Restrictions
72 Spaces	Paved	30Width/90Length

| Internet, Shower, Laundry | Rentals, Pool, Playground | Pavilion, Fire Rings, Tables |

Sugar Mill RV Park
Stay here to avoid the higher prices in Florida.

4857 Mcmillan Rd, Ochlocknee, GA 3177	(229) 227-1451 sugarmillrvcampground.com/	All Year
$30	Military/Good Sam	Pet Breed
121 Spaces	Paved/Gravel	30Width/65Length
Internet, Shower, Laundry	Rentals, LP Gas, Rec. Hall	Pavilion, Shuffleboard

Fair Harbor RV Park
An easily accessible park located along a well-stocked fishing lake.

515 Marshallville Rd, Perry, GA 31069	(478) 988-8844 https://fairharborrvpark.com/	All Year
$44-$49	Military/Good Sam	No Restrictions
260 Spaces	Paved	28Width/75Length
Internet, Shower, Laundry	Fishing, Cable, Firewood	Supplies, Rentals, Rec. Hall

Crossroads Travel Park
Walking distance to several restaurants and a short drive to more dining and attractions.

1513 Sam Nunn Blvd, Perry, GA 31069	(478) 987-3141 crossroadstravelpark.com/	All Year
$45	Military/Good Sam	Pet Breed
72 Spaces	Paved	26Width/60Length
Internet, Shower, Laundry	Cable, Pool, Rec. Hall	Games, Tables

Pine Mountain RV Resort
Here is a luxury experience awaiting you.

8804 Hamilton Road, Pine Mountain, GA 31822	(706) 663-4329 https://pinemountainrvresort.com/	All Year
$50-$80	Military/Good Sam	No Restrictions
202 Spaces	Paved/Gravel	30Width/70Length
Internet, Shower, Laundry	Supplies, Cable, Rentals, Gym	Fire Rings, Rec. Hall, Pool

Whispering Pines RV Park
There are plenty of things to keep you busy inside and outside the park.

1755 Hodgeville Rd, Rincon, GA 31326	(912) 728-7562 whisperingpinesrvpk.com/	All Year
$30-$55	Military/Good Sam	Pet Breed
88 Spaces	Paved/Gravel	28Width/60Length
Internet, Shower, Laundry	Cable, Firewood	Games, Playground

Biltmore RV Park

Simple access to the city bus line so you can get to attractions and activities easily.

4707 Ogeechee Rd, Savannah, GA 31405	(912) 236-4065 http://biltmorerv.com/	All Year
$45-$50	Good Sam	Pet Breed
38 Spaces	Paved	30Width/60Length
Firewood	Cable	Bus Line Access

CreekFire RV Resort

Surround yourself with nature while enjoying resort amenities.

275 Fort Argyle Rd, Savannah, GA 31419	(912) 897-2855 https://www.creekfirerv.com/	All Year
$52-$99	Military/Good Sam	Pet Breed
103 Spaces	Paved	30Width/100Length
Internet, Shower, Laundry	Firewood, Cable, Rentals	Pavilion, Tennis, Patios

Savannah Oaks RV Resort

A great base camp to explore the coast and historic Savannah.

805 Fort Argyle Rd, Savannah, GA 31419	(912) 748-4000 https://savannahoaksrvresort.com/	All Year
$44-$49	Military/Good Sam	No Restrictions
139 Spaces	Paved/Gravel	24Width/60Length
Internet, Shower, Laundry	Snack Bar, Rentals, Pool	Game Room, Playground

Red Gate Campground

This is the closest park to historic Savannah and makes a great base camp.

136 Red Gate Farm Trl, Savannah, GA 31405	(912) 272-8028 redgatecampground.com/	All Year
$40-$75	Military/Good Sam	No Restrictions
31 Spaces	Paved/Gravel	30Width/60Length
Internet, Shower, Laundry	Pool, Firewood, Pavilion	Playground, Gym, Tables

Parkwood RV Park

A brief description.

12188 US Highway 301 S, Statesboro, GA 30458	(912) 681-3105 http://parkwoodrv.com/	All Year
$38-$43	Military/Good Sam	Pet Breed
48 Spaces	Paved	30Width/80Length
Internet, Shower, Laundry	Firewood, Rentals, Cable	Pool, Games

Pines RV Park I-75

Easy access on and off the interstate. The best park to stay at in the area.

18 Casseta Rd, Tifton, GA 31793	(229) 382-3500 pinesrvparki75.com/	All Year
$30-$33	Military/Good Sam	No Restrictions
55 Spaces	Gravel	25Width/60Length
Internet, Shower, Laundry	Firewood, Cable, Ice	Rec. Hall, Games

Lake Harmony RV Park

Quietly nestled in the woods, you can enjoy a vacation on a lake.

1088 Lake Harmony Dr. SW, Townsend, GA 31331	(912) 832-4338 lakeharmonypark.com/	All Year
$39	Military/Good Sam	No Restrictions
54 Spaces	Gravel	25Width/60Length
Internet, Shower, Laundry	Cable, Ice, Gated, Firewood	Rec. Hall, Games, Tables

McIntosh Lake RV Park

A brief description.

1093 Mcintosh Lake Ln SW, Townsend, GA 31331	(912) 832-6215 mcintoshlakervpark.com/	All Year
$39	Military/Good Sam	Pet Breed
37 Spaces	Gravel	33Width/70Length
Internet, Shower, Laundry	Rec. Hall, Rentals, Cable	Tables, Fire Rings

Rivers End Campground

A place to stay any time of the year; beaches, history, and plenty of outdoor adventures await.

5 Fort Ave, Tybee Island, GA 31328	(912) 786-5518 riversendcampground.com/	All Year
$49-$99	Military/Good Sam	Pet Quantity
92 Spaces	Paved	20Width/45Length
Internet, Shower, Laundry	ATM, LP Gas, Cable, Ice	Cabins, Gym, Pool

Valdosta Oaks RV Park

A brief description.

4630 N Valdosta Rd, Valdosta, GA 31602	(229) 247-0494 valdostaoaksrv.com/	All Year
$32	Military/Good Sam	Pet Quantity
76 Spaces	Paved/Gravel	35Width/60Length
Internet, Shower, Laundry	Cable	RV Wash

Idaho

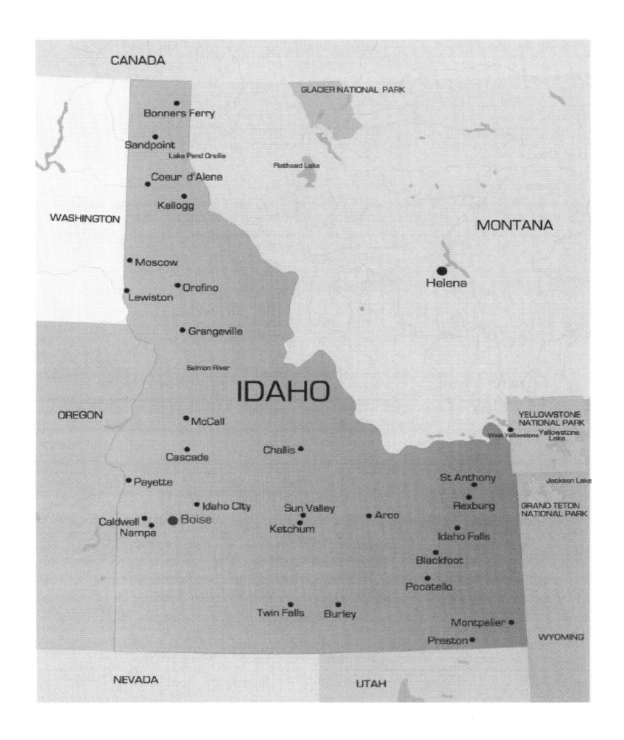

Idaho – Western

Western Idaho puts you close to a wide range of outdoor fun. The parks in this part of Idaho allow you to quickly access a range of amenities and services after a long day of fun.

Mountain View RV Park
After a long day in the city, enjoy a well maintained and friendly park.

2040 W Airport Way, Boise, ID 83705	(208) 345-4141	All Year
$45	Military/Good Sam	No Restrictions
60 Spaces	Paved	20Width/65Length
Internet, Showers, Laundry	Ice, RV Service	RV Wash, Tables

Hi Valley RV Park
This park puts you close to scenic rivers and mountain valleys.

10555 Horseshoe Bend Rd, Boise, ID 83714	(208) 939-8080 g7rvresorts.com/rv-park/hi-valley-rv-park/	All Year
$45	Military/Good Sam	Pet Breed
194 Spaces	Paved	24Width/70Length
Internet, Showers, Laundry	ATM, Ice, Cable, Supplies	Pool, Rec. Hall, Patios

Boise Riverside RV Park
Located right along the Boise River, there are plenty of nearby attractions to enjoy.

6000 N Glenwood St, Boise, ID 83714	(208) 375-7432 boiseriversidervpark.com/	All Year
$40-$49	Military/Good Sam	Pet Quantity
139 Spaces	Gravel	36Width/46Length
Internet, Showers, Laundry	Supplies, Rentals, LP Gas	Playground, Games

Canyon Springs RV Resort
Stay in a rural setting in southwestern Idaho.

21965 Chicago St, Caldwell, ID 83607	(208) 402-6630 https://canyonspringsrvresort.com/	All Year
$42-$49	Military/Good Sam	RV Age, Pet Breed
136 Spaces	Paved	25Width/70Length
Internet, Shower, Laundry	Rentals, Rec. Hall, Cable	Playground, Gym

Caldwell Campground

A pet-friendly park with a number of outdoor activities to enjoy.

21830 Town Cir Ste 34, Caldwell, ID 83607	(208) 454-0279 caldwellcampgroundandrvparkllc.com/	All Year
$30	No Discounts	Pet Breed
108 Spaces	Paved/Gravel	27Width/65Length
Internet, Shower, Laundry	Firewood, Cable, RV Wash, Supplies	Horseshoes, Games

Ambassador RV Resort

First-class amenities and customer service ensures a stay of both class and comfort.

615 Smeed Pkwy, Caldwell, ID 83605	(208) 454-8584 g7rvresorts.com/rv-park/ambassador/	All Year
$45	Military/Good Sam	Pet Breed
187 Spaces	Paved	33Width/80Length
Internet, Shower, Laundry	ATM, Supplies, Ice, LP Gas	Cable, Rec.Hall, Sauna, Pool

Country Corners RV Park

Easy access to the interstate and a wide range of amenities.

17671 Oasis Rd, Caldwell, ID 83607	(208) 453-8791 countrycornersrvpark.com/	All Year
$39-$43	Military/Good Sam	Pet Breed
62 Spaces	Gravel	30Width/66Length
Internet, Shower, Laundry	Firewood, Grocery, Ice	Rec. Hall, Games, Tables

Alpine Country Store & RV Park

Close to a casino and an amusement park.

17568 N Highway 95, Hayden, ID 83835	(208) 772-4305 http://nirvpark.com/	April 15 to October 15
$49-$52	Good Sam	No Restrictions
36 Spaces	Paved/Gravel	42Width/90Length
Internet, Shower, Laundry	Firewood, Grocery, SnackBar	Games, Tables, Ice

Wolf Lodge Campground

Relax at this fun campground and have an enjoyable vacation.

12329 E Frontage Rd, Coeur D Alene, ID 83814	(208) 664-2812 wolflodgecampground.com/	May 15 to September 30
$40-$45	Military/Good Sam	No Restrictions
53 Spaces	Gravel	23Width/70Length
Internet, Shower, Laundry	Grocery, Firewood, Rentals	Pavilion, PedalCarts, Rentals

Chalet RV Park
Easy access to a number of outdoor mountain activities.

418 N Main St, Donnelly, ID 83615	(208) 325-8223 https://www.g7rvresorts.com/	May 1 to October 1
$38	Military/Good Sam	No Restrictions
76 Spaces	Gravel	22Width/48Length
Internet, Shower, Laundry	Supplies, Ice, Cable	RVWash, Horseshoes, Rec.Hall

Neat Retreat RV Park
This park offers the best experience with easy access and great accommodations.

2701 N Alder Dr, Fruitland, ID 83619	(208) 452-4324 https://www.neatretreatrvpark.com/	All Year
$42-$44	Military/Good Sam	Pet Breed
80 Spaces	Paved	30Width/75Length
Internet, Shower, Laundry	Cable, Ice, RV Wash/Service	Activities, Games, Patios

Trail Break RV Park
The friendly atmosphere of this park is a short drive to the old Oregon Trail.

432 N Bannock St, Glenns Ferry, ID 83623	(208) 366-7745 https://trailbreakrvpark.com	All Year
$30	Military/Good Sam	No Restrictions
30 Spaces	Gravel	27Width/65Length
Internet, Shower, Laundry	Firewood, Ice, Cable	Pavilion, Fire Rings, Tables

Bear Den RV Park
This peaceful park offers wonderful views of the prairies.

16967 Hwy 95 S, Grangeville, ID 83530	(208) 983-0140 https://beardenrv.com/	All Year
$27-$35	Military/Good Sam	No Restrictions
34 Spaces	Gravel	26Width/78Length
Internet, Shower, Laundry	Firewood, Supplies, Rentals	Games, Pavilion, Rec. Hall

Long Camp RV Park
Camp right along the banks of the Clearwater River.

4192 Highway 12, Kamiah, ID 83536	(208) 935-7922 http://longcamprvpark.com/	All Year
$35-$39	Good Sam	No Restrictions
22 Spaces	Gravel	24Width/60Length
Internet, Shower, Laundry	Restaurant, Rentals, Fishing	Pavilion, Games, Patios

McCall RV Resort
Located in a luxurious mountain setting, this is the ideal summer retreat.

200 Scott St, McCall, ID 83638	(208) 634-5646 g7rvresorts.com/rv-park/mccall-rv-resort/	All Year
$42-$52	Military/Good Sam	No Restrictions
157 Spaces	Paved	45Width/75Length
Internet, Shower, Laundry	Pool, Ice, LP Gas, Cable	Rec. Hall, Pavilion, Games

Mountain Home RV Resort
This quiet park is beautifully landscaped. Enjoy resort-style amenities and services.

2295 American Legion Blvd, Mountain Home, ID 83647	(208) 580-1211 g7rvresorts.com/rv-park/mountain-home/	All Year
$45	Military/Good Sam	Pet Breed
179 Spaces	Paved	32Width/90Length
Internet, Shower, Laundry	Supplies, ATM, Ice, LP Gas	Playground, Pavilion, Cable

Gem State RV Park
A convenient base camp to explore nearby towns, cities, and state parks.

220 E 10th N, Mountain Home, ID 83647	(208) 587-5111 http://www.gemstatervpark.com/	All Year
$35	Military/Good Sam	No Restrictions
61 Spaces	Paved	34Width/87Length
Internet, Shower, Laundry	Supplies, Cable, Rentals	Playground, Rec. Hall

The Hemlocks RV and Lodging
The perfect location to explore the Northern Rockies.

73400 Highway 2, Moyie Springs, ID 83845	(208) 267-4363 https://hemlockslodging.com/	All Year
$35	Military/Good Sam	Pet Quantity
20 Spaces	Gravel/Dirt	35Width/76Length
Internet, Shower, Laundry	Restaurant, Rentals, Firewood	Playground, Games, Pavilion

Clearwater Crossing RV Park
Offering a full range of amenities and services.

500 Riverfront Ave, Orofino, ID 83544	(208) 476-4800 https://clearwatercrossingrvpark.com/	All Year
$29-$40	Military/Good Sam	No Restrictions
50 Spaces	Paved	24Width/50Length

| Internet, Shower, Laundry | Cable, RV Wash, Pavilion | Games, Patios, Tables |

Blue Anchor RV Park
Enjoy a variety of unique attractions in the area around you.

300 W Mullan Ave, Osburn, ID 83849	(208) 752-3443 https://www.blueanchorrvpark.com/	All Year
$37	Military/Good Sam	No Restrictions
60 Spaces	Paved	27Width/60Length
Internet, Shower, Laundry	Cable, Ice, Rentals, Rec. Hall	Games, RV Wash, Tables

Canyon Pines RV Resort
Located near the white water capital of Idaho, this park is your destination for water-based fun.

159 Barn Rd, Pollock, ID 83547	(208) 628-4006 http://www.canyonpinesrv.com/	All Year
$34	Good Sam	No Restrictions
54 Spaces	Paved	30Width/70Length
Internet, Shower, Laundry	Supplies, Snack Bar, Firewood	Rec. Hall, Games, Fishing

Monroe Creek Campground
Stay here, and you'll be at the gateway to many outdoor adventures.

822 Highway 95, Weiser, ID 83672	(208) 549-2026 http://www.monroecreek.com/	All Year
$29	Military/Good Sam	No Restrictions
53 Spaces	Gravel	22Width/66Length
Internet, Shower, Laundry	Firewood, Ice, RV Wash	Games, Pavilion, Tables

Swiftwater RV Park
This pet-friendly park offers access to many outdoor activities at an affordable price.

3154 Salmon River Ct, White Bird, ID 83554	(208) 839-2700 https://swiftwaterrv.com/	All Year
$34-$37	Military/Good Sam	No Restrictions
24 Spaces	Gravel	15Width/60Length
Internet, Shower, Laundry	Ice, Firewood, RV Wash	Games, Pavilion, Tables

Eastern Idaho

Eastern Idaho is a land of rugged beauty. Here you'll find natural sites such as Yellowstone. You can easily spend days at the parks in this area while enjoying a range of outdoor activities. You're sure to find an amazing place to stay.

Indian Springs Resort & RV
Experience both beauty and community at this park.

3249 Indian Springs Rd, American Falls, ID 83211	(208) 226-7700 http://indianspringsresortandrv.com/	April 1 to October 31
$19-$38	Military/Good Sam	No Restrictions
138 Spaces	Gravel	20Width/42Length
Firewood, Shower, Laundry	Supplies, Pool, Snack Bar	Waterslide, Game Room

Mountain View RV Park
. Visit the Sawtooth Mountains or the nearby hot springs.

705 W Grand Ave, Arco, ID 83213	(208) 527-3707 https://www.mountainviewarco.com/	All Year
$45-$48	Military/Good Sam	No Restrictions
35 Spaces	Gravel	51Width/72Length
Internet, Shower, Laundry	Restaurant, RV Service, Lounge	Mini Golf, Tables, Patios

Challis RV Park
Enjoy water activities on the Salmon River or explore nearby ghost towns.

210 Golf Club Lane, Challis, ID 83226	(208) 879-5300 https://www.golfcourserv.com/	April 15 to October 15
$35-$38	Good Sam	No Restrictions
30 Spaces	Gravel	25Width/6067 Length
Internet, Shower, Laundry	Snack Bar, Lounge, RV Wash	Golf, Driving Range

Round Valley Park
A beautiful park with spacious sites at an affordable price.

211 Ramshorn Dr, Challis, ID 83226	(208) 879-2393 http://www.roundvalleyrv.com/	April 15 to November 30
$36	Military/Good Sam	No Restrictions
67 Spaces	Paved/Gravel	54Width/90Length
Internet, Shower, Laundry	Firewood, Fishing, Pavilion	Playground, Games, Tables

Village of Trees RV Resort

Camp along the Snake River. A variety of outdoor adventures await you.

274 Highway 25 I-84 Exit 216, Declo, ID 83323	(208) 654-2133 villageoftreesrvresort.com/	All Year
$32	Military/Good Sam	Pet Breed
84 Spaces	Gravel	30Width/70Length
Internet, Shower, Laundry	Restaurant, Grocery, Ice	Fishing, Rentals, Pool

Hagerman RV Village

It offers wonderful sites with plenty of unique attractions in the surrounding area.

18049 Highway 30, Hagerman, ID 83332	(208) 837-4906 hagermanrvvillage.com/	All Year
$35	Good Sam	Pet Breed
72 Spaces	Gravel	30Width/75Length
Internet, Shower, Laundry	Supplies, Rentals, Ice	LPGas, Rec.Hall, GameRoom

Heyburn Riverside RV Park

Conveniently located in the city and offers quick access to several attractions.

941 18th St, Heyburn, ID 83336	(208) 431-2977	March 1 to November 30
$26-$28	Good Sam	No Restrictions
29 Spaces	Paved/Gravel	51Width/64Length
Internet, Shower, Playground	RV Wash, Pavilion, Boats	Patios, Tables, BBQ

Snake River RV Park

A brief description.

1440 Lindsay Blvd, Idaho Falls, ID 83402	(208) 523-3362 https://snakeriverrvpark.com/	All Year
$37-$52	Military/Good Sam	No Restrictions
145 Spaces	Paved/Gravel	24Width/72Length
Internet, Shower, Laundry	Rentals, Grocery, Ice	Firewood, Games, Fire Rings

Yellowstone RV Park

Stay just 20 minutes from Yellowstone. Walk to family-friendly activities.

4270 Old Highway 191, Island Park, ID 83429	(208) 716-5959 https://yellowstonervpark.com/	June 1 to September 30
$50-$60	Military/Good Sam	No Restrictions
70 Spaces	Gravel	40Width/65Length
Internet, Shower, Laundry	Rentals, Firewood, Games	Fire Ring, Tables, Ice

RedRock RV & Camping Park

Get away from the crowds and surround yourself with beauty.

3707 Red Rock Rd, Island Park, ID 83429	(208) 558-7442 http://www.redrockrvpark.com/	May 10 to September 25
$58-$68	Military/Good Sam	No Restrictions
90 Spaces	Paved/Gravel	32Width/75Length
Internet, Shower, Laundry	Rec. Hall, Firewood, Activities	Playground, Games, Pavilion

Buffalo Run RV Park

Plenty of nearby activities, so everyone is sure to find something they like to do.

3402 N Highway 20, Island Park, ID 83429	(208) 558-7112 https://buffalorunrvpark.com/	May 15 to October 15
$45	Good Sam	No Restrictions
28 Spaces	Gravel	30Width/65Length
Internet, Shower, Laundry	Rentals, Fishing, RV Wash	Restaurant, Ice, Tables

Wagonhammer RV Park

A great way to get back to nature and enjoy some time in the outdoors.

1826 Highway 93 N, North Fork, ID 83466	(208) 865-2477 http://wagonhammercampground.com/	April 25 to November 10
$37	Military/Good Sam	No Restrictions
49 Spaces	Gravel	25Width/80Length
Internet, Shower, Laundry	Firewood, Rentals, Ice, Fishing	Driving Range, Pavilion

Buck's Gas & RV

A small park with ample amenities and services to make any length of stay enjoyable.

3781 Hwy 26, Irwin, ID 83428	(208) 483-3581 http://bucksgasandrv.com/	March 1 to November 30
$35-$40	Military/Good Sam	No Restrictions
28 Spaces	Gravel	20Width/45Length
Internet, Shower, Laundry	Firewood, Snack Bar, Fishing	Rentals, Horseshoes, Tables

Cowboy RV Park

You can have fun year-round at this park with a wide range of outdoor activities.

845 Barton Rd, Pocatello, ID 83204	(208) 232-4587	All Year
$40-$44	Good Sam	No Restrictions
77 Spaces	Paved	25Width/60Length
Internet, Shower, Laundry	Playground	Patios, Tables

Wakeside Lake RV Park
Located along a lake within an hour of Yellowstone.

2245 South 2000 West, Rexburg, ID 83440	(208) 356-3681 https://www.wakesidelakerv.com/	April 1 to October 31
$33-$43	Military/Good Sam	No Restrictions
32 Spaces	Gravel	36Width/70Length
Internet, Shower, Laundry	RV Wash, Rentals, Firewood	Horseshoes, Tables

Intermountain RV Camp
No matter how long you stay, you'll have a comfortable and relaxing time.

1894 North Frontage Rd, Wendell, ID 83355	(208) 536-2301	March 1 to November 15
$33	Military/Good Sam	No Restrictions
25 Spaces	Gravel	33Width/63Length
Internet, Shower, Laundry	Supplies, Firewood, Breakfast	Playground, Activities

Illinois

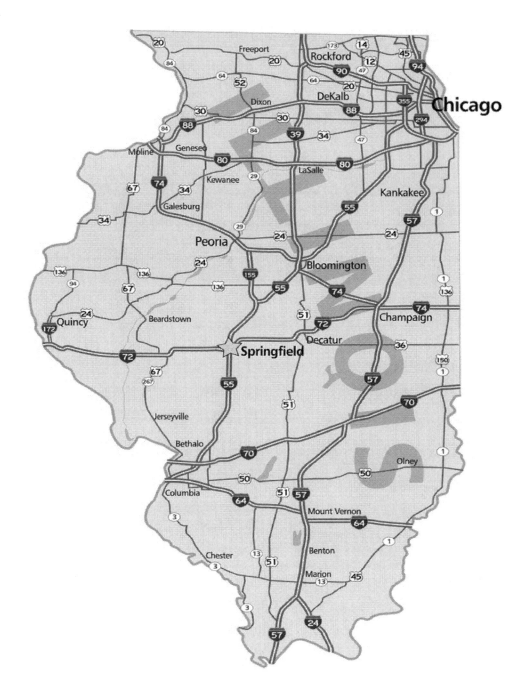

O'Connell's Yogi Bear Park
Featuring a world-class water park for you to enjoy during your stay.

| 970 Green Wing Road, Amboy, IL 61310 | (800) 367-9644 | April 21 to October 15 |

$54-$85	Military/Good Sam	No Restrictions
668 Spaces	Paved/Gravel	45Width/65Length
Internet, Shower, Laundry	Firewood, SnackBar, Grocery	Rentals, Pool, ATM

Mendota Hills Campground

A family-friendly campground where you can sit back and relax while enjoying nature.

642 US Highway 52, Amboy, IL 61310	(815) 849-5930 mendotahillscampground.com/	April 15 to October 15
$44	Good Sam	No Restrictions
189 Spaces	Gravel	40Width/70Length
Internet, Shower, Laundry	Fishing, Rentals, Rec. Hall	Game Room, Activities

Cahokia RV Parque

A brief description.

4060 Mississippi Ave, Cahokia, IL 62206	(618) 332-7700 http://www.cahokiarvparque.com/	All Year
$45-$50	Military/Good Sam	No Restrictions
119 Spaces	Paved/Gravel	22Width/55Length
Internet, Shower, Laundry	Firewood, Supplies, Ice, Pool	Playground, Games

Millpoint RV Park

Situated on the beautiful Upper Peoria Lake along the Illinois River.

310 Ash Ln, East Peoria, IL 61611	(309) 231-6497 https://millpointrvpark.com/	All Year
$40	Military/Good Sam	No Restrictions
85 Spaces	Gravel	60Width/100Length
Internet, Shower, Laundry	Rentals, Firewood, Games	Fire Rings, Tables

Camp Lakewood Campground

The best place to relax and camp year-round in Illinois.

1217 W Rickelman Ave, Effingham, IL 62401	(217) 342-6233 camplakewoodcampground.com/	All Year
$45-$56	Military/Good Sam	No Restrictions
65 Spaces	Gravel	27Width/60Length
Internet, Shower, Laundry	Supplies, Firewood, Fishing	Rentals, Playground

Galesburg East Campground

Located just off the highway and a short drive to the town of Knoxville.

| 1081 E US Highway 150, Knoxville, IL 61448 | (309) 289-2267 galesburgeastcampground.com/ | April 1 to October 31 |

$34-$38	Military/Good Sam	No Restrictions
67 Spaces	Gravel	30Width/60Length
Internet, Shower, Laundry	Rentals, Firewood, Pool, Ice	Playground, Rec. Hall

Geneseo Campground
Quiet camping in the middle of nature.

22978 Illinois Highway 82, Geneseo, IL 61254	(309) 944-6465 https://geneseocampground.com/	April 1 to October 31
$27-$33	No Discounts	No Restrictions
62 Spaces	Gravel	30Width/65Length
Internet, Shower, Laundry	Rentals, Grocery, Snack Bar, Ice	Rec. Hall, Fire Rings, Table

Leisure Lake Resort
Located near Route 66 and all the attractions it offers.

21900 SW Frontage Rd, Joliet, IL 60404	(815) 741-9405 http://leisurelakeresort.com	March 1 to November 30
$54	Good Sam	No Restrictions
265 Spaces	Gravel	30Width/70Length
Internet, Shower, Laundry	Golf Carts, Firewood, Pool	Game Room, Activities

RV Park at Hollywood Casino
Enjoy the same amenities as the casino hotel guests.

777 Hollywood Blvd, Joliet, IL 60436	(815) 927-2500 hollywoodcasinojoliet.com/	All Year
$39-$69	Military/Good Sam	No Restrictions
80 Spaces	Paved	40Width/70Length
Internet, Shower, Laundry	Casino, Breakfast, Lounge	Rec. Hall, Guest Services

Lehman's Lakeside RV Resort
Conveniently located between Chicago and Rockford.

19609 Harmony Rd, Marengo, IL 60152	(815) 923-4533	All Year
$45-$50	Good Sam	No Restrictions
295 Spaces	Paved/Gravel	50Width/75Length
Internet, Shower, Laundry	Firewood, Supplies, Ice	Grocery, Rec. Hall, Games

Marion Campground & RV Park
This park offers what you need to stay in comfort and convenience.

119 N 7th St, Marion, IL 62959	(618) 997-3484 http://marioncampground.weebly.com/	All Year
$39	Good Sam	No Restrictions

58 Spaces	Gravel	30Width/60Length
Internet, Shower, Laundry	Firewood, Rec. Hall, Cable	Playground, Pavilion

Glenwood RV Resort

Located in the Illinois River Valley near Starved Rock State Park.

551 Wilson St, Marseilles, IL 61341	(815) 795-6000 http://glenwoodrvresort.com/	All Year
$36-$45	Military	No Restrictions
580 Spaces	Gravel	28Width/80Length
Internet, Shower, Laundry	Grocery, Firewood, Tennis	Rec. Hall, Pool, Playground

Indiana

Northern Indiana

Northern Indiana offers plenty of fun outdoor activities, but still, many parks offer you to be within easy travel distance of larger cities. So no matter what you are looking to do on your vacation, you'll find it in Northern Indiana.

Peaceful Waters Campground
This place has it all: recreation, camping, and shopping.

3325 N US Highway 41, Bloomingdale, IN 47832	(765) 592-6458 peacefulwaterscampground.com/	April 25 to November 1
$35-$40	Military/Good Sam	Pet Breed
63 Spaces	Gravel	30Width/60Length
Internet, Shower, Laundry	Rentals, Fishing, Playground	Activities, Games, Tables

Eby's Pines RV Park
Here you can have economic fun for the whole family.

14583 State Road 120, Bristol, IN 46507	(574) 848-4583 http://ebyspines.com/	April 1 to November 1
$40-$55	No Discounts	RV Age
300 Spaces	Paved/Gravel	30Width/60Length
Internet, Shower, Laundry	Supplies, Pool, Rentals	Waterslide, Game Room

Horseshoe Lakes RV Campground
A family-oriented park in a beautiful setting among spring-fed lakes and wooded landscapes.

12962 S 225 W, Clinton, IN 47842	(765) 832-2487	April 22 to October 19
$48-$68	Military/Good Sam	Pet Quantity
124 Spaces	Gravel	12Width/65Length
Gated, Shower, Laundry	Rec. Hall, Pool, LP Gas, Ice	Playground, Activities

Elkhart Campground
Close to some unique attractions: Amish Acres and Notre Dame.

25608 County Road 4, Elkhart, IN 46514	(574) 264-2914 http://elkhartcampground.com/	March 15 to November 25
$42-$48	Military/Good Sam	No Restrictions
278 Spaces	Paved/Gravel	30Width/70Length
Internet, Shower, Laundry	Cable, Pool, Firewood	Gym, Rec. Hall, Playground

Heartland Resort
Located in central Indiana near Indianapolis.

1613 W 300 N,	(317) 326-3181	All Year

Greenfield, IN 46140	http://www.heartlandresort.com/	
$45	Military	No Restrictions
290 Spaces	Paved/Gravel	25Width/60Length
Internet, Shower, Laundry	Golf, Pavilion, Playground	Pool, Firewood, Ice

Twin Mills RV Resort

This northern Indiana park offers you a full-time recreational program.

1675 W. Sr 120, Howe, IN 46746	1 (888) 408-5093	April 15 to November 1
$31-$63	Military/Good Sam	Pet Quantity
534 Spaces	Paved	34Width/68Length
Internet, Shower, Laundry	Rentals, Pool, Golf Carts	Firewood, Rec.Hall, Game Room

Lake Haven Retreat

Conveniently located near the highway and just 2 miles from Indianapolis.

1951 W Edgewood Ave, Indianapolis, IN 46217	(317) 783-5267 lakehavenretreat.com/	All Year
$37	Military/Good Sam	No Restrictions
138 Spaces	Paved/Gravel	28Width/65Length
Internet, Shower, Laundry	Gated, Firewood, Cable	Rec.Hall, Playground, Tables

Indiana Beach Campgrounds

Here you can get a free ride to the boardwalk amusement park.

2732 N West Shafer Dr, Monticello, IN 47960	(574) 583-4141 http://www.indianabeach.com/	May 1 to October 31
$46-$52	Military	Pet Quantity
946 Spaces	Paved/Gravel	25Width/55Length
Internet, Shower, Laundry	ATM, Supplies, Cable, Ice	Firewood, SnackBar, Rec.Hall

Caboose Lake Campground

Located along a spring-fed and well-stocked lake.

3657 W US Highway 24, Remington, IN 47977	(219) 261-3828 http://cabooselake.com/	All Year
$46	Military/Good Sam	Pet Breed
125 Spaces	Gravel	30Width/75Length
Internet, Shower, Laundry	Firewood, Gated, ATM, Ice	Firewood, Supplies, Grocery

Deer Ridge Camping Resort

Easy access on and off the interstate ensures you can easily visit many nearby attractions.

3696 Smyrna Rd, Richmond, IN 47374	(765) 939-0888 deerridgecampingresort.com/	May 1 to October 31

$41-$46	Military/Good Sam	No Restrictions
62 Spaces	Gravel	25Width/80Length
Showers, Laundry, Firewood	Playground, Pavilion, Ice	Rec. Room, Pavilion

Grandpa's Farm
A brief description.

4244 IN-227 N, Richmond, IN 47374	(765) 962-7907 http://grandpasfarmcamp.com/	April 1 to November 1
$38	Military/Good Sam	No Restrictions
95 Spaces	Paved/Gravel	30Width/70Length
Internet, Shower, Laundry	Grocery, Firewood, Supplies	Pool, Game Room, Tables

Lakeview Campground
Offering a range of services and activities, plus plenty of nearby attractions.

7781 E 300 N, Rochester, IN 46975	(574) 353-8114 https://lakeviewcampingfun.com/	April 15 to October 15
$33	Military	No Restrictions
105 Spaces	Gravel	25Width/50Length
Internet, Shower, Laundry	Firewood, Supplies, Rentals	Rec. Hall, Activities, Games

Old Mill Run Park
With great amenities and services, you'll be very comfortable and happy here.

8544 W 690 N, Thorntown, IN 46071	(765) 436-7190 http://www.oldmillrun.com/	April 1 to October 15
$35-$38	Good Sam	No Restrictions
321 Spaces	Paved/Gravel	45Width/65Length
Showers, Laundry, Gated	Supplies, Rentals, Rec. Hall	Game Room, Playground

Southern Indiana

Indian Lakes RV Campground
A place where families and groups can go to enjoy nature.

7234 E State Rd 46, Batesville, IN 47006	(812) 934-5496	April 1 to November 1
$46-$50	Military/Good Sam	Pet Quantity
1100 Spaces	Paved/Gravel	30Width/80Length
Internet, Showers, Laundry	Grocery, Ice, Restaurant	Rentals, Pool, Supplies

Louisville North Campground
The closest place to stay in downtown Louisville if you want to explore all the city has to offer.

900 Marriott Dr, Clarksville, IN 47129	(812) 282-4474 louisvillenorthcampground.com/	All Year
$50	Military/Good Sam	No Restrictions
108 Spaces	Paved	18Width/60Length
Internet, Showers, Laundry	Snack Bar, Grocery, ATM	Rentals, GameRoom, Tables

Ceraland Park & Campground
You can find everything you ever wanted at this park.

3989 S 525 E, Columbus, IN 47203	(812) 377-5849 https://www.ceraland.org	April 1 to October 31
$47-$51	Good Sam	No Restrictions
308 Spaces	Paved/Gravel	25Width/70Length
Internet, Showers, Laundry	Fishing, Rentals, Pool	Playground, Games, Pavilion

Follow the River RV Resort
The perfect base to stay while exploring the surrounding area.

12273 Markland Town Rd, Florence, IN 47020	(812) 427-3330 followtheriverrvresort.com/	All Year
$43-$53	Good Sam	No Restrictions
130 Spaces	Paved/Gravel	40Width/85Length
Internet, Showers, Laundry	Laundry, Firewood, Ice, Pool	Playground, Activities

Bill Monroe Campground
This park has featured music for over 50 years.

5163 N State Road 135, Morgantown, IN 46160	(812) 988-6422	May 1 to November 1

$38	Military/Good Sam	No Restrictions
260 Spaces	Gravel	20Width/40Length
Showers, Laundry, Firewood	Rentals, Grocery, ATM	Activities, Music, Pavilion

Brown County KOA

This park puts you within minutes of a variety of attractions and activities.

2248 State Road 46 E, Nashville, IN 47448	(812) 988-4675 koa.com/campgrounds/brown-county/	April 1 to November 1
$50-$83	No Discounts	No Restrictions
41 Spaces	Paved/Gravel	21Width/50Length
Internet, Showers, Laundry	Supplies, Cable, Rentals	Pool, Playground, Patios

New Vision RV Park

Offering the basic amenities to help you relax before you head out and see the sites.

13552 N US Highway 41, Oaktown, IN 47561	(812) 745-2125 newvisionrvpark.com/	All Year
$29	Military/Good Sam	No Restrictions
39 Spaces	Gravel	36Width/65Length
Internet, Showers, Laundry	LP Gas, Firewood, Ice	RV Service, Fishing Supplies

Rising Star Casino Resort & RV Park

A great stopover or a place for an extended getaway.

777 Rising Star Dr, Rising Sun, IN 47040	(812) 438-1234 https://risingstarcasino.com/	All Year
$19-$35	Military/Good Sam	10 Day Max
56 Spaces	Paved	30Width/50Length
Internet, Showers, Laundry	Restaurant, Cable, Lounge	Snack Bar, Golf, Gym

Little Farm on the River RV Park

Come stay in comfort at this wonderful camping getaway.

1343 E Bellview Ln, Rising Sun, IN 47040	(812) 438-9135 http://littlefarmresort.com/	All Year
$40-$52	Military/Good Sam	No Restrictions
192 Spaces	Gravel	35Width/90Length
Internet, Showers, Laundry	Grocery, Supplies, Rentals	Activities, Rec. Hall

Iowa

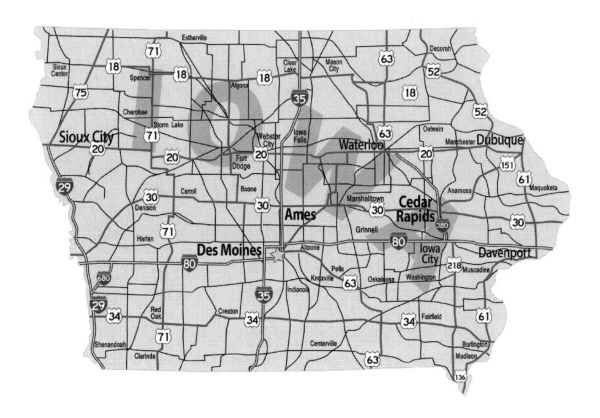

Amana RV Park
Stay at a great park while exploring the historic villages of the Amana Colonies.

3850 C St, Amana, IA 52203	(319) 622-7616 https://amanarvpark.com/	April 1 to October 31
$36-$39	Good Sam	No Restrictions
450 Spaces	Gravel	30Width/75Length
Internet, Showers, Laundry	Supplies, Rec. Hall, Ice	Playground, Games, Fire Rings

Lakeshore RV Resort
Located on Lake Oelwein in Northeast Iowa.

1418 Q Ave, Oelwein, IA 50662	(319) 800-9968 https://www.lakeshoreiowa.com/	May 1 to October 15
$35	Good Sam	No Restrictions
85 Spaces	Gravel	30Width/80Length
Internet, Showers, Laundry	Firewood, Activities, RV Wash	Shuffleboard, Fire Rings

On-Ur-Wa RV Park
Enjoy a pleasant stay here.

1111 28th St, Onawa, IA 51040	(712) 423-1387 http://www.onurwarvpark.com/	April 15 to October 15
$36-$39	Military/Good Sam	Pet Breed
44 Spaces	Gravel	28Width/100Length
Internet, Showers, Laundry	Supplies, Firewood, LP Gas	Rec. Hall, Tables, Ice

Sleepy Hollow RV Park
A family-friendly park in eastern Iowa.

3340 Black Hawk Ave NW, Oxford, IA 52322	(319) 828-4900 https://www.sleepyhollowia.com/	All Year
$33-$42	Good Sam	Pet Breed
120 Spaces	Gravel	28Width/65Length
Internet, Showers, Laundry	Supplies, Firewood, LP Gas	Ice, Snack Bar, Groceries

Kellogg RV Park
A solar-powered and eco-friendly park.

1570 Highway 224 S, Kellogg, IA 50135	(641) 526-8535 http://iowasbestburgercafe.com/	All Year
$33	Good Sam	No Restrictions
38 Spaces	Gravel	27Width/85Length
Shower, Laundry, Firewood	Snack Bar, Restaurant, Ice	RV Wash, Fishing Supplies

Crossroads RV Park
Centrally located in southeast Iowa.

708 S Iris St, Mount Pleasant, IA 52641	(319) 385-9737 http://www.xrdsrv.com/	All Year
$36	Military/Good Sam	Pet Quantity, Breed
34 Spaces	Gravel	34Width/90Length
Internet, Showers, Laundry	Firewood, Cable, Playground	Rec. Hall, Fire Rings, Tables

Newton/Des Moines East KOA
Basic amenities make this a great place to recharge.

1601 East 36th Street South, Newton, IA 50208	(641) 792-2428 koa.com/campgrounds/newton/	April 1 to October 31
$42-$47	Military	Pet Breed
77 Spaces	Gravel	24Width/62Length
Internet, Showers, Laundry	Rentals, Pool, Firewood	Playground, Game Room

Timberline Campground

This is a delightful place to stay.

31635 Ashworth Rd, Waukee, IA 50263	(515) 987-1714 https://www.timberlineiowa.com/	April 1 to November 1
$44-$49	Good Sam	Pet Breed
105 Spaces	Gravel	25Width/60Length
Internet, Showers, Laundry	Rentals, Supplies, Game Room	Playground, Pavilion, Rec. Hall

Kansas

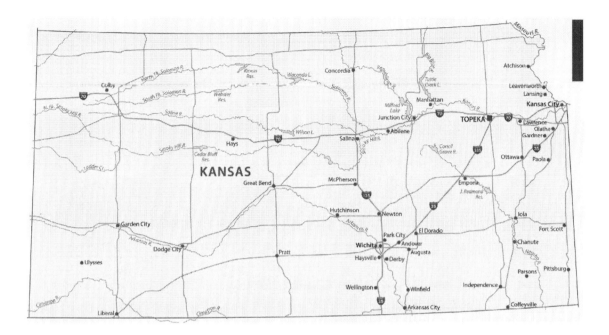

Kansas is a state of variety; you can visit large cities or enjoy an outdoor adventure. There are plenty of great RV parks that you can enjoy during any length of time you need to stay. Consider some of the many activities you can enjoy while in the state of Kansas.

Covered Wagon RV Resort
A brief description.

803 S Buckeye Ave, Abilene, KS 67410	(785) 263-2343	All Year
$38	Military/Good Sam	No Restrictions
50 Spaces	Gravel	25Width/70Length
Internet, Showers, Laundry	Pool, Cable, Playground	Games, Pavilion, Tables

Deer Grove RV Park
This park is rustic but elegant and offers plenty of amenities to help you enjoy your stay.

2873 SE US Highway 54, El Dorado, KS 67042	(316) 321-6272 http://deergrovervpark.com/	All Year
$36-$39	Good Sam	Pet Breed
49 Spaces	Gravel	25Width/65Length
Internet, Showers, Laundry	Cable, RV Wash, Firewood	Rec.Hall, DogRun, StormShelter

Spring Lake RV Resort

At this picturesque park, you can choose from a range of outdoor activities.

1308 S Spring Lake Rd, Halstead, KS 67056	(316) 835-3443 springlakervresort.com/	All Year
$30-$32	Military/Good Sam	No Restrictions
179 Spaces	Paved/Gravel	30Width/70Length
Internet, Showers, Laundry	Rec. Hall, Pool, Rentals	GameRoom, Playground, Tennis

Lighthouse Landing RV Park

This park is a fun frontier town with replicas of old prairie cabins.

9 Heartland Dr, South Hutchinson, KS 67505	(800) 921-1236 http://lighthouselandingrvpark.com/	All Year
$34	Military/Good Sam	No Restrictions
46 Spaces	Gravel	35Width/70Length
Internet, Shower, Laundry	Rentals, Horseshoes	Rec. Hall, Fire Ring, Tables

Seven Winds RV Park

A quality atmosphere with good service at an affordable price.

4910 W US Highway 54, Liberal, KS 67901	(620) 624-5581 sevenwindsrvpark.com/pc/	All Year
$32	Military/Good Sam	No Restrictions
33 Spaces	Gravel	23Width/58Length
Internet, Shower, Laundry	Firewood, Ice, Horseshoes	Playground, Tables

Rutlader Outpost RV Park

This historical park allows you to stay on beautiful grounds.

33565 Metcalf Rd, Louisburg, KS 66053	(866) 888-6779 https://www.rutladeroutpost.com/	All Year
$40	Military/Good Sam	No Restrictions
82 Spaces	Gravel	30Width/70Length
Internet, Shower, Laundry	Supplies, Ice, Grocery	Rec.Hall, Playground, Games

Crossroads RV Park

Relax while being surrounded by nature or choose to do an outdoor adventure.

23313 S US Highway 75, Lyndon, KS 66451	(785) 221-5482 http://www.crossroadsrvpark.com/	All Year
$32	Military/Good Sam	No Restrictions
45 Spaces	Gravel	30Width/65Length
Internet, Shower, Laundry	Firewood, Grocery, Rentals	Rec.Hall, Playground, Tables

McPherson RV Ranch
A brief description.

2201 E Northview Ave, McPherson, KS 67460	(620) 241-5621 mcphersonrvranchandhorse.com/	All Year
$33	Military/Good Sam	No Restrictions
27 Spaces	Gravel	30Width/70Length
Internet, Shower, Laundry	Supplies, Firewood	Rec. Hall, Fire Rings

Walnut Grove RV Park
Tucked away in the heart of downtown Merriam is this wonderful RV park.

10218 Johnson Dr, Merriam, KS 66203	(913) 262-3023 https://walnutgroverv.com	All Year
$50-$100	Military/Good Sam	No Restrictions
51 Spaces	Paved	24Width/65Length
Internet, Shower, Laundry	Firewood, Ice, Guest Service	Rec. Hall, Fire Ring

High Plains Camping
This convenient park is your place to rejuvenate for a night or more.

462 US Highway 83, Oakley, KS 67748	(785) 672-3538 highplainscamping.com/	All Year
$44	Military/Good Sam	No Restrictions
68 Spaces	Paved/Gravel	36Width/70Length
Internet, Shower, Laundry	Snack Bar, Cable, Grocery	Restaurant, Lounge, Pool

Bailey's RV Resort
Fish at the private lake or spend some time seeing local attractions.

1701 North St, Seneca, KS 66538	(785) 294-1208 https://baileysrvresort.com/	All Year
30-$35	Military/Good Sam	No Restrictions
34 Spaces	Gravel	24Width/60Length
Internet, Shower, Laundry	RV Service, Rec. Hall	Playground, Pavilion

All Seasons RV Park
Stay just 20 minutes from downtown Wichita in a country setting.

15520 W Maple St, Goddard, KS 67052	(316) 722-1154 allseasonsrvcampground.com/	All Year
$38-$45	Military/Good Sam	Pet Breed
48 Spaces	Gravel	24Width/65Length
Internet, Shower, Laundry	Grocery, Ice, Cable	Playground, Activities

USI RV Park
Kid and pet-friendly, this park has constantly been rated as one of the top parks in Wichita.

2920 E 33rd St N, Wichita, KS 67219	(316) 838-8699 http://www.usirvpark.com/	All Year
$37-$53	Military/Good Sam	Pet Quantity, Breed
75 Spaces	Gravel	24Width/60Length
Internet, Shower, Laundry	LP Gas, RV Wash, Ice	Rec. Hall, Playground

Air Capital RV Park
Located within 10 minutes of many attractions in Wichita.

609 E 47th St S, Wichita, KS 67216	(316) 201-1250 aircapital-rvpark.com/	All Year
$49-$59	Military/Good Sam	No Restrictions
90 Spaces	Paved	25Width/70Length
Internet, Shower, Laundry	Cable, RV Wash, Rentals	Rec. hall, Playground

Kentucky

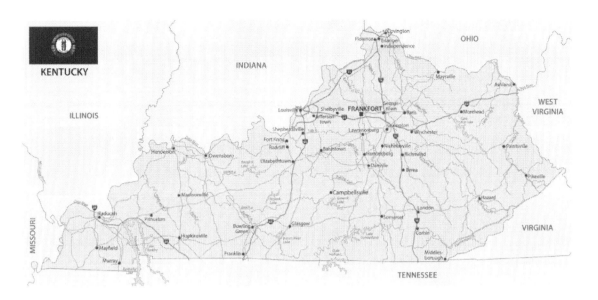

Kentucky is a land of rolling green hills and historic towns. No matter what your interest, you'll find plenty of activities to keep you busy during an activity here.

Lakeside Campground
Located along Jonathan Creek, an inlet of the scenic Kentucky Lake.

12363 US Highway 68 E, Benton, KY 42025	(270) 354-8157 visitlakesidecampground.com/	March 17 to October 31
$30-$35	Military/Good Sam	Pet Breed
133 Spaces	Gravel	30Width/80Length
Internet, Showers, Laundry	Onsite Meat Storage Facilities	Pool, Game Room, Boats

White Acres Campground
This pet-friendly park offers monthly rates for those who want a long-term stay.

3022 Boston Rd, Bardstown, KY 40004	(502) 348-9677	All Year
$43	Military/Good Sam	No Restrictions
89 Spaces	Paved/Gravel	30Width/80Length
Internet, Showers, Supplies	Rentals, Playground, Games	Pavilion, Fire Ring, Tables

Stagecoach Station Campground
A pet-friendly park that offers rates for any length of stay.

230 Easy St, Benton, KY 42025	(270) 410-2267 http://stagecoachcampground.com/	All Year
$28-$33	Good Sam	No Restrictions

32 Spaces	Gravel	30Width/70Length
Internet, Showers, LP Gas	Firewood, Rec. Hall, Ice	GameRoom, FireRing, Tables

Cave Country RV Campground

The perfect place to stay while you explore Mammoth Cave National Park.

216 Gaunce Dr, Cave City, KY 42127	(270) 773-4678 http://www.cavecountryrv.com/	All Year
$41-$44	Military/Good Sam	Pet Quantity
51 Spaces	Gravel	40Width/65Length
Internet, Showers, Laundry	Cable, Supplies, Firewood	Rec. Hall, Game Room

Yogi Bear's Jellystone Park

This park has fun as its main focus. There is a wide range of activities to choose from.

950 Mammoth Cave Rd, Cave City, KY 42127	(270) 773-3840 jellystonemammothcave.com/	All Year
$46-$123	Military	Pet Breed
227 Spaces	Paved/Gravel	35Width/80Length
Internet, Showers, Laundry	Cable, Guest Services, Rentals	Pavilion, Golf, Gym

Singing Hills RV Park

Located in the heart of a beautiful cave country just outside Mammoth Cave National Park.

4110 Mammoth Cave Rd, Cave City, KY 42127	(270) 773-3789	All Year
$36-$44	Military/Good Sam	No Restrictions
29 Spaces	Gravel	20Width/70Length
Internet, Showers, Supplies	Firewood, LP gas, Ice	RV Wash, Games, Fire Rings

Falls Creek Campground

No matter what type of outdoor activity you enjoy, you'll be sure to find it at this park.

1943 KY-90, Corbin, KY 40701	(800) 541-7238 https://www.fallscreekcc.com/	All Year
$33-$46	Good Sam	No Restrictions
13 Spaces	Gravel	40Width/80Length
Internet, Showers, Laundry	Firewood, Snack Bar, Ice	Playground, Games, Tables

Laurel Lake Camping Resort

Conveniently located off the interstate make this a great base camp for your daily activities.

80 Robert Blair Rd, Corbin, KY 40701	(606) 526-7876 laurellakecampingresort.com/	April 1 to November 1

$45-$65	Military/Good Sam	No Restrictions
78 Spaces	Gravel	30Width/80Length
Internet, Shower, Laundry	Snack Bar, Gated, Cable	Rentals, Games, Fire Rings

Three Springs Campground
Stay at the tranquil foothills of the Appalachian Mountains.

595 Campground Rd, Corinth, KY 41010	(859) 823-0258 threespringscampgroundandrvpark.com/	All Year
$50	Military/Good Sam	Restrictions
25 Spaces	Gravel	35Width/60Length
Internet, Showers, Ice	Laundry, Grocery, Rentals, Rec. Hall	Playground, Games

Murphy's Outback RV Resort
Just 2 miles from the marina at Lake Barkley.

4481 State Route 93 S, Eddyville, KY 42038	(270) 388-4752 http://www.murphysrv.com/	April 1 to November 1
$43	Good Sam	No Restrictions
88 Spaces	Paved	25Width/65Length
Internet, Showers, Laundry	Pool, Playground, Pavilion	Fire Rings, Games, Tables

Elizabethtown Crossroads Campground
This park has beautiful landscaping to provide a naturally peaceful place to stay.

209 Tunnel Hill Rd, Elizabethtown, KY 42701	(270) 737-7600 elizabethtowncrossroadscampgroundky.com/	All Year
$34-$45	Military/Good Sam	RV Age, Pet Breed
47 Spaces	Gravel	25Width/70Length
Internet, Laundry	Showers, Firewood, Supplies, Playground	Rentals, Game Room

Elkhorn Campground
Located along the banks of Elkhorn Creek.

165 N Scruggs Ln, Frankfort, KY 40601	(502) 695-9154 elkhorncampground.com/	All Year
$37-$42	Military/Good Sam	Pet Breed
125 Spaces	Paved	25Width/80Length
Internet, Shower, Laundry	Snack Bar, Cable, Grocery	Activities, Games, Pavilion

Westgate RV Campground
A great overnight spot to stop or for a long term stay.

254 Russell Dyche Memorial Highway, London, KY 40741	(606) 878-7330 westgatecampground.com/	All Year

$34-$39	Military/Good Sam	No Restrictions
14 Spaces	Gravel	25Width/45Length
Internet, Showers, ATM, Ice	Grocery, Restaurant, Rentals	Pool, Playground, Tables

Duck Creek RV Park
Two nearby lakes give you plenty of fishing and water sport activity options.

2540 John L Puryear Dr, Paducah, KY 42003	(270) 415-0404 http://www.duckcreekrv.com	All Year
$34-$39	Military/Good Sam	No Restrictions
96 Spaces	Gravel	30Width/80Length
Internet, Showers, Laundry	Grocery, Fishing, Pool	Rec. Hall, Pavilion, Games

Fern Lake Campground
A variety of amenities will make your stay a pleasant one.

5535 Cairo Rd, Paducah, KY 42001	(270) 444-7939 fernlakecampground.net/	All Year
$30-$38	Military/Good Sam	No Restrictions
60 Spaces	Paved/Gravel	22Width/60Length
Internet, Showers, Laundry	Playground, Games, Firewood	Fire Rings, Tables, Ice

4 Guys RV Park
Located between two state parks, so you have plenty of opportunities for outdoor activities.

10137 Campton Rd, Stanton, KY 40380	(606) 481-1611 http://www.4guysrvpark.com/	All Year
$39	Military/Good Sam	Pet Breed
45 Spaces	Gravel	30Width/70Length
Internet, Showers, Laundry	Grocery, Rentals, Pool	Rec. Hall, Games, Pavilion

Oak Creek Campground
The basic amenities will keep you comfortable while you explore the surrounding area.

13329 Oak Creek Rd, Walton, KY 41094	(859) 485-9131 http://oakcreekcampground.com/	All Year
$36	Military/Good Sam	No Restrictions
102 Spaces	Paved	22Width/65Length
Internet, Showers, Laundry	Supplies, Firewood, Ice	Grocery, Pavilion, FireRings

Louisiana

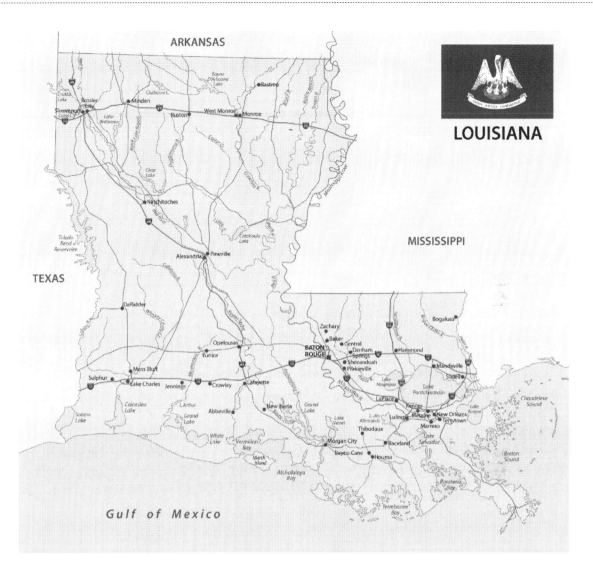

Louisiana is a beautiful and rich state with vibrant and unique cultures and cities. There are plenty of great RV parks throughout the state that will provide you an excellent place to stay while exploring all that the area around you has to offer.

Natalbany Creek Campground
Conveniently located near New Orleans and a variety of coastal cities and attractions.

30218 Highway 16, Amite, LA 70422	(985) 748-4311 natalbanycreekcampground.net/	All Year
$35-$45	Military/Good Sam	No Restrictions
123 Spaces	Paved	24Width/60Length
Internet, Restrooms, Showers	Golf Carts, Supplies, Gated	Game Room, Pool, Mini

| | | | Golf |

DiamondJacks Casino & RV Park
Experience both fun and leisure time at this RV park.

711 Diamondjacks Blvd, Bossier City, LA 71111	(318) 678-7777 diamondjacks.com/	All Year
$29-$34	Good Sam	No Restrictions
32 Spaces	Paved	30Width/65Length
Restaurant, Guest Services	Snack Bar, GameRoom, Pool	Gym, Patios, Tables

Poche's RV Park
The place to go to enjoy the peace and quiet of the great outdoors.

1080 Sawmill Hwy, Breaux Bridge, LA 70517	(337) 332-0326 Website	All Year
$40	Good Sam	Pet Breed
89 Spaces	Paved/Gravel	30Width/70Length
Internet, Showers, Laundry	Fishing, Rentals, Pool	Rec. Hall, Playground

Poche Plantation RV Resort
Located less than an hour from New Orleans and Baton Rouge.

6554 State Highway 44, Convent, LA 70723	(225) 562-7728	All Year
$40-$45	Good Sam	No Restrictions
165 Spaces	Gravel	25Width/60Length
Internet, Showers, Laundry	Restaurant, Cable, Pool	Rec. Hall, Pavilion, Patios

Frog City RV Park
Located deep in the beautiful Cajun countryside.

3003 Daulaut Dr, Duson, LA 70529	(337) 223-2307 http://www.lafayettervpark.com/	All Year
$40	Military/Good Sam	Pet Quantity, Breed
62 Spaces	Paved	30Width/70Length
Internet, Showers, Laundry	Cable, Pool, RV wash	Rec.Hall, Playground, Tables

Cajun Palms RV Resort
Located close to the best of Louisiana.

1055 N Barn Rd, Henderson, LA 70517	(337) 667-7772 http://www.cajunpalms.com	All year
$35-$79	Good Sam	Pet Breed
400 Spaces	Paved	40Width/65Length

| Internet, Showers, Laundry | Gated, ATM, Supplies | Firewood, Games, Pool |

Cypress Bend RV Park
Whether an overnight stay or longer, this is your place to stay.

717 N Thomson Ave, Iowa, LA 70647	(337) 582-1722	All Year
$45	Good Sam	No Restrictions
129 Spaces	Paved	30Width/75Length
Internet, Showers, Laundry	ATM, Supplies, Snack Bar	Restaurant, Cable, Ice

Evangeline Oaks RV Park
A one of a kind place to stay near Lake Charles.

21125 Louisiana Cotton Dr, Iowa, LA 70647	(337) 288-0032 https://evangelineoaksrvpark.com/	All Year
$50	Good Sam	No Restrictions
111 Spaces	Paved	30Width/82Length
Internet, Showers	Laundry	Patios, Tables

Blue Heron RV Park
Just nine miles from Lake Charles.

601 W Highway 90, Iowa, LA 70647	(337) 508-0600 https://www.blueheronrv.com/	All Year
$40-$45	Good Sam	No Restrictions
50 Spaces	Paved	24Width/70Length
Internet	Showers	Laundry

Coushatta Luxury RV Resort
A true luxury RV resort right outside a casino.

777 Coushatta Dr, Kinder, LA 70648	1 (888) 774-7263 coushattacasinoresort.com/	All Year
$25-$65	Good Sam	14 Day Max Stay
107 Spaces	Paved	35Width/70Length
Internet, Showers, Laundry	Rentals, Pool, Casino	Cable, Restaurant, Lounge

Twelve Oaks RV Park
Just one mile off the interstate and easy access to anything you need or want.

2736 Conoco St, Lake Charles, LA 70615	(337) 439-2916 http://twelveoaksrv.com/	All Year
$45-$50	Good Sam	Pet Breed
107 Spaces	Paved	28Width/70Length
Internet, Showers, Laundry	Cable, Breakfast, RV Wash	Rec. Hall, Pavilion, Patios

Lakeside RV Park

Conveniently located so you can easily get to both New Orleans and Baton Rouge.

28370 S Frost Rd, Livingston, LA 70754	(225) 686-7676 http://lakeside-rvpark.com/	All Year
$38-$55	Military/Good Sam	Pet Breed
139 Spaces	Paved	28Width/85Length
Internet, Showers, Laundry	Fishing, Rentals, Pool	Activities, Gym, Pavilion

Toledo Bend RV Resort

The perfect place for a planned, fun-filled vacation.

114 Shamrock Lane, Many, LA 71449	(318) 256-0002 toledobendrvresortandcabins.com/	All Year
$30-$55	Military/Good Sam	Pet Breed
48 Spaces	Paved/Gravel	35Width/65Length
Internet, Shower, Laundry	Rentals, Pool. Paddle Boats	Rec. Hall, Pavilion, Patio

Paragon Casino RV Resort

Stay near a casino and all the amenities it offers.

711 Paragon Pl, Marksville, LA 71351	(800) 946-1946 paragoncasinoresort.com/	All Year
$25-$35	Good Sam	14 Day Max Stay
205 Spaces	Paved	35Width/80Length
Internet, Showers, Laundry	ATM, Ice, Snack Bar	Rentals, Playground, Golf

Cinnamon Creek RV Park

Centrally located in northern Louisiana, this park puts you close to all the popular attractions.

12996 Highway 371, Minden, LA 71055	(318) 371-5111 cinnamoncreekrvpark.com/	All Year
$36	Good Sam	No Restrictions
81 Spaces	Gravel	24Width/65Length
Internet, Showers	Laundry, Cable	Pavilion, Tables

Nakatosh Campground

Top-quality amenities ensure a pleasant stay here.

5428 Highway 6, Natchitoches, LA 71457	(318) 352-0911 http://nakatoshcampgrounds.com/	All Year
$34	Good Sam	No Restrictions
44 Spaces	Gravel	25Width/55Length
Internet, Showers	Laundry, RV wash	Rec. Hall

Grand Ecore RV Park

Stay high on a bluff overlooking the Red River.

1071 Tauzin Island Rd, Natchitoches, LA 71457	(318) 238-7446 https://grandecorervpark.com/	All Year
$40	Good Sam	No Restrictions
59 Spaces	Paved	65Width/70Length
Internet, Showers, Gated	Laundry, Rec. Hall, Ice	Pavilion, Patios, Fire Fings

KOC Kampground

Come for an enjoyable vacation. Offering enjoyable events and nearby attractions.

3104 Curtis Ln, New Iberia, LA 70560	(337) 364-6666 kockampground.com/	All Year
$30-$33	Military/Good Sam	Pet Breed
200 Spaces	Paved/Gravel	30Width/50Length
Internet, Showers, Laundry	Ice, Cable, Grocery	Rentals, Playground, Patios

Isle of Iberia RV Resort

A quiet and peaceful park offering basic amenities.

713 NW Bypass, Hwy 3212, New Iberia, LA 70560	(337) 256-8681 https://www.isleofiberia.com/	All Year
$45-$55	Good Sam	No Restrictions
185 Spaces	Paved/Gravel	25Width/75Length
Internet, Showers, Laundry	Gated, Pool, Rec. Hall	Activities, Pavilion, Fire Rings

Jude Travel Park of New Orleans

The perfect family vacation destination.

7400 Chef Menteur Hwy, New Orleans, LA 70126	(504) 241-0632 https://judetravelpark.com/	All Year
$35-$65	Military/Good Sam	No Restrictions
46 Spaces	Gravel	20Width/45Length
Internet, Showers, Laundry	Gated, Ice, Pool	Hot Tub, Tables

Shreveport/Bossier KOA

A beautiful park with easy access off the interstate.

6510 West 70th Street, Shreveport, LA 71129	(318) 687-1010 koa.com/campgrounds/shreveport/	All Year
$42-$49	None	Pet Breed
100 Spaces	Paved/Gravel	35Width/90Length
Internet, Shower, Laundry	Grocery, Cable, Rentals	Playground, Pavilion

Pine Crest RV Park

Close to New Orleans and Gulf Coast beaches.

2601 Old Spanish Trl, Slidell, LA 70461	(985) 649-3181 http://pinecrestrv.com/	All Year
$39-$44	Good Sam	Pet Breed
202 Spaces	Paved	30Width/65Length
Internet, Showers, Laundry	LP Gas, Ice, Rec. Hall	Shuttle Service, Patios

A+ Motel & RV Park

Just 2 miles from the interstate and at the entrance to the Creole Nature Trail.

4631 Highway 27 S, Sulphur, LA 70665	(337) 583-2631 http://a-plusmotel.com/	All Year
$40-$45	Military/Good Sam	Pet Breed
134 Spaces	Paved	30Width/70Length
Internet, Showers, Laundry	Pool, Rec. Hall, Playground	Games, Sauna, Gym, BBQ's

River View RV Park & Resort

Take a river walk, ride a historic paddleboat, or engage in an outdoor activity.

100 Riverview Pkwy, Vidalia, LA 71373	(318) 336-1400	All Year
$33-$45	Military/Good Sam	Pet Breed
145 Spaces	Paved/Gravel	30Width/60Length
Internet, Showers, Laundry	Rentals, Pool, Firewood, Ice	Rec. Hall, Playground

Maine

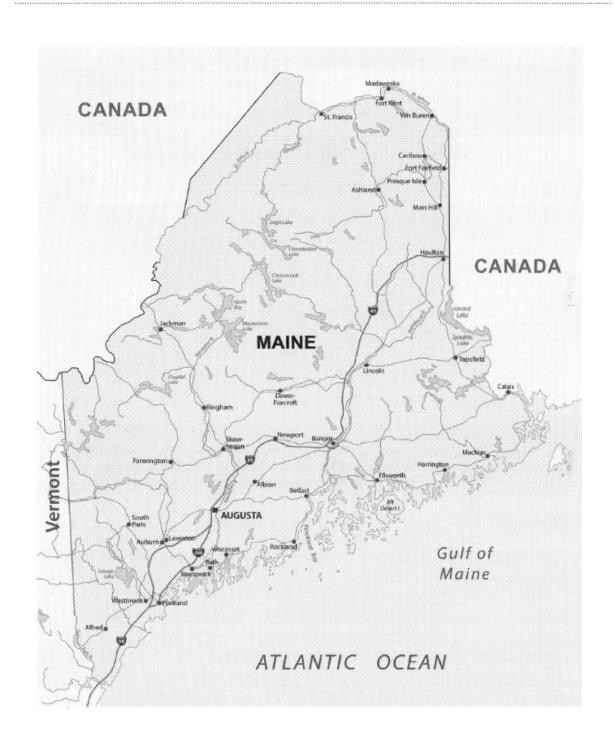

Maine – Northern

Woodland Acres Campground
A great place for a relaxing vacation or a base camp to explore the beautiful Saco River Valley.

33 Woodland Acres Dr, Brownfield, ME 04010	(207) 935-2529 https://woodlandacres.com/	May 15 to October 15
$40-$50	Good Sam	None
90 Spaces	Gravel	30Width/79Length
Internet, Showers, Laundry	Firewood, Gated, Ice	Fishing, Rentals, Pool

Point Sebago Resort
This park provides first-class family vacations.

261 Point Sebago Rd, Casco, ME 04015	(800) 655-1232 https://www.covecommunities.com/rv-resorts/maine/point-sebago	May 1 to October 31
$80-$125	Military/Good Sam	Pet Quantity
223 Spaces	Paved/Gravel	30Width/60Length
Internet, Showers, Laundry	Firewood, Gated, Ice, Driving Range, Golf, ATM Supplies	Playground, Rentals, Lodge

Cold River Campground
A short drive away, and you can visit Arcadia National Park.

211 Riverside Dr, Eddington, ME 04428	(207) 922-2551 coldrivercampground.com	May 15 to October 15
$44	Military/Good Sam	Pet Breed
77 Spaces	Gravel	30Width/62Length
Internet, Showers, Laundry	Supplies, Grocery, Cable	Rentals, Game Room, Pool

My Brother's Place Campground
From this park, you can easily cross the border and enjoy some time in Canada.

659 North St, Houlton, ME 04730	(207) 532-6739 mybrothersplace.mainerec.com/	May 10 to October 15
$38-$41	Good Sam	None
77 Spaces	Paved	28Width/100Length
Internet, Shower, Laundry	Rentals, Paddle Boats, Rec. Hall	Playground, Games, Tables

Katahdin Shadows Campground

Events are available all summer that everyone in the family can enjoy.

118 Katahdin Shadows, Medway, ME 04460	(207) 746-9349 https://katahdinshadows.com/	May 1 to November 1
$37-$39	Good Sam	None
105 Spaces	Paved/Gravel	26Width/74Length
Internet, Showers, Laundry	Supplies, Firewood, Ice	Rentals, GameRoom, Fire Rings

Two Lakes Camping Area

A family camping spot on Hogan Pond.

215 Campground Ln, Oxford, ME 04270	(207) 539-4851 Website	May 1 to October 14
$40-$55	Good Sam	Pet Quantity
125 Spaces	Gravel	24Width/64Length
Internet, Showers, Laundry	Rentals, Rec.Hall, GameRoom	Playground, Pavilion, Games

Kokatosi Campground

Located on the crystal clear, beautiful Crescent Lake.

635 Webbs Mills Rd, Raymond, ME 04071	(207) 627-4642 http://kokatosicampground.com/	May 15 to October 9
$45-$49	Military/Good Sam	No Restrictions
156 Spaces	Gravel	30Width/60Length
Internet, Showers, Laundry	Snack Bar, Cable, Rentals	Playground, Game Room

Two Rivers Campground

Located on the banks of the Kennebec River and Wesserunsett Stream.

327 Canaan Rd, Skowhegan, ME 04976	(207) 474-6482 http://www.tworvrs.com/	May 15 to October 15
$45-$49	Military/Good Sam	No Restrictions
65 Spaces	Gravel	30Width/100Length
Internet, Showers, Laundry	Cable, Fishing, Rentals	Game Room, Playground

Acres of Wildlife Campground

There are plenty of choices so you can spend your vacation however you want.

60 Acres Of Wildlife Rd, Steep Falls, ME 04085	(207) 675-2267 https://www.acresofwildlife.com/	May 1 to October 19
$32-$72	None	None
270 Spaces	Gravel	30Width/60Length
Internet, Showers, Laundry	Snack Bar, Lounge, Fishing	Rentals, Golf Carts

Augusta-West Lakeside Kampground

Enjoy the great outdoors from the heart of Maine.

183 Holmes Brook Ln, Winthrop, ME 04364	(207) 377-9993 augustawestkampground.com/	May 15 to October 15
$39-$46	Good Sam	None
90 Spaces	Gravel	40Width/80Length
Internet, Showers, Gated	Laundry, Fishing, Grocery	Game Room, Activities

Maine- Southern

Southern Maine is full of beautiful coastal RV parks. See plenty of sites while enjoying the great outdoors or just sit back and relax.

Walnut Grove Campground
Country camping at its finest. A family-friendly campground in beautiful Southern Maine.

599 Gore Rd, Alfred, ME 04002	(207) 324-1207 walnutgrovecampground.net/	May 8 to October 15
$38-$54	None	None
90 Spaces	Gravel	30Width/60Length
Internet, Showers, Laundry	Snack Bar, Grocery, Rentals	Pool, Playground, Fire Rings

Pumpkin Patch RV Resort
There are plenty of interesting things to see, such as museums like Stephen King's home.

149 Billings Rd, Hermon, ME 04401	(207) 848-2231 pumpkinpatchrvresort.com/	May 1 to October 15
$38-$42	Military/Good Sam	Pet Breed
85 Spaces	Gravel	40Width/75Length
Internet, Showers, Laundry	Ice, Rentals, Horseshoes	Rec. Hall, Game Room

Pleasant Hill Campground
Easy day trip access to some nearby attractions.

45 Mansell Rd, Hermon, ME 04401	(207) 848-5127 pleasanthillcampground.com/	May 1 to October 13
$45-$50	Military/Good Sam	Pet Breed
107 Spaces	Paved/Gravel	30Width/70Length
Internet, Showers, Laundry	Supplies, Firewood, Rentals	Pool, Game Room, Mini Golf

Paul Bunyan Campground
A family-friendly campground located on rolling terrain.

1858 Union St, Bangor, ME 04401	(207) 941-1177 paulbunyancampground.com/	May 1 to October 15
$36-$48	Military/Good Sam	Pet Size, Quantity, Breed
52 Spaces	Paved/Gravel	30Width/72Length
Internet, Showers, Laundry	Grocery, Pool, Rec. Hall	Activities, Pavilion, Fire Rings

Mt Desert Narrows Camping Resort
This coastal RV park in Maine offers panoramic views of the ocean.

1219 State Hwy 3,	(888) 408-5658	May 15 to October 10

Bar Harbor, ME 04609		
$42-$116	Military/Good Sam	No Restrictions
143 Spaces	Paved/Gravel	30Width/48Length
Internet, Showers, Laundry	Rentals, Pool, Rec. Hall	Game Room, Playground

Narrows Too Camping Resort
Enjoy the good life at this park. Overlooking Mt. Desert Island.

1150 Bar Harbor Rd., Trenton, ME 04605	(888) 459-2610	May 1 to October 21
$48-$129	Military/Good Sam	No Restrictions
206 Spaces	Paved/Gravel	30Width/68Length
Internet, Showers, Laundry	Rentals, Grocery, Cable	Boat Rental, Activities

Hadley's Point Campground
A fun place to camp with access to Acadia National Park and historic Bar Harbor.

33 Hadley Point Rd, Bar Harbor, ME 04609	(207) 288-4808 http://www.hadleyspoint.com/	May 15 to October 15
$39-$50	None	None
130 Spaces	Paved/Gravel	32Width/60Length
Internet, Showers, Laundry	Rentals, Pool, Firewood, Ice	Activities, Games, Tables

Meadowbrook Camping Area
Choose from sites in the sun or secluded in the woods.

33 Meadowbrook Rd, Phippsburg, ME 04562	(207) 443-4967 http://www.meadowbrookme.com/	May 1 to October 1
$38-$48	Military/Good Sam	No Restrictions
105 Spaces	Gravel	30Width/80Length
Internet, Showers, Laundry	Rentals, Pool, Boat Rental	Rec. Hall, Game Room

Shore Hills Campground
Located in the mid-region coastal area of Maine, known as the boating capital of the world.

553 Wiscasset Rd, Boothbay, ME 04537	(207) 633-4782 http://www.shorehills.com/	May 15 to October 14
$49-$57	Good Sam	Pet Breed
136 Spaces	Paved/Gravel	30Width/84Length
Internet, Showers, Laundry	Rentals, Lodge, Cable	Boat Rental, Rec. Hall

Seaview Campground
Located on the bay near the easternmost city in the United States

16 Norwood Rd,	(207) 853-4471	May 15 to October 13

Eastport, ME 04631	https://eastportmaine.com/	
May 15 to October 13	May 15 to October 13	May 15 to October 13
80 Spaces	Paved/Gravel	24Width/60Length
Internet, Showers, Laundry	Restaurant, Cable, Fishing	Playground, Games, Tables

Patten Pond Camping Resort

This peaceful resort offers you a classic East Coast vacation.

1470 Bucksport Rd, Ellsworth, ME 04605	(877) 667-7376	May 15 to October 14
$44-$70	Military/Good Sam	No Restrictions
130 Spaces	Gravel	26Width/70Length
Internet, Showers, Laundry	Rentals, Fishing, Cable	Paddle Boats, Playground

Forest Ridge Campground

A great base camp for your day trips to historic Bar Harbor and Acadia National Park.

3566 Loleta Road, Marienville, PA 16239	(814) 927-8340	May 1 to October 15
$50-$60	Military/Good Sam	Pet Quantity, Breed
60 Spaces	Gravel	30Width/65Length
Internet, Showers, Laundry	Cable, Rentals, RV Wash	Pool, Games, Pavilion

Cedar Haven Family Campground

The closest camping resort to downtown Freeport.

39 Baker Rd, Freeport, ME 04032	(207) 865-6254 cedarhavenfamilycampground.com/	May 1 to October 31
$60-$71	Good Sam	None
74 Spaces	Gravel	30Width/60Length
Internet, Shower, Laundry	Snack Bar, Rentals, Paddle Boats	Playground, Games

Blueberry Pond Campground

Spend your time in the deep green woods of Maine.

218 Poland Range Rd, Pownal, ME 04069	(207) 688-4421 blueberrycampground.com/	May 15 to October 30
$44	Military	None
29 Spaces	Gravel	40Width/60Length
Internet, Shower, Laundry	Pool, Rentals, Activities	Games, Playground

Red Apple Campground

The ideal camping location, just five minutes from the coast.

111 Sinnott Rd, Kennebunkport, ME 04046	(207) 967-4927 redapplecampground.com/	May 11 to October 8

$65-$69	None	None
131 Spaces	Paved	35Width/68Length
Internet, Shower, Laundry	Cable, Rentals, Guest Services	Playground, Games, Pavilion

Sandy Pines Campground

A beautiful wooded campground with resort-style amenities.

277 Mills Rd, Kennebunkport, ME 04046	(207) 967-2483 https://sandypinescamping.com/	May 11 to October 14
$55-$92	Military	Pet Quantity
101 Spaces	Gravel	30Width/60Length
Internet, Shower, Laundry	Gated, Rentals, Firewood, ATM	Pool, Boat Rentals, Patios

. Lazy Frog Campground

This family-friendly park offers a quiet and clean environment.

75 Cemetery Rd, Lebanon, ME 04027	(207) 457-1260 http://lazyfrogcampground.com/	May 18 to October 8
$45-$52	Good Sam	None
71 Spaces	Gravel	25Width/50Length
Internet, Shower, Laundry	Rec. Hall, Game Room, Rental	Activities, Playground, Game

Salmon Falls/Lebanon KOA

A classic campground just 30 minutes from Boston.

21 Flat Rock Bridge Road, Lebanon, ME 04027	(207) 339-9465 koa.com/campgrounds/salmon-falls/	May 5 to October 14
$59-$119	Military/Good Sam	Pet Quantity, Breed
221 Spaces	Gravel	30Width/40Length
Internet, Shower, Laundry	Firewood, Snack Bar, Ice	Supplies, Cable, Rentals

Sebasticook Lake Campground

Located on the shores of Sebasticook Lake in Central Maine.

52 Tent Village Rd, Newport, ME 04953	(207) 368-5047 https://www.mainervpark.com	May 11 to October 7
$33-$39	Good Sam	None
60 Spaces	Paved/Gravel	24Width/84Length
Internet, Shower, Laundry	Grocery, Rentals, Golf Carts	Game Room, Playground

Old Orchard Beach Campground

There are many things to do at this campground.

27 Ocean Park Rd, Old Orchard Beach, ME 04064	(207) 934-4477 https://www.gocamping.com/	May 1 to October 31
$55-$115	Military/Good Sam	No Restrictions
276 Spaces	Paved	40Width/80Length
Internet, Shower, Laundry	Cable, Grocery, Rec. Hall	Playground, Game Room

Wagon Wheel RV Resort

Minutes from the top attractions of Old Orchard Beach.

3 Old Orchard Rd, Old Orchard Beach, ME 04064	(207) 934-2160	May 1 to October 15
$50-$87	Military/Good Sam	No Restrictions
267 Spaces	Paved	30Width/60Length
Internet, Shower, Laundry	Gated, Splash Pad, Cable	Playground, Game Room

Wild Acres RV Resort

Enjoy picturesque grounds and a wonderful selection of amenities.

179 Saco Ave, Old Orchard Beach, ME 04064	(207) 934-2535	April 30 to October 13
$59-$106	Military/Good Sam	Pet Quantity, Breed
587 Spaces	Paved	30Width/60Length
Internet, Shower, Laundry	Fishing, Cable, Pool, Rentals	Activities, Pavilion, Games

Pinehirst RV Resort

Located deep in the woods, you can relax in a peaceful setting.

7 Oregon Ave, Old Orchard Beach, ME 04064	(866) 679-3819	May 1 to October 31
$78	Military/Good Sam	No Restrictions
537 Spaces	Paved	28Width/45Length
Internet, Shower, Laundry	Cable, Pool, Rec. Hall	Games, Tennis, Gym

Wassamki Springs Campground

Located on a private lake with one mile of sandy beach.

56 Saco St, Scarborough, ME 04074	(207) 839-4276 https://wassamkisprings.com/	May 1 to October 15
$40-$70	Military/Good Sam	Pet Breed
265 Spaces	Paved/Gravel	30Width/60Length
Internet, Shower, Laundry	Gated, Cable, Grocery	Playground, Pavilion, Games

Wild Duck Adult Campground

This park is for ages 21 and up only.

39 Dunstan Landing Rd, Scarborough, ME 04074	(207) 883-4432 wildduckcampground.com/	April 26 to October 21
$35-$70	Military/Good Sam	Age 21+ only
57 Spaces	Paved	20Width/80Length
Internet, Shower, Laundry	Firewood, Cable, Supplies	Fishing, Games, Fire Rings

Timberland Acres RV Park

Just minutes from Bar Harbor and Acadia National Park.

57 Bar Harbor Rd, Trenton, ME 04605	(207) 667-3600 timberlandacresrvpark.com/	May 11 to October 21
$41-$55	Military/Good Sam	No Restrictions
218 Spaces	Paved	30Width/100Length
Internet, Shower, Laundry	Pool, Rec. Hall, Game Room	Playground, Pavilion, Tables

Wells Beach Resort

Come stay along the inviting shores of Wells Beach.

1000 Post Rd, Wells, ME 04090	(800) 640-2267 https://wellsbeach.com/	May 15 to October 15
$57-$98	None	Pet Quantity
231 Spaces	Paved	30Width/65Length
Internet, Shower, Laundry	Grocery, Cable, Pool	Playground, Games, Gym

Sea-Vu Campground

This is an older campground but still offers an excellent experience when camping in Maine.

1733 Post Rd, Wells, ME 04090	(207) 646-7732 sea-vucampground.com/	May 10 to October 14
$50-$78	None	Pet Quantity
229 Spaces	Paved	40Width/60Length
Internet, Shower, Laundry	Pool, Cable, Grocery, Games	Playground, Mini Golf

York Beach Camper Park

This is a wonderful family park with activities for all ages.

Route 1A, 11 Cappy's Lane, York Beach, ME 03910	(207) 363-1343	May 22 to October 15
$49	Military	None
46 Spaces	Gravel	20Width/64Length
Internet, Shower, Laundry	Firewood, Playground, Games	Fire Rings, Tables, BBQ's

Libby's Oceanside Camp

The location and beaches of this park are the main attraction.

US Route 1A, York Harbor, York, ME	(207) 363-4171 libbysoceancamping.com/	May 15 to October 15
$65-$108	None	None
85 Spaces	Paved	20Width/65Length
Internet, Shower, Laundry	Supplies, Firewood	Cable, Fire Rings

Maryland

Maryland is a state of historic sites, big cities, and beautiful countryside. Choose to relax or view the city sites, but you also have the option of plenty of good outdoor activities depending on your interests.

Bar Harbor RV Park
Stay at a waterfront site and enjoy spectacular views.

4228 Birch Ave, Abingdon, MD 21009	(410) 679-0880 barharborrvpark.com/	All Year
$65-$75	None	Pet Breed
93 Spaces	Paved/Gravel	30Width/50Length
Internet, Shower, Laundry	Grocery, Fishing, Pool	Boat Rental, Playground

Brunswick Family Campground
Sit back and enjoy the nature around you or take part in outdoor activities.

100 S Maple Ave, Brunswick, MD 21716	(301) 834-9950 potomacrivercampground.com/	March 25 to November 1
$50-$65	Military/Good Sam	14 Day Max
48 Spaces	Paved/Gravel	25Width/60Length
Internet, Shower, Laundry	Supplies, Rentals, Horseshoes	Playground, Pavilion

Cherry Hill Park

The closest RV park to Washington D.C.

9800 Cherry Hill Rd, College Park, MD 20740	(301) 937-7116 https://www.cherryhillpark.com/	All Year
$77-$98	Military/Good Sam	Pet Breed
350 Spaces	Paved	30Width/70Length
Internet, Shower, Laundry	Cable, Golf Carts, Gated	Game Room, Playground

Merry Meadows Recreation Farm

This is your choice for camping in Maryland.

1523 Freeland Rd, Freeland, MD 21053	(410) 357-4088 merrymeadows.com/	February 1 to November 30
$32-$62	Military/Good Sam	Pet Breed
225 Spaces	Paved	25Width/75Length
Internet, Shower, Laundry	Rentals, Cable, Pool	Playground, Activities

Bay Shore Campground

Located on the scenic Chesapeake Bay.

4228 Eastern Neck RD, Rock Hall, MD 21661	(410) 639-7485 http://bayshorecamping.com/	All Year
$57-$80	None	Pet Breed
135 Spaces	Gravel	30Width/65Length
Internet, Shower, Laundry	Supplies, Golf Carts	Bike Rentals, Fire Rings

Yogi Bear's Jellystone Park Camp

This is a beautiful family-friendly park.

9550 Jellystone Park Way, Williamsport, MD 21795	(301) 223-7117 https://jellystonemaryland.com/	April 12 to December 1
$49-$163	None	14 Day Max Stay
155 Spaces	Paved/Gravel	40Width/75Length
Internet, Shower, Laundry	Rentals, Pool, Golf Carts	Activities, Games, Pavilion

Ramblin Pines Family Campground

This family campground is located in a quiet and peaceful wooded setting.

801 Hoods Mill Rd, Woodbine, MD 21797	(410) 795-5161	All Year
$65	Military/Good Sam	Pet Breed
200 Spaces	Paved	30Width/70Length
Internet, Shower, Laundry	Fishing, Rentals, Pool	Activities, Playground

Massachusetts

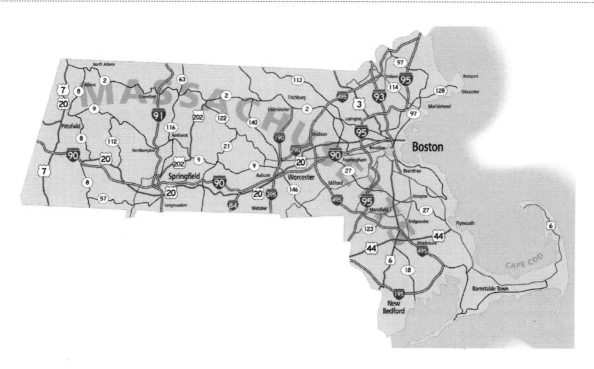

The state of Massachusetts features mountains, valleys, and beautiful coastlines. There are quaint villages and historical sites to visit. Above all, there is a range of enjoyable outdoor activities to take part in around the state

Circle CG Farm Campground
A quiet and full-service RV park with a western theme.

131 N Main St, Bellingham, MA 02019	(508) 966-1136 https://circlecgfarm.com/	All Year
$40-$60	Military/Good Sam	Pet Breed
150 Spaces	Paved	27Width/63Length
Internet, Showers, Laundry	Cable, Grocery, Game Room	Games, Mini Golf, Tennis

Shady Knoll Campground
There are plenty of water-based activities if that is your interest.

1709 Main St, Brewster, MA 02631	(508) 896-3002	May 15 to October 15
$30-$73	Good Sam	Pet Quantity
100 Spaces	Gravel	29Width/67Length
Internet, Showers, Laundry	Cable, Guest Services	Game Room, Playground

Campers Haven RV Resort

Enjoy a number of amenities and activities right within the park.

184 Old Wharf Rd, Dennis Port, MA 02639	(508) 398-2811	May 1 to October 31
$74-$110	Military/Good Sam	No Restrictions
270 Spaces	Paved	30Width/75Length
Internet, Showers, Laundry	Activities, Rentals, Cable	Games, Mini Golf, Tables

Cape Cod Campresort

Located in scenic Olde Cape Cod, you can relax at your site and enjoy the ocean.

176 Thomas B Landers Rd, East Falmouth, MA 02536	(508) 548-1458	May 1 to October 15
$69-$105	Military/Good Sam	Pet Breed
230 Spaces	Paved	30Width/80Length
Internet, Showers, Laundry	Pool, Fishing, Firewood	Gated, GameRoom, Rec.Hall

Atlantic Oaks

Just minutes from the Cape Cod Rail Trail.

3700 State Hwy, Eastham, MA 02642	(508) 255-1437 https://atlanticoaks.com/	May 1 to November 1
$61-$78	Good Sam	Pet Quantity
100 Spaces	Gravel	30Width/70Length
Internet, Showers, Laundry	Gated, Supplies, Firewood	Rec. Hall, Game Room

Normandy Farms Family Campground

Located deep in the woods between Boston and Cape Cod.

72 West St, Foxboro, MA 02035	(866) 673-2767 normandyfarms.com/	April 1 to November 30
$62-$118	Military/Good Sam	No Restrictions
387 Spaces	Gravel	40Width/60Length
Internet, Showers, Laundry	Guest Services, Fishing	Rentals, Games, Sauna

Cape Ann Camp Site

Located at the fishing port and whale watching capital of the world.

80 Atlantic St, Gloucester, MA 01930	(978) 283-8683 http://capeanncampsite.com/	May 15 to October 15
$58-$68	None	None
230 Spaces	Paved/Gravel	22Width/45Length
Restrooms, Showers, Supply	Firewood, Ice, Grocery	Fire Ring, Tables

Mt Greylock Campsite Park

Both family and pet-friendly, this park offers wooded sites.

15 Scott Rd, Lanesborough, MA 01237	(413) 447-9419 mtgreylockcampsitepark.com	April 15 to November 15
$40-$50	Good Sam	Pet Quantity
112 Spaces	Gravel	40Width/64Length
Internet, Showers, Laundry	RV Wash, Firewood, Gated	Rec. Hall, Playground

Boston Minuteman Campground

A peaceful getaway located close to everything.

264 Ayer Rd, Littleton, MA 01460	(978) 772-0042 minutemancampground.com/	May 4 to October 19
$51-$64	Military/Good Sam	No Restrictions
93 Spaces	Gravel	30Width/54Length
Internet, Shower, Laundry	Guest Services, Game Room	Playground, Games, Cable

Sunsetview Farm Camping Area

A family fun campground.

57 Town Farm Rd, Monson, MA 01057	(413) 267-9269 https://sunsetview.com/	April 15 to October 15
$45-$66	None	Pet Quantity
200 Spaces	Gravel	30Width/60Length
Showers, Laundry, Gated	Snack Bar, Firewood, Pool	Game Room, Activities

Pine Acres Family Camping Resort

Enjoy boating or fishing at the lake or simply relax at your site and enjoy nature.

203 Bechan Rd, Oakham, MA 01068	(508) 882-9509 https://pineacresresort.com/	All Year
$60-$95	Military	$60-$95
350 Spaces	Paved	30Width/60Length
Internet, Showers, Laundry	ATM, Gated, Firewood	Playground, Activities, Tennis

Lamb City Campground

Enjoy a peaceful setting or travel into the mountains for breathtaking views.

85 Royalston Rd, Phillipston, MA 01331	(978) 249-2049 http://lambcity.com/	All Year
$40-$55	None	Pet Breed
230 Spaces	Gravel	30Width/67Length
Internet, Showers, Laundry	Rentals, Grocery, Fishing	Firewood, Playground

Sandy Pond Campground

Surround yourself with green trees and crystal clear lake water.

834 Bourne Rd, Plymouth, MA 02360	(508) 759-9336 http://sandypond.com/	April 15 to October 15
$54-$63	Military/Good Sam	Pet Breed
225 Spaces	Gravel	38Width/63Length
Internet, Showers, Laundry	Rentals, Cable, Restaurant	Game Room, Rec. Hall

Pinewood Lodge Campground
Located in historic Plymouth between Boston and Cape Cod.

190 Pinewood Rd, Plymouth, MA 02360	(508) 746-3548 http://www.pinewoodlodge.com/	May 1 to October 30
$65-$90	Military	Pet Quantity
283 Spaces	Paved/Gravel	25Width/60Length
Internet, Showers, Laundry	Snack Bar, Cable, Lounge	Playground, Boat Rental

Black Bear Campground
Minutes to the beaches of Hampton and Salisbury.

54 Main St, Salisbury, MA 01952	(978) 462-3183 https://blackbearcamping.com/	May 15 to September 30
$45-$60	None	Pet Size
262 Spaces	Gravel	32Width/65Length
Internet, Showers, Laundry	Gated, Firewood, Cable, Pool	Game Room, Playground

Peters Pond RV Resort
One of the best campgrounds in the Cape Cod area.

185 Cotuit Rd, Sandwich, MA 02563	(508) 477-1777	April 15 to October 15
$45-$110	Military/Good Sam	Pet Quantity
362 Spaces	Paved	33Width/87Length
Internet, Showers, Laundry	Lounge, Cable, Firewood	Playground, Game Room

Old Chatham Road RV Campground
Luxury campsites in the heart of Cape Cod.

310 Old Chatham Rd., South Dennis, MA 02660	(866) 679-3823	April 15 to October 31
$62-$84	Good Sam	Pet Breed
301 Spaces	Paved	24Width/42Length
Internet, Showers, Laundry	Pool, Game Room, Ice	Playground, Pavilion, Tables

Pine Lake RV Resort
Located close to Old Sturbridge Village. Great facilities complete with wonderful amenities.

30 River Rd,	(508) 347-9570	All Year

Sturbridge, MA 01566	https://pinelakervresortandcottages.com/	
$40-$91	Military	Pet Quantity
363 Spaces	Paved/Gravel	24Width/45Length
Showers, Laundry, Ice	Firewood, Gated, Fishing, Snack Bar	Pool, Rec. Hall, Hot Tub

Sturbridge RV Resort
This quaint New England park is located in the woods.

19 Mashapaug Rd., Sturbridge, MA 01566	508) 347-7156	April 8 to October 25
$57-$76	Good Sam	None
175 Spaces	Paved/Gravel	30Width/70Length
Internet, Showers, Laundry	Grocery, Supplies, Gated	Game Room, Activities

Martha's Vineyard Family Campground
Get to this site by automobile ferry in just 45 minutes.

569 Edgartown Rd, Vineyard Haven, MA 02568	(508) 693-3772 https://campmv.com/	May 16 to October 16
$73-$78	Military/Good Sam	Pet Quantity
48 Spaces	Gravel	45Width/60Length
Internet, Showers, Laundry	Cable, Grocery, Firewood	Playground, Games, Rentals

Oak Haven Family Campground
Leave the crowds behind and enjoy your vacation.

22 Main St, Wales, MA 01081	(413) 245-7148 https://oakhavencampground.com/	May 1 to October 15
$44-$52	Military/Good Sam	Pet Quantity
140 Spaces	Gravel	36Width/60Length
Internet, Shower, Laundry	Gated, Supplies	Firewood, Ice, LP Gas

Cape Cod's Maple Park Campground
Centrally located in the Cape Cod area.

290 Glen Charlie Rd, East Wareham, MA 02538	(508) 295-4945 capecodmaplepark.com/	May 1 to October 15
$45-$88	None	None
424 Spaces	Paved/Gravel	30Width/70Length
Shower, Laundry, Gated	Supplies, Firewood, Golf Cart	Playground, Game Room

Michigan

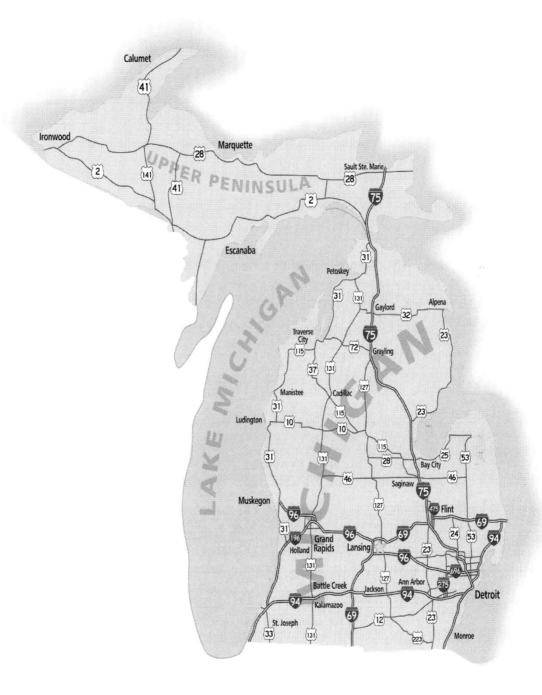

Michigan – Upper Peninsula

The Upper Peninsula of Michigan is set aside from the southern portion of Michigan by the Great Lakes. There are plenty of outdoor activities to enjoy while you stay at amenity-filled sites with excellent views.

Big Cedar Campground

The best place to set up camp while exploring the attractions of the eastern Upper Peninsula.

7936 State Highway M77, Germfask, MI 49836	(906) 586-6684 http://bigcedarcampground.com/	May 1 to October 20
$26-$31	Good Sam	Pet Breed
50 Spaces	Gravel	30Width/65Length
Shower, Laundry, Firewood	BoatRental, Games, Playground	Fire Rings, Pavilion

Summer Breeze Campground

Located along the northwestern edge of Iron Mountain.

W8576 Twin Falls Rd, Iron Mountain, MI 49801	(906) 774-7701 summerbreezecampground.com/	May 1 to October 15
$30-$34	Good Sam	None
70 Spaces	Gravel	40Width/100Length
Internet, Showers, Laundry	Grocery, Rentals, Pool	Playground, Pavilion

Manistique Lake Campground

This state of the art park is located on the shores of Lake Michigan.

320 Traders Point, Manistique, MI 49854	(906) 286-1696 manistiquelakeshorecampground.org/	May 1 to October 31
$40-$50	None	None
50 Spaces	Paved	60Width/60Length
Internet, Shower, Laundry	Playground, Pavilion, Firewood	Fire Rings, Tables

Indian Lake Travel Resort

Located in the natural woods with nearby sandy beaches and government land for hunting.

2025 County Road 455, Manistique, MI 49854	(906) 341-2807	May 16 to September 12
$28-$30	Good Sam	None
60 Spaces	Gravel	24Width/65Length
Internet, Shower, Laundry	Firewood, Supplies, Ice	Rec. Hall, Playground

Newberry Campground

Located in the heart of the eastern Upper Peninsula.

13724 State Highway M28, Newberry, MI 49868	(906) 293-5762 newberrycampground.com/	May 1 to October 15
$45-$55	Military/Good Sam	No Restrictions
77 Spaces	Gravel	30Width/58Length
Internet, Shower, Laundry	Snack Bar, Rentals, Games	Playground, Mini Golf, Tables

Kritter's Northcountry Campground

Surround yourself with the tranquil and wildlife-rich wilderness.

13209 State Highway M123, Newberry, MI 49868	(906) 293-8562 northcountrycampground.com/	May 1 to October 15
$40-$44	Military/Good Sam	No Restrictions
40 Spaces	Gravel	35Width/75Length
Internet, Shower, Laundry	Rentals, Firewood, Ice	Games, Pavilion, Fire Rings

Castle Rock Lakefront Mackinac Trail Camp Park

Located across from Castle Rock and featuring about a half-mile of lakefront.

2811 Mackinac Trl, Saint Ignace, MI 49781	(906) 643-9222 Website	May 15 to October 15
$38-$50	Military/Good Sam	No Restrictions
99 Spaces	Paved/Gravel	30Width/60Length
Internet, Shower, Laundry	Playground, Horseshoes	Games, Tables

Lakeshore RV Park

Close to all the major attractions and just minutes from downtown St Ignace.

W1226 Pointe Labarbe Rd, Saint Ignace, MI 49781	(906) 984-2097 Website	May 1 to October 15
$42	Military/Good Sam	No Restrictions
55 Spaces	Gravel	30Width/60Length
Internet, Shower, Laundry	Firewood, Ice, Games	Pavilion, Fire Rings

Michigan – North

Just over the Great Lakes from the Upper Peninsula lies the other half of the state of Michigan. The northern part of Michigan is filled with great seasonal spots to stay while you enjoy the great outdoors and all the activities it affords.

Chain O'Lakes Campground
A wonderful smaller park within minutes to many attractions in Northern Michigan.

7231 South M 88 Hwy, Bellaire, MI 49615	(231) 533-8432 http://chainolakescamp.com/	All Year
$41	Good Sam	None
49 Spaces	Paved/Gravel	30Width/100Length
Internet, Showers, Laundry	Grocery, Rentals, Pool, Ice	Firewood, Playground

Indigo Bluffs RV Park
Stay at a place where food, art, and events are in plentiful supply.

6760 W Empire Hwy, Empire, MI 49630	(231) 326-5050 https://www.indigobluffs.com/	May 15 to October 15
$30-$62	None	Pet Quantity
205 Spaces	Paved/Gravel	35Width/60Length
Internet, Showers, Laundry	Rentals, Firewood, Supplies	Pavilion, Rec. Hall, Patios

Countryside Campground
Get away from it all with fun and relaxation at this family-friendly campground.

805 Byfield Dr, Harrison, MI 48625	(989) 539-5468 countrysidecampgroundandcabins.com/	May 1 to October 15
$41-$44	Good Sam	None
73 Spaces	Gravel	35Width/70Length
Internet, Shower, Laundry	Rentals, Pool, Rec. Hall, Games	Pavilion, Fire Rings

Hidden Hill Family Campground
Enjoy camping in northern Michigan in a quiet, shady, and family-friendly setting.

300 North Clare Ave, Harrison, MI 48625	(989) 539-9372 hiddenhillcampground.com/	April 15 to October 31
$40-$42	Good Sam	Pet Quantity
40 Spaces	Gravel	50Width/60Length
Internet, Showers, Laundry	Supplies, Firewood, RVWash	Pavilion, Shuffleboard

Michigan Oaks Camping Resort

The place for a relaxing and fun-filled getaway.

2201 E M-68, Indian River, MI 49749	(231) 238-8259 https://michiganoaks.com/	May 1 to October 30
$40-$50	Military/Good Sam	Pet Quantity/Pet Breed
144 Spaces	Gravel	30Width/50Length
Showers, Laundry, Supplies	Rentals, Activities, Playground	Mini Golf, Pavilion, Games

Kalkaska RV Park

A quiet wooded park with serene walking trails.

580 M 72 E, Kalkaska, MI 49646	(231) 258-9863 http://kalkaskacampground.com/	April 21 to October 15
$39-$43	Good Sam	Pet Quantity
96 Spaces	Gravel	30Width/60Length
Internet, Showers, Laundry	Supplies, Firewood, Grocery	Playground, Pedal Carts

Poncho's Pond

The center of the park features a 3-acre pond stocked with fish.

5335 W Wallace Ln, Ludington, MI 49431	(888) 308-6602 https://poncho.com/	April 1 to October 31
$40-$60	None	Pet Quantity
265 Spaces	Paved	30Width/80Length
Internet, Showers, Laundry	Fishing, Golf Carts, Pool	Playground, Gym, Patios

Mackinaw Mill Creek Camping

Surround yourself with thousands of acres of wilderness.

9730 US Highway 23, Mackinaw City, MI 49701	(231) 436-5584 https://www.campmackinaw.com/	May 1 to October 25
$30-$84	None	Pet Breed
562 Spaces	Paved	40Width/70Length
Internet, Showers, SnackBar	Grocery, Firewood, Supplies	Playground, Game Room, Golf

Little River Casino Resort RV Park

Stay at deluxe sites with several amenities.

2700 Orchard Hwy, Manistee, MI 49660	(231) 723-1535 https://www.lrcr.com/	April 1 to November 1
$35-$50	Good Sam	None
95 Spaces	Paved	30Width/70Length
Internet, Showers, Laundry	SnackBar, Cable, Restaurant	Games, Playground, Gym

The Bluffs on Manistee Lake

This 55+ park is open year-round.

956 Tennessee Avenue, Manistee, MI 49660	231-887-4512 thebluffsonmanisteelake.com/	All Year
$40-$58	Good Sam	55+, No Class B, RV age, Pet Qty
36 Spaces	Paved	55Width/100Length
Showers, Laundry	Pool, Rec. Hall	Pickle Ball, Patios

Insta Launch Campground

An RV camp for all budgets and comforts.

20 Park Ave, Manistee, MI 49660	(231) 723-3901 http://instalaunch.com/	April 1 to November 15
$39	Good Sam	Pet Quantity
170 Spaces	Gravel	30Width/80Length
Internet, Showers, Laundry	Grocery, Rentals, Fishing	Rec.Hall, Firewood, SnackBar

Petoskey RV Resort

Located near the shores of Lake Michigan, this is your chance for a luxury vacation.

5505 Charlevoix Ave, Petoskey, MI 49770	(231) 348-2400	May 1 to October 31
$62-$120	Good Sam	Pet Quantity
135 Spaces	Paved	30Width/90Length
Internet, Showers, Laundry	Gated, Cable, Breakfast	Pool, Game Room, Tennis

Holiday Park Campground

A short ten-minute drive to downtown Traverse City.

4860 US Highway 31 S, Traverse City, MI 49685	(231) 943-4410 https://www.holidayparktc.com/	April 25 to October 25
$42-$70	Good Sam	None
217 Spaces	Paved	40Width/65Length
Internet, Showers, Laundry	Grocery, Firewood, Fishing	Rentals, Playground, Tables

Traverse Bay RV Resort

Here you can enjoy world-class amenities rivaled only by the beautiful scenery around you.

5555 M-72 East, Williamsburg, MI 49690	(231) 938-5800 http://traversebayrv.com/	May 1 to October 31
$69-$99	Good Sam	55+, No Class B or C, RV Age
217 Spaces	Paved	48Width/100Length
Internet, Showers, Laundry	Cable, Guest Services	RV Wash, Pool, Rec. Hall

Michigan – Central

Central Michigan is further from the Great Lakes, but still provides some great lakes for outdoor water activities. Besides, there are plenty of other outdoor experiences to have.

Lakeside Camp Park
A modern campground in a suburban setting. There is something for every age at this park.

13677 White Creek Ave, Cedar Springs, MI 49319	(616) 696-1735 http://www.lakesidecamppark.com/	April 28 to October 7
$37-$39	Good Sam	Pet Breed
155 Spaces	Paved	30Width/50Length
Internet, Shower, Laundry	Fishing Supplies, Rentals	Games, Pavilion

Yogi Bear's Jellystone Park
The number one priority here is family fun.

03403 64th Street, South Haven, MI 49090	(269) 637-6153 southhavenjellystone.com/	March 1 to December 31
$58-$83	Military/Good Sam	No Restrictions
196 Spaces	Paved/Gravel	25Width/65Length
Internet, Shower, Laundry	Snack Bar, Grocery, Pool	Activities, Games, Pavilion

Eastpointe RV Resort
This is the perfect place to have your vacation.

200 N Beechtree St, Grand Haven, MI 49417	(616) 414-8137 http://eastpointervresort.com/	May 1 to October 1
$58-$78	None	RV Age
121 Spaces	Paved	30Width/80Length
Internet, Shower, Laundry	Playground, Rec. Hall	Pavilion, Gym, Patios

Silver Creek RV Resort
This is your place for adventure.

1441 N 34th Ave, Mears, MI 49436	(231) 873-9200	April 1 to October 31
$38-$100	Military/Good Sam	No Restrictions
258 Spaces	Paved	50Width/80Length
Internet, Shower, Laundry	Grocery, Cable, Firewood	Games, Gym, Rec. Hall

Soaring Eagle Hideaway RV Park
Located next to a 42-acre lake, this is a great destination for water-based fun.

5514 E Airport Rd,	(989) 817-4803	April 1 to October 31

Mount Pleasant, MI 48858	soaringeaglehideaway.com/	
$35-$80	Military/Good Sam	No Restrictions
67 Spaces	Paved	30Width/65Length
Internet, Shower, Laundry	Lounge, Supplies, ATM, Ice	Snack Bar, Sauna, Rec. Hall

Lake Sch-nepp-a-ho Family Campground
This family fun park has plenty of beautiful sites to enjoy.

390 East Tyler Rd, Muskegon, MI 49445	(231) 766-2209	May 1 to September 30
$40-$55	Military/Good Sam	Pet Breed
84 Spaces	Gravel	30Width/50Length
Internet, Shower, Laundry	Snack Bar, Grocery	Rec. Hall, Boat Rental

Stony Haven Campground
Located at the heart of the western Michigan coastline.

8079 W Stony Lake Rd, New Era, MI 49446	(231) 861-5201 https://campstonyhaven.com/	May 1 to October 30
$30-$40	Military/Good Sam	No Restrictions
48 Spaces	Gravel	30Width/40Length
Internet, Shower, Laundry	Firewood, Rentals, Playground	Games, Pavilion, Tables

Ber Wa Ga Na Campground
Whether you enjoy outdoor sports or a leisurely hike, you'll find it here.

2601 W Sanilac Rd, Vassar, MI 48768	(989) 673-7125 berwaganacampground.com	May 1 to November 1
$36	Good Sam	None
184 Spaces	Gravel	25Width/60Length
Internet, Shower, Laundry	On-Site Meat Storage	Rec.Hall, Games, Firewood

Michigan – South

Although farther away from the lakes, southern Michigan still has plenty of water-based activities to enjoy. If the water isn't your thing, just consider some of the many other outdoor activities you can enjoy in the area.

Wayne County Fairgrounds RV Park
Offering daily, weekly, and extended stay options.

10871 Quirk Rd, Belleville, MI 48111	(734) 697-7002	All Year
$39-$44	Military/Good Sam	Pet Quantity
107 Spaces	Gravel	30Width/68Length
Internet, Showers, Laundry	Firewood, Ice, RV Wash	Rec. Hall, Pavilion

Eden Springs Park
Located next to a historic park and several other local attractions.

793 M 139, Benton Harbor, MI 49022	(269) 927-3302 http://www.edenspringspark.org/	All Year
$38-$45	Military/Good Sam	No Restrictions
43 Spaces	Gravel	24Width/80Length
Internet, Shower, Firewood	Supplies, Rentals	Playground, Games

Fuller's Clear Lake Resort
A little hideaway secret.

1622 E Clear Lake Rd, Buchanan, MI 49107	(269) 695-3785 http://fullersresort.com/	April 15 to November 1
$40-$75	None	Pet Breed
155 Spaces	Gravel	30Width/60Length
Internet, Showers, Laundry	Restaurant, Snack Bar	Guest Services, Rentals

Bear Cave Resort
Relax, have an adventure, or be a part of history at this resort.

4085 Bearcave Rd, Buchanan, MI 49107	(269) 695-3050	May 1 to October 31
$55	Military/Good Sam	Pet Quantity
124 Spaces	Gravel	24Width/40Length
Showers, Laundry, Gated	Fishing, Rentals, Pool	Playground, Games

Waffle Farm Campgrounds

Seven lakes within easy distance provide great fishing opportunities.

790 N Union City Rd Ste B, Coldwater, MI 49036	(517) 278-4315 http://wafflefarm.com/	April 15 to October 15
$35-$50	Good Sam	Pet Breed
355 Spaces	Gravel	25Width/75Length
Internet, Showers, Firewood	Fishing, Rentals, Playground	Games, Mini Golf, Tables

Hungry Horse Campground

Family camping at its best with a great outdoor experience.

2016 142nd Ave, Dorr, MI 49323	(616) 681-9843 hungryhorsecampground.com/	May 1 to October 15
$36-$45	Good Sam	None
98 Spaces	Paved/Gravel	30Width/70Length
Internet, Showers, Laundry	Rentals, Pool, Game Room	Pavilion, Pedal Carts

Apple Creek Campground

Plan a quiet or fun-filled weekend, you can have both here.

11185 Orban Rd, Grass Lake, MI 49240	(517) 522-3467 Website	April 15 to November 30
$35-$40	Military/Good Sam	No Restrictions
180 Spaces	Gravel	30Width/60Length
Internet, Showers, Laundry	Supplies, Rentals, Pool	Playground, Pavilion

Hidden Ridge RV Resort

Centrally located between Kalamazoo and Grand Rapids.

2306 12th St, Hopkins, MI 49328	(269) 682-8838	April 1 to October 30
$52-$67	Good Sam	RV Age, Pet Breed
335 Spaces	Paved	45Width/80Length
Internet, Showers, Laundry	Gated, ATM, Firewood	Golf Carts, Game Room

Lansing Cottonwood Campground

A clean and friendly park where you're guaranteed to have a great time.

5339 Aurelius Rd, Lansing, MI 48911	(517) 393-3200 lansingcottonwoodcampground.com/	April 15 to October 29
$29-$39	None	None
110 Spaces	Gravel	30Width/60Length
Internet, Shower, Laundry	Grocery, ATM, Firewood, Ice	Rentals, Game Room

Camp Lord Willing RV Park

Nightly, weekly, and monthly rates available.

1600 Stumpmier Rd, Monroe, MI 48162	(734) 243-2052 https://camplordwilling.com/	All Year
$40-$50	Military/Good Sam	No Restrictions
100 Spaces	Paved/Gravel	40Width/80Length
Internet, Shower, Laundry	Firewood, Ice, Supplies	Playground, Games, Tables

Indian Creek Camp

This is your best place for a family camping experience in Southern Michigan.

9415 Tangent Rd, Tecumseh, MI 49286	(517) 423-5659 indiancreekcampingmichigan.com/	April 15 to October 15
$45-$60	Military/Good Sam	None
251 Spaces	Gravel	25Width/70Length
Internet, Shower, Laundry	Rentals, Pool, Firewood, Ice	Playground, Fire Rings

Detroit/Greenfield RV Park

Relax at your site or explore the surrounding area.

6680 Bunton Rd, Ypsilanti, MI 48197	(734) 482-7722 http://detroitgreenfield.com/	April 1 to October 31
$48-$52	None	Pet Breed
193 Spaces	Gravel	30Width/60Length
Internet, Shower, Laundry	Firewood, Grocery, Rentals	Games, Pavilion, Mini Golf

Minnesota

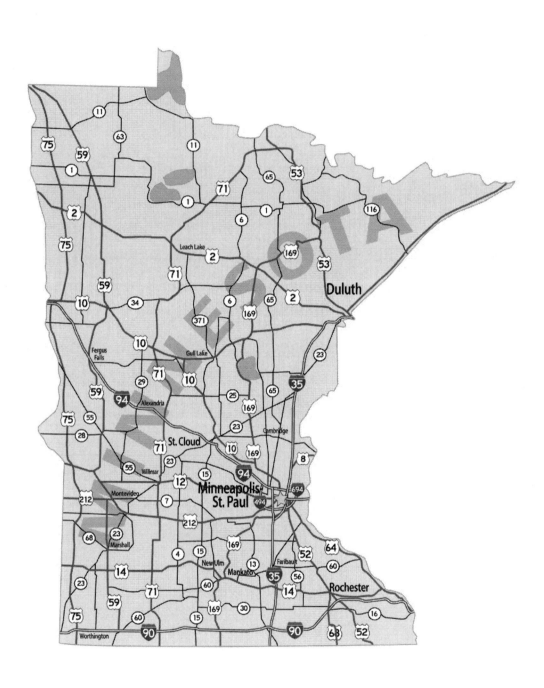

Minnesota – North

Northern Minnesota is a great place to get away from city life and get back to nature. There are plenty of opportunities to simply relax and enjoy nature, but there are also plenty of activities you can do in the great outdoors.

Royal Oaks RV Park
Convenient location in a quiet area near the headwaters of the Mississippi.

2860 Washington Ave SE, Bemidji, MN 56601	(218) 751-8357 https://royaloaksrvpark.com/	April 15 to October 15
$42-$47	Good Sam	None
64 Spaces	Gravel	30Width/80Length
Internet, Showers, Laundry	Supplies, Firewood, Grocery	Games, Playground

Stony Point Resort RV Park
A brief description.

5510 US 2 NW, Cass Lake, MN 56633	(218) 335-6311 stonyptresortcasslake.com	May 1 to October 15
$40-$45	Military/Good Sam	No Restrictions
175 Spaces	Paved	30Width/85Length
Internet, Showers, Laundry	Firewood, ATM, Supplies	Grocery, Fishing, Sauna

A-J Acres
A safe, gated community where you can relax among woods, flowers, trails, and lakes.

1300 195th St E, Clearwater, MN 55320	(320) 558-2847 ajacrescampground.com/	May 1 to October 1
$43	Good Sam	None
200 Spaces	Gravel	35Width/70Length
Showers, Laundry, Gated	Grocery, Rec. Hall, Activities	Playground, Fire Rings

St Cloud/Clearwater RV Park
Get away from it all and truly reconnect with nature at this park.

2454 County Road 143, Clearwater, MN 55320	(320) 558-2876 https://www.time2camp.com/	May 1 to October 15
$43-$52	Military/Good Sam	No Restrictions
100 Spaces	Gravel	30Width/70Length
Internet, Showers, Laundry	Firewood, Grocery, Rentals	Games, Pavilion, Mini Golf

Duluth Indian Point Campground
Stay high above Spirit Bay.

7000 Pulaski St,	(855) 777-0652	May 1 to October 20

Duluth, MN 55807	duluthindianpointcampground.com/	
$39-$61	None	Pet Breed
82 Spaces	Gravel	30Width/80Length
Internet, Firewood, Ice	Showers, Snack Bar, Laundry	Pavilion, Fire Rings

Oak Park Kampground
Easy access off the interstate.

9561 County Rd 8 NW, Garfield, MN 56332	(320) 834-2345 oakparkcampground.com/	April 15 to October 1
$40-$43	Military/Good Sam	Pet Breed
60 Spaces	Gravel	45Width/70Length
Showers, Firewood, Supplies	Grocery, Pool, Paddle Boats	Rec. Hall, Playground

St Croix River Resort
A beautiful family vacation retreat.

40756 Grace Lake Rd, Hinckley, MN 55037	(320) 655-0016 midwestoutdoorresorts.com/	May 1 to October 20
$50-$70	Good Sam	None
168 Spaces	Gravel	30Width/50Length
Showers, Laundry, Firewood	Rentals, Pool, Rec. Hall	Playground, Pavilion

Grand Casino Hinckley RV Resort
A casino nearby means you have plenty of amenities.

1326 Fire Monument Rd, Hinckley, MN 55037	(800) 472-6321 https://grandcasinomn.com	All Year
$29-$79	Military/Good Sam	No Restrictions
271 Spaces	Paved	35Width/65Length
Internet, Showers, Laundry	Gated, Supplies, Firewood	Rentals, Golf, Games

Camp S'more Campground
Overnight, weekly, monthly, and seasonal camping are available here.

24797 Us 71, Long Prairie, MN 56347	(320) 732-2517 http://www.campsmoremn.com/	May 1 to October 15
$34	Good Sam	None
26 Spaces	Gravel	40Width/50Length
Showers, Firewood	Rec. Hall, Playground	Games, Fire Rings

Big Pines RV Park
A scenic park along the banks of Fish Hook River.

501 Central Ave S,	(218) 237-8815	May 1 to September 30

Park Rapids, MN 56470	https://www.sceniclodging.com/	
$45-$55	Good Sam	None
60 Spaces	Gravel	50Width/100Length
Internet, Showers, Laundry	Firewood, Cable, Rec. Hall	Game Room, Rentals

St Cloud Campground

Enjoy the park amenities or enjoy the activities in the outdoor area surrounding the park.

2491 2nd St SE, Saint Cloud, MN 56304	(320) 251-4463 stcloudcampground.com/	May 1 to October 12
$42-$46	Good Sam	None
95 Spaces	Gravel	35Width/70Length
Internet, Showers, Laundry	Supplies, Firewood, Rec. Hall	Snack Bar, Playground

Wildwood Campground

Stay here and choose your adventure.

20078 Lake Blvd, Shafer, MN 55074	(651) 465-7162 wildwoodcamping.com	May 1 to October 15
$50-$55	Military	Pet Quantity
200 Spaces	Gravel	50Width/70Length
Internet, Showers, Firewood	Grocery, Pool, Game Room	Playground, Games

Trails RV Park

A full-service park in Southern Minnesota in the Chippewa National Forest.

9424 State 371 NW, Walker, MN 56484	(218) 547-1138 http://www.trailsrvpark.com/	May 1 to October 6
$47-$52	Good Sam	No Class C
106 Spaces	Gravel	50Width/130Length
Showers, Laundry, Firewood	Pool, Rec. Hall, Game Room	Playground, Pavilion

Minnesota – South

Southern Minnesota is a wonderful place to stay where you can sit back and relax for your vacation. There is still plenty to do if you choose to get up and get active. Also, a great place to see history and make memories.

Lebanon Hills Campground
The perfect place for a weekend getaway or a longer vacation.

12100 Johnny Cake Ridge Rd, Apple Valley, MN 55124	(651) 688-1376 co.dakota.mn.us	May 1 to October 20
$22-$40	None	14 Day Max Stay
93 Spaces	Paved/Gravel	30Width/50Length
Internet, Showers, Laundry	Firewood, Playground	Fire Rings, Ice, Tables

Camp Faribo
A family-oriented park for both a fun adventure and relaxation.

21851 Bagley Ave, Faribault, MN 55021	(507) 332-8453 http://campfaribo.com/	April 15 to October 15
$40-$45	Good Sam	Pet Quantity
71 Spaces	Paved/Gravel	30Width/60Length
Internet, Showers, Laundry	Rentals, Pool, Rec. Hall	Game Room, Pavilion

Prairie View RV Park
Stay and play at this park that has room for the largest RVs.

5616 Prairies Edge Ln, Granite Falls, MN 56241	(866) 293-2121 prairiesedgecasino.com/	April 15 to October 15
$30-$35	None	None
42 Spaces	Paved	50Width/75Length
Internet, Showers, Laundry	Rentals, Pool, Game Room	Playground, Games, Sauna

Ham Lake Resort
Stay just 30 minutes from the Twin Cities.

2400 Constance Blvd NE, Ham Lake, MN 55304	(763) 434-9492 midwestoutdoorresorts.com/	May 1 to October 31
$45	None	Pet Quantity
135 Spaces	Gravel	35Width/60Length
Internet, Showers, Laundry	Firewood, Grocery, Rentals	Playground, Activities

Money Creek Haven
When you're ready, there are plenty of outdoor activities to enjoy.

18502 County 26,	(507) 896-3544	April 15 to October 15

Houston, MN 55943	https://moneycreekhaven.com/	
$35-$50	Good Sam	None
205 Spaces	Paved/Gravel	55Width/55Length
Internet, Showers, Laundry	Rentals, Pool, Game Room	Activities, Games, Tables

Eagle Cliff Campground
This is your place to relax and rejuvenate.

35455 State Highway 16, Lanesboro, MN 55949	(507) 467-2598 https://eagle-cliff.com/	April 15 to October 20
$32-$40	Good Sam	None
236 Spaces	Gravel	45Width/55Length
Internet, Showers, Laundry	Grocery, Firewood, Ice	Playground, Activities

River View Campground
Stay for a fun and friendly getaway.

2554 SW 28th St, Owatonna, MN 55060	(507) 451-8050 riverviewcampgroundminnesota.com/	April 15 to October 15
$27-$53	Good Sam	None
115 Spaces	Gravel	25Width/60Length
Internet, Shower, Laundry	Rentals, Pool, Rec. Hall, Playground	Grocery, Games, Patios

The Old Barn Resort
Featuring a golf course and a restaurant, this is a great place to spend your vacation.

24461 Heron Rd, Preston, MN 55965	(507) 467-2512 Website	April 1 to October 31
$36-$51	Military/Good Sam	No Restrictions
246 Spaces	Gravel	30Width/60Length
Showers, ATM, Golf Carts	Restaurant, Firewood, Ice	Golf, Games, Playground

Big River Resort
Comfort and convenience are the focus of your stay here.

1110 Hiawatha Dr. E, Wabasha, MN 55981	(651) 565-9932 http://www.bigriverresort.com/	April 15 to October 15
$55-$60	Good Sam	None
30 Spaces	Gravel	12Width/90Length
Internet, Shower, Laundry	Cable, Rentals, Firewood	Rec.Hall, Patios, Fire Rings

Mississippi

Mississippi – East

Bay Hide Away RV Park
This park is tucked away but still puts you close to everything.

8360 Lakeshore Rd, Bay Saint Louis, MS 39520	(228) 466-0959	All Year
$44-$60	Military/Good Sam	Pet Breed
40 Spaces	Gravel	30Width/65Length
Internet, Showers, Laundry	Supplies, Firewood, Ice	Pool, Playground, Pavilion

Hollywood Casino RV Park
When you stay here, you have access to a golf course, three restaurants, and a casino.

711 Hollywood Blvd, Bay St. Louis, MS 39520	(866) 758-2591 hollywoodgulfcoast.com/	All Year
$35-$49	Good Sam	None
100 Spaces	Paved	25Width/60Length
Internet, Showers, Laundry	Lounge, Fishing, Pool	Game Room, Golf, Pavilion

Cajun RV Park
Come enjoy this beautiful RV park across from a beach.

1860 Beach Boulevard, Biloxi, MS 39531	(228) 388-5590 http://www.cajunrvpark.com/	All Year
$45-$89	Military/Good Sam	RV Age, Pet Breed
130 Spaces	Gravel	24Width/60Length
Internet, Showers, Laundry	Cable, Breakfast, Pool	Rec. Hall, Activities

Boomtown Casino RV Park
Stay at this smaller park and take the trolley to the casino.

676 Bayview Ave, Biloxi, MS 39530	(228) 435-7000 boomtownbiloxi.com/	All Year
$29-$45	Good Sam	None
50 Spaces	Paved	22Width/90Length
Internet, ATM, Snack Bar	Restaurant, Cable, Lounge	Guest Services, Tables

Mazalea Travel Park
Close to a casino, beaches, shopping, and restaurants.

8220 W Oaklawn Rd, Biloxi, MS 39532	(228) 392-8575 http://southernrvparks.com/	All Year
$32	Good Sam	Restrictions
140 Spaces	Paved	25Width/80Length
Internet, Showers, Laundry	Grocery, Supplies, Cable	Rec. Hall, Playground

Oaklawn RV Park
When you stay here, you get a safe and pleasant environment.

8400 W Oaklawn Rd, Biloxi, MS 39532	(228) 392-1233 https://oaklawnrvpark.net/	All Year
$30-$32	Military/Good Sam	Pet Breed
49 Spaces	Paved	22Width/60Length
Internet, Showers	Laundry	Ice, Tables

Indian Point RV Resort
Conveniently located between Mobile and New Orleans, just minutes from Biloxi.

1600 Indian Point Pkwy, Gautier, MS 39553	(228) 497-1011 http://www.indianpt.com	All Year
$25-$32	Good Sam	Pet Breed
175 Spaces	Paved	35Width/75Length
Internet, Showers, Laundry	LP Gas, Restaurant, Cable	Rec. Hall, Rentals, Pool

Frog Hollow Campground
Offering the best place to rest and relax in Eastern Mississippi.

601 Hwy 7 N, Grenada, MS 38901	(662) 226-9042 https://frog-hollow.com/	All Year
$32-$33	Good Sam	Pet Quantity, Pet Breed
49 Spaces	Gravel	30Width/70Length
Internet, Showers, Supplies	LP Gas, Ice, Rentals	Rec. Hall, Games, Patios

Campgrounds of the South
Relax on the beach, head into Gulfport for shopping and dining.

10406 Three Rivers Rd, Gulfport, MS 39503	(228) 539-2922 campgroundsofthesouth.com/	All Year
$28	Military, Good Sam	Pet Breed
140 Spaces	Paved	25Width/70Length
Internet, Showers, Laundry	Cable, RV Service	RV Wash, Rec. Hall

Baywood RV Park
Stay close to casinos, beaches, shopping, and restaurants.

1100 Cowan Rd, Gulfport, MS 39507	(228) 896-4840 http://southernrvparks.com/	All Year
$32-$34	Good Sam	Pet Quantity, Breed
114 Spaces	Paved	24Width/60Length
Internet, Showers, Laundry	Supplies, Grocery, Cable	Pool, Rec. Hall, Playground

Countryside RV Park

Stay in a warm and comfortable environment.

20278 Highway 49, Saucier, MS 39574	(228) 539-0807 Website	All Year
$28	Military/Good Sam	RV Age, Pet Breed
32 Spaces	Gravel	30Width/75Length
Internet, Showers, Laundry	Snack Bar, Cable, Lounge	Pool, Rec. Hall, Pavilion

Okatoma Resort

A peaceful and relaxing environment awaits you.

221 Okatoma River Rd, Hattiesburg, MS 39401	(601) 520-6631 https://okatomaresort.com/	All Year
$38	Military/Good Sam	RV Age, Pet Quantity
70 Spaces	Gravel	30Width/60Length
Showers, Laundry, Firewood	Grocery, Rentals, Pool	Rec. Hall, Playground

Memphis Jellystone Camp Resort

Stay just minutes from the wonderful city of Memphis.

1400 Audubon Point Dr, Horn Lake, MS 38637	(662) 280-8282 memphisjellystone.com/	All Year
$50-$70	Military	Pet Quantity
135 Spaces	Paved	32Width/70Length
Internet, Showers, Laundry	Firewood, Grocery, Cable	Pool, Rec. Hall, Pavilion

Little Black Creek Campground

Stay at one of the most beautiful campgrounds in Mississippi.

2159 Little Black Creek Rd, Lumberton, MS 39455	(601) 794-2957 http://lbccampground.com/	All Year
$30-$33	Military/Good Sam	RV Age
124 Spaces	Paved	25Width/60Length
Showers, Firewood, Ice	Fishing, Hunting Facilities	Pavilion, Games, Tables

Benchmark Coach & RV Park

A clean and quiet park for you to enjoy your vacation.

6420 Dale Dr, Marion, MS 39342	(601) 483-7999 http://benchmarkrv.net/	All Year
$30-$33	Military/Good Sam	Pet Breed
35 Spaces	Gravel	25Width/75Length

| Internet, Showers, Laundry | Ice, Cable, LP Gas | RV Wash, Tables |

Green Tree RV Park
This high-quality service park is a great place to stay.

2169 Highway 80, Morton, MS 39117	(601) 278-4823 greentreeparkms.net/	All Year
$30-$35	Good Sam	RV Age, Pet Breed
19 Spaces	Gravel	27Width/70Length
Internet, Laundry, RV Wash	Guest Services, Games	Pavilion, Fire Rings

Sun Roamers RV Resort
A beautiful park located among the tall pines.

41 Mississippi Pines Blvd, Picayune, MS 39466	(601) 798-5818 http://www.sunroamers.com/	All Year
$35-$38	Military/Good Sam	Pet Quantity
154 Spaces	Paved	25Width/60Length
Internet, Showers, Laundry	Rentals, Pool, Playground	Pavilion, Gym, Mini Golf

EZ Daze RV Park
First-class amenities ensure you'll enjoy your stay.

536 WE Ross Pkwy, Southaven, MS 38671	(662) 342-7720	All Year
$50-$65	Military/Good Sam	Pet Breed
136 Spaces	Paved	25Width/75Length
Storm Shelter, Internet	Firewood, Cable, Pool	Laundry, Gym, Playground

Southaven RV Park
Located on the Tennessee and Mississippi state line.

270 Stateline Rd W, Southaven, MS 38671	(662) 393-8585 https://southavenrvpark.com/	All Year
$45	Military/Good Sam	Pet Breed
44 Spaces	Paved	20Width/65Length
Internet, Showers, Laundry	LP Gas, Ice, Cable	RV Wash, Patios

Campground at Barnes Crossing
A quiet, secluded, and beautiful park.

125 Campground Rd, Tupelo, MS 38804	(662) 844-6063 http://cgbarnescrossing.com/	All Year

$40-$45	Good Sam	None
55 Spaces	Paved	30Width/68Length
Internet, Showers, Laundry	Cable, Guest Services	Horseshoes, Games, Tables

Natchez Trace RV Park

Stay at the beautiful hills of the Natchez Trace Parkway.

189 County Road 506, Shannon, MS 38868	(662) 767-8609 http://natcheztracervpark.com/	All Year
$29	Military/Good Sam	No Restrictions
25 Spaces	Gravel	25Width/65Length
Showers, Laundry, Firewood	Ice, RV Wash, Pool	Rec. Hall, Games

Mississippi – West

Western Mississippi is on the other side of the mighty Mississippi River. There are some great outdoor activities for those who want an adventure. Otherwise, you can simply relax and get back to enjoying nature.

Sunset Marina and RV Park
Located on the beautiful Ross Barnett Reservoir.

4269 Highway 43 N, Brandon, MS 39047	(601) 829-1513 sunsetmarinaat43.com/	All Year
$35	Military/Good Sam	No Restrictions
89 Spaces	Paved	32Width/60Length
Showers, Laundry, RV Wash	Patios	Tables

Movietown RV Park
This is your home away from home.

109 Movietown Dr, Canton, MS 39046	(601) 859-7990	All Year
$30	Military/Good Sam	No Restrictions
114 Spaces	Paved/Gravel	45Width/65Length
Internet, Showers, Laundry	Guest Services, Rentals	Playground, Horseshoes

Springridge RV Park
Located near historic Vicksburg.

499 Springridge Rd, Clinton, MS 39056	(601) 924-0947 http://springridgemhp.com/	All Year
$33	Military/Good Sam	Pet Breed
92 Spaces	Paved	20Width/55Length
Showers, Laundry	Snack Bar, Pool	Ice, Rec. Hall, Playground

Plantation RV Park
The closest RV park to the historic town of Natchez.

Highway 61S, Natchez, MS 39120	(601) 442-5222	All Year
$35-$40	Military/Good Sam	No Restrictions
38 Spaces	Paved	25Width/65Length
Internet, Showers, Laundry	Guest Services, Patios	Fire Rings, Tables

Yogi on the Lake

This is your premier family destination in the south.

143 Campground Rd, Pelahatchie, MS 39145	(601) 854-6621 https://jellystonems.com/	All Year
$39-$78	Military/Good Sam	Pet Breed
164 Spaces	Paved/Gravel	30Width/50Length
Showers, Laundry, Gated	Firewood, Restaurant	Rentals, Rec. Hall, Pool

River Town Campground

Close enough to have fun in town, but far enough away to relax and enjoy nature.

5900 Highway 61 S, Vicksburg, MS 39180	(601) 630-9995 rivertown-campground.com/	All Year
$31	Military/Good Sam	RV Age
109 Spaces	Gravel	45Width/62Length
Internet, Showers, Laundry	Supplies, RV Wash, Ice	Pool, Rec. Hall, Playground

Magnolia RV Park Resort

This park focuses on service and quality.

211 Miller St, Vicksburg, MS 39180	(601) 631-0388 magnoliarvparkresort.com/	All Year
$26-$31	Military/Good Sam	No Restrictions
66 Spaces	Paved/Gravel	20Width/65Length
Internet, Showers, Laundry	Supplies, Ice, LP Gas	Pool, Playground, Tables

Ameristar Casino & RV Park

Offering wonderful services and amenities near the Mississippi River.

725 Lucy Bryson St, Vicksburg, MS 39180	(601) 638-1000	All Year
$30-$35	Military/Good Sam	No Restrictions
67 Spaces	Paved	25Width/55Length
Internet, Showers, Laundry	Cable, RV Wash, Pool	Gym, Tables, Casino

Missouri

Missouri – North

Missouri offers some great historical areas among rolling plains. Stay at an RV park in the northern part of Missouri, and you can choose between relaxing, having an outdoor adventure, or stepping back in time.

Cozy C RV Campground
Located among the hills close to the Mississippi River.

16733 Highway 54, Bowling Green, MO 63334	(573) 324-3055 cozyccampground.com	All Year
$32	Good Sam	Pet Breed
45 Spaces	Gravel	25Width/60Length
Internet, Showers, Laundry	Supplies, Firewood, LP Gas	Rec. hall, Games, Pavilion

Lazy Day Campground
The perfect place to have a quiet and relaxing vacation.

214 Highway J, Danville, MO 63361	(573) 564-2949 lazydaycampground.com/	All Year
$39	Military/Good Sam	No Restrictions
62 Spaces	Gravel	26Width/70Length
Internet, Showers, Laundry	Firewood, Supplies, Ice	Pool, Rec. Hall, Playground

Eagle Ridge RV Park
A quiet and quaint little RV park oasis.

22708 W 182nd St, Eagleville, MO 64442	(660) 867-5518 https://eagleridgervpark.webs.com/	March 1 to November 30
$35	Military/Good Sam	No Restrictions
23 Spaces	Gravel	24Width/70Length
Showers, Laundry, Ice	Pool, Paddle Boats, Games	Shuffleboard, Fire Rings

Trailside RV Park
A quiet place to relax and close to all the popular attractions.

1000 R D Mize Rd, Grain Valley, MO 64029	(800) 748-7729 http://trailsidervpark.com/	All Year
$38-$40	None	Pet Size, PetBreed, 28 Day Max
69 Spaces	Paved	24Width/65Length
Internet, Showers, Laundry	Grocery, Pool, Rec. Hall	Playground, Games

Jonesburg Gardens Campground

Close proximity to a number of outdoor activities.

15 Highway E, Jonesburg, MO 63351	(636) 488-5630 jonesburggardenscampground.com	All Year
$36	Military/Good Sam	None
45 Spaces	Gravel	24Width/60Length
Internet, Shower, Laundry	Fishing, Rentals, Pool	Paddle Boats, Playground

Mark Twain Landing

A great family park with a playland and water park.

42819 Landing Ln, Monroe City, MO 63456	(573) 735-9422 https://marktwainlanding.com/	All Year
$55-$78	Military/Good Sam	Pet Breed
65 Spaces	Paved	42Width/65Length
Internet, Showers, Laundry	Gated, ATM, Supplies, Ice	Firewood, Snack Bar, Pool

Country Gardens RV Park

Easy access on and off the interstate means you can easily access area attractions.

7089 Outer Rd, Odessa, MO 64076	(816) 633-8720 countrygardensrv.com/	All Year
$32-$43	Good Sam	None
45 Spaces	Paved	28Width/70Length
Internet, Showers	Laundry, LP Gas	Grocery, Rec. Hall

Peculiar Park Place

Conveniently located near the Kansas City area.

22901 SE Outer Rd, Peculiar, MO 64078	(816) 779-6300 peculiarparkplacervpark.com/	All Year
$34	Military/Good Sam	Pet Breed
81 Spaces	Gravel	30Width/75Length
Internet, Showers, Laundry	RV Service, Games, Ice	Pavilion, Patios, Tables

Basswood Resort

A nice, secluded RV resort with a country-modern atmosphere.

15880 Interurban Rd, Platte City, MO 64079	(816) 858-5556 https://basswoodresort.com/	All Year
$56	Good Sam	Pet Breed
149 Spaces	Paved	24Width/80Length
Internet, Showers, Laundry	ATM, Supplies, LP Gas	Firewood, Grocery, SnackBar

Sundermeier RV Park

Historic St Charles allows you to relieve the spirit of early America.

111 Transit St, Saint Charles, MO 63301	(636) 940-0111 https://sundermeierrvpark.com/	All Year
$59	Military/Good Sam	Pet Breed
110 Spaces	Paved	28Width/80Length
Internet, Showers, Laundry	Supplies, LP Gas, Rec. Hall	Patios, Tables

AOK Campground

Conveniently located near the interstate.

12430 County Road 360, Saint Joseph, MO 64505	(816) 324-4263 https://aokcamping.com/	All Year
$28-$32	Military/Good Sam	Pet Breed
53 Spaces	Gravel	24Width/75Length
Internet, Showers, Laundry	Firewood, Supplies, Pool	Playground, Games, Gym

370 Lakeside Park

Leave your worries behind and enjoy nature at this park.

1000 Lakeside Park Dr, Saint Peters, MO 63376	(636) 387-5253 stpetersmo.net/	All Year
$30-$45	None	None
75 Spaces	Paved	35Width/71Length
Internet, Showers, Laundry	Firewood, Supplies, Rentals	Pavilion, Patios, Fire Rings

Missouri – Central

Just minutes from Columbia, Rock Bridge Memorial State Park gives visitors the chance to scramble, hike, and bicycle through a scenic environment – and lets them peek into Missouri's underworld.

Cottonwoods RV Park
Located in the heart of Central Missouri.

5170 N Oakland Gravel Rd, Columbia, MO 65202	(573) 474-2747 https://cottonwoodsrvpark.com/	All Year
$40	Military/Good Sam	No Restrictions
97 Spaces	Paved	30Width/60Length
Internet, Showers, Laundry	Supplies, Firewood, Ice	Grocery, Games, Rec.Hall

Cedar Creek Resort
The ideal vacation destination that allows you to spend time with your family.

3251 Pinetree Dr, Columbia, MO 65201	(573) 239-8340 https://cedarcreekresort.org/	All Year
$48	Good Sam	None
37 Spaces	Gravel	27Width/80Length
Internet, Showers, Laundry	Rentals, Games, Rec. Hall	Pavilion, Patios, Tables

Boiling Spring Campground
Family camping and fishing opportunities abound here.

18700 Cliff Rd, Dixon, MO 65459	(573) 759-7294 https://www.bscoutdoors.com/	May 15 to October 15
$35	Military/Good Sam	No Restrictions
38 Spaces	Gravel	26Width/65Length
Internet, Showers, Laundry	Grocery, Firewood, Fishing	Boat Rentals, Games, Tables

Riverview RV Park
Located in the hills along the Osage River.

398 Woodriver Rd, Lake Ozark, MO 65049	(573) 365-1122 http://www.riverviewrvparkllc.com/	All Year
$35	Military/Good Sam	No Restrictions
74 Spaces	Gravel	34Width/45Length
Internet, Shower, Laundry	Snack Bar, Firewood, LP Gas	Playground, Pavilion

Hidden Valley Outfitters
Located along Niangua River beside Bennett Spring State Park.

27101 Marigold Dr, Lebanon, MO 65536	(417) 533-5628 http://www.hvoutfitters.com/	March 1 to October 31
$34-$39	Military/Good Sam	No Restrictions
115 Spaces	Gravel	40Width/52Length
Shower, Laundry, Firewood	Snack Bar, Grocery	Pavilion, Games

Missouri – Southwest

The southwest portion of Missouri includes the popular Branson destination with numerous entertainment options. Outside of Branson, there is no shortage of beautiful places where you can get back to nature and enjoy outdoor adventures.

Musicland Kampground

Located in the heart of Branson within walking distance to some great entertainment.

116 Gretna Rd, Branson, MO 65616	(417) 334-0848 musiclandkampground.com/	March 1 to December 30
$48	Military/Good Sam	No Restrictions
102 Spaces	Paved	24Width/60Length
Internet, Showers, Laundry	Gated, Rentals, Pool	Rec.Hall, Playground, Ice

America's Best Campground

Close to the city, but far enough away to offer country quiet.

499 Buena Vista Rd, Branson, MO 65616	(800) 671-4399 abc-branson.com/	All Year
$45	Military/Good Sam	No Restrictions
160 Spaces	Paved	28Width/70Length
Internet, Showers, Laundry	Cable, Guest Services, Ice	Grocery, Rec. Hall, Games

Branson Lakeside RV Park

Definitely consider this park when planning a Branson vacation.

300 Box Car Willie Dr, Branson, MO 65616	(417) 334-2915 bransonlakesidervpark.com	All Year
$36-$55	Military/Good Sam	No Restrictions
135 Spaces	Paved	24Width/90Length
Internet, Showers, Laundry	Cable, Rentals, Rec. Hall	Pavilion, Tables

Cooper Creek Resort

Stay at this park, and you'll experience the Ozarks as they were meant to be.

471 Cooper Creek Rd, Branson, MO 65616	(417) 334-4871 https://coopercreekresort.com	March 10 to December 1
$41-$51	Military/Good Sam	No Restrictions
74 Spaces	Paved	28Width/70Length
Internet, Showers, Laundry	Firewood, Grocery, Cable	Fishing, Pool, Game Room

Tall Pines Campground

Located in the Ozark Mountains near Silver Dollar City.

5558 State Highway 265, Branson, MO 65616	(417) 338-2445 https://campinmissouri.com	March 1 to December 1
$36	Military/Good Sam	No Restrictions
71 Spaces	Paved	24Width/65Length
Internet, Showers, Laundry	Supplies, Firewood, Fishing	Pool, Game Room, Pavilion

Ozark Country Campground

A relaxing and enjoyable stay is what you get when you come here.

679 Quebec Dr, Branson, MO 65616	(417) 334-4681	All Year
$32-$47	Military/Good Sam	No Restrictions
69 Spaces	Paved/Gravel	28Width/60Length
Internet, Showers, Laundry	Supplies, Firewood, Ice	Cable, Rec. Hall, Playground

Branson View Campground

This full-service campground is known for its spectacular views.

2362 State Highway 265, Branson, MO 65616	(417) 338-1038 thebransonviewcampground.com/	All Year
$50	Military/Good Sam	Pet Quantity
36 Spaces	Paved	24Width/90Length
Internet, Showers, Laundry	Cable, Rentals, Pool, GameRoom	Playground, Pavilion

Branson Treehouse Adventures

This unique park offers something for everyone.

159 Acorn Acres Ln, Branson West, MO 65737	(800) 338-2504 bransontreehouseadventures.com/	All Year
$42-$62	Military/Good Sam	No Restrictions
63 Spaces	Gravel	34Width/70Length
Internet, Shower, Laundry	Rentals, Firewood, Pool, Rec. Hall	Playground, Games

Bar M Resort

Located in a private cove of Table Rock Lake.

207 Bar M Ln, Branson West, MO 65737	(417) 338-2593 http://www.barmresort.com/	April 1 to November 1
$35-$50	Good Sam	Pet Breed
22 Spaces	Gravel	34Width/60Length

| Internet, Showers, Laundry | Firewood, Ice, Fishing, Pool | Games, Pavilion, GameRoom |

Big Red Barn RV Park
There is a range of amenities and attractions to help you enjoy your vacation.

13625 Elm Road, Carthage, MO 64836	(417) 358-2432 https://brbrv.com/	All Year
$40	Military/Good Sam	Pet Breed
63 Spaces	Gravel	30Width/70Length
Internet, Showers, Laundry	Rec. Hall, Cable, Ice	Firewood, Games, Supplies

Coachlight RV Park
A small yet great place to stay, whether you need an overnight stop or a long term stay.

5327 South Garrison Rd, Carthage, MO 64836	(417) 358-3666	All Year
$32	None	None
80 Spaces	Paved	24Width/80Length
Internet, Laundry, Ice	Supplies, Cable, Rec. Hall	Pavilion, Games, Activities

Osage Prairie RV Park
Enjoy this family-friendly park all season long.

1501 N Osage Blvd, Nevada, MO 64772	(417) 667-2267 https://osageprairie.com/	All Year
$35-$38	Military/Good Sam	No Restrictions
45 Spaces	Gravel	24Width/60Length
Internet, Showers, Laundry	Firewood, Pool, Rec. Hall	Playground, Mini Golf

Beagle Bay RV Haven
A rustic park in a natural setting.

2041 Cimarron Rd, Sarcoxie, MO 64862	(417) 548-0000 http://www.beaglebayrv.com/	All Year
$25	Military/Good Sam	No Restrictions
36 Spaces	Gravel	24Width/70Length
Internet, Showers, Laundry	Firewood, Rentals, Pool	Game Room, Playground

Missouri – Southeast

The southeast portion of Missouri is a great place to go when you want to get back to nature. Whether you want to relax at your site or plan an outdoor adventure, there is plenty of things to do in this area.

Big Creek RV Park
A relaxing environment with fun and unique activities.

47247 Hwy. 49　Annapolis, MO 63620	(573) 598-1064　https://bigcreekrvpark.com/	All Year
$37-$43	Military/Good Sam	No Restrictions
65 Spaces	Gravel	35Width/85Length
Internet, Showers, Laundry	Gated, Supplies, Firewood	Rentals, Game Room

Stone Park Resort
This park meets all of your RV vacation needs in one place.

8614 Berry Rd,　Bonne Terre, MO 63628	(317) 769-2283　http://www.stoneparkmo.com/	All Year
$40	Good Sam	None
31 Spaces	Gravel	30Width/65Length
Showers, Laundry, Firewood	Rentals, Rec. Hall	Pavilion, Fire Rings

Lady Luck Casino & RV Park
Conveniently located along the banks of the Mississippi River.

777 E 3rd St,　Caruthersville, MO 63830	(573) 333-6000　ladyluckcaruthersville.com/	All Year
$40	Good Sam	14 Day Max Stay
27 Spaces	Paved	30Width/75Length
Internet, Showers, Laundry	Gated, ATM, Restaurant	Lounge, Rec.Hall, GameRoom

Camelot RV Campground
Stay for a night or make a long term vacation stop while you relax and enjoy the area.

4728 Highway 67 N,　Poplar Bluff, MO 63901	(573) 785-1016　camelotrvcampground.com/	All Year
$35	Military/Good Sam	Pet Breed
76 Spaces	Gravel	30Width/65Length
Internet, Showers, Laundry	Supplies, LP Gas, Cable, Ice	Pavilion, Tables

Montana

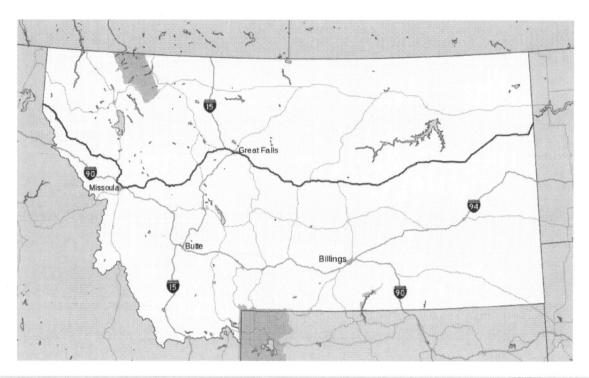

Montana - Glacier Country

Glacier Country covers the western tip of Montana. It is home to beautiful natural parks, beautiful scenery, and several small mountain towns.

Outback Montana RV Park
Minutes from Flathead Lake, the largest freshwater lake west of the Mississippi.

13772 Outback Ln, Bigfork, MT 59911	(406) 837-6973 outbackmontana.com/	All Year
$31-$39	Military/Good Sam	No Restrictions
49 Spaces	Gravel	20Width/80Length
Internet, Showers, Supplies	Firewood, Rentals	Playground, Games

Bearmouth Chalet RV Park
Wonderful nearby attractions and fun activities with this park as your base camp.

1611 Drummond Frontage Rd, Clinton, MT 59825	(406) 825-9950	May 1 to October 31
$35-$40	Good Sam	None
45 Spaces	Gravel	31Width/75Length
Showers, Laundry, ATM	Rentals, Snack Bar, Ice	Firewood, Rec. Hall, Games

La Salle RV Park

This pet-friendly park is open year-round for your vacation fun.

5618 Us Highway 2 W, Columbia Falls, MT 59912	(406) 892-4668 https://lasallervpark.webs.com/	All Year
$54-$60	Military/Good Sam	Pet Qty, Breed
47 Spaces	Paved/Gravel	30Width/70Length
Internet, Laundry, Supplies	Firewood, LP Gas, Ice	Playground, Games

Mountain View RV Park

Located between Whitefish and Columbia Falls with easy access on and off the highway.

3621 MT Highway 40 W, Columbia Falls, MT 59912	(406) 892-2500 http://rvparkmontana.com/	All Year
$54-$60	Military/Good Sam	Pet Qty, Breed
45 Spaces	Paved	32Width/62Length
Internet, Showers, Laundry	Supplies, Tables, Ice	RV Wash, Games

Columbia Falls RV Park

A full-service RV park that is your gateway to Glacier National Park.

103 US Highway 2 E, Columbia Falls, MT 59912	(406) 892-1122 https://columbiafallsrvpark.com/	April 1 to October 31
$49-$70	Military/Good Sam	No Restrictions
77 Spaces	Gravel	27Width/90Length
Internet, Showers, Laundry	Supplies, Cable, RV Service	Rentals, Games

Black Rabbit RV Park

The park and the area around it are beautiful and filled with fun activities.

2101 North 1st St, Hamilton, MT 59840	(406) 363-3744 https://blackrabbitrv.com/	All Year
$38	Military/Good Sam	Pet Breed
59 Spaces	Gravel	23Width/60Length
Internet, Showers, Laundry	Firewood, Cable, Supplies	RV Wash, Tables

Rocky Mountain 'Hi' RV Park

Stay here, and Glacier National Park is in your backyard.

825 Helena Flats Rd, Kalispell, MT 59901	(406) 755-9573 glaciercamping.com/	All Year
$42	Military/Good Sam	No Restrictions
98 Spaces	Paved/Gravel	27Width/80Length
Internet, Showers, Laundry	ATM, Supplies, Firewood, Ice	Playground, Games, Pavilion

Spruce Park on the River

Located on scenic Flathead River, just a short drive to West Glacier Entrance.

1985 Hwy 35, Kalispell, MT 59901	(406) 752-6321 https://www.spruceparkrv.com/	April 1 to November 15
$40-$63	Military/Good Sam	No Restrictions
84 Spaces	Paved	30Width/60Length
Internet, Showers, Laundry	Firewood, Cable, Grocery	Playground, Games, Tables

Edgewater RV Resort

A friendly park on Flathead Lake.

7140 US Highway 93 S, Lakeside, MT 59922	(406) 844-3644 https://edgewaterrv.com/	May 1 to September 30
$59	Military/Good Sam	Pet Breed
38 Spaces	Paved	21Width/70Length
Internet, Showers, Laundry	Rentals, Rec. Hall, RV Wash	Games, Pavilion

Woodland RV Park

A beautiful, quaint park located in Kootenai National Forest.

31480 US Highway 2, Libby, MT 59923	(406) 293-8395 woodlandrvpark.com/	April 15 to October 15
$40-$45	Good Sam	None
50 Spaces	Gravel	35Width/90Length
Internet, Showers, Laundry	Fishing, Rentals, Cable	Rec. Hall, Games, Patios

Jellystone RV Park

This is a great destination if you want to explore Montana.

9900 Jellystone Dr, Missoula, MT 59808	(406) 543-9400 http://www.jellystonemt.com/	May 1 to October 15
$40-$50	Military/Good Sam	No Restrictions
110 Spaces	Paved	40Width/65Length
Internet, Showers, Laundry	Firewood, Grocery, Rentals	Pool, Game Room, Mini Golf

Jim & Mary's RV Park

Enjoy beautiful flower gardens in the park or plan an outdoor adventure.

9800 US Highway 93 N, Missoula, MT 59808	(406) 549-4416 http://jimandmarys.com/	All Year
$47	Military/Good Sam	No Restrictions
69 Spaces	Paved	38Width/80Length
Internet, Showers, Laundry	Supplies, Cable, Horseshoes	Rec. Hall, Games, Pavilion

Eagle Nest RV Resort

Stay at the most fun RV park in Montana.

35800 Eagle Nest Dr, Polson, MT 59860	(406) 883-5904 https://eaglenestrv.com/	May 1 to October 15
$42-$69	Military/Good Sam	No Restrictions
56 Spaces	Paved	28Width/64Length
Internet, Showers, Laundry	Pool, Activities, Playground	Games, Gym, Patios

Campground St Regis

Come here and make your getaway memorable.

44 Frontage Rd W, Saint Regis, MT 59866	(406) 649-2470 campgroundstregisrvpark.com/	April 1 to October 1
$30-$44	Military/Good Sam	No Restrictions
75 Spaces	Paved/Gravel	32Width/100Length
Internet, Showers, Laundry	Grocery, Firewood, LP Gas	Game Room, Playground

Nugget RV Park

Surround yourself with beautiful mountain ranges and flowing rivers.

1037 Old Highway 10 E, Saint Regis, MT 59866	(406) 649-2122 thenuggetrvpark.com/	May 1 to November 15
$43-$52	Military/Good Sam	No Restrictions
86 Spaces	Gravel	30Width/75Length
Internet, Showers, Laundry	Playground, Games, Pool	Firewood, Ice, Rec. Hall

West Glacier RV Park

Stay at one of the most beautiful travel destinations in North America.

200 Going-to-the-Sun Road West Glacier, MT 59936	(844) 868-7474 glacierparkcollection.com	May 15 to October 1
$85	Good Sam	None
102 Spaces	Paved	40Width/80Length
Internet, Showers, Laundry	Restaurant, Grocery, Firewood	Playground, Games

North American RV Park

The hub of all activities in Montana's Glacier Country.

10640 Highway 2 E, Coram, MT 59913	(800) 704-4266 northamericanrvpark.com/	April 15 to October 15
$55	Military/Good Sam	No Restrictions
60 Spaces	Paved/Gravel	30Width/62Length
Internet, Showers, Laundry	Rentals, Firewood, Ice	Game Room, Playground

Montana – Eastern

Eastern Montana is pretty much every part of the state not covered in the western tip of Glacier Country. It truly is big sky country with beautiful scenery and national parks. Stay at any of the parks in this area, and enjoy a range of outdoor activities.

Fairmont RV Resort

The perfect stop when visiting Glacier or Yellowstone parks.

1700 Fairmont Rd, Anaconda, MT 59711	(406) 797-3505 fairmontrvresort.com/	All Year
$48-$54	Military	None
116 Spaces	Gravel	31Width/75Length
Internet, Showers, Laundry	Grocery, Fishing, Hunting	Games, Tables, Ice

Spring Creek Campground

Stay among the pines along Boulder River.

257 Main Boulder Rd, Big Timber, MT 59011	(406) 932-4387 springcreekcampground.com/	April 1 to September 30
$40-$47	Military/Good Sam	No Restrictions
57 Spaces	Gravel	40Width/70Length
Internet, Showers, Laundry	Firewood, Grocery, RV Wash	Rentals, Playground, Games

Yellowstone River RV Park

From tourist attractions to National Parks, there is everything in this area.

309 Garden Ave, Billings, MT 59101	(406) 259-0878 yellowstoneriverrvpark.com/	All Year
$39-$80	Military/Good Sam	No Restrictions
105 Spaces	Paved	18Width/65Length
Internet, Showers, Laundry	Firewood, Cable, Rentals	Pool, Game Room, Pavilion

Billings Village RV Park

Stay here and visit all of the popular sites and attractions in Billings.

325 S Billings Blvd, Billings, MT 59101	(406) 248-8685 billingstrailervillagervpark.com/	All Year
$54-$60	Military/Good Sam	Pet Size
81 Spaces	Paved	30Width/60Length
Internet, Showers, Laundry	Cable, RV Wash	Playground, Games

Sunrise Campground

Enjoy fun, sun, and outdoor life by staying here.

31842 Frontage Rd, Bozeman, MT 59715	(406) 587-4797 sunriservcampground.com/	April 1 to October 30
$42-$45	None	None
50 Spaces	Paved/Gravel	21Width/64Length
Internet, Showers, Laundry	LP Gas, Ice, RV Wash	Rec. Hall, Playground

Indian Creek RV Park

Explore the historic Deer Lodge Valley.

745 Maverick Ln, Deer Lodge, MT 59722	(406) 846-3848 indiancreekcampground.net/	All Year
$35-$37	Military/Good Sam	No Restrictions
72 Spaces	Gravel	25Width/75Length
Internet, Showers, Laundry	Restaurant, ATM, Firewood	Lounge, Cable, Ice

Countryside RV Park

Pet-friendly with easy access on and off the freeway.

30 Sawmill Rd, Dillon, MT 59725	(406) 683-9860 https://www.csrvmt.com/	All Year
$25-$48	Military/Good Sam	No Restrictions
44 Spaces	Paved/Gravel	32Width/70Length
Internet, Showers, Laundry	Firewood, Horseshoes	Games, Rentals

Southside RV Park

Walk just 9 blocks to visit historic downtown Dillon.

104 E Poindexter St, Dillon, MT 59725	(406) 683-2244 http://southsidervpark.com/	March 1 to December 1
$40-$44	Military/Good Sam	Pet Breed
40 Spaces	Gravel	26Width/85Length
Internet, Showers, Laundry	Fishing, Rentals, Games	Activities, Tables

Ennis RV Village

Enjoy fishing or relaxing on the river.

15 Geyser St, Ennis, MT 59729	(406) 682-5272 https://ennisrv.com/	April 1 to November 1
$28-$38	Good Sam	None
112 Spaces	Gravel	32Width/78Length
Internet, Showers, Laundry	Horseshoes, RV Wash	Rec. Hall, Tables

Yellowstone RV Park

This park is unequaled in its setting along the Yellowstone River.

121 Highway 89 S, Gardiner, MT 59030	(406) 848-7496 rvparkyellowstone.com/	May 1 to October 30
$48-$72	Military/Good Sam	No Restrictions
46 Spaces	Gravel	26Width/55Length
Internet, Showers, Laundry	Supplies, Playground	RV Wash, Tables

Rocky Mountain RV Park

Surround yourself with spectacular mountain views.

14 Jardine Rd, Gardiner, MT 59030	(406) 848-7251 rockymountainrvpark.com/	May 1 to September 30
$49-$71	Military/Good Sam	Pet Quantity
65 Spaces	Gravel	28Width/60Length
Internet, Showers, Laundry	Cable, Supplies, Ice	Rentals, Mini Golf, Tables

Bernie and Sharon's Riverfront RV Park

This park offers VIP services.

115 Riverfront Ln, Garrison, MT 59731	(406) 846-2158 riverfrontrvparkmt.com/	All Year
$33-$35	Military/Good Sam	No Restrictions
50 Spaces	Paved	26Width/110Length
Internet, Showers, Laundry	Firewood, LP gas, RV Wash	Rentals, Game Room, Ice

7th Ranch RV Camp

A brief description.

662 Reno Creek Rd, Garryowen, MT 59031	(406) 638-2438	May 1 to October 1
$41-$47	Military/Good Sam	No Restrictions
66 Spaces	Gravel	30Width/80Length
Internet, Showers, Laundry	Gated, Rentals, RV Wash	Playground, Games, Tables

Dick's RV Park

A brief description.

1403 11th St SW, Great Falls, MT 59404	(406) 452-0333 http://www.dicksrvpark.com/	All Year
$45	Good Sam	None
114 Spaces	Gravel	30Width/65Length
Internet, Showers, Laundry	ATM, Supplies, Ice	RV Service, Mini Golf

Grandview Camp & RV Park

Quick access on and off the interstate. Stay here and explore all the area has to offer.

1002 N Mitchell Ave, Hardin, MT 59034	(406) 665-2489 grandviewcamp.com/	All Year
$28-$42	Military/Good Sam	No Restrictions
56 Spaces	Gravel	30Width/90Length
Internet, Showers, Laundry	Cable, Rentals, Rec. Hall	Activities, Playground

Helena North KOA

Located exactly halfway between Glacier and Yellowstone.

850 Lincoln Road West, Helena, MT 59602	(406) 458-3725 koa.com/campgrounds/helena-north/	All Year
$45-$65	Military/Good Sam	No Restrictions
78 Spaces	Gravel	24Width/77Length
Internet, Showers, Laundry	Supplies, LP Gas	Patios, Tables, Ice

Osen's RV Park

A picturesque, quiet, and convenient location.

20 Merrill Ln, Livingston, MT 59047	(406) 222-0591 montanarvpark.com/	April 15 to October 10
$44-$55	Military/Good Sam	Pet Quantity
45 Spaces	Gravel	30Width/75Length
Internet, Showers, Laundry	Supplies, Cable, RV Service	Games, Tables

Trails West RV Park

Just a short drive from Glacier, Great Falls, and Canada.

770 Adamson Rd, Shelby, MT 59474	(406) 424-8436 http://trailswestrvpark.com/	All Year
$35-$40	Military/Good Sam	No Restrictions
32 Spaces	Paved/Gravel	30Width/60Length
Internet, Showers, Laundry	Snack Bar, Ice, ATM	Rentals, Snack Bar

Shelby RV Park & Resort

A casino and several amenities are within walking distance to this park.

455 Mckinley Ave, Shelby, MT 59474	(406) 434-2233 shelbymtrvpark.com/	All Year
$35-$50	Military/Good Sam	No Restrictions
27 Spaces	Gravel	42Width/80Length
Internet, Showers, Laundry	Rentals, Pool, Lounge	Gym, Sauna, Tables

Lewis & Clark RV Park
A clean and quiet park with easy interstate access.

1535 Oilfield Ave, Shelby, MT 59474	(406) 434-2710 http://lewisandclarkrvpark.com/	April 15 to September 30
$30-$36	Good Sam	Pet Quantity
62 Spaces	Gravel	25Width/65Length
Internet, Showers, Laundry	Supplies, LP Gas	Ice, Tables

Buffalo Crossing RV Park
The newest park in West Yellowstone.

101 BS Canyon St., West Yellowstone, MT 59758	(406) 646-4300 buffalocrossingrvpark.com/	May 11 to October 17
$40-$65	Military/Good Sam	No Restrictions
25 Spaces	Gravel	30Width/70Length
Internet, Showers, Laundry	Supplies, Snack Bar	RV Service, Patios, Tables

Yellowstone Grizzly RV Park
Easy walking distance to dining, shopping, and attractions.

210 S Electric St, West Yellowstone, MT 59758	(406) 646-4466 https://grizzlyrv.com/	May 1 to October 15
$45-$90	Military/Good Sam	No Restrictions
227 Spaces	Paved	30Width/70Length
Internet, Showers, Laundry	Grocery, Supplies, RV Wash	Rec. Hall, Playground, Patios

Nebraska

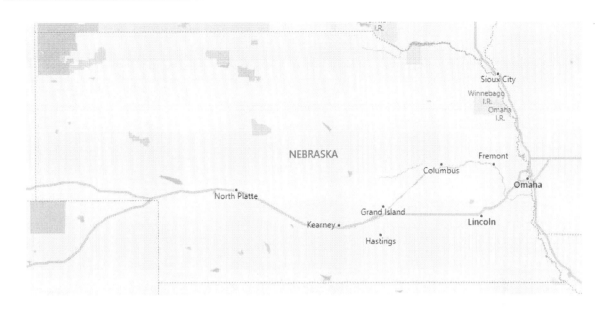

Nebraska is a state with wide-open plains. There are plenty of outdoor activities throughout the state, but you can also just sit back and relax on your vacation. Consider the options available.

Robidoux RV Park
Located at the base of historic Scotts Bluff National Monument.

585 Five Rocks Rd, Gering, NE 69341	(308) 436-2046 gering.org/robidoux-rv-park	All Year
$27-$33	Military/Good Sam	No Restrictions
42 Spaces	Paved	35Width/65Length
Internet, Showers, Laundry	Playground, Rec. Hall	Patios, Tables, Cable

Gothenburg Blue Heron Campground
A natural retreat just off the interstate in central Nebraska.

1102 S Lake Ave, Gothenburg, NE 69138	(308) 537-7387	April 1 to October 30
$30-$39	Military/Good Sam	No Restrictions
44 Spaces	Gravel	25Width/40Length
Internet, Showers, Laundry	Ice, Snack Bar, Pool	Firewood, Playground

Pine Grove RV Park
A country setting with many fun things to do.

23403 Mynard Rd, Greenwood, NE 68366	(402) 944-3550 https://pinegrovervpark.com/	All Year
$32-$63	Military/Good Sam	No Restrictions

100 Spaces	Gravel	44Width/80Length
Internet, Showers, Laundry	Pool, Lounge, Snack Bar	Grocery, Firewood, Tennis

Prairie Oasis Campground
A great place to rest and relax after a busy day.

913 Road B, Henderson, NE 68371	(402) 723-5227 prairieoasiscampground.com/	All Year
$39-$42	Military/Good Sam	Pet Quantity
31 Spaces	Gravel	20Width/90Length
Internet, Showers, Laundry	Rentals, Snack Bar, Ice	Rec. Hall, Playground

Kearney RV Park
The only full-service park in Kearney with easy access on and off the interstate.

1140 East 1st Street Kearney, NE 68847	308-237-PARK https://www.kearneyrv.com	All Year
$40-$45	Military/Good Sam	No Restrictions
96 Spaces	Gravel	30Width/100Length
Internet, Showers, Laundry	Supplies, LPGas, Horseshoes	Rec. Hall, Playground

Camp A Way RV Park
The best campground in the area for 50 years.

200 Campers Cir, Lincoln, NE 68521	(402) 476-2282	All Year
$35-$89	Military/Good Sam	No Restrictions
92 Spaces	Paved/Gravel	35Width/70Length
Internet, Showers, Laundry	Firewood, Cable, Grocery	Snack Bar, Games, Pool

Victorian Acres RV Park
A quiet and beautiful park. Monthly and yearly rates available.

6591 Highway 2, Nebraska City, NE 68410	(402) 873-6866 victorianacresrvpark.com/	March 1 to November 30
$37	Military/Good Sam	No Restrictions
88 Spaces	Gravel	30Width/75Length
Internet, Showers, Laundry	Firewood, Rec. Hall, Ice	Playground, Pavilion

Holiday RV Park
Stay here for relaxation and family fun.

601 Halligan Dr, North Platte, NE 69101	(800) 424-4531 holidayparkne.com/	All Year
$32-$41	Military/Good Sam	Pet Breed

92 Spaces	Gravel	30Width/70Length
Internet, Showers, Laundry	Grocery, Cable, Pool	Games, Playground

I-80 Lakeside Campground

A private lake and amenities to help you have a comfortable stay.

3800 Hadley Dr, North Platte, NE 69101	(308) 534-5077 i80lakesidecampground.com/	All Year
$40	Military/Good Sam	No Restrictions
86 Spaces	Gravel	26Width/70Length
Showers, Laundry, Firewood	Grocery, Supplies, Rentals	Games, Playground

Sleepy Sunflower RV Park

The goal here is to provide you with a comfortable stay in a clean and friendly park.

221 Rd E 85, Ogallala, NE 69153	(308) 284-1300 sleepysunflower.com	All Year
$38	Military/Good Sam	Pet Breed
37 Spaces	Gravel	24Width/70Length
Internet, Showers, Laundry	Snack Bar, Cable, Pool	Firewood, Playground

Area's Finest Country View Campground

A quaint RV park that provides the basic amenities.

120 Rd East 80, Ogallala, NE 69153	(308) 284-2415 cvcampground.com/	April 1 to November 1
$39	Military/Good Sam	No Restrictions
51 Spaces	Gravel	24Width/100Length
Internet, Showers, Laundry	Firewood, Fire Rings	Horseshoes, Pavilion

Fishberry Campground

Offering you an old west adventure. A full amenity park in a great outdoor setting.

90440 US Highway 83, Valentine, NE 69201	(866) 376-1662	All Year
$38	Military/Good Sam	No Restrictions
22 Spaces	Gravel	25Width/100Length
Internet, Showers, Laundry	Firewood, Horseshoes	Pavilion, Fire Rings

Nevada

Nevada – Reno/Tahoe Area

The Reno-Tahoe area along the western edge of the state is a popular tourist stop, second only to Las Vegas. There is less city glamour in the area, but there are ample outdoor activities to enjoy.

Gold Dust West Casino & RV Park
Located near Lake Tahoe and Virginia City

2171 E William St, Carson City, NV 89701	(775) 885-9000 gdwcasino.com/Carson/	All Year
$40-$45	Good Sam	RV Age, Pet Breed
47 Spaces	Paved	21Width/46Length
Internet, Showers, Laundry	ATM, Ice, Snack Bar, Cable	Rentals, Lounge, Pool

Comstock Country RV Resort
Stay just 30 minutes from Reno, Lake Tahoe, and Virginia City.

5400 S Carson St, Carson City, NV 89701	(775) 882-2445 http://www.comstockrv.com/	All Year
$38-$44	Good Sam	None
150 Spaces	Paved	28Width/60Length
Showers, Laundry, Supplies	LP Gas, Grocery, Cable	Pool, Games, Pavilion

Dayton RV Park
This boutique park is easily located off the highway and pet-friendly.

75 E Pike St, Dayton, NV 89403	(775) 246-9300 https://www.daytonrvpark.com/	All Year
$50-$52	Good Sam	None
50 Spaces	Paved	26Width/65Length
Internet, Showers, Laundry	Ice, Cable, Games	Tables, Horseshoes

Carson Valley RV Resort & Casino
Stay here and take a day trip to Tahoe, Virginia City, or Carson City.

1639 US Highway 395 N, Minden, NV 89423	(800) 321-6983 https://carsonvalleyinn.com/	All Year
$32-$60	Good Sam	None
59 Spaces	Paved	25Width/54Length
Internet, Showers, Laundry	ATM, Ice, Snack Bar, Cable	Rec. Hall, Rentals, Gym

Keystone RV Park
Close to the city, yet provides you a quiet environment.

1455 W 4th St,	(775) 324-5000	All Year

Reno, NV 89503	http://keystonervpark.com/	
$49-$52	Good Sam	RV Age
102 Spaces	Paved	23Width/40Length
Internet, Showers	Laundry, Cable	Lodge Room Rentals

Silver Sage RV Park
The most deluxe and convenient RV park in Reno.

2760 S Virginia St, Reno, NV 89502	(775) 829-1919 silversagervparkreno.com	All Year
$39-$60	Military/Good Sam	No Restrictions
43 Spaces	Paved	23Width/50Length
Internet, Showers	Laundry, Gated, Ice	Cable, Pavilion, Patios

Grand Sierra Resort RV Park
Enjoy all that Reno and Tahoe have to offer.

2500 2nd St, Reno, NV 89595	(775) 789-2000 grandsierraresort.com/	All Year
$65-$75	Military/Good Sam	RV Age, 14 Day Max
165 Spaces	Paved	30Width/65Length
Internet, Showers, Laundry	ATM, Supplies, Ice, Pool	Snack Bar, Games, Sauna

Bordertown Casino & RV Resort
This is a full-service, high mountain resort.

19575 Highway 395 N, Reno, NV 89508	(775) 972-1309 bordertowncasinorv.com	All Year
$30-$55	Military/Good Sam	No Restrictions
50 Spaces	Paved	24Width/70Length
Internet, Showers, Laundry	Supplies, Snack Bar, Cable	Lounge, Rec. Hall, Games

Shamrock RV Park
Located just minutes from downtown Reno with beautiful views of the Sierras.

260 Parr Blvd., Reno, NV 89512	(775) 329-5222 https://shamrockrv.com	All Year
$38-$45	Good Sam	None
121 Spaces	Paved	28Width/56Length
Internet, Showers, Laundry	Cable, Pool, Game Room	Activities, Games, Gym

Bonanza Terrace RV Park
An RV park that is affordable and comfortable.

4800 Stoltz Rd, Reno, NV 89506	(775) 329-9624 https://bonanzaterracervp.com	All Year

$42-$45	Military/Good Sam	Pet Breed
79 Spaces	Paved	24Width/45Length
Showers, Restrooms	Laundry, Cable	RV Wash

Victorian RV Park
Beautiful grounds, great location, exceptional service.

205 Nichols Blvd, Sparks, NV 89431	(775) 356-6400 http://victorianrvpark.com/	All Year
$41-$52	Military/Good Sam	No Restrictions
85 Spaces	Paved	24Width/60Length
Internet, Showers, Laundry	Grocery, Cable, Pool, Ice	Pavilion, Tennis, Gym

Sparks Marina RV Park
Serving Reno and Sparks at an affordable rate.

1200 E Lincoln Way, Sparks, NV 89434	(775) 851-8888 sparksmarinarvpark.com	All Year
$37-$94	Military/Good Sam	RV Age, Pet Breed, 28 Day Max
204 Spaces	Paved	30Width/65Length
Internet, Showers, Laundry	Gated, Supplies, Rec. Hall	Games, Pool, Cable

Gold Ranch Casino & RV Resort
A pet-friendly park offering daily and weekly rates.

350 Gold Ranch Rd, Verdi, NV 89439	(775) 345-6789 goldranchrvcasino.com	All Year
$43-$60	Military/Good Sam	Pet Quantity, 28 Day Max
105 Spaces	Paved	30Width/75Length
Internet, Showers, Laundry	SnackBar, Grocery, Restaurant	Pool Rec. Hall, Cable

Nevada – North

Gold Country RV Park
Whether you want a fun getaway or a relaxing vacation, this is your destination.

2050 Idaho St., Elko, NV 89801	(800) 621-1332 goldcountryinnelko.com/	All Year
$30-$32	Good Sam	None
26 Spaces	Paved	24Width/40Length
Internet, Showers, Laundry	Restaurant, Lounge, Ice	ATM, Pool, Gym

Iron Horse RV Resort
Located along the beautiful Ruby Mountains.

3400 E Idaho St, Elko, NV 89801	(775) 777-1919 ironhorservresort.com	All Year
$33-$48	Good Sam	Pet Breed
92 Spaces	Paved	28Width/75Length
Internet, Showers, Laundry	Rentals, Pool, Rec. Hall	Game Room, Activities

Double Dice RV Park
The nearby area offers outdoor activities for every season.

3730 E Idaho St, Elko, NV 89801	(775) 738-5642 doubledicervpark.com	All Year
$45	Military/Good Sam	Pet Quantity
120 Spaces	Paved/Gravel	30Width/65Length
Internet, Showers, Laundry	ATM, Supplies, LP Gas, Ice	Restaurant, Cable, Lounge

Elko RV Park
Conveniently located just off the interstate and bordering the Humboldt River.

507 Scott Rd, Elko, NV 89801	(775) 738-3448 elkorvparkatryndon.com	All Year
$32-$40	Military/Good Sam	Pet Breed
120 Spaces	Gravel	30Width/60Length
Internet, Showers, Laundry	Firewood, Snack Bar, Ice	Grocery, Lounge, Games

Fallon RV Park
Offering all the comforts of home so you won't want to leave the park.

5787 Reno Hwy, Fallon, NV 89406	(775) 867-2332 http://fallonrv.com/	All Year
$48-$51	Military/Good Sam	Pet Breed
64 Spaces	Paved	30Width/70Length
Internet, Showers, Laundry	Supplies, LP Gas, Firewood	Grocery, Cable, Tables

Cold Springs Station Resort

Stay in beautiful Central Nevada near the site of the original Pony Express.

52300 Austin Hwy, Fallon, NV 89406	(775) 423-1233 http://cssresort.com/	All Year
$30-$40	Good Sam	None
24 Spaces	Gravel	20Width/50Length
Internet, Showers, Laundry	Firewood, Grocery, Lounge	Game Room, Pavilion

Desert Rose RV Park

Offering beautiful and spacious sites with wonderful amenities.

3285 US Highway 50 E, Fernley, NV 89408	(775) 575-9399 https://www.desertroserv.com	All Year
$35-$40	Military/Good Sam	Pet Breed
124 Spaces	Paved/Gravel	35Width/65Length
Internet, Showers, Laundry	Supplies, Cable, Rec. Hall	Pavilion, Gym, Patios

Angel Lake RV Park

Your gateway to Angel Lake and offering reduced rates if you need longer to explore the area.

124 S Humboldt Ave, Wells, NV 89835	(775) 752-2745 http://www.angellakerv.com	All Year
$35-$40	Military/Good Sam	No Restrictions
48 Spaces	Gravel	24Width/70Length
Internet, Showers, Laundry	SnackBar, Grocery, RVWash	Games, Horseback Riding

Silver State RV Park

Here, modern camping meets the excitement of the Old West.

5575 E Winnemucca Blvd, Winnemucca, NV 89445	(775) 623-4513 https://www.silverstaterv.com	All Year
$42	Good Sam	None
151 Spaces	Paved	27Width/63Length
Internet, Showers, Laundry	Snack Bar, Cable, Grocery	Pool, Rec. Hall, Playground

Winnemucca RV Park

Your hidden gem out west and your place for work or fun.

5255 E Winnemucca Blvd, Winnemucca, NV 89445	(775) 623-4458 winnemuccarv.com	All Year
$42	Military/Good Sam	No Restrictions
100 Spaces	Gravel	22Width/70Length
Internet, Showers, Laundry	Cable, Pool, Ice, Supplies	Horseshoes, Games, Tables

Nevada – South

Southern Nevada is home to many popular tourist destinations. You can spend days enjoying all there is in Las Vegas. For the more outdoor-minded, there is Lake Mead. Plus, the Grand Canyon and Death Valley are just day trips from most parks in this area. Just consider some of the many outdoor activities you can have here.

Canyon Trail RV Park

This park has it all when it comes to amenities.

1200 Industrial Rd, Boulder City, NV 89005	(702) 293-1200 http://www.canyontrailrvpark.com	All Year
$48-$58	Military/Good Sam	Pet Quantity
156 Spaces	Paved	30Width/50Length
Internet, Showers, Laundry	Supplies, Cable, Pool, RV Wash	Rec. Hall, Games, Pavilion

Lake Mead RV Village

Centrally located near the Hoover Dam and just 30 miles from Las Vegas.

268 Lake Shore Dr, Boulder City, NV 89005	(702) 293-2540 lakemeadrvvillage.com	All Year
$34-$50	Military/Good Sam	Pet Quantity
97 Spaces	Paved	24Width/100Length
Internet, Showers, Laundry	Snack Bar, Grocery, Cable	Rec. Hall, Firewood, Supplies

Whiskey Flats RV Park

Come see why this area is known as a desert wonderland.

3045 Highway 95, Hawthorne, NV 89415	(775) 945-1800 http://www.whiskeyflats.net	All Year
$31	Good Sam	None
60 Spaces	Gravel	26Width/60Length
Internet, Showers, Laundry	Grocery, Cable, Fishing	Horseshoes, Games, Tables

Oasis Las Vegas RV Resort

Park your RV and then get out to explore all of Las Vegas.

2711 W Windmill Ln, Las Vegas, NV 89123	(702) 260-2001 oasislasvegasrvresort.com	All Year
$47-$84	Military/Good Sam	Pet Quantity, Pet Breed
700 Spaces	Paved	24Width/90Length
Internet, Showers, Laundry	Gated, ATM, Supplies	Snack Bar, Restaurant

Las Vegas Motorcoach (LVM) Resort

A luxury Class A RV resort, offering you the best in motorcoach accommodations.

8175 Arville St, Las Vegas, NV 89139	(702) 897-9300 https://www.lvmresort.com	All Year No Class B or C
$70-$120	Military/Good Sam	RV Age, Pet Quantity, Breed
407 Spaces	Paved	30Width/65Length
Internet, Showers, Laundry	Restaurant, Pool, Sauna, Tennis	Gym, Patios, Activities

Duck Creek RV Park

Spread out at this park and enjoy Las Vegas.

6635 Boulder Hwy, Las Vegas, NV 89122	(702) 454-7090 https://duckcreekrvparklv.com	All Year
$32-$55	Military/Good Sam	Pet Breed
207 Spaces	Paved	20Width/73Length
Internet, Showers, Laundry	Grocery, Pool, Ice, Supplies	Rec. Hall, Activities, Games

Hitchin' Post RV Park

A highly rated gate access park with affordable rates.

3640 Las Vegas Blvd N, Las Vegas, NV 89115	(888) 433-8402 http://www.hprvp.com	All Year
$38	Good Sam	Pet Size
196 Spaces	Paved	25Width/70Length
Internet, Showers, Laundry	Ice, ATM, Gated, Restaurant	Cable, Lounge, Pool

Las Vegas RV Resort

Resort-style living close to the action and entertainment of the Las Vegas Strip.

3890 S Nellis Blvd, Las Vegas, NV 89121	(866) 846-5432 lasvegasrvresort.com	All Year
$29-$63	Good Sam	RV Age, Pet Breed
384 Spaces	Paved	30Width/60Length
Internet, Showers, Laundry	Rentals, Pool, Rec. Hall	Game Room, Gym, Tables

Arizona Charlie's Boulder RV Park

Offering all the comforts of home with the action of casinos.

4445 Boulder Hwy, Las Vegas, NV 89121	(702) 951-5911 arizonacharliesboulder.com/	All Year
$34-$36	Military/Good Sam	Pet Breed
221 Spaces	Paved	20Width/70Length
Internet, Showers, Laundry	Restaurant, Cable, Pool	Rec. Hall, Games, Gym

Riviera RV Park

Close to the Grand Canyon, Lake Mead, and Hoover Dam.

2200 Palm St, Las Vegas, NV 89104	(702) 457-8700 http://rivierarvlv.com/	All Year
$33	Good Sam	Pet Breed
137 Spaces	Paved	30Width/65Length
Internet, Showers, Laundry	Pool, RV Wash, Game Room	Gym, Patios, Tables

Thousand Trails Las Vegas RV Resort

Stay here to explore the area in a new and exciting way.

4295 Boulder Hwy, Las Vegas, NV 89121	(702) 451-2719	All Year
$45-$55	Good Sam	None
203 Spaces	Paved	20Width/60Length
Internet, Showers, Laundry	Gated, Rentals, Pool, Ice	Rec. Hall, Activities, Tables

Desert Skies RV Resort

No matter what you like to do, you'll find it here.

350 E Highway 91, Mesquite, NV 89027	(928) 347-6000 http://desertskiesresorts.com/	All Year
$35-$49	Good Sam	RV Age
321 Spaces	Paved	32Width/65Length
Internet, Showers, Laundry	Cable, Pool, Rec.Hall	Activities, Mini Golf, Gym

Sun Resorts RV Park

Mesquite, Nevada is a golf lovers paradise.

400 Hillside Dr, Mesquite, NV 89027	(702) 346-6666 http://www.sunresortsrv.com	All Year
$32-$45	Good Sam	Pet Quantity
71 Spaces	Paved	33Width/87Length
Internet, Showers, Laundry	Supplies, Cable	Rec. Hall, Pavilion, Putting

Lakeside Casino & RV Park

This park is designed to help you relax and enjoy the area.

5380 Homestead Rd, Pahrump, NV 89048	(775) 751-7770 https://lakesidecasinopahrump.com	All Year
$35-$70	Military/Good Sam	RV Age, Pet Breed
159 Spaces	Paved	30Width/70Length
Internet, Showers, Laundry	Firewood, Supplies, Grocery	Pool, Paddle Boats

Wine Ridge RV Resort

Offering great amenities and easy access to all the area has to offer.

3800 Winery Rd, Pahrump, NV 89048	(775) 751-7805 https://wineridgervresort.com	All Year
$22-$45	Military/Good Sam	No Restrictions
129 Spaces	Paved	33Width/60Length
Internet, Showers, Laundry	Restaurant, Rentals, Pool	Rec. Hall, Activities, Gym

Preferred RV Resort

Offering you the best location by being hidden in the downtown area.

1801 Crawford Way, Pahrump, NV 89048	(775) 727-4414 http://www.preferredrv.com	All Year
$40	Good Sam	RV Age
270 Spaces	Gravel	20Width/60Length
Internet, Showers, Laundry	Rentals, Pool, Game Room	Playground, Pavilion, Sauna

Nevada Treasure RV Resort

This park is known as a jewel in the desert.

301 W Leslie St, Pahrump, NV 89060	(800) 429-6665 http://nevadatreasurervresort.com/	All Year
$44-$66	Good Sam	RV Age, Pet Breed
202 Spaces	Paved	36Width/50Length
Internet, Showers, Laundry	Lounge, Snack Bar, Pool, Ice	Games, Sauna, Gym

New Hampshire

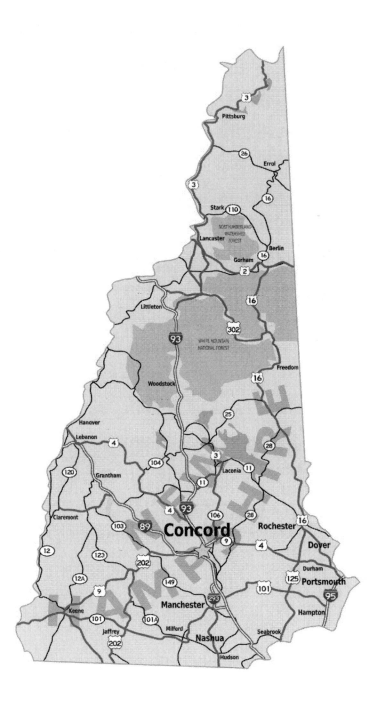

New Hampshire – North

Ames Brook Campground
A clean and quiet campground nestled in the valleys and hills of the White Mountains.

104 Winona Rd, Ashland, NH 03217	(603) 968-7998 https://www.amesbrook.com	May 12 to October 14
$46-$48	Military/Good Sam	Pet Quantity
89 Spaces	Gravel	37Width/64Length
Internet, Showers, Laundry	Firewood, Supplies, Cable	Rec. Hall, Playground, Gym

Newfound RV Park
Located between the New Hampshire Lake Region and the White Mountains.

792 Mayhew Tpke, Bristol, NH 03222	(603) 744-3344 http://www.newfoundrvpark.com	May 1 to October 31
$42-$50	Military/Good Sam	Pet Quantity
45 Spaces	Gravel	33Width/99Length
Internet, Showers, Laundry	Firewood, Cable, Ice, Rec. Hall	Playground, Games

Chocorua Camping Village KOA
Make your family camping adventure a memorable one.

893 White Mountain Hwy, Chocorua, NH 03817	(603) 323-8536	May 1 to October 16
$58-$99	Military	Pet Quantity
135 Spaces	Paved/Gravel	30Width/60Length
Internet, Showers, Laundry	Gated, Rentals, Pool	Pavilion, Games, Fire Rings

The Bluffs RV Resort
Located between the Lakes Region of New Hampshire and the White Mountains.

196 Shawtown Rd, Freedom, NH 03836	603.539.2069 danforthbay.com/the-bluffs	April 18 to November 2
$57-$66	None	55+, Pet Quantity
313 Spaces	Gravel	30Width/65Length
Internet, Showers, Laundry	Firewood, Snack Bar, Gated	Fishing, Rec. Hall, Games

Danforth Bay Camping
A brief description.

196 Shawtown Rd, Freedom, NH 03836	(603) 539-2069 https://www.danforthbay.com	All Year
$49-$84	Military	Pet Quantity
310 Spaces	Gravel	30Width/60Length
Internet, Showers, Laundry	Firewood, SnackBar, Ice, ATM	Tennis, Pavilion, Playground

Mountain Lake Camping Resort
Conveniently located between Maine and Vermont.

485 Prospect St, Lancaster, NH 03584	(603) 788-4509 mtnlakecampground.com	May 15 to October 15
$58-$82	Good Sam	Pet Breed
82 Spaces	Gravel	32Width/60Length
Internet, Showers, Laundry	Rentals, Pool, Snack Bar	Paddle Boats, Rec. Hall

Riverside Camping & RV Resort
Camping at a beautiful riverside setting in scenic northern New Hampshire.

4280 Boyds Creek Hwy, Sevierville, TN 37876	(865) 453-7299	May 1 to October 15
$45-$50	Good Sam	None
95 Spaces	Gravel	45Width/85Length
Internet, Showers, Laundry	Firewood, Pool, Activities	Games, Shuffleboard

Crazy Horse Family Campground
Just 12 miles away from lake access with plenty of water activities.

788 Hilltop Rd, Littleton, NH 03561	(603) 444-2204 https://www.crazyhorsenh.com	All Year
$48	Military/Good Sam	No Restrictions
175 Spaces	Gravel	32Width/64Length
Internet, Showers, Laundry	Firewood, Grocery, Cable	Pool, Playground, Games

Meredith Woods 4 Season Camping Area
This is a four-season campground offering year-round fun.

551 New Hampshire Route 104, Meredith, NH 03253	(603) 279-5449 meredithwoods.com	All Year
$55	Military	None
100 Spaces	Paved	28Width/Length
Internet, Showers, Laundry	Breakfast, Firewood, Pool	Rec. Hall, Game Room

Twin Tamarack Family Camping
A brief description.

41 Twin Tamarack Rd, New Hampton, NH 03256	(603) 279-4387 twintamarackcampground.com	May 17 to October 14
$38-$48	Good Sam	None
240 Spaces	Gravel	30Width/60Length
Internet, Showers, Laundry	Firewood, Cable, Rentals	Pool, Rec.Hall, Game Room

Mi-Te-Jo Campground
Just an hour's drive from the White Mountains.

111 Mitejo Rd, Milton, NH 03851	(603) 652-9022 https://mi-te-jo.com/	May 15 to October 10
$53-$105	None	None
202 Spaces	Gravel	35Width/80Length
Showers, Laundry, Gated	Firewood, Cable, Rentals	Tennis, Pavilion, Games

Long Island Bridge Campground
Offering both waterfront and backwoods camping, depending on your taste.

29 Long Island Rd, Moultonborough, NH 03254	(603) 253-6053 longislandbridgecampgroundnh.com	May 15 to October 10
$41-$50	None	Pet Breed, 21 Day Max
96 Spaces	Gravel	24Width/45Length
Internet, Showers, Laundry	Firewood, Gated, Cable, Games	Rentals, Playground

Crow's Nest Campground
A wooded wonderland awaits you at this Newport campground.

529 S Main St, Newport, NH 03773	(603) 863-6170 http://crowsnestcampground.com/	May 15 to October 10
$39-$43	None	Pet Quantity
103 Spaces	Gravel	27Width/75Length
Internet, Showers, Laundry	Pool, Rentals, Rec. Hall	Game Room, Playground

Westward Shores RV Resort
Seasonal, weekly, and overnight camping are available.

110 Nichols Rd, Ossipee, NH 03864	(603) 539-6453 https://www.westwardshores.com	May 15 to October 15
$97-$109	Military	None
381 Spaces	Gravel	30Width/40Length
Internet, Showers, Laundry	ATM, Gated, Ice, Snack Bar	Rentals, Games, Tennis

Strafford/Lake Winnipesaukee South KOA
Your opportunity to escape to the lake regions of New Hampshire.

79 1st Crown Point Rd, Strafford, NH 03884	(603) 332-0405 https://koa.com/campgrounds/strafford/	May 10 to October 14
$69-$99	None	Pet Quantity
135 Spaces	Gravel	24Width/60Length
Internet, Shower, Laundry	Firewood, Supplies, Gated, Cable, Ice	Rec. Hall, Game Room

Tamworth Camping Area
Located between the Lake and White Mountain regions.

194 Depot Rd, Tamworth, NH 03886	(603) 323-8031 https://tamworthcamping.com	May 15 to October 15
$50-$55	Good Sam	None
100 Spaces	Gravel	35Width/50Length
Showers, Laundry, Cable	Gated, Firewood, Rec. Hall	Games, Mini Golf, Tables

Beech Hill Campground
Come and relax in the White Mountains.

970 Route 302 W, Carroll, NH 03598	(603) 846-5521 http://beechhillcampground.com/	May 15 to October 15
$39-$49	None	None
107 Spaces	Gravel	30Width/60Length
Showers, Laundry, Gated	Firewood, Grocery, Rec. Hall	Game Room, Cable

New Hampshire - South

Field & Stream RV Park
Open to all ages, but focusing on providing services for adult travelers.

7 Dupaw Gould Rd, Brookline, NH 03033	(603) 673-4677 http://www.fsrvp.com	All Year
$47	Military/Good Sam	Pet Breed
54 Spaces	Gravel	29Width/64Length
Internet, Shower, Laundry	Playground, Gated, Firewood	Cable, Pavilion, Tables

Sandy Beach RV Resort
This park is the best-kept secret in New Hampshire.

677 Clement Hill Rd, Contoocook, NH 03229	(866) 281-3076	May 5 to October 10
$38-$49	Military/Good Sam	No Restrictions
182 Spaces	Paved/Gravel	35Width/60Length
Internet, Shower, Laundry	Firewood, Grocery, Cable	Rentals, Paddle Boats, Ice

Green Gate Campground
Located in the beautiful forests of Exeter.

Route 108, Exeter, NH 03833	(603) 772-2100	May 1 to October 1
$55-$59	Good Sam	Pet Quantity
74 Spaces	Gravel	26Width/130Length
Internet, Shower, Laundry	Gated, Firewood, Pool	Rentals, Playground

Tidewater Campground
Located just minutes to Hampton Beach.

160 Lafayette Rd, Hampton, NH 03842	(603) 926-5474 tidewatercampgroundnh.com	May 15 to October 15
$54	None	**No Pets**
228 Spaces	Paved/Gravel	25Width/60Length
Internet, Showers, Gated	Firewood, Grocery, Pool	Playground, Fire Rings

Wakeda Campground
Just 8 miles to Hampton Beach, a great place to make camping memories.

294 Exeter Rd, Hampton Falls, NH 03844	(603) 772-5274	May 15 to October 1
$52-$57	Military	None
377 Spaces	Paved	22Width/86Length
Showers, Laundry, Firewood	Snack Bar, Grocery, Rentals	Playground, Games

Hinsdale Campground at Thicket Hill Village
Ideally located in southwestern New Hampshire along the Connecticut River.

29 Pine St, Hinsdale, NH 03451	(603) 336-8906 https://www.campingnow.com	April 17 to October 31
$50	Good Sam	Pet Quantity
88 Spaces	Gravel	35Width/60Length
Internet, Shower, Laundry	Rec. Hall, Cable, Pool	Game Room, Activities

Friendly Beaver Campground
Offering plenty of amenities, including planned activities.

99 Cochran Hill Rd, New Boston, NH 03070	(603) 487-5570 https://www.friendlybeaver.com	All Year
$64	Military	Pet Breed
288 Spaces	Gravel	30Width/45Length
Internet, Shower, Laundry	ATM, Ice, Firewood, Snack Bar	Rentals, Game Room

Great Bay Camping
Enjoy staying in the beauty of this park along the Squamscott River.

56 Rte 108 Ste 60, Newfields, NH 03856	(603) 778-0226 https://www.greatbaycamping.com	May 15 to October 1
$45	None	Pet Quantity
68 Spaces	Gravel	45Width/72Length
Internet, Shower, Laundry	Snack Bar, Pool, Boat Rental	Games, Playground

Pine Acres Resort
Located in the heart of the Seacoast Region of New Hampshire.

74 Freetown Road, Raymond, NH 03077	(603) 895-2519	April 15 to October 15
$51-$69	Good Sam	None
381 Spaces	Paved	32Width/48Length
Internet, Shower, Laundry	Firewood, SnackBar	Game Room, Rec. Hall

Cold Springs Camp Resort
This is the most fun campground in New Hampshire.

62 Barnard Hill Rd, Weare, NH 03281	(603) 529-2528 coldspringscampresort.com	May 1 to October 10
$69-$83	None	Pet Breed
380 Spaces	Paved	33Width/64Length

New Jersey

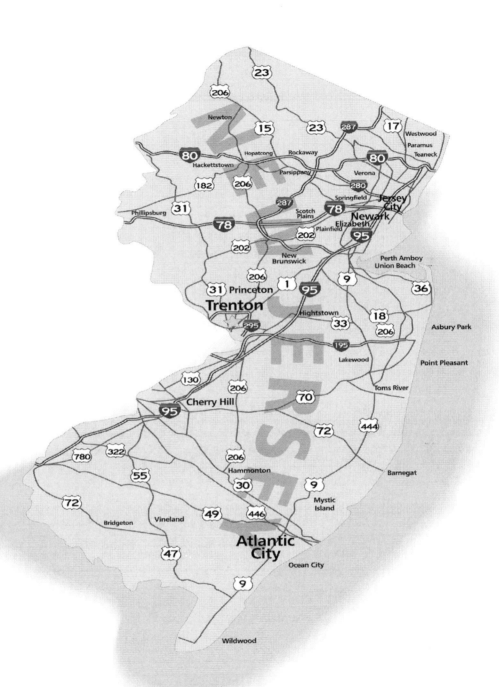

New Jersey is a state of variety. In the northern areas, you can enjoy beautiful and rugged outdoors. Then there are larger, bustling cities with plenty of attractions and even some casinos. No matter what you want to do on your vacation, you'll find it here.

Long Beach RV Resort
The best destination to see both the Jersey Shore and Long Beach Island.

30 Rte 72, Barnegat, NJ 08005	(609) 698-5684 Website	April 1 to November 1
$54-$68	Military	None
188 Spaces	Gravel	22Width/46Length
Internet, Shower, Laundry	Firewood, Gated, Snack Bar	Playground, Games, Tables

The Depot Travel Park
The closest campground to Cape May beaches.

800 Broadway, West Cape May, NJ 08204	(609) 884-2533 https://thedepottravelpark.com/	May 1 to October 14
$43-$63	None	None
240 Spaces	Paved	30Width/60Length
Internet, Shower, Laundry	Gated, Firewood, Cable	Rentals, Playground

Big Timber Lake RV Camping Resort
Stay at a fabulous location and a great vacation destination.

116 Swainton Goshen Rd, Cape May Court House, NJ 08210	(609) 465-4456	April 15 to October 21
$58-$98	Good Sam	None
469 Spaces	Paved/Gravel	25Width/50Length
Internet, Shower, Laundry	Firewood, SnackBar, Restaurant	Game Room, Activities, Pool

Avalon Campground
Stay minutes away from beautiful beaches.

1917 Rte 9 N, Cape May Court House, NJ 08210	(609) 624-0075 http://avaloncampground.com/	April 14 to October 15
$45-$77	Military	None
320 Spaces	Paved	25Width/40Length
Internet, Shower, Laundry	Rentals, Pool, Rec. Hall	Game Room, Playground

Wading Pines Camping Resort
A brief description.

85 Godfrey Bridge Rd, Chatsworth, NJ 08019	(609) 726-1313 https://wadingpines.com	April 15 to November 15
$40-$70	None	None
284 Spaces	Gravel	25Width/60Length
Showers, Laundry, Gated	Firewood, Snack Bar, Ice	Pool, Game Room, Tennis

Driftwood RV Resort
Avalon and Woodlands offer beaches and boardwalks full of activities and fun.

1955 Route 9, Clermont, NJ 08210	(609) 624-1899	April 8 to October 9
$43-$88	Good Sam	None
663 Spaces	Paved	30Width/60Length
Internet, Shower, Laundry	Rentals, Pool, Rec. Hall	Game Room, Playground

Country Oaks Campground
A brief description.

13 S Jersey Ave, Dorothy, NJ 08317	(609) 476-2143 countryoakscampground.com	April 15 to October 15
$58-$62	Good Sam	Pet Breed
140 Spaces	Gravel	30Width/70Length
Internet, Shower, Laundry	Gated, Supplies, Firewood	Pool, Cable, Rentals

Holly Acres Campground
Have a peaceful camping experience while still being close to attractions.

218 S Frankfurt Ave, Egg Harbor City, NJ 08215	(609) 965-2287 hollyacresrvpark.com	April 15 to October 31
$45-$65	Military	Pet Breed
166 Spaces	Gravel	25Width/45Length
Pool, Rec. Hall	Playground	Mini Golf

Fla-net Park
Conveniently and centrally located just off the interstate.

10 Flanders Netcong Rd, Flanders, NJ 07836	(973) 347-4467 http://flanetpark.com/	All Year
$45-$60	Good Sam	None
89 Spaces	Gravel	25Width/55Length
Internet, Shower, Laundry	Playground, Firewood, Ice	Playground, Game Room

Shady Pines RV Resort
A peaceful retreat near two nature preserves.

443 S 6th Ave, Galloway Township, NJ 08205	(609) 652-1516	All Year
$57	Military/Good Sam	55+, Pet Quantity
140 Spaces	Paved	30Width/60Length
Internet, Shower, Laundry	Playground, Pool, Rec. Hall	Shuffleboard, Gym

Pomona RV Park
Great family camping in the heart of the southern New Jersey shore area.

536 S Pomona Rd, Pomona, NJ 08240	(609) 965-2123 https://pomonarvpark.com	All Year
$55-$63	Military/Good Sam	None
100 Spaces	Gravel	35Width/60Length
Internet, Shower, Laundry	Firewood, Cable, Rentals	Game Room, Playground

Timberland Lake Campground
The best option for family camping.

1335 Reed Rd, Jackson, NJ 08527	(732) 928-0500 http://timberlandlakecampground.com/	All Year
$55-$65	Military/Good Sam	No Restrictions
220 Spaces	Gravel	35Width/60Length
Showers, Gated, Ice	Supplies, Cable, Paddle Boats	Playground, Mini Golf

Tip Tam Camping Resort
A family camping experience with endless activities and amenities, both indoor and outdoor.

301 Brewers Bridge Rd, Jackson, NJ 08527	(732) 363-4036 https://tiptam.com/	April 15 to October 31
$49-$67	Military/Good Sam	Pet Breed
192 Spaces	Paved/Gravel	30Width/50Length
Internet, Shower, Laundry	Game Room, Pool, Rec. Hall	Playground, Games, Mini Golf

Indian Rock RV Park
Close to the Jersey Shore, Six Flags, and more.

920 W Veterans Hwy, Jackson, NJ 08527	(732) 928-0034 https://indianrockrvpark.com	All Year
$60-$70	Military/Good Sam	Pet Breed
150 Spaces	Gravel	30Width/65Length
Internet, Shower, Laundry	Firewood, Pool, Rec. Hall	Game Room, Playground

Liberty Harbor Marina RV Park
The closest RV park to New York City.

11 Luis Munoz Marin Blvd, Jersey City, NJ 07302	(201) 516-7500 http://libertyharborrv.com/	All Year
$110-$120	None	None
70 Spaces	Paved	18Width/45Length
Internet, Shower, Laundry	Gated, Restaurant, Ice	RV Service, Boat Rental

Winding River Campground
The finest campground in the Atlantic City area.

6752 Weymouth Rd, Mays Landing, NJ 08330	(609) 625-3191 windingrivercampground.com	May 1 to October 15
$50-$56	Military/Good Sam	No Restrictions
132 Spaces	Gravel	40Width/68Length
Showers, Laundry, Gated	Fishing, Boat Rental, Pool	Firewood, Game Room, Ice

Mays Landing Campground
Located in southern New Jersey, this campground offers outstanding accommodations.

1079 12th Avenue, Mays Landing, NJ 08330	(609) 476-2811	April 1 to October 31
$44-$78	Good Sam	Pet Quantity
148 Spaces	Gravel	30Width/60Length
Internet, Shower, Laundry	Rentals, Pool, Game Room	Firewood, Snack Bar, Ice

Ocean View Resort Campground
This is a top-rated, family-operated resort campground.

2555 N Rte 9, Ocean View, NJ 08230	(609) 624-1675 https://ovresort.com	April 13 to October 8
$42-$98	None	None
1175 Spaces	Paved	30Width/62Length
Internet, Shower, Laundry	Rentals, Snack Bar, Cable	Rec.Hall, GameRoom, Tennis

Lake & Shore RV
Your family fun destination, offering cozy wooded sites and amenities.

515 Corson Tavern Road, Ocean View, NJ 08230	(609) 624-1494	All Year
$54	Military/Good Sam	No Restrictions
396 Spaces	Paved/Gravel	30Width/45Length
Internet, Shower, Laundry	Cable, Firewood, Rentals	Pool, Rec. Hall, Game Room

Echo Farms RV Resort

The perfect vacation destination near the Jersey Shore.

3066 North Route 9, Ocean View, NJ 08230	(609) 624-3589	April 15 to October 31
$52	Good Sam	Pet Quantity
240 Spaces	Paved/Gravel	30Width/60Length
Internet, Shower, Laundry	Rentals, Pool, Gated, Cable	Playground, Fire Rings

Frontier Campground

A family campground located between Ocean City and Sea Isle City

84 Tyler Road Ocean View, NJ 08230	(609) 390-3649 https://frontiercampground.com/	April 15 to October 13
$60-$120	Good Sam	Pet Size
192 Spaces	Gravel	25Width/45Length
Internet, Shower, Laundry	Firewood, Cable, Rentals, Ice	Rec. Hall, Game Room

Sea Grove Camping Resort

Located in the heart of Cape May County and just minutes from the beach.

2665 N Rte 9, Ocean View, NJ 08230	(609) 624-3529 https://seagroveresort.com/	April 1 to November 1
$38-$64	None	None
170 Spaces	Paved/Gravel	30Width/47Length
Internet, Shower, Laundry	Grocery, Cable, Pool, Ice	Snack Bar, Game Room

Chestnut Lake RV Campground

A tranquil park in the pine barrens.

631 Chestnut Neck Rd, Port Republic, NJ 08241	(609) 652-1005	April 22 to October 31
$58	Good Sam	Pet Quantity
185 Spaces	Gravel	28Width/60Length
Internet, Shower, Laundry	Firewood, Rec. Hall, Pool	Playground, Cable, Mini Golf

Atlantic Shore Pines Campground

A family-friendly campground located in the pine barrens.

450 Ishmael Rd, Tuckerton, NJ 08087	(609) 296-9163 https://atlanticshorepines.com/	All Year
$58-$65	Military/Good Sam	No Restrictions
176 Spaces	Gravel	30Width/80Length
Showers, Laundry, ATM	Snack Bar, Pool, Grocery	Game Room, Mini Golf

New Mexico

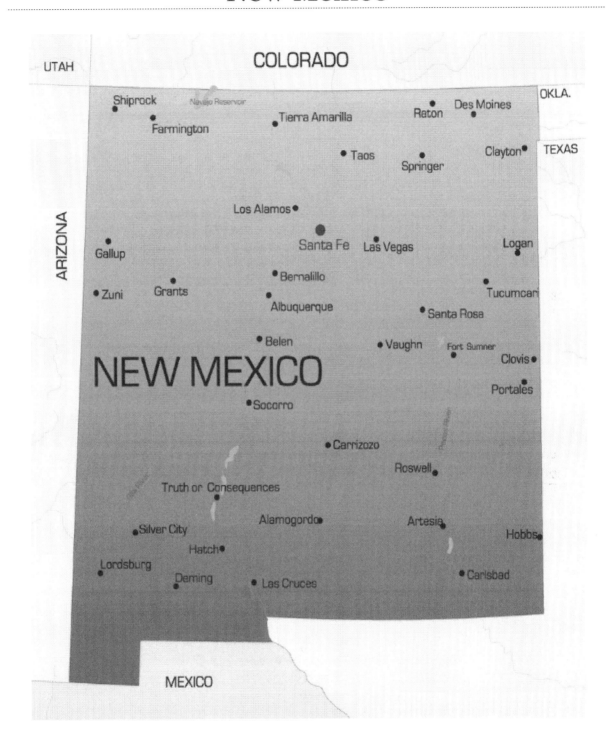

New Mexico – North

New Mexico North offers you plenty of outdoor experiences along with cultural sites and Historic Route 66. There is no shortage of things to keep you busy while on vacation here. Or just come for the winter to enjoy your time at a great RV park.

Sky City RV Park
Located next to the Sky City Casino Hotel so you can enjoy 24-hour gaming.

Interstate 40 Exit 102, Pueblo Of Acoma, NM 87034	(505) 552-7965 https://www.skycity.com	All Year
$22	Military	None
42 Spaces	Gravel	30Width/85Length
Casino, ATM, Cable	Internet, Showers, Laundry	Lounge, Pool, Gym

Angel Fire RV Resort
A family-friendly destination in the Southern Rockies.

27500 US Highway 64, Angel Fire, NM 87710	(855) 421-0308 https://angelfirervresort.com/	All Year
$50-$80	Military	RV Age
102 Spaces	Paved	40Width/90Length
Internet, Showers, Laundry	Gated, Cable, Breakfast	Supplies, Pool, Ice

Moore's RV Park
A relaxing park with all the amenities you need.

1900 E Blanco Blvd, Bloomfield, NM 87413	(505) 632-8339 http://mooresrvpark.com/	All Year
$40-$45	Military	None
62 Spaces	Gravel	27Width/60Length
Internet, Showers, Laundry	Pool, Firewood, Rentals	Rec.Hall, Games, Pavilion

Sky Mountain Resort RV Park
This park is located in the quiet village of Chama.

HC 75 2743, Chama, NM 87520	(575) 756-1100 https://skymountainresort.com/	May 15 to October 15
$38-$46	Military/Good Sam	Pet Breed
46 Spaces	Gravel	30Width/60Length
Internet, Showers, Laundry	Fishing Guides, Firewood	Games, Pavilion, Fire Rings

Golden Eagle RV Resort

Conveniently located along the Enchanted Circle Scenic Byway.

540 W Therma Dr, Eagle Nest, NM 87718	(800) 388-6188 https://www.goldeneaglerv.com/	All Year
$42-$46	Military/Good Sam	No Restrictions
65 Spaces	Gravel	24Width/65Length
Internet, Showers, Laundry	Firewood, Supplies, Grocery	Horseshoes, Rec. Hall, Gym

USA RV Park

A brief description.

2925 W Historic Highway 66, Gallup, NM 87301	(505) 863-5021 http://www.usarvpark.com/	All Year
$33-$35	Military/Good Sam	Pet Breed
136 Spaces	Paved	27Width/80Length
Internet, Showers, Laundry	Rentals, Pool, Activities	Playground, Games, Patios

Lavaland RV Park

Easy access on and off the interstate.

1901 E Santa Fe Ave, Grants, NM 87020	(505) 287-8665 http://lavalandrvpark.com/	All Year
$29	Good Sam	None
39 Spaces	Gravel	30Width/75Length
Brewery, Supplies, Lounge	Horseshoes, Rec. Hall	Internet, Showers, Laundry

Bar S RV Park

Located near a golf course and many wonderful attractions.

1860 Pinon Dr, Grants, NM 87020	(505) 876-6002 campingandcampgrounds.com	All Year
$22-$23	Military/Good Sam	Pet Breed
50 Spaces	Gravel	27Width/70Length
Internet, Showers, Laundry	Supplies, Ice	Cable, Rec. Hall

Homestead RV Park

Stay where each day is a new adventure.

11 Road 6432, Kirtland, NM 87417	(505) 598-9181 homesteadrvparknm.com/	All Year
$36	Military/Good Sam	Pet Breed
64 Spaces	Gravel	30Width/65Length
Internet, Showers, Laundry	Supplies, Rentals	Tables, Ice

Santa Fe Skies RV Park
Experience views and sunsets, within easy travel to Santa Fe attractions.

14 Brown Castle Rnch, Santa Fe, NM 87508	(505) 473-5946 http://santafeskiesrvpark.com/	All Year
$54-$75	Military/Good Sam	No Restrictions
98 Spaces	Paved/Gravel	31Width/75Length
Internet, Showers, Laundry	Rec. Hall, Ice, Game Room	Pavilion, Patios, Supplies

Rancheros de Santa Fe Campground
A quiet and wooded campground just minutes from Old Downtown Santa Fe.

736 Old Las Vegas Hwy, Santa Fe, NM 87505	(505) 466-3482 https://www.rancheros.com/	All Year
$35-$59	Military/Good Sam	No Restrictions
124 Spaces	Paved/Gravel	24Width/55Length
Internet, Showers, Laundry	Supplies, Firewood, Cable	Rentals, Pool, Rec. Hall

Los Suenos de Santa Fe RV Resort
Located minutes from Santa Fe Plaza by car or bus.

3574 Cerrillos Rd, Santa Fe, NM 87507	(505) 473-1949 https://lossuenosrv.com/	All Year
$39-$55	Military/Good Sam	Pet Breed
95 Spaces	Paved	25Width/70Length
Internet, Showers, Laundry	Playground, Rentals, Ice	Pavilion, Patios, Tables

Roadrunner RV Park
Just 15 miles north of Santa Fe and easily accessible off the highway.

55 Ogo Wii, Santa Fe, NM 87506	(505) 455-2626 http://roadrunnerrvparknm.com/	All Year
$35	Military/Good Sam	None
60 Spaces	Gravel	35Width/60Length
Internet, Lounge, Snack Bar	ATM, Supplies, Ice, RV Wash	Pool, Waterslide, Tables

Santa Rosa Campground
Get all the amenities of home with the beauty of camping.

2136 Rte 66, Santa Rosa, NM 88435	(575) 472-3126 santarosacampground.com/	All Year
$32-$43	Military/Good Sam	Pet Quantity, Pet Breed
91 Spaces	Gravel	25Width/75Length
Internet, Showers, Laundry	Cable, Restaurant, Firewood	Pool, Playground, Ice

Taos Valley RV Park

There is plenty of outdoor activities to be had in the surrounding area here.

120 Este Es Rd, Taos, NM 87571	(575) 758-4469 https://taosrv.com/	All Year
$38-$51	Military/Good Sam	Pet Breed
64 Spaces	Gravel	25Width/65Length
Internet, Showers, Laundry	Game Room, Playground	Pavilion, Tables, BBQ's

Blaze-in-Saddle RV Park

Come here for high quality and personal service. Accommodates both pets and horses.

2500 E Route 66 Blvd, Tucumcari, NM 88401	(575) 815-4085 blaze-in-saddle.com/	All Year
$27-$29	Military/Good Sam	None
51 Spaces	Gravel	24Width/65Length
Internet, Showers, Laundry	Supplies, Firewood	Ice, RV Wash

New Mexico – Central

Central New Mexico offers plenty of activities around the Albuquerque area. There are rich cultural diversity and historical sites to enjoy. You can also take part in several outdoor activities.

Isleta Lakes & RV Park
Experience the natural beauty of the Southwest.

11000 Broadway SE Albuquerque, NM 87105	505-244-8102 http://www.isleta.com	All Year
$38	Good Sam	Pet Breed
50 Spaces	Paved/Gravel	30Width/60Length
Internet, Showers, Laundry	Gated, Snack Bar, Ice	Pavilion, Sauna, Golf

Route 66 RV Resort
Just minutes west of Albuquerque along Route 66.

14500 Central Ave. SW, Albuquerque, NM 87121	(505) 352-8000 http://rt66rvresort.com/	All Year
$50-$60	Military/Good Sam	RV Age, 28 Day Max Stay
100 Spaces	Paved	45Width/85Length
Internet, Showers, Laundry	Lounge, Guest Services, Ice	Firewood, Playground

Coronado Village RV Resort
Enjoy the best of a resort lifestyle here.

8401 Pan American Fwy NE, Albuquerque, NM 87113	(505) 823-2515 http://thesman.com/coronado-albuquerque	All Year
$45-$125	Good Sam	Pet Size, Pet Quantity, Breed
321 Spaces	Paved	25Width/60Length
Showers, Laundry, Gated	Pool, Rec. Hall, Activities	Playground, Gym, Patios

American RV Resort
Enjoy wonderful amenities just off the interstate and near old Route 66.

13500 Central Ave SW, Albuquerque, NM 87121	(505) 831-3545 https://americanrvpark.com/	All Year
$35-$150	Military/Good Sam	Pet Breed
218 Spaces	Paved	25Width/65Length
Internet, Showers, Laundry	Rentals, Gated, Supplies, Ice	Cable, Breakfast, Rec. Hall

Enchanted Trails RV Park
Get amazing views from beautiful sunsets to desert vistas.

14305 Central Ave NW, Albuquerque, NM 87121	(505) 831-6317 http://www.enchantedtrails.com/	All Year
$34-$37	Military/Good Sam	None
135 Spaces	Paved/Gravel	25Width/80Length
Internet, Showers, Laundry	Pool, Supplies, Hot Tub	Rec. Hall, Game Room

Balloon View RV Park
Stay here to explore the hidden treasures of the Albuquerque area.

500 Tyler Rd NE, Albuquerque, NM 87113	(505) 345-3716 http://www.balloonviewrv.com/	All Year
$45	Good Sam	Pet Breed
87 Spaces	Gravel	25Width/40Length
Internet, Showers, Laundry	Pool, Cable, Gym	Pavilion, Patios

Stagecoach Stop RV Park
A brief description.

3650 State Hwy 528 NE, Rio Rancho, NM 87144	(505) 867-1000 stagecoachstoprv.com/	All Year
$41-$49	Military/Good Sam	Pet Breed
85 Spaces	Paved	27Width/60Length
Internet, Showers, Laundry	Cable, Pool, Rec.Hall	Pavilion, Game Room

New Mexico – South

Southern New Mexico offers you a quiet and restful solitude for your vacation. For the adventurous sort, there is plenty of outdoor activities. Plus, you can see culture and history all around you.

Boot Hill RV Resort
Enjoy an excellent climate when you visit here for either a short stay or a long term winter stay.

1 Dog Ranch Rd, Alamogordo, NM 88310	(575) 439-6224 http://www.boothillrv.com/	All Year
$32-$41	Good Sam	RV Age
50 Spaces	Gravel	32Width/83Length
Internet, Showers, Laundry	Supplies, Rentals, Rec. Hall	Games, Pavilion, Gym

Kiva RV Park
Relax and enjoy your time in the southwest. Pet-friendly and horse-friendly as well.

21 Old Highway 60 W, Bosque, NM 87006	(505) 861-0693 kivarvparkandhorsemotel.com/	All Year
$35	Military/Good Sam	None
34 Spaces	Gravel	28Width/60Length
Horse Motel, Internet	Showers, Laundry	Game Room, Activities

Bud's Place RV Park
Just 15 minutes to the popular Carlsbad Caverns.

900 Standpipe Rd, Carlsbad, NM 88220	(575) 200-1865 Website	All Year
$45	Military/Good Sam	None
91 Spaces	Gravel	30Width/70Length
Internet, Showers, Laundry	Cable, Rentals, Playground	Fire Rings, Tables

Carlsbad RV Park
A gated community close to many area attractions.

4301 National Parks Hwy, Carlsbad, NM 88220	(505) 885-6333 carlsbadrvpark.com/	All Year
$35-$43	Military/Good Sam	None
144 Spaces	Gravel	22Width/55Length
Internet, Showers, Laundry	Gated, GameRoom, Supplies	Grocery, Cable, Rentals

Clovis RV Park

Located on the north side of Clovis, this place aims to be your home away from home.

3009 N Prince St, Clovis, NM 88101	575-742-5035 https://clovisrvpark.co/	All Year
$36-$38	Military/Good Sam	None
64 Spaces	Paved/Gravel	25Width/75Length
Internet, Showers, Laundry	Cable, Supplies, LP Gas	Rec. Hall, Tables

Travelers World RV Park

A safe, quiet, friendly, and full-service RV park.

1361 US Hwy 60/84, Clovis, NM 88101	(575) 763-8153 travelersworldcampground.com/	All Year
$50	None	Restrictions
65 Spaces	Gravel	27Width/70Length
Internet, Showers, Laundry	Supplies, Ice, Cable, LP Gas	Playground, Tables

Little Vineyard RV Resort

The perfect base camp for exploring historic Deming and the region around you.

2901 E Pine St, Deming, NM 88030	(575) 546-3560 http://littlevineyard.com/	All Year
$35	Good Sam	Pet Quantity, Pet Breed
144 Spaces	Gravel	32Width/70Length
Internet, Showers, Laundry	Cable, Pool, Supplies	Rec. Hall, Game Room

Elephant Butte Lake RV Resort

The perfect base camp for exploring Sierra County and the Geronimo Trail.

402 Highway 195 Elephant Butte, NM 87935	(575) 744-5996 elephantbuttelakervresort.com/	All Year
$43-$71	Military/Good Sam	None
132 Spaces	Paved	30Width/70Length
Internet, Showers, Laundry	Game Room, Rec.Hall	Cable, Pool, Gym

Cedar Cove RV Park

With two locations at Elephant Butte Lake, you are sure to find a great site to enjoy.

48 Yapple Canyon Rd, Elephant Butte, NM 87935	(575) 744-4472 https://cedarcovervpark.com/	All Year
$40-$50	Military/Good Sam	None
140 Spaces	Gravel	32Width/80Length
Internet, Showers, Laundry	Guest Services, Rentals, Ice	Game Room, Activities, Gym

Sunny Acres RV Park
A quiet RV park paradise for a great stay in New Mexico.

595 N Valley Dr, Las Cruces, NM 88005	(575) 524-1716 http://lascrucesrvpark.com/	All Year
$45-$55	Military/Good Sam	Pet Quantity/Pet Breed
100 Spaces	Gravel	33Width/85Length
Internet, Showers, Laundry	Rec. Hall, Activities, Games	Patios, Tables, Cable

Hacienda RV Resort
Majestic views of the Organ Mountains.

740 Stern Dr, Las Cruces, NM 88005	(575) 528-5800 https://www.haciendarv.com/	All Year
$34-$63	Military/Good Sam	None
113 Spaces	Paved	25Width/60Length
Internet, Showers, Laundry	Ice, Cable, Rec. Hall	Gym, Hot Tub

Trailer Village RV Park
Conveniently located near the downtown center of Roswell.

1706 East 2nd St - Hwy 380 E, Roswell, NM 88201	(575) 623-6040 trailervillagervpark.com/	All Year
$33-$39	Military/Good Sam	None
68 Spaces	Gravel	30Width/65Length
Internet, Showers, Laundry	Supplies, Rentals, Cable	Patios, Tables

Town & Country RV Park
A great RV park where you can get away from it all.

331 West Brasher Rd, Roswell, NM 88203	(505) 624-1833 townandcountryrvpark.com/	All Year
$35	Military/Good Sam	Pet Quantity/Pet Breed
122 Spaces	Paved	24Width/85Length
Internet, Showers, Laundry	Pool, Cable, Rec. Hall	Activities, Gym, Tables

Circle B RV Park
The best RV park in Ruidoso and the closest to all the activities.

26514 US Highway 70 E, Ruidoso Downs, NM 88346	(505) 378-4990 http://www.circlebrv.com/	May 1 to October 31
$40-$45	Good Sam	None
135 Spaces	Paved	35Width/65Length
Internet, Showers, Laundry	Rentals, Cable, RV Wash	Rec. Hall, Activities, Gym

Eagle Creek RV Resort

An abundance of outdoor recreation can be enjoyed here.

159 Ski Run Road, Alto, NM 88312	(575) 336-1131 eaglecreekrvresort.com/	April 1 to November 1
$35-$45	Military/Good Sam	None
48 Spaces	Gravel	30Width/60Length
Internet, Laundry, Gated, Ice	Rentals, Pavilion	Putting Green, Tables

Twin Spruce RV Park

A conveniently located park that can serve as your base camp.

25995 US Highway 70, Ruidoso, NM 88345	(575) 257-4310 twinsprucervpark.com/	All Year
$35-$47	Military/Good Sam	None
111 Spaces	Paved/Gravel	27Width/60Length
Internet, Showers, Laundry	Cable, Restaurant, Pool	Pavilion, Activities

Rainbow Lake RV Resort

The perfect place to relax and have a good time.

806 Carrizo Canyon Rd, Ruidoso, NM 88345	(575) 630-2267 rainbowlakecabinandrv.com/	All Year
$38-$45	Military/Good Sam	None
49 Spaces	Paved/Gravel	25Width/45Length
Internet, Showers, Laundry	Rentals, Supplies, Cable, Ice	Rec. Hall, Pavilion, Tables

Midtown Mountain Campground

Close to midtown and all the best activities and attractions.

302 Mechem Dr., Ruidoso, NM 88345	575-964-8555 midtownmountaincampground.com/	All Year
$39-$59	Good Sam	Pet Quantity
24 Spaces	Gravel	30Width/60Length
Internet, Showers, Laundry	Rentals, Games, Sauna	Pavilion, Tables

Rose Valley RV Ranch

The perfect park to get comfortable and enjoy your vacation.

2040 Memory Ln, Silver City, NM 88061	(505) 534-4277 http://www.rosevalleyrv.com/	All Year
$34-$38	Military/Good Sam	Pet Breed
68 Spaces	Gravel	35Width/70Length
Internet, Showers, Laundry	Rentals, Rec. Hall	Games, Pavilion, Tables

New York

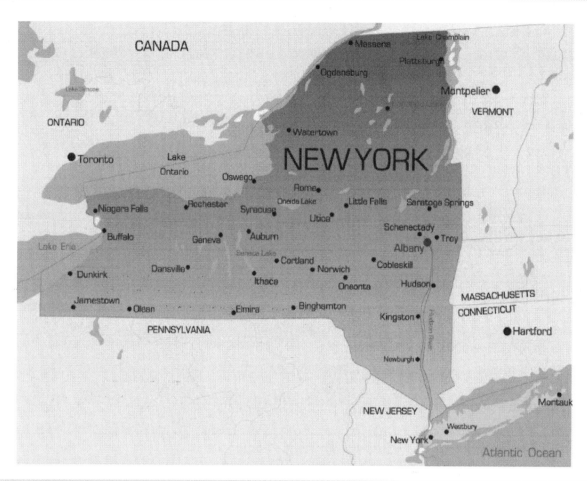

New York – West

Western New York is far removed from the bustling cities and coastal areas. Instead, you get to enjoy a range of beautiful outdoor experiences and attractions such as Niagara Falls. This is a great place to come when you want to enjoy a range of outdoor activities.

Sunflower Acres Family Campground
Stay in the country between Addison and Lindley.

1488 Sunflower Blvd, Addison, NY 14801	(607) 523-7756 sunfloweracresfamilycampground.com/	May 1 to October 15
$35	Good Sam	None
100 Spaces	Gravel	40Width/50Length
Internet, Shower, Laundry	Firewood, Supplies, Pool, Grocery	Activities, Tennis, Ice

Conesus Lake Campground

The best place for family camping on Conesus Lake.

5609 E Lake Rd, Conesus, NY 14435	(585) 346-5472 conesuslakecampground.com/	May 15 to October 15
$50	Good Sam	None
143 Spaces	Paved	35Width/40Length
Internet, Shower, Laundry	Golf Carts, Firewood, Cable	Snack Bar, Rec. Hall

Camp Bell Campground

A family-friendly park in the Finger Lakes area.

8700 State Route 415, Campbell, NY 14821	(607) 527-3301 https://campbellcampground.com/	May 1 to October 22
$34-$45	Military/Good Sam	None
89 Spaces	Gravel	25Width/55Length
Internet, Shower, Laundry	Guest Services, Rentals, Pool	Playground, Activities

Ferenbaugh Campground

Offering the amenities needed for a comfortable and convenient stay.

4248 State Route 414, Corning, NY 14830	(607) 962-6193 http://ferenbaugh.com/	May 1 to October 30
$32-$75	Military	None
149 Spaces	Gravel	50Width/75Length
Internet, Shower, Laundry	Cable, Firewood, Snack Bar	Game Room, Rec. Hall

Skyline RV Resort

Conveniently located between Buffalo and Rochester.

10933 Town Line Road, Darien Center, NY 14040	(585) 591-2033 https://www.skylinervresort.com	May 2 to October 13
$47-$60	Military/Good Sam	Pet Quantity, Pet Breed
325 Spaces	Paved/Gravel	35Width/60Length
Internet, Showers, Gated	Snack Bar, Pool, Game Room	Activities, Tennis, Ice

Chautauqua Lake KOA

A fun place to stay with incredible views.

5652 Thumb Rd, Dewittville, NY 14728	(716) 386-3804 https://chautauqualakekoa.com/	May 1 to October 15
$39-$92	Military	Pet Breed
246 Spaces	Gravel	50Width/80Length
Internet, Shower, Laundry	Game Room, Pool, Splash Pad	Pedal Carts, Mini Golf

Triple R Camping Resort
A pet and kid-friendly RV park in western New York.

3491 Bryant Hill Rd, Franklinville, NY 14737	(716) 676-3856 https://www.triplercamp.com/	April 15 to October 15
$57-$79	Military/Good Sam	None
218 Spaces	Gravel	45Width/70Length
Internet, Shower, Laundry	Firewood, Grocery, Snack Bar	Pavilion, Pool, Fire Rings

Shamrock Pines Campground
A family-friendly park located among lush green pines.

3900 Jarecki Rd, Franklinville, NY 14737	(716) 676-2776 https://shamrockpines.com/	May 1 to October 15
$40-$52	Military/Good Sam	Pet Quantity
126 Spaces	Gravel	35Width/60Length
Internet, Shower, Laundry	ATM, Firewood, Grocery, Ice	Game Room, Activities

Woodstream Campsite
Offering the basic amenities to help you enjoy your stay.

5440 School Rd, Gainesville, NY 14066	(585) 493-5643 woodstreamcampsite.com	May 1 to October 15
$46	Military/Good Sam	None
220 Spaces	Gravel	50Width/70Length
Guest Services, Showers, Ice	Firewood, Rentals, Rec. Hall	Playground, Games, Tables

Red Rock Ponds RV Resort
Enjoy a tranquil getaway on the Erie Canal.

16097 Canal Rd, Holley, NY 14470	(585) 638-2445 https://redrockponds.com/	May 1 to October 18
$50-$65	Military	Pet Quantity, Pet Breed
132 Spaces	Gravel	40Width/65Length
Internet, Shower, Laundry	Game Room, Rec.Hall, Cable	Playground, Pavilion

Spruce Row Campground
Located above Cayuga Lake in the heart of the Finger Lakes area.

2271 Kraft Rd, Ithaca, NY 14850	(607) 387-9225 http://www.sprucerow.com/	May 1 to October 12
$40-$50	Military/Good Sam	Pet Breed
180 Spaces	Gravel	50Width/65Length
Internet, Rentals, Boats	Game Room, Firewood	Rentals, Mini Golf, Ice

Hidden Valley Camping Area

Offering large sites with basic amenities.

299 Kiantone Rd, Jamestown, NY 14701	(716) 569-5433 hiddenvalleycampingarea.com/	April 15 to October 15
$40-$52	Military	None
225 Spaces	Gravel	28Width/60Length
Internet, Shower, Laundry	Horseshoes, Cable, Pool	Tennis, Playground, Tables

Beaver Meadow Family Campground

Offering a quiet and family-oriented atmosphere.

1455 Beaver Meadow Rd, Java Center, NY 14082	(585) 457-3101 beavermeadowcampground.com/	May 8 to October 14
$40-$60	Good Sam	None
270 Spaces	Gravel	40Width/40Length
Internet, Shower, Laundry	Rentals, Pool, Rec. Hall, Ice	Firewood, Game Room

Niagara County Camping Resort

Enjoy some quiet time in between exploring all the area has to offer.

7369 Wheeler Rd, Lockport, NY 14094	(716) 434-3991 http://www.niagaracamping.com/	May 10 to October 13
$51	Military/Good Sam	Pet Quantity
240 Spaces	Gravel	30Width/55Length
Internet, Firewood, Grocery	Cable, Fishing, Rentals	Playground, Pavilion, Ice

AA Royal Motel and Campground

A brief description.

3333 Niagara Falls Blvd, N. Tonawanda, NY 14120	(716) 693-5695 http://royalmotelandcampground.com/	All Year
$60-$70	Military/Good Sam	None
28 Spaces	Paved	30Width/80Length
Internet, Shower, Laundry	Firewood, Ice, RV Service	Lodge Room, Tables

Niagara Falls Campground

Stay at the closest campground to Niagara Falls.

2405 Niagara Falls Blvd, Niagara Falls, NY 14304	(716) 731-3434 niagarafallscampground.com/	April 1 to November 1
$50-$80	Military/Good Sam	Pet Quantity
64 Spaces	Gravel	25Width/75Length
Internet, Shower, Laundry	Firewood, Supplies, Playground	Pool, Fire Rings, Tables

Cheerful Valley Campground
Located in a beautiful river valley.

1412 State Route 14, Phelps, NY 14532	(315) 781-1222 cheerfulvalleycampground.com/	May 1 to October 15
$50-$59	Good Sam	Pet Quantity
125 Spaces	Paved	50Width/70Length
Internet, Shower, Laundry	Firewood, Grocery, Rentals	Game Room, Playground

Junius Ponds Campground
Stay in a peaceful and family-friendly campground setting.

1475 West Townline Rd, Phelps, NY 14532	(315) 781-5120	April 15 to October 15
$46	Good Sam	None
231 Spaces	Paved	45Width/80Length
Internet, Shower, Laundry	Grocery, Pool, Firewood, Ice	Playground, Game Room

Holiday Hill Campground
Your place for a peaceful family getaway.

7818 Marvin Hill Rd, Springwater, NY 14560	(585) 669-2600 holidayhillcampground.com/	May 1 to October 11
$40-$50	Good Sam	Pet Quantity
167 Spaces	Gravel	40Width/50Length
Internet, Shower, Laundry	Cable, Grocery, Firewood	Playground, Mini Golf

Cherry Grove Campground
Offering you a unique Lake Ontario camping experience.

12669 Ridge Rd, Wolcott, NY 14590	(315) 594-8320 cherrygrovecampground.com/	April 15 to October 15
$42-$47	Good Sam	Pet Quantity, Pet Breed
105 Spaces	Gravel	30Width/75Length
Internet, Shower, Laundry	Pool, Firewood, Ice, Rentals	Playground, Rec.Hall

New York – North

Northern New York is full of beautiful lakes, lush river valleys, and stunning mountains.

Swan Bay Resort
Located in the heart of the 1000 Islands Region.

43615 State Route 12, Alexandria Bay, NY 13607	(315) 482-7926 https://www.swanbayresort.com/	May 1 to October 31
$55-$129	Military/Good Sam	None
150 Spaces	Paved	40Width/80Length
Internet, Showers, Laundry	Lounge, Fishing, Rentals	Activities, Playground

Merry Knoll 1000 Islands Campground
Here you'll enjoy a pleasant camping experience with views of the St. Lawrence River.

38115 Rt 12E, Clayton, NY 13624	(315) 686-3055 merryknollcampground.com/	May 1 to October 15
$38-$55	Military/Good Sam	Pet Breed
75 Spaces	Paved	30Width/60Length
Internet, Showers, Laundry	Pool, Grocery, Rentals	Playground, Pavilion, Tables

Lake George Escape Camping Resort
This large resort offers you direct access to the Schroon River.

74 State Route 149, Lake George, NY 12845	(518) 792-3775 lakegeorgervpark.com/	May 15 to October 15
$72-$110	Military/Good Sam	None
575 Spaces	Paved	30Width/75Length
Internet, Showers, Laundry	Firewood, Playground, Pool	Tennis, Pavilion, Cable

King Phillips Campground
The place to go for an outdoor adventure.

14 Bloody Pond Rd, Lake George, NY 12845	(518) 668-5763 kingphillipscampground.com/	May 1 to October 31
$49-$74	Military/Good Sam	None
222 Spaces	Gravel	35Width/60Length
Internet, Showers, Laundry	Gated, Playground, Pool	Snack Bar, Games, Patios

Ledgeview RV Park
The best place to stay while enjoying the great outdoors.

1 Rockland Dr, Lake George, NY 12845	(518) 798-6621 https://www.ledgeview.com/	May 5 to October 10
$56-$65	Good Sam	**No Pets**
214 Spaces	Paved	50Width/75Length
Internet, Showers, Laundry	Cable, Rentals, Firewood	Playground, Pavilion, Games

Lake George Riverview Campground
Enjoy the beauty and outdoor activities along the Schroon River.

3652 State Route 9, Lake George, NY 12845	(518) 623-9444 http://lakegeorgeriverview.com/	May 15 to October 15
$54-$75	Military/Good Sam	None
94 Spaces	Paved/Gravel	30Width/50Length
Internet, Showers, Laundry	Gated, Supplies, Pool	Game Room, Mini Golf

Yogi Bear's Jellystone Park
Just 2 miles from Lake Ontario and a range of outdoor fun.

601 County Route 16, Mexico, NY 13114	(315) 963-7096 https://jellystonecny.com/	April 26 to October 20
$60-$82	Military	Pet Quantity
125 Spaces	Gravel	40Width/75Length
Internet, Showers, Laundry	ATM, Gated, Pool, Cable	Horseshoes, Pavilion

Brennan Beach RV Resort
Enjoy the comforts of home with a relaxing beach vacation along Lake Ontario.

80 Brennan Beach, Pulaski, NY 13142	(888) 891-5979	May 1 to October 15
$59-$90	Good Sam	None
1400 Spaces	Paved/Gravel	40Width/70Length
Showers, Laundry, Gated	Firewood, Snack Bar, Cable	Activities, Game Room

Lake George Schroon Valley Resort
Your home away from home along the banks of the Schroon River.

1730 Schroon River Rd., Warrensburg, NY 12885	(800) 958-2267	May 10 to October 15
$68-$78	Military/Good Sam	None
119 Spaces	Gravel	40Width/55Length
Showers, Laundry, Gated	Firewood, Grocery, Pool	Game Room, Playground

Babbling Brook RV Park

Located along the Salmon River and close to many local attractions.

1623 County Rt. 4, Ft, Covington, NY 12937	(518) 358-4245 babblingbrookrvparkny.com/	April 15 to October 15
$35-$38	Good Sam	Pet Quantity, Pet Breed
57 Spaces	Gravel	25Width/75Length
Internet, Showers, Laundry	Rec. Hall, Firewood	Fire Rings, Playground

North Pole Resorts

Located on the banks of the Ausable River at the base of Whiteface Mountain.

5644 Nys Rte 86, Wilmington, NY 12997	(518) 946-7733 https://northpoleresorts.com/	April 25 to October 25
$57-$72	Good Sam	Pet Quantity, Pet Breed
113 Spaces	Gravel	30Width/80Length
Internet, Showers, Laundry	Rentals, Pool, Game Room	Rec. Hall, Game Room

New York – Central

Central New York offers a range of outdoor activities. No matter what you like to do, you'll find it in this area. Choose a wonderful park with great amenities and then get out and explore the area.

Tall Pines Campground
A fun, family campground with an old fashioned atmosphere.

2715 County Road 35, Bainbridge, NY 13733	(607) 563-8271 http://tallpinescampgroundny.com/	May 3 to October 14
$41-$55	Good Sam	None
98 Spaces	Gravel	35Width/70Length
Internet, Showers, Laundry	Activities, Rec. Hall, Fishing, Pool	Playground, Games, Ice

Cider House Campground
Far enough away from the highway, so you aren't bothered by the noise.

3570 Canal Rd, Bouckville, NY 13310	(315) 825-8477 ciderhousecampground.com/	May 20 to October 1
$25-$45	Good Sam	None
39 Spaces	Gravel	30Width/70Length
Internet, Showers, Laundry	Rentals, RecHall, Playground	Pavilion, Games, Fire Rings

Cooperstown Shadow Brook Campground
Stay in a clean, fun, and safe environment.

2149 County Highway 31, Cooperstown, NY 13326	(607) 264-8431 https://cooperstowncamping.com/	May 6 to October 15
$52-$72	Military/Good Sam	Pet Breed
97 Spaces	Gravel	30Width/50Length
Internet, Showers, Laundry	Game Room, Pool, Firewood	Games, Pavilion, Rentals

Meadow-Vale Campsites
A brief description.

505 Gilbert Lake Rd, Mount Vision, NY 13810	(607) 293-8802 https://meadow-vale.com/	May 12 to October 9
$42-$46	Military/Good Sam	None
95 Spaces	Gravel	35Width/70Length
Internet, Showers, Laundry	PaddleBoats, Pool, Rentals	Fishing, Game Room, Ice

Cooperstown Beaver Valley

Just five miles to Cooperstown.

138 Towers Rd, Cooperstown, NY 13326	(607) 293-7324 beaver-valley.com/	May 20 to October 14
$35-$50	Military/Good Sam	None
54 Spaces	Gravel	25Width/60Length
Internet, Showers, Laundry	Grocery, Firewood, Fishing	Pool, Paddle Boats, Rentals

Hartwick Highlands Campground

Located on a peaceful country road just 5 miles south of Cooperstown.

131 Burke Hill Rd, Milford, NY 13807	(607) 547-1996 hartwickhighlandscg.com/	May 15 to October 12
$49	None	None
57 Spaces	Gravel	40Width/80Length
Internet, Showers, Laundry	Rentals, Firewood, ATM	Gated, Playground, Pool

Alpine Lake RV Resort

Located at the foothills of the Adirondack Mountains.

78 Heath Rd, Corinth, NY 12822	(800) 576-8541	May 1 to October 12
$68-$77	Military/Good Sam	None
480 Spaces	Gravel	35Width/70Length
Internet, Showers, Laundry	Cable, Restaurant, Firewood	Game Room, Pool, Patios

Black Bear Campground

Offering a complete camping experience with wonderful amenities.

197 Wheeler Rd, Florida, NY 10921	(845) 651-7717 blackbearcampground.com/	All Year
$80-$100	Military/Good Sam	Pet Quantity, Pet Breed
154 Spaces	Paved	30Width/75Length
Internet, Showers, Laundry	Firewood, Games, Playground	Pool, Fishing, Game Room

Adirondack Gateway Campground

Enjoy an outdoor adventure, or just relax at your site.

427 Fortsville Rd, Gansevoort, NY 12831	(518) 792-0485	May 1 to October 15
$46-$65	Military/Good Sam	Pet Quantity
339 Spaces	Paved	35Width/50Length
Internet, Showers, Laundry	Rec.Hall, Game Room, Cable	Playground, Pool, Firewood

Country Roads Campground

If you enjoy nature and peaceful surroundings, then this campground is right for you.

144 Peaceful Ln, Gilboa, NY 12076	(518) 827-6397 countryroadscampground.com/	May 15 to October 12
$43-$46	Good Sam	None
102 Spaces	Gravel	30Width/60Length
Internet, Showers, Laundry	Pool, Rentals, Firewood	Game Room, Activities

Belden Hill Campground

Stay at a clean, quiet, and beautiful park while you explore the nearby area.

1843 State Route 7, Harpursville, NY 13787	(607) 693-1645 http://beldenrvpk.com/	April 1 to October 30
$45	Good Sam	None
123 Spaces	Gravel	35Width/80Length
Internet, Showers, Laundry	Snack Bar, Firewood, Ice	Playground, Activities

Arrowhead RV Park

Located on the Mohawk River as a part of the Erie Canal.

2 Van Buren Ln, Glenville, NY 12302	(518) 382-8966 https://arrowheadmrvp.com/	May 15 to October 15
$37-$40	Good Sam	None
60 Spaces	Paved/Gravel	40Width/100Length
Internet, Showers, Laundry	Firewood, Cable, Ice	Activities, Patios

The Villages at Turning Stone RV Park

Stay at this top-rated park and enjoy nature's playground around you.

5218 Patrick Rd, Verona, NY 13478	(315) 361-7275 https://turningstone.com	May 3 to October 15
$45-$60	Good Sam	None
175 Spaces	Paved	50Width/60Length
Internet, Showers, Laundry	Pool, Fishing, Casino	Playground, Golf, Tennis

Lakeside Campground

Enjoy a number of activities in a serene, outdoor setting.

336 Hargrave Rd, Windsor, NY 13865	(607) 655-2694 Website	May 1 to October 1
$49	Military/Good Sam	Pet Quantity
110 Spaces	Gravel	30Width/75Length
Internet, Showers, Laundry	Rentals, Playground, Tennis	Pavilion, Golf, Game Room

New York – South

Southern New York doesn't have many RV parks, but the ones that are there offer excellent amenities and close proximity to a number of outdoor activities. If you want to get away from it all and enjoy an outdoor adventure, then plan your next vacation at one of these parks.

Rondout Valley Resort

Drive a short distance to historic villages or enjoy an outdoor adventure.

105 Mettacahonts Rd, Accord, NY 12404	(845) 626-5521	April 1 to November 1
$68-$78	Good Sam	None
373 Spaces	Gravel	40Width/90Length
Internet, Showers, Laundry	Rentals, Pool, Playground	Firewood, Gated, Rec.Hall

Woodland Hills Campground

Enjoy a quiet, comfortable, and pet-friendly camping experience nestled in the mountains.

386 Fog Hill Rd, Austerlitz, NY 12017	(518) 392-3557 http://whcg.net/	May 15 to October 10
$45-$51	None	None
190 Spaces	Gravel	30Width/45Length
Internet, Showers, Laundry	Grocery, Firewood, Game Room	Activities, Rec. Hall

Waubeeka Family Campground

Have a time filled with fun and excitement while enjoying all the amenities of home.

133 Farm Rd, Copake, NY 12516	(518) 329-4681 waubeekafamilycampground.com/	May 1 to October 15
$55-$75	Military/Good Sam	Pet Quantity
408 Spaces	Gravel	35Width/60Length
Internet, Cable, Showers	Gated, Snack Bar, Firewood, Ice	GuestServices, PedalCarts

Brook N Wood Family Campground

Enjoy a beautiful, clean, quiet, and relaxing vacation.

1947 County Route 8, Elizaville, NY 12523	(518) 537-6896	April 25 to October 31
$54-$59	Military/Good Sam	Pet Breed
150 Spaces	Gravel	35Width/60Length
Internet, Showers, Laundry	Rentals, Pool, Rec. Hall	Activities, Playground

Yogi Bear's Jellystone Park
Come to this park and enjoy both mountain and river views.

50 Bevier Rd, Gardiner, NY 12525	(845) 255-5193 https://www.lazyriverny.com/	April 16 to November 1
$52-$168	Military	None
223 Spaces	Paved	30Width/80Length
Internet, Showers, Laundry	Cable, Firewood, Grocery	Game Room, Pool, Rec.Hall

Interlake RV Park
Enjoy the park after a long day exploring the surrounding area.

428 Lake Dr, Rhinebeck, NY 12572	(845) 266-5387 https://interlakervpark.com/	April 15 to October 19
$50-$62	Military/Good Sam	None
159 Spaces	Paved	35Width/60Length
Internet, Showers, Laundry	Rentals, Pool, Cable, Firewood	Game Room, Rec. Hall

Rip Van Winkle Campgrounds
A relaxing camping experience in the Catskills Mountains.

149 Blue Mountain Rd Saugerties, NY 12477	845-246-8334 ripvanwinklecampgrounds.com/	April 1 to October 15
$66	Military/Good Sam	None
176 Spaces	Gravel	40Width/75Length
Internet, Showers, Laundry	Rentals, Pool, Cable, Ice	Game Room, Rec. Hall

North Carolina

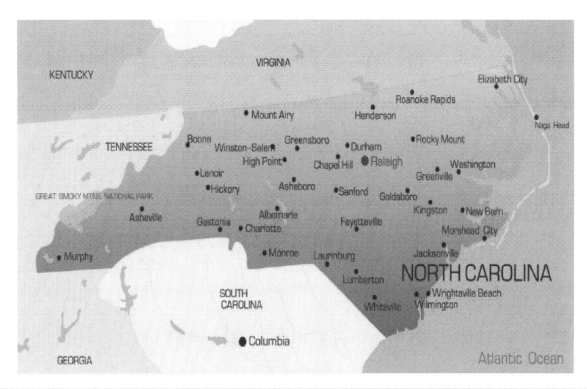

North Carolina – West

Western North Carolina is a land dominated by the Great Smoky Mountains. There are quaint mountain towns to explore and plenty of outdoor activities. Many parks can serve as a great base camp for your day excursions into the surrounding area.

Asheville Bear Creek RV Park
At the end of the day, come back to a park full of peace and quiet.

81 South Bear Creek Road. Asheville, Nc 28806	828-253-0798 ashevillebearcreek.com	All Year
$50-$55	Good Sam	Pet Quantity, Pet Breed
114 Spaces	Paved	30Width/60Length
Internet, Showers, Laundry	Supplies, Pool, Cable, LPGas	Playground, Games, Tables

Campfire Lodgings
Find serenity in the heart of the Blue Ridge Mountains.

116 Appalachian Village Rd, Asheville, NC 28804	(828) 658-8012 campfirelodgings.com/	All Year

$55-$75	Military	None
17 Spaces	Gravel	30Width/65Length
Internet, Showers, Laundry	Supplies, Firewood, Cable	Rentals, Games, Patios

Boone KOA
This is the highest-rated KOA east of the Mississippi.

123 Harmony Mountain Lane, Boone, NC 28607	(828) 264-7250 koa.com/campgrounds/boone/	May 1 to October 31
$44-$75	Military	None
135 Spaces	Gravel	30Width/60Length
Internet, Showers, Laundry	Grocery, Firewood, Pool	Rec. Hall, Fire Rings, Games

Smoky Mountain Meadows Campground
Leave the hustle of your everyday life behind when you enter this campground.

755 E Alarka Rd, Bryson City, NC 28713	(828) 488-3672 http://smokymtnmeadows.com/	April 1 to October 30
$40-$45	Military/Good Sam	None
28 Spaces	Gravel	26Width/68Length
Internet, Showers, Laundry	Rentals, Playground, Firewood	Games, Pavilion, Fire Rings

Fort Wilderness Campground
A brief description.

284 Fort Wilderness Rd, Whittier, NC 28789	(828) 497-9331 http://www.fortwilderness.net/	All Year
$40-$50	Military/Good Sam	None
97 Spaces	Paved	20Width/55Length
Internet, Showers, Laundry	Cable, Rentals, Pool, Ice	Firewood, Game Room

Yogi in the Smokies
Enjoy a beautiful and comfortable campsite deep in the Smoky Mountains.

317 Galamore Rd, Cherokee, NC 28719	(828) 497-9151 https://jellystonecherokee.com/	April 1 to November 1
$55-$72	Military/Good Sam	Pet Breed
127 Spaces	Gravel	18Width/58Length
Internet, Showers, Laundry	Cable, Firewood, Grocery	Game Room, Rec.Hall, Games

Byrd's Branch Campground
Connects the Mountains to Sea Trail through Elkin.

225 Martin Byrd Rd, Elkin, NC 28621	(336) 366-9955 http://byrdsbranchcampground.com/	All Year

$30-$39	Good Sam	None
14 Spaces	Gravel	40Width/80Length
Internet, Showers	Supplies, Firewood, Grocery	Playground, Games

The Great Outdoors RV Resort
Enjoy resort amenities with panoramic mountain views.

321 Thumpers Trl, Franklin, NC 28734	(828) 349-0412 http://gorvresort2.com/	All Year
$49-$55	Military/Good Sam	Pet Breed
63 Spaces	Paved	35Width/60Length
Internet, Showers, Laundry	Cable, Firewood, Grocery	Game Room, Activities

Franklin RV Park
Your gateway to exploring the Smoky Mountains and local historic villages.

230 Old Addington Bridge Rd, Franklin, NC 28734	(828) 349-6200 https://franklinrvpark.com/	April 1 to November 15
$47-$59	Military/Good Sam	Pet Breed
27 Spaces	Gravel	35Width/70Length
Internet, Showers, Firewood	Cable, Activities, Pavilion	Fire Rings, Tables, BBQ's

Lakewood RV Resort
This 55+ park is focused on the active senior.

15 Timmie Ln, Flat Rock, NC 28731	(828) 697-9523 lakewoodrvresort.com/	All Year
$56-$66	Military/Good Sam	55+, Pet Quantity, Pet Breed
78 Spaces	Paved	30Width/75Length
Internet, Showers, Laundry	Lodge Room, Pavilion, Pool	Activities, Gym, Patios

Stonebridge RV Resort
The perfect location to enjoy the mountain towns and many unique places in the area.

1786 Soco Rd Hwy 19, Maggie Valley, NC 28751	(828) 926-1904 stonebridgecampgrounds.com/	All Year
$30-$60	Military/Good Sam	Pet Breed
230 Spaces	Paved/Gravel	25Width/60Length
Internet, Showers, Laundry	Cable, Firewood, Supplies	Game Room, Activities

Valley River RV Resort
Located in the heart of the Great Smokies.

65 Old Tomotla Rd, Marble, NC 28905	(828) 385-4220 http://www.valleyriverrv.com/	All Year
$53-$57	Military/Good Sam	Pet Quantity

93 Spaces	Paved	40Width/65Length
Internet, Showers, Laundry	Firewood, Pool, Rec. Hall	Game Room, Activities

Peachtree Cove Rv Park
Visit the mountains of North Carolina and enjoy amenities for a comfortable stay.

68 Old Peachtree Rd, Marble, NC 28905	(828) 557-2722 https://www.peachtreecove.com/	All Year
$42	Military/Good Sam	Pet Breed
23 Spaces	Paved	30Width/70Length
Internet, Showers, Laundry	Fire Rings, Horseshoes	Firewood, Tables

Buck Creek RV Park
Stay where you can enjoy peace, serenity, and tranquility.

2576 Tom's Creek Road, Marion, NC 28752	(828) 724-4888 http://buckcreekrvparknc.com/	April 1 to November 1
$40-$52	Military/Good Sam	Pet Breed
74 Spaces	Gravel	30Width/62Length
Internet, Showers, Laundry	Firewood, Supplies, Cable	Pavilion, Fire Rings, Ice

Riverside RV Park
This park is a paradise for the golf lover.

611 Independence Blvd, Morganton, NC 28655	(828) 433-6464 riversidegolfrvpark.com/	All Year
$35	Military/Good Sam	Pet Breed
30 Spaces	Paved/Gravel	26Width/67Length
Golf, Cable, Internet	Horseshoes, Mini Golf	Driving Range

Bear Den Family Campground
Come here for a mountain adventure.

600 Bear den Mountain Rd, Spruce Pine, NC 28777	(828) 765-2888 https://bear-den.com/	March 15 to November 30
$47-$54	Military/Good Sam	Pet Quantity, 21 Day Max
60 Spaces	Gravel	20Width/50Length
Internet, Showers, Laundry	FishingSupplies, GameRoom	Rentals, Firewood, Ice

Mama Gertie's Hideaway Campground
This park preserves the beauty of the natural state in the surrounding area.

15 Uphill Rd, Swannanoa, NC 28778	(877) 686-4258 https://www.mamagerties.com/	All Year
$43-$80	Military/Good Sam	None

44 Spaces	Paved	30Width/60Length
Internet, Showers, Laundry	Cable, Rentals, Gated	Firewood, Games, Gym

Fort Tatham RV Resort
Your home away from home in the heart of the Smoky Mountains.

175 Tathams Creek Rd, Sylva, NC 28779	(828) 586-6662	April 1 to October 31
$50	Military/Good Sam	None
87 Spaces	Paved/Gravel	22Width/64Length
Internet, Showers, Laundry	Pool, Rec. Hall, Firewood, Ice	Playground, Games, Pavilion

Moonshine Creek Campground
Enjoy back to nature camping in the Great Smoky Mountains.

2486 Dark Ridge Rd, Sylva, NC 28779	(828) 586-6666 https://moonshinecreek.com/	April 1 to November 1
$49	None	Pet Breed
60 Spaces	Gravel	30Width/50Length
Showers, Laundry, Grocery	Fishing Supplies, Rentals, Ice	Rec. Hall, Playground

Creekwood Farm RV Park
Offering great RV sites that meet any need.

4696 Jonathan Creek Rd, Waynesville, NC 28785	(828) 926-7977 https://creekwoodfarmrv.com/	All Year
$35-$85	Military/Good Sam	Pet Breed
122 Spaces	Gravel	30Width/90Length
Internet, Showers, Laundry	Cable, Rentals, Firewood	Rec. Hall, Activities

Flaming Arrow Campground
Family camping in the Great Smoky Mountains.

283 Flaming Arrow Dr, Whittier, NC 28789	(828) 497-6901 flamingarrowcampground.com/	All Year
$45	Military/Good Sam	Pet Breed
65 Spaces	Paved	28Width/85Length
Internet, Showers, Laundry	Cable, Pool, Playground	Firewood, Games, Pavilion

North Carolina – Central

Central North Carolina has it all. You can be close to attractions, historic sites, bustling cities, and natural beauty. This area is truly a paradise for those who want to get back to rustic nature and enjoy the peace and quiet.

Zooland Family Campground
Close to the North Carolina Zoo and many other local attractions.

3671 Pisgah Covered Bridge Rd, Asheboro, NC 27205	(336) 381-3422 http://www.zoolandfc.com	All Year
$40-$45	MilitaryGood Sam	None
146 Spaces	Gravel	30Width/65Length
Internet, Showers, Laundry	Pool, Firewood, Game Room	Playground, Activities

Spring Hill RV Park
Be close to it all, yet feel far away from everything.

3500 Old Greensboro Rd Lot 1A, Chapel Hill, NC 27516	(919) 967-4268 http://springhillpark.com/	All Year
$40	None	None
66 Spaces	Gravel	30Width/100Length
Internet, Metered LP Gas	Cable, Playground	Tables, Trash Pickup

Camping World Racing Resort
This is a full-service RV resort located at Charlotte Motor Speedway.

6600 Bruton Smith Blvd, Concord, NC 28027	(704) 455-4445 charlottemotorspeedway.com	All Year
$25-$30	Good Sam	None
380 Spaces	Paved	30Width/100Length
Internet, Showers, Laundry	Firewood, ATM, Ice	Pavilion, Playground

Four Oaks Lodging
This park offers something for everyone.

4606 US Highway 301 S, Four Oaks, NC 27524	(919) 963-3596 fouroakslodging.com	All Year
$30-$50	Military/Good Sam	Pet Breed
25 Spaces	Gravel	25Width/80Length
Internet, Showers, Laundry	Firewood, Rentals, Cable	Lodge Room, Playground

Raleigh Oaks RV Resort
Wonderful resort-style amenities ensure you have a great stay.

527 US Highway 701 S, Four Oaks, NC 27524	(919) 934-3181 https://raleighoaksrvresort.com/	All Year
$50-$78	Military/Good Sam	Pet Quantity
150 Spaces	Gravel	35Width/80Length
Internet, Showers, Laundry	Cable, Firewood, Rentals, Pool	Activities, Playground

Cross Winds Family Campground
This is the place to make your campground memories.

160 Campground Ln, Linwood, NC 27299	(336) 853-4567 crosswindsfamilycampground.com/	All Year
$43-$46	None	None
94 Spaces	Paved/Gravel	40Width/90Length
Internet, Shower, Laundry	Gated, Cable, Firewood, Ice	Playground, Pavilion

Lake Myers RV Resort
This family-oriented park is spacious and has it all for your vacation needs.

2862 U.S. 64 West, Mocksville, NC 27028	(888) 361-1731	All Year
$45-$80	Good Sam	None
444 Spaces	Paved/Gravel	25Width/40Length
Internet, Shower, Laundry	Firewood, Cable, Grocery	Snack Bar, Waterslide, Ice

Mayberry Campground
Great rates and basic amenities.

114 Bunker Rd, Mount Airy, NC 27030	(336) 789-6199 mayberrycampground.com/	All Year
$38	Military/Good Sam	None
128 Spaces	Gravel	32Width/73Length
Internet, Shower, Laundry	Firewood, Cable, Supplies	Fishing Supplies, RV Wash

Greystone RV Park
Stay here while enjoying all the area has to offer.

1166 Pilot Knob Park Rd, Pinnacle, NC 27043	(336) 368-5588 greystonervpark.com/	All Year
$58	Military/Good Sam	None
10 Spaces	Gravel	38Width/60Length
Internet, Shower, Laundry	Games, Firewood, Ice	Fire Rings, Tables

Midway Campground

This is the perfect setting for a peaceful retreat.

114 Midway Dr, Statesville, NC 28625	(704) 546-7615 midwaycampground.com/	All Year
$41-$50	Military/Good Sam	Pet Breed
62 Spaces	Gravel	30Width/60Length
Internet, Shower, Laundry	Firewood, Cable, Rentals	Games, Pool, Mini Golf

Van Hoy Farms Family Campground

Offering full amenities for a great vacation experience.

742 Jericho Rd, Harmony, NC 28634	(704) 539-5493 https://vanhoyfarms.com/	All Year
$50-$55	Military/Good Sam	None
94 Spaces	Paved	30Width/65Length
Internet, Shower, Laundry	Firewood, RV Wash, Ice	Pool, Games, Pavilion

Fayetteville RV Resort

Easy access on and off the interstate so you can easily explore all the area has to offer.

6250 Wade Stedman Rd, Wade, NC 28395	(910) 484-5500 https://fayettevillervresort.com/	All Year
$50-$73	Military/Good Sam	Pet Quantity
110 Spaces	Gravel	35Width/90Length
Internet, Shower, Laundry	Pool, Firewood, Rentals, Ice	Playground, Gym, Mini Golf

Kamper's Lodge

Here you'll find many amenities, premium sites, and convenient facilities.

3465 US Highway 301 N, Wilson, NC 27893	(252) 237-0905 https://kamperslodge.com/	All Year
$35	Good Sam	Pet Quantity
51 Spaces	Gravel	30Width/70Length
Internet, Shower, Laundry	Pool, Firewood, Rentals, Ice	Playground, Mini Golf

North Carolina – East

East North Carolina is a place of islands and beautiful white-sand beaches.

Cape Woods Campground

A family-oriented park in a secluded and quiet spot on Hatteras Island.

47649 Buxton Back Rd, Buxton, NC 27920	(252) 995-5850 http://www.capewoods.com/	March 15 to December 1
$48-$58	Military/Good Sam	Pet Quantity
106 Spaces	Gravel	25Width/65Length
Internet, Showers, Laundry	Cable, Gated, Rentals	Playground, Fire Rings

Frisco Woods Campground

Located on Pamlico Sound within the Cape Hatteras National Seashore.

53124 Highway 12, Frisco, NC 27936	(252) 995-5208 thefriscowoodscampground.com/	March 1 to December 1
$46-$80	Military/Good Sam	Pet Quantity
215 Spaces	Paved/Gravel	30Width/60Length
Internet, Showers, Laundry	Fishing, Pool, Rentals	Games, Pavilion

Hatteras Sands Campground

The only campground near Hatteras Village in the scenic Outer Banks.

57316 Eagle Pass Rd, Hatteras, NC 27943	(252) 986-2422 hatterassandsrvpark.com/	April 1 to November 1
$53-$97	Military/Good Sam	None
62 Spaces	Paved	30Width/50Length
Showers, Internet, Laundry	Fishing, Rentals, Cable	Rec. Hall, Pool

Deep Creek RV Resort

Conveniently located just off the highway and a short drive to both Jacksonville and Swansboro.

1090 West Deep Creek Rd, Bryson City, NC 28713	(828) 488-6055	All Year
$50	Military/Good Sam	Pet Breed
98 Spaces	Paved/Gravel	40Width/70Length
Showers, Internet, Laundry	Ice, Grocery, Gated Access	Pool, Games, Fishing Supplies

Cabin Creek Campground
The perfect home away from home with white sand beaches at a family-friendly park.

3200 Wilmington Hwy, Jacksonville, NC 28540	(800) 699-5305 http://properties.camping.com	All Year
$33-$39	Military/Good Sam	Pet Quantity, Pet Breed
99 Spaces	Paved/Gravel	24Width/85Length
Internet, Showers, Laundry	Cable, Firewood, Rentals	Playground, Games, Mini Golf

Camp Hatteras RV Resort
You're sure to make lifelong memories here.

24798 NC Highway 12, Rodanthe, NC 27968	(252) 987-2777 https://www.camphatteras.com/	All Year
$46-$135	Military/Good Sam	None
403 Spaces	Paved	30Width/60Length
Internet, Showers, Laundry	Pool, Rec. Hall, Firewood, Ice	Playground, Pavilion, Games

Brunswick Beaches Camping Resort
Relax at one of three family beaches just down the road from the resort.

7200 Koa Dr. SW, Sunset Beach, NC 28468	(910) 579-7562	All Year
$55-$70	Military/Good Sam	None
84 Spaces	Paved/Gravel	30Width/68Length
Internet, Showers, Laundry	Firewood, Supplies, Grocery	Cable, Rentals, Tables

Lanier's Campground
Stay on the beautiful Intercoastal Waterway.

1161 Spot Ln, Surf City, NC 28445	(910) 328-9431 lanierscampground.com/	All Year
$40-$65	Military/Good Sam	Pet Breed
483 Spaces	Paved/Gravel	40Width/90Length
Showers, Laundry, Gated	Restaurant, Snack Bar	Game Room, Playground

Twin Lakes RV Resort
A family-friendly atmosphere with southern hospitality will ensure a great experience.

1618 Memory Lane, Chocowinity, NC 27817	(866) 315-9339	All Year
$43-$61	Military/Good Sam	Pet Breed
496 Spaces	Paved/Dirt	28Width/65Length
Showers, Laundry, Gated	Grocery, Fishing Supplies	Rentals, Pool, Game Room

Green Acres Family Campground
Your place for wholesome family camping fun with a unique experience.

1679 Green Acres Rd, Williamston, NC 27892	(252) 792-3939 http://greenacresnc.com/	All Year
$31-$35	Military/Good Sam	None
153 Spaces	Gravel/Dirt	30Width/56Length
Internet, Showers, Laundry	Firewood, Snack Bar, Ice	Grocery, RV Wash

North Dakota

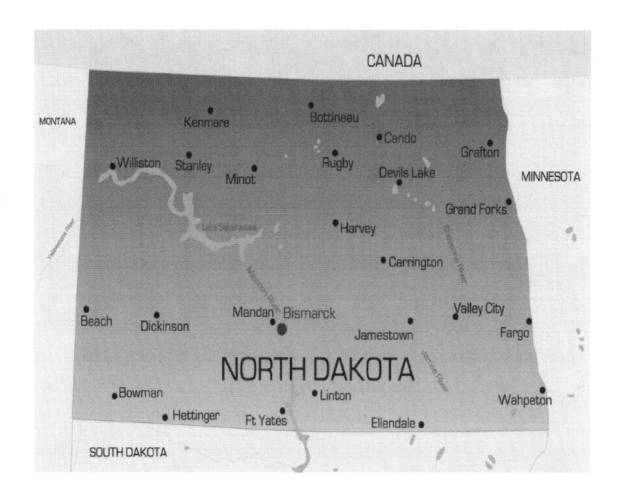

North Dakota is a place full of the great outdoors and provides plenty of opportunities to have fun. There are a handful of great parks in key locations to help you enjoy the great outdoors.

Bismarck KOA
Your standard KOA campground with the basic amenities.

3720 Centennial Road, Bismarck, ND 58503	(701)222-2662 koa.com/campgrounds/bismarck/	All Year
$42-$52	Military	None
94 Spaces	Gravel	30Width/60Length
Internet, Showers, Laundry	Snack Bar, Pool, Playground	Games, Pavilion, Tennis

North Park RV Campground
Affordable camping in a clean, safe, and quiet environment.

2320 Buckskin Dr, Dickinson, ND 58601	(701) 227-8498 https://campnorthpark.com/	All Year
$39	Military/Good Sam	Pet Size, Quantity, Breed
102 Spaces	Gravel	24Width/90Length
Internet, Showers, Laundry	Games, Guest Services	Bike Rentals, Games

Red Trail Campground
Professional service ensures you have a pleasant stay while here.

250 E River Rd S, Medora, ND 58645	(701) 623-4317 http://redtrailcampground.com/	May 15 to September 30
$36-$51	Good Sam	None
120 Spaces	Paved/Gravel	28Width/60Length
Internet, Showers, Laundry	Grocery, Cable, Playground	Games, Pavilion

Roughrider Campground
A family-friendly park that can accommodate most needs.

500 54th St NW, Minot, ND 58703	(701) 852-8442 http://roughridercampground.com/	All Year
$45	Military/Good Sam	Pet Breed
117 Spaces	Gravel	21Width/55Length
Internet, Showers, Laundry	Firewood, Guest Services	Frisbee Golf, Tables

Ohio

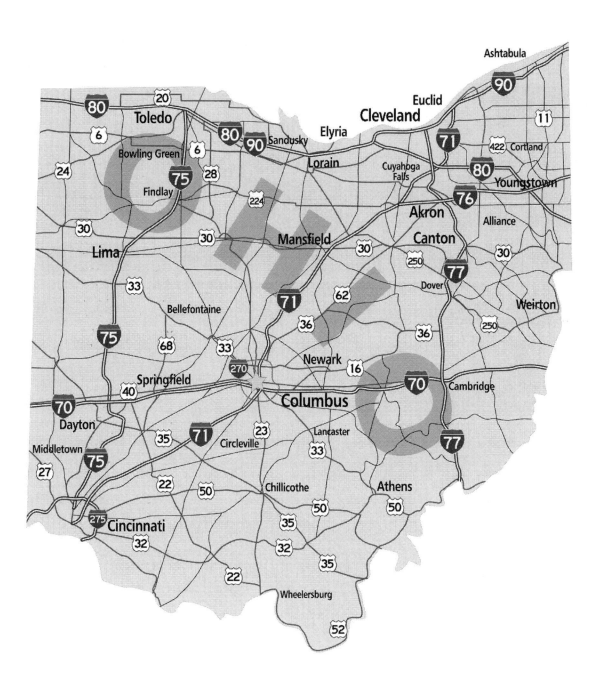

Ohio – North

Sauder Village Campground
There are plenty of unique hands-on activities to enjoy.

22611 Oh-2, Archbold, OH 43502	(800) 590-9755 https://saudervillage.org	April 15 to October 31
$26-$51	Military/Good Sam	None
77 Spaces	Paved	34Width/75Length
Internet, Showers, Laundry	SnackBar, Pool, Game Room	Playground, Sauna, Tables

Gotta Getaway RV Park
The perfect destination halfway between Toledo and Cleveland.

4888 US Highway 20 E, Bellevue, OH 44811	(419) 483-3177 gottagetawayrvpark.com/	May 1 to October 31
$38-$45	Good Sam	Pet Quantity
84 Spaces	Paved/Gravel	30Width/60Length
Showers, Laundry, Ice	Firewood, Rec. Hall, Pool	Game Room, Pavilion

Scenic Hills RV Park
Located in the heart of Amish country.

4483 Township Road 367, Millersburg, OH 44654	(330) 893-3607 scenichillsrvpark.com/	April 1 to November 1
$38-$45	Good Sam	Pet Breed
112 Spaces	Gravel	30Width/86Length
Internet, Laundry, Firewood	Rec. Hall, RV Service	Fire Rings, Tables

Berlin RV Park
Great rates and convenient amenities are available at this park.

5898 Ohio 39, Millersburg, OH 44654	(330) 674-4774 http://www.berlinrvpark.com/	April 1 to December 1
$29-$47	Military/Good Sam	None
52 Spaces	Gravel	52Width/46Length
Internet, Showers, Laundry	Firewood, RV Wash, Ice	Playground, Games

Leafy Oaks Campground
Outstanding amenities in an ideal setting.

6955 State Route 101, Clyde, OH 43410	(419) 639-2887 https://www.leafyoaks.com/	April 15 to October 15
$32-$47	Military	None
235 Spaces	Gravel	34Width/40Length

| Rentals, Internet, Showers | Laundry, Gated, Supplies | Firewood, Ice, LP Gas |

Evergreen Lake Park

Stay in beautiful wooded countryside sites.

703 Center Rd, Conneaut, OH 44030	(440) 599-8802 evergreenlakecampground.com/	May 1 to October 15
$34-$39	Military/Good Sam	None
280 Spaces	Paved/Gravel	35Width/63Length
Gated, Internet, Showers	Snack Bar, Grocery, Rentals	Activities, Mini Golf, Patios

Indian Creek Camping Resort

A one-stop campground with everything you'll need during your stay.

4710 Lake Rd E, Geneva, OH 44041	(440) 466-8191	All Year
$57-$87	Military/Good Sam	None
533 Spaces	Paved/Gravel	40Width/75Length
Internet, Showers, Laundry	Gated, ATM, Firewood	Playground, Lounge, Cable

American Wilderness Campground

Just 25 minutes to downtown Cleveland with easy access to a number of local attractions.

17273 Avon Belden Rd., Grafton, OH 44044	(440) 926-3700 americanwildernesscampground.com/	May 1 to October 15
$40-$48	Military/Good Sam	None
166 Spaces	Gravel	38Width/95Length
Internet, Showers, Gated	Laundry, Rentals, Paddle Boats	Pavilion, Game Room

Kenisee Lake

Staying here will put you in touch with nature.

2021 Mill Creek Rd, Jefferson, OH 44047	(440) 576-9030	April 22 to October 19
$49-$62	Military/Good Sam	None
132 Spaces	Gravel	38Width/98Length
Showers, Gated, Firewood	Laundry, Pool, Rentals	Rec. Hall, Playground

Evergreen Park RV Resort

Enjoy exploring the nearby Amish community and other wonderful activities.

16359 Dover Rd, Dundee, OH 44624	(330) 359-2787 evergreenparkrvresort.com/	All Year
$62	Good Sam	Pet Breed
87 Spaces	Paved	30Width/65Length

| Internet, Showers, Laundry | Snack Bar, Firewood, Cable | Rentals, Golf Carts, Ice |

Baylor Beach Park
This well-maintained park will be a pleasure for your vacation.

8725 Manchester Ave SW, Navarre, OH 44662	(330) 767-3031 baylorbeachpark.com/	May 1 to October 15
$36-$45	Military/Good Sam	Pet Qty, Breed, 14 Day Max
60 Spaces	Paved	30Width/90Length
Internet, Showers, Gated	Snack Bar, Waterslide	Rec.Hall, Playground, Mini Golf

Clay's Park Resort
A great outdoor camping destination with a water park.

13190 Patterson Rd, North Lawrence, OH 44666	(330) 854-6691 https://clayspark.com/	May 1 to November 1
$70-$105	None	Pet Quantity
550 Spaces	Paved/Gravel	50Width/90Length
Internet, Showers, Laundry	Restaurant, Rentals, Pool	SnackBar, Playground, Tennis

Cedarlane RV Park
Just one mile from Lake Erie, this beautiful park is conveniently located.

2926 NE Catawba Rd., Port Clinton, OH 43452	(419) 797-9907 http://cedarlanervpark.com/	May 1 to October 15
$55-$70	Military/Good Sam	None
285 Spaces	Paved/Gravel	30Width/60Length
Gated, Internet, Firewood	Grocery, Snack Bar, Pool	Playground, Pavilion

The Resort at Erie Landing
Located on the Portage River near Lake Erie.

4495 Darr-Hopfinger Road, Port Clinton, OH 43452	(419) 734-2460 https://www.erielanding.com	April 15 to October 15
$50-$65	Military/Good Sam	Pet Quantity
102 Spaces	Paved/Gravel	50Width/90Length
Internet, Showers, Laundry	Snack Bar, Pool, Golf Carts	Game Room, Pavilion

Milan Travel Park
Located on the outskirts of the historic town of Milan.

11404 US Highway 250 N, Milan, OH 44846	(419) 499-4627 travelpark.staycolonial.com/	May 1 to November 1
$48	Military/Good Sam	Pet Breed
85 Spaces	Paved	27Width/64Length
Internet, Showers, Laundry	Firewood, Supplies, Ice	Rentals, Game Room

Camp Sandusky

Just a short drive from Cedar Point Amusement Park.

3518 Tiffin Ave, Sandusky, OH 44870	(419) 626-1133 https://www.campsandusky.com/	May 6 to October 21
$32-$95	Military/Good Sam	None
115 Spaces	Paved/Gravel	25Width/60Length
Internet, Showers, Laundry	Firewood, Rentals, Pool	Pedal Carts, Tables, Fire Rings

Maple Lakes Recreational Park

Conveniently located just 5 minutes off the interstate.

4275 Blake Rd, Seville, OH 44273	(330) 336-2251 https://www.maplelakes.com/	April 15 to October 1
$50	Military/Good Sam	Pet Quantity
198 Spaces	Paved/Dirt	30Width/60Length
Internet, Showers, Gated	Rentals, Supplies, Pool	Rec.Hall, Pavilion, Playground

Woodside Lake Park

Camp in a scenic park near Cleveland.

2486 Frost Rd, Streetsboro, OH 44241	(330) 626-4251 https://woodsidelake.com/	April 15 to October 31
$50-$60	Military/Good Sam	Pet Quantity
250 Spaces	Gravel	25Width/70Length
Internet, Showers, Laundry	Firewood, Snack Bar, Ice	Rentals, Waterslide

Clinton Lake Camping

Located in Seneca County, and this park focuses on providing unique experiences.

4990 E Township Road 122, Republic, OH 44867	(419) 585-3331 http://clintonlake.tripod.com/	May 1 to October 15
$29	None	None
160 Spaces	Gravel	30Width/40Length
Showers, Firewood, Grocery	Game Room, Activities	Playground, Pavilion

Austin Lake RV Park

A family-friendly park with lots of space for outdoor activities.

1002 Township Road 285A, Toronto, OH 43964	(740) 544-5253 https://austinlakepark.com/	May 1 to October 31
$55-$75	Good Sam	None
250 Spaces	Paved/Gravel	34Width/75Length
Gated, Snack Bar, Firewood	Rentals, Paddle Boats, Ice	Playground, Games, Tables

Clare Mar Lakes Campground

Enjoy several outdoor activities just outside Wellington.

47571 New London Eastern Rd, New London, OH 44851	(440) 647-3318 https://www.claremar.com/	May 1 to October 15
$40-$43	Military	None
350 Spaces	Gravel	35Width/70Length
Internet, Showers, Gated	Firewood, Supplies, Ice	Fishing Supplies, RV Wash

Ohio – South

Sun Valley Campground
Located in historic Ross County just four miles from town.

10105 County Road 550, Chillicothe, OH 45601	(740) 775-3490 sunvalleycampground.freeservers.com/	All Year
$45-$50	Military/Good Sam	None
56 Spaces	Paved/Gravel	24Width/100Length
Internet, Showers, Games	Playground, Firewood	Pavilion, Patios, Tables

Cross Creek Camping Resort
Just twenty minutes from Columbus.

3190 S Old State Rd, Delaware, OH 43015	(740) 549-2267 alumcreek.com/	All Year
$35-$80	Military/Good Sam	Pet Quantity, Breed
200 Spaces	Paved	40Width/65Length
Internet, Showers, Laundry	ATM, RV Supplies	LP Gas, Firewood, Ice

Alton RV Park
Conveniently located in central Ohio off Route 40.

6552 W Broad St, Galloway, OH 43119	(614) 878-9127 https://altonrvpark.com/	All Year
$43	Good Sam	Pet Breed
35 Spaces	Gravel	24Width/60Length
Internet	RV Service, RV Wash	Tables

Olive Branch Campground
Enjoy endless recreational adventures.

6985 Wilmington Rd, Oregonia, OH 45054	(513) 932-2267 https://www.olivebranchcg.com/	All Year
$42-$47	Military	Pet Quantity, Breed
137 Spaces	Gravel	50Width/60Length
Internet, Showers, Laundry	Fishing Supplies, Pool, Ice	Playground, Firewood, Tables

Cardinal Center Campground
The perfect family vacation located in the country.

616 OH-61, Marengo, OH 43334	(419) 253-0800 thecardinalcenter.com/	All Year
$33-$42	Military	None

400 Spaces	Paved/Gravel	55Width/105Length
Internet, Showers, Laundry	Supplies, Firewood, Ice	Restaurant, Golf Carts

Arrowhead Campground

Located in beautiful, rolling, wooded terrain.

1361 Thomas Rd, New Paris, OH 45347	(937) 996-6203 arrowhead-campground.com/	April 15 to October 27
$44-$56	Military/Good Sam	Pet Breed
131 Spaces	Gravel	35Width/70Length
Firewood, Showers, Laundry	Internet, Rentals, Rec. Hall	Game Room, Playground

Tomorrow's Stars RV Resort

It doesn't get any better than this!

6716 E National Rd, South Charleston, OH 45368	(937) 324-2267 https://aarvparks.com	All Year
$43	Military/Good Sam	None
210 Spaces	Gravel	40Width/80Length
Showers, Laundry	Firewood, Snack Bar	Rec. Hall, Mini Golf

Enon Beach Campground

Your place to camp, fish, swim, and canoe.

2401 Enon Rd, Springfield, OH 45502	(937) 882-6431 http://www.enonbeach.com/	All Year
$43	None	Pet Breed
117 Spaces	Paved	40Width/54Length
Showers, Laundry, Firewood	Snack Bar, Ice, Supplies	Paddle Boats, Pavilion

Sunbury/Columbus North KOA

You won't get bored when you stay here.

8644 Porter Central Road, Sunbury, OH 43074	(740) 625-6600 koa.com/campgrounds/sunbury/	April 15 to October 15
$41-$86	None	None
178 Spaces	Paved	30Width/63Length
Gym, Pool, Fire Rings	Internet, Showers, Boat Rental	Pedal Carts, Patios, Tables

Thousand Trails Wilmington

Located between Cincinnati and Dayton, it is a natural preserve in Ohio.

1786 State Route 380, Wilmington, OH 45177	(937) 382-5883	April 17 to October 21
$59	Good Sam	None

168 Spaces	Gravel	23Width/76Length
Showers, Laundry, Gated	Fishing Supplies, Rentals	Playground, Pavilion, Tennis

Wolfies Campground
A safe, secure, and well-maintained park for a wonderful vacation.

101 Buckeye Dr, Zanesville, OH 43701	(740) 454-0925 wolfiescampground.com/	All Year
$43-$45	Military/Good Sam	None
54 Spaces	Gravel	30Width/65Length
Internet, Showers, Laundry	Grocery, Pool, Rec. Hall	Game Room, Playground

Oklahoma

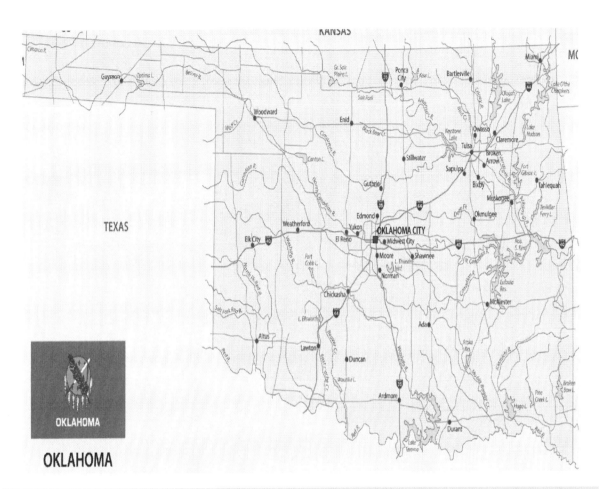

OKLAHOMA

Oklahoma – North

Large cities like Oklahoma City offer a range of things to see and do. Then there are plenty of quaint towns and outdoor areas, with plenty of adventures to be had. Consider what you can enjoy at a range of parks in the Northern part of Oklahoma.

Monkey Island RV Resort
Located in the heart of Grand Lake O' The Cherokees.

56140 E 280 Rd, Afton, OK 74331	(918) 257-6400 https://monkeyislandrv.com/	All Year
$35-$45	Military/Good Sam	None
72 Spaces	Paved	45Width/85Length
Internet, Shower, Laundry	Supplies, Snack Bar, Rentals	Pavilion, Bike Rentals, Pool

Riverside RV Resort

A shaded park on the Caney River.

1211 SE Adams Blvd, Bartlesville, OK 74003	(918) 336-6431 https://resortrv.com/	All Year
$35	Military/Good Sam	Pet Quantity
72 Spaces	Paved/Gravel	24Width/60Length
Internet, Showers, Laundry	Firewood, Cable, Pool, Ice	Games, Pavilion, Tables

Tulsa RV Ranch

Enjoy your stay at this ranch and its many wonderful amenities.

2548 Highway 75, Beggs, OK 74421	(918) 267-7569 http://tulsarvranch.com/	All Year
$35	Military/Good Sam	None
97 Spaces	Paved	30Width/70Length
Internet, Showers, Laundry	Restaurant, Grocery, Ice	Rec. Hall, Playground, Gym

Oak Glen RV Park

Located between Tulsa and Oklahoma City.

347203 E Highway 66, Chandler, OK 74834	(405) 258-2994 http://www.oakglenrv.com/	All Year
$27-$29	Good Sam	None
53 Spaces	Gravel	24Width/80Length
Rec. Hall, Playground	Grocery, Internet, Showers	Laundry, Supplies, Ice

Pecan Grove RV Resort

Located within the city limits of Chickasha.

600 W Almar Dr, Chickasha, OK 73018	(405) 224-0500 http://pecangrovervresort.com/	All Year
$35-$40	Military/Good Sam	Pet Quantity, Breed
94 Spaces	Paved	45Width/107Length
Games, Pavilion, Patios	Rentals, Game Room, Ice	Internet, Showers, Laundry

Xtreme RV Resort

This is your best destination for relaxation.

203 Adams St, Eufaula, OK 74432	(918) 707-5636 https://xtremeresortok.com/	All Year
$45-$50	Military/Good Sam	Pet Breed
100 Spaces	Paved	30Width/65Length
Gated, Grocery, Boat Rentals	Fishing Guides, Rec. Hall	Internet, Showers, Laundry

Little Turtle RV
Next to Lake Eufaula.

114161 Highway 69, Eufaula, OK 74432	(918) 618-2140 http://littleturtlerv.com/	All Year
$43-$53	Good Sam	None
120 Spaces	Gravel	35Width/80Length
Internet, Showers, Laundry	Pool, Rec. Hall, Playground	Gym, Patios, Tables

Marval Resort
The place where families go to create vacation memories.

445140 E 1011 Rd, Gore, OK 74435	(918) 489-2295 https://marvalresort.com/	All Year
$37-$59	Military/Good Sam	Pet Quantity
155 Spaces	Paved/Gravel	38Width/70Length
Mini Golf, Fire Rings, Tables	Rentals, Pool, Golf Carts	Gated, Laundry, Internet

Cedar Oaks RV Park
The best in lake-front camping with over thirty acres of private lakefront access.

1550 83rd St NW, Grove, OK 74344	(918) 786-4303 https://www.cedaroaksrvpark.com/	All Year
$30-$35	Military/Good Sam	None
123 Spaces	Paved/Gravel	26Width/60Length
Rec. Hall, Pavilion, Firewood	Rentals, Lodge, Horseshoes	Internet, Showers, Laundry

Cedar Valley RV Park
Just four miles from the historic town of Guthrie.

725 Masters Dr, Guthrie, OK 73044	(405) 282-4478 cedarvalleyrvpark.com	All Year
$40	Good Sam	RV Age
91 Spaces	Paved	25Width/70Length
Golf, Pavilion	LP Gas, Horseshoes, Ice	Internet, Showers, Rec. Hall

Crooked Creek RV Park
A newer luxury RV park in the Grand Lake area.

2036 N 3rd St, Langley, OK 74350	(918) 770-6111 360grandlake.com/RV/Crooked-Creek-RV-Park.html	All Year
$35	Good Sam	RV Age
50 Spaces	Paved	30Width/65Length
Game Room, Restaurant	Rentals, Paddle Boats	Internet, Lounge, Laundry

Hidden Valley RV Park
Relax and enjoy a pleasant stay at this family-friendly park.

6388 HWY-69, Porter, OK 74454	(918) 681-4457 https://hiddenvalleyok.com/	All Year
$30	Good Sam	None
60 Spaces	Gravel	30Width/75Length
Internet, Showers, Laundry	Firewood, Rec. Hall, Ice	Playground, Pavilion

Rockwell RV Park
Just minutes from downtown Oklahoma City.

720 S Rockwell Ave, Oklahoma City, OK 73128	(405) 787-5992 http://www.rockwellrvpark.com/	All Year
$40-$45	Military/Good Sam	None
170 Spaces	Paved	28Width/70Length
Cable, Internet, Showers	Breakfast, Rentals, Pool	Rec. Hall, Sauna, Games

Council Road RV Park
The most conveniently located park in all of Oklahoma City.

8108 SW 8th St, Oklahoma City, OK 73128	(405) 789-2103 https://councilrdrvpark.com/	All Year
$40	Military/Good Sam	Pet Breed
102 Spaces	Paved/Gravel	25Width/60Length
Pavilion, Patios, Tables	Snack Bar, Cable, Ice	Internet, Showers, Laundry

Mustang Run RV Park
Featuring wonderful amenities in a well-kept park.

11528 W I-40 Service Rd, Oklahoma City, OK 73099	(405) 577-6040 mustangrunrvpark.com/	All Year
$49	Military/Good Sam	None
61 Spaces	Paved	30Width/75Length
Rec. Hall, Pavilion, Tables	Cable, Pool, Ice, Supplies	Internet, Showers, Laundry

Twin Fountains RV Resort
The ultimate RV vacation experience with both comfort and convenience.

2727 NE 63rd St, Oklahoma City, OK 73111	(405) 475-5514 https://twinfountainsrvresort.com/	All Year
$50	Military/Good Sam	None
192 Spaces	Paved	34Width/75Length
Gated, Internet, Showers	Laundry, Firewood, ATM	Snack Bar, Grocery, Sauna

Mingo RV Park

Located in the heart of Indian Country and the closest park to downtown Tulsa.

801 N Mingo Rd, Tulsa, OK 74116	(918) 832-8824 https://mingorvpark.com/	All Year
$40	Military/Good Sam	None
250 Spaces	Paved	30Width/80Length
Internet, Showers, Laundry	Cable, Rec. Hall, Playground	Pavilion, Horseshoes

Oklahoma – South

Antlers RV Park
Relax in peace and quiet whether you are spending the night or looking for a long term place.

220 NW J St, Antlers, OK 74523	(580) 298-9008 http://www.antlersrvparkok.com/	All Year
$28	Good Sam	None
29 Spaces	Gravel	26Width/100Length
Internet	Laundry	Pavilion

By the Lake RV Park Resort
Stop by for a night or stay for a weekend getaway.

1031 Lodge Rd, Ardmore, OK 73401	(580) 798-4721 http://bythelakerv.com/	All Year
$43-$48	Military/Good Sam	None
128 Spaces	Paved	40Width/75Length
Internet, Showers, Laundry	Snack Bar, Cable, Firewood	Rec. Hall, Game Room

Red River Rose RV Resort
Relax and enjoy the amenities.

4661 Hedges Rd, Ardmore, OK 73401	(580) 220-2900 https://www.hiddenlakerv.com/	All Year
$34-$39	Military/Good Sam	Pet Quantity, Breed
90 Spaces	Gravel	33Width/70Length
Pool, Fishing, Firewood, Ice	Cable, Showers, Laundry	Fire Rings, Waterslide

Tiny Town OK
Located just across the street from the beautiful Beaver Bend Park.

6773 N US Highway 259, Broken Bow, OK 74728	(580) 301-4898 tinytownokcabins.com/	All Year
$35-$50	Good Sam	None
23 Spaces	Gravel	30Width/65Length
Rentals, Playground	Internet, Laundry	Fire Rings, Tables

Smokin' Joe's RV Park
Enjoy the great outdoors with all the modern conveniences.

3184 Jollyville Rd, Davis, OK 73030	(580) 247-9714 smokinjoesribranch.com/	All Year
$35	Good Sam	None
44 Spaces	Dirt	30Width/75Length
Internet, Showers	Restaurant, Laundry, Ice	Horseshoes, Rec. Hall

Chisholm Trail RV Park
Located just south of the town of Duncan.

3000 S Highway 81, Duncan, OK 73533	(580) 252-7200 https://chisholmtrailrvpark.com	All Year
$30	Good Sam	None
80 Spaces	Gravel	24Width/60Length
Internet, Showers	Laundry, Ice	Rec. Hall

Choctaw RV Park KOA
The number one KOA in all of Oklahoma.

3650 Enterprise Dr, Durant, OK 74701	(580) 920-0160 koa.com/campgrounds/durant/	All Year
$45-$55	None	Pet Breed
77 Spaces	Paved	30Width/80Length
Internet, Showers, Laundry	Restaurant, Firewood, Ice	Game Room, Playground

Elk Creek RV Park
Spend your days exploring historic sites along Route 66.

317 E 20th St, Elk City, OK 73644	(580) 225-7865 http://elkcreekrvpark.com/	All Year
$33-$36	Military/Good Sam	None
78 Spaces	Paved	21Width/65Length
Rec.Hall, Horseshoes, Internet	Laundry, Supplies, Ice	Cable, RV Wash

Buffalo Bob's RV Park
Relax and enjoy this park near Fort Sill.

1508 SE Tower Rd, Lawton, OK 73501	(580) 699-3534 http://buffalobobsrvpark.net/	All Year
$35	Military/Good Sam	Pet Quantity
38 Spaces	Paved	34Width/65Length
Internet, Showers, Laundry	Cable, RV Wash	Rec. Hall, Gym, Patios

Red River Ranch RV Resort
Offering nightly, weekly, and monthly rates.

19691 US Highway 77, Thackerville, OK 73459	(580) 276-4411 redriverranchrvresort.org/	All Year
$40	Military/Good Sam	Pet Quantity
367 Spaces	Paved/Gravel	24Width/75Length
Internet, Showers, Laundry	Pool, Ice, Hot Tub	Rec. Hall, Mini Golf

Oregon

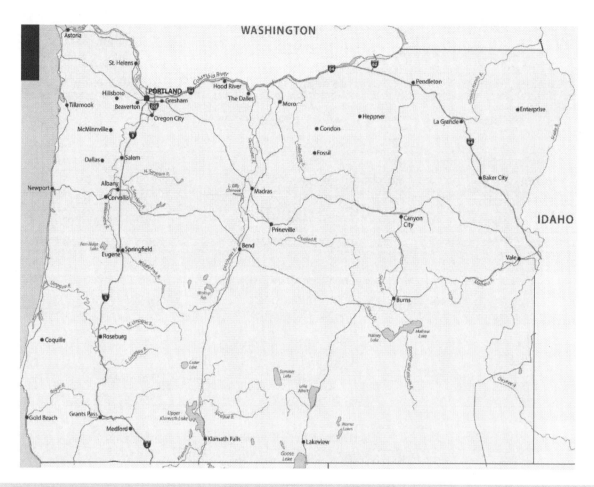

Oregon – Coast

Bandon RV Park
A short walk takes you to old town Bandon.

935 2nd St SE, Bandon, OR 97411	(541) 347-4122 https://bandonrvpark.com/	All Year
$48	Good Sam	None
44 Spaces	Paved	21Width/65Length
Internet, Showers	Laundry, Supplies	Patios and Tables

Bandon by the Sea RV Park
Located on the Southern Oregon Coast.

49612 Highway 101,	(541) 347-5155	All Year

Bandon, OR 97411	http://bandonbythesearvpark.com/	
$47	Military/Good Sam	None
90 Spaces	Paved/Gravel	30Width/70Length
Internet, Showers	Laundry, Supplies, Cable	Rec. Hall, Tables

Coquille River RV Park
The park caters to those looking to enjoy the many outdoor activities in the area.

83202 N Bank Ln, Bandon, OR 97411	(451) 207-1730 coquilleriverrv.com/	All Year
$35-$40	Good Sam	RV Age
50 Spaces	Gravel/Dirt	30Width/55Length
Internet, Showers	Firewood, Rentals	Games, Internet

AtRivers Edge RV Resort
This park offers you a true resort feel from the buildings to the view around you.

98203 S Bank Chetco River Rd, Brookings, OR 97415	(541) 469-3356 https://www.atriversedge.com/	All Year
$45-$53	Military/Good Sam	Pet Quantity
110 Spaces	Paved	24Width/60Length
Internet, Showers, Laundry	Cable, Rentals, Ice	Horseshoes, Activities

Driftwood RV Park
The beauty of the Wild Rivers Coast awaits you here.

16011 Lower Harbor Rd, Brookings, OR 97415	(541) 469-9089 driftwoodrvpark.com/	All Year
$45-$49	Military/Good Sam	Pet Quantity
108 Spaces	Paved	26Width/60Length
Internet, Showers, Laundry	Grocery, Rec.Hall, Games	Pavilion, Patios, Tables

Brookings RV Park
Offering excellent views and standard amenities.

96707 E Harris Heights Rd, Brookings, OR 97415	(541) 469-6849 http://brookingsrv.com/	All Year
$36	Good Sam	None
38 Spaces	Paved	20Width/50Length
Internet, Showers, Laundry	Cable, RV Wash, Rentals	Rec.Hall, Games

Cannon Beach RV Resort
Escape to the coast and stay at the beach.

340 Elk Creek Rd, Cannon Beach, OR 97110	(503) 436-2231 http://cbrvresort.com/	All Year

$40-$60	Military /Good Sam	None
99 Spaces	Paved	30Width/60Length
Internet, Firewood, Laundry	Showers, LP Gas, Cable	Playground, Game Room

Oceanside Beachfront RV Resort
Enjoy the nearby pet-friendly beach or other activities in the surrounding area.

90281 Cape Arago Hwy, Coos Bay, OR 97420	(541) 888-2598	All Year
$40-$92	Military/Good Sam	Pet Quantity, 21 Day Max
64 Spaces	Paved	30Width/60Length
Internet, Showers	Laundry, Firewood	Rentals, Fire Rings

Charleston Marina & RV Park
Buy your seafood fresh or enjoy some fishing on your own.

63402 Kingfisher Rd, Coos Bay, OR 97420	(541) 888-9512	All Year
$39-$43	Good Sam	RV Age
100 Spaces	Paved	27Width/50Length
Fishing, Rentals	Laundry, Cable	Internet, Rec. Hall

Bay Point Landing
Located in the wetlands of Coos Bay.

92443 Cape Arago Hwy, Coos Bay, OR 97420	(541) 351-9160 https://baypointlanding.com/	All Year
$49-$85	Military/Good Sam	RV Age, Pet Quantity
142 Spaces	Gravel	41Width/70Length
Internet, Showers	Laundry, Firewood	Pool, Game Room

Alder Acres RV Park
Pet-friendly and a short distance to Pacific beaches.

1800 S 28th Ct, Coos Bay, OR 97420	(541) 269-0999 http://alderacres.com/	All Year
$50	Good Sam	RV Age
88 Spaces	Paved	28Width/60Length
Internet, Showers	Ice, Grocery	Recreation Area, Gym

Sea & Sand RV Park
All sites have beautiful ocean views where you can make your home away from home.

4985 N Highway 101, Depoe Bay, OR 97341	(541) 764-2313 Website	All Year
$44-$82	Military/Good Sam	Pet Qty, Breed, 14 Day Max

108 Spaces	Gravel	26Width/44Length
Games, Fire Rings	Cable, Firewood	Internet, Showers

Elkton RV Park
Located along the beautiful Umpqua River with boat pull access.

450 River Rd, Elkton, OR 97436	(541) 584-2832 http://www.elktonrvpark.com/	All Year
$40	Military/Good Sam	None
45 Spaces	Gravel	25Width/45Length
Fishing/Hunting Guides	Laundry, Internet	Games, Rentals

Woahink Lake RV Resort
View and hike the unique Oregon Dunes just outside the park.

83570 Highway 101, Florence, OR 97439	(541) 997-6454 http://www.woahinklakerv.com/	All Year
$44	Military/Good Sam	Pet Breed
75 Spaces	Paved	31Width/65Length
Internet, Showers	Laundry, Rentals	Game Room, Rec. Hall

South Jetty RV Resort
Stay here and enjoy comfort and relaxation.

05010 S Jetty Rd, Florence, OR 97439	(888) 459-9831	All Year
$55-$70	Military/Good Sam	14 Day Max Stay
188 Spaces	Paved/Dirt	34Width/50Length
Rentals, Firewood, Gated	Pool, Rec. Hall, Activities	Playground, Sauna

Heceta Beach RV Park
Enjoy a range of coastal activities right outside the park.

4636 Heceta Beach Road, Florence, OR 97439	(541) 997-7664 hecetabeachrvpark.com/	All Year
$47	Military/Good Sam	None
50 Spaces	Gravel	34Width/60Length
Internet, Beach Access	Firewood, Grocery	Rec. Hall, Gym

Port of Garibaldi RV Park
Experience a small seaside town with plenty of activities.

606 Biak Ave, Garibaldi, OR 97118	(503) 322-3292 http://portofgaribaldi.org/	All Year
$38-$42	Military/Good Sam	RV Age
48 Spaces	Gravel	30Width/45Length

Turtle Rock RV Resort
Walking distance to the beach and ocean.

28788 Hunter Creek Loop, Gold Beach, OR 97444	(541) 247-9203 turtlerockresorts.com/	All Year
$37-$83	Military/Good Sam	Pet Quantity
76 Spaces	Gravel	35Width/60Length
Internet, Restaurant	Lounge, Rentals	Rec. Hall, Games

Osprey Point RV Resort
Stay near two beautiful mountain lakes.

1505 N Lake Rd, Lakeside, OR 97449	(541) 759-2801 http://ospreypointrvresort.com/	All Year
$35-$50	Military/Good Sam	Pet Breed
134 Spaces	Paved	31Width/60Length
Firewood, Supplies	Restaurant, Lounge	Cable, Game Room

Logan Road RV Park
The only RV park in Lincoln City west of Highway 101.

4800 NE Logan Rd, Lincoln City, OR 97367	(541) 994-4261 https://loganroadrvpark.com/	All Year
$42-$48	Military/Good Sam	Pet Quantity
51 Spaces	Paved	28Width/45Length
Internet	Lounge, Pool	Game Room

Premier RV Resorts - Lincoln City
Located within the historic Taft District.

4100 SE Highway 101, Lincoln City, OR 97367	(541) 996-2778 http://www.premierrvresorts.com/	All Year
$57-$69	Military/Good Sam	None
92 Spaces	Paved	23Width/50Length
Internet, Showers	Cable, Rec.Hall	Game Room, Gym

Pacific Shores Motorcoach Resort
Located on the bluffs overlooking the ocean.

6225 N Coast Hwy, Newport, OR 97365	(541) 265-3750 pacificshoresmotorcoachresort.com/	All Year
$55-$140	Good Sam	No Class B, Pet Quantity
210 Spaces	Paved	35Width/70Length
Gated, Showers	Pool, Rec. Hall	Sauna, Gym

Port of Newport Marina & RV Park
Located on the south side of Yaquina Bay.

2120 Se Marine Science Dr, Newport, OR 97365	(541) 867-3321 portofnewport.com/	All Year
$46-$53	Military/Good Sam	Pet Quantity
92 Spaces	Paved	27Width/60Length
Internet	Restaurant	Fishing

The Mill Casino Hotel & RV Park
Offering all the basic amenities you need to enjoy your stay.

3201 Tremont St, North Bend, OR 97459	(541) 756-8800 https://www.themillcasino.com/	All Year
$45-$70	Military/Good Age	RV Age, 28 Day Max Stay
102 Spaces	Paved	28Width/62Length
Laundry	Restaurant/Lounge	Guest Services, Pool

Cape Kiwanda RV Resort
Simply walk across the street to be at the beach.

33305 Cape Kiwanda Dr, Pacific City, OR 97135	(503) 965-6230 https://capekiwandarvresort.com	All Year
$37-$62	Good Sam	None
113 Spaces	Paved	25Width/60Length
Pool	Firewood	Rec. Hall

Hart's Camp
Experience the great outdoors with amenities to make you feel at home.

33145 Webb Park Rd, Pacific City, OR 97135	(503) 965-7006 https://www.hartscamp.com/	All Year
$29-$59	Good Sam	44 Day Max
16 Spaces	Paved	22Width/50Length
Gated	Restaurant	Fire Rings

Port Orford RV Village
A clean and tranquil setting just off Highway 101.

2855 Port Orford Loop Rd, Port Orford, OR 97465	(541) 332-1041 http://www.portorfordrv.com/	All Year
$40	Military/Good Sam	None
38 Spaces	Paved	29Width/70Length
Laundry	Rec.Hall	Gym

Loon Lake Lodge & RV Resort
Located near the Central Oregon Coast.

9011 Loon Lake Rd, Reedsport, OR 97467	(541) 599-2244 https://loonlakerv.com/	April 15 to October 31
$43-$55	Military/Good Sam	Pet Quantity, 28 Day Max
31 Spaces	Gravel/Dirt	31Width/65Length
Internet	Firewood	Rentals

Remote Outpost RV Park
Enjoy a relaxing getaway here in a friendly environment.

23146 Highway 42, Remote, OR 97458	(541) 572-5105 http://www.remoteoutpostrv.com/	All Year
$44	Military/Good Sam	RV Age, Pet Size, Breed
26 Spaces	Paved	30Width/55Length
Internet	Rentals	Games

Seaside RV Resort
Surround yourself with scenic and historic sites.

1703 12th Avenue, Seaside, OR 97138	(888) 399-9095 Website	All Year
$49-$67	Military/Good Sam	Pet Quantity
232 Spaces	Gravel/dirt	25Width/50Length
Internet	Gated, Rentals	Firewood, Tennis

Circle Creek RV Resort
From here, you can explore all that the Northern Oregon Coast has to offer.

85658 Highway 101, Seaside, OR 97138	(503) 738-6070 https://circlecreekrv.com/	All Year
$42-$56	Military/Good Sam	None
44 Spaces	Paved	40Width/55Length
Internet	Grocery	Rec. Hall

Tillamook Bay City RV Park
There are plenty of things to see and do in the surrounding area.

7805 Alderbrook Rd, Tillamook, OR 97141	(503) 377-2124 http://tillamookbaycityrvpark.com/	All Year
$35-$44	Good Sam	RV Age, Pet Quantity
43 Spaces	Gravel	25Width/60Length
Firewood	Rentals	Playground

Netarts Bay Garden RV Resort

Get away from the crowds and stay off the beaten path.

2260 Bilyeu St, Tillamook, OR 97141	(503) 842-7774 http://www.netartsbay.com/	All Year
$34-$49	Military/Good Sam	Pet Quantity
83. Spaces	Paved	24Width/55Length
Internet	Restaurant, Fishing	Rec. Hall, Games

Sea Perch RV Resor

Located right on the water between the seaside towns of Yachats and Florence.

95480 Highway 101 S, Yachats, OR 97498	(541) 547-3505 http://www.seaperchrvresort.com/	All Year
$80-$100	Good Sam	RV Age, Pet Quantity
28 Spaces	Paved	28Width/60Length
Gym, Patios	Rec.Hall	Internet

Oregon – North

Home to larger cities like Portland; Northern Oregon is a great place to go for wilderness and cities. Often plenty of activities are within driving distance to your park so you can see and do anything you desire. There are still some great outdoor adventures to be had in this area.

Aurora Acres RV Resort

This is a beautiful setting to stay when in the northern Oregon area.

21599 Dolores Way NE, Aurora, OR 97002	(503) 678-2646 http://www.auroraacresrv.com/	All Year
$37-$42	Good Sam	Pet Quantity
128 Spaces	Paved	21Width/60Length
Internet	Laundry	Pool, Rec. Hall

Portland Fairview RV Park

This park is so much more than a place to park your RV.

21401 NE Sandy Blvd, Fairview, OR 97024	(503) 661-1047	All Year
$59	Military/Good Sam	RV Age, Pet Breed
407 Spaces	Paved	25Width/60Length
Internet	Laundry	Pool, Rec. Hall

Jantzen Beach RV Park

Located along the Columbia River in the beautiful Portland area.

1503 N Hayden Island Dr, Portland, OR 97217	(503) 289-7626 http://www.jantzenbeachrv.com/	All Year
$50	Military/Good Sam	Pet Breed
169 Spaces	Paved	27Width/68Length
Laundry	Pool, Rec. Hall	Game Room

Columbia River RV Park

Perfect for travelers and long-term stays.

10649 NE 13th Ave, Portland, OR 97211	(503) 285-1515 https://www.columbiariverrv.com/	All Year
$40-$45	Good Sam	RV Age, Pet Size, Qty, Breed
198 Spaced	Paved	25Width/60Length
Internet	Cable, Rec. Hall	Gym, Patios

Sandy Riverfront RV Resort
A beautiful park with friendly people.

1097 E Historic Columbia River Hwy, Troutdale, OR 97060	(503) 665-6722 http://sandyrv.com/	All Year
$53-$60	Good Sam	RV Age
113 Spaces	Paved	24Width/60Length
Internet	Cable	Games

Mt Hood Village Resort
The outdoor activities abound in this area.

65000 E. Hwy 26, Welches, OR 97067	(888) 416-5536	All Year
$53-$72	Military/Good Sam	Pet Quantity
406 Spaces	Paved/Dirt	35Width/60Length
Gated	Rentals	Playground

Pheasant Ridge RV Resort
Experience scenic beauty and convenience.

8275 SW Elligsen Rd, Wilsonville, OR 97070	(503) 682-7829 http://pheasantridge.com/	All Year
$58-$71	Military/Good Sam	Pet Quantity
130 Spaces	Paved	30Width/65Length
Internet	Cable, Games	Gym, Pool

Portland/Woodburn RV Park
Located right off the interstate and a close drive to Portland and Salem.

115 Arney Rd, Woodburn, OR 97071	(503) 981-0002 http://www.woodburnrv.com/	All Year
$52	Good Sam	Pet Breed
148 Spaces	Paved	25Width/60Length
Internet	Grocery	Horseshoes

Oregon – Willamette Valley

This is the beautiful wine country region of Oregon. Enjoy rolling hills and valleys as you plan an excellent vacation. Either enjoy outdoor activities, a leisure day of wine tasting, or simply take in the nature around you from the comfort of your site.

The Blue Ox RV Park
Located just outside of Albany, where you can find plenty of activities to keep you busy.

4000 Blue Ox Dr. SE, Albany, OR 97322	(541) 926-2886 http://theblueoxrvpark.com/	All Year
$40-$43	Military/Good Sam	None
149 Spaces	Paved	29Width/70Length
Internet, Cable	Showers	Pool, Rec. Hall

Patio RV Park
Located in Central Oregon on the Mackenzie River.

55636 Mckenzie River Dr, Blue River, OR 97413	(541) 822-3596 http://patiorv.com/	All Year
$34-$41	Military/Good Sam	Pet Size, Pet Breed
58 Spaces	Paved/Gravel	30Width/60Length
Laundry	Firewood	Game Room

Dexter Shores RV Park
Just eleven miles from the interstate.

39140 Dexter Rd, Dexter, OR 97431	(541) 937-3711 http://dextershoresrv.com/	All Year
$34-$38	Military/Good Sam	Pet Size, Qty, Breed
53 Spaces	Paved/Gravel	24Width/60Length
Internet	Cable, Laundry	Putting Green

Premier RV Resorts Eugene
Easy access on and off the interstate.

33022 Van Duyn Rd, Eugene, OR 97408	(541) 686-3152 http://www.premierrvresorts.com/	All Year
$58-$68	Military/Good Sam	None
193 Spaces	Paved	33Width/64Length
Showers	Rentals, Pool	Activities

Eugene Kamping World RV Park
A clean, quiet, and family-oriented park near Eugene.

90932 S Stuart St, Coburg, OR 97408	(541) 343-4832 eugenekampingworld.com/	All Year
$44-$49	Military/Good Sam	Pet Breed
110 Spaces	Paved	22Width/65Length
Showers	Laundry	Playground

Guaranty RV Park
Located in the Willamette Valley wine country area.

93668 Oregon 99, Junction City, OR 97448	(541) 234-0970 https://www.guaranty.com	All Year
$40-$45	Military/Good Sam	RV Age
55 Spaces	Paved	30Width/70Length
ATM, Supplies	Grocery	Restaurant

Olde Stone Village RV Park
There is no shortage of things to see and do in this area.

4155 NE Three Mile Ln, McMinnville, OR 97128	(503) 472-4315 oldestonevillage.com/	All Year
$54	Good Sam	RV Age, Pet Size, Breed
71 Spaces	Paved	30Width/65Length
Laundry	Pavilion	Playground

Hee Hee Illahee RV Resort
Located in the heart of Willamette Valley.

4751 Astoria St NE, Salem, OR 97305	(503) 463-6641 https://heeheeillahee.com/	All Year
$49	Military/Good Sam	Pet Quantity, Pet Breed
139 Spaces	Paved	30Width/75Length
Internet	Laundry	Playground

Phoenix RV Park
A well-kept and clean park.

4130 Silverton Rd NE, Salem, OR 97305	(503) 581-2497 https://phoenixrvpark.com/	All Year
$52	Military/Good Sam	RV Age, Pet Quantity, Breed
107 Spaces	Paved	32Width/60Length
Laundry	Gym	Playground

Premier RV Resorts - Salem
Located next to Rickreall Creek.

4700 Salem Dallas Highway NW, Salem, OR 97304	(503) 364-7714 http://www.premierrvresorts.com	All Year
$57-$63	Military/Good Sam	Pet Quantity
188 Spaces	Paved	25Width/60Length
Playground	Gym	Rec. Hall

Silver Spur RV Park & Resort
Perfect for a family or group getaway.

12622 Silverton Rd NE, Silverton, OR 97381	503-873-2020 https://www.silverspurrvpark.com/	All Year
$46-$60	Military/Good Sam	Pet Quantity
200 Spaces	Gravel	30Width/60Length
Firewood	Cable	Rentals

Casey's Riverside RV Park
Rest and relax by rivers and mountains while viewing native wildlife.

46443 Westfir Rd, Westfir, OR 97492	(541) 782-1906 http://www.caseysrvpark.com/	All Year
$50	None	Restrictions
56 Spaces	Paved	31Width/75Length
Internet	Pool	Pavilion

Oregon – Central

Central Oregon is home to quaint, historic towns with lots of charm to explore. For the outdoor person, there are mountain ranges and valleys to spend your days exploring. There are many wonderful parks in the area to help you recharge at the end of a long day.

Bend/Sisters Garden RV Resort
Mild summers and spectacular views await you.

67667 Highway 20, Bend, OR 97703	(541) 516-3036 bendsistersgardenrv.com/	All Year
$45-$76	Good Sam	Pet Quantity
99 Spaces	Paved	30Width/70Length
Internet	Firewood	Mini Golf

Bend Sunriver RV
Located on the Little Deschutes River.

17480 South Century Dr, Bend, OR 97707	(888) 367-3616	All Year
$40-$65	Military/Good Sam	None
290 Spaces	Gravel	40Width/55Length
Laundry	Pool	Rentals

Scandia RV Park
Bend is a great vacation town, and this RV park is in the middle of it.

61415 Hwy 97 Ste 59, Bend, OR 97702	(541) 382-6206 http://www.scandiarv.com/	All Year
$39-$64	Military/Good Sam	None
111 Spaces	Paved	25Width/60Length
Cable	Horseshoes	Gym, Laundry

Crown Villa RV Resort
Wonderful large sites allow you to spread out at this resort.

60801 Brosterhous Rd, Bend, OR 97702	(541) 388-1131 http://crownvillarvresort.com	All Year
$40-$109	Military/Good Sam	RV Age, Pet Breed
106 Spaces	Paved	55Width/130Length
Showers	Cable	Rentals

Boardman Marina & RV Park
The best place to go if you want to enjoy a wide range of water activities.

1 W Marina Dr,	(541) 481-7217	All Year

Boardman, OR 97818	http://boardmanmarinapark.com/	
$25-$36	Military/Good Sam	14 Day Max Stay
63 Spaces	Paved	31Width/80Length
Showers	Firewood	Mini Golf

Hoodoo's Camp Sherman RV Park & Motel

Enjoy the beauty of nature all around you.

25635 SW Forest Service Rd, Camp Sherman, OR 97730	(541) 595-6514 http://campshermanrv.com/	All Year
$34-$38	Military/Good Sam	Pet Size, Quantity, Breed
31 Spaces	Paved	25Width/55Length
Firewood	Laundry	Lodge Room

Crooked River Ranch RV Park

Fun and activity for the whole family.

14875 Hays Rd, Crooked River Ranch, OR 97760	(541) 923-1441 crookedriverranch.com/	All Year
$38-$42	Military/Good Sam	Pet Breed
83 Spaces	Paved/Gravel	24Width/60Length
Restaurant	Lounge	Playground

Expo Center RV Park

Next door to the Cascade Mountains and a golf course.

3800 SW Airport Way, Redmond, OR 97756	(541) 548-2711 https://expo.deschutes.org/	All Year
$35	Good Sam	None
105 Spaces	Paved	28Width/70Length
Showers	ATM, Patios	Activities

Oregon – South

Southern Oregon is home to historic and unique parks with a range of outdoor activities. Whether you want to get back to nature and just relax or you want to do an outdoor adventure, this is your place to go.

Ashland's Creekside Campground
A great location near downtown Ashland.

5310 Highway 66, Ashland, OR 97520	(541) 488-1785 https://ashlandcreeksiderv.com/	All Year
$40	Military/Good Sam	None
48 Spaces	Paved	24Width/60Length
Internet	Firewood	Recreation Hall

Seven Feathers RV Resort
Located in a canyon of Douglas fir and pine trees.

325 Quintioosa Blvd, Canyonville, OR 97417	(541) 839-3599 sevenfeathersrvresort.com	All Year
$66-$74	Military/Good Sam	Pet Quantity, 28 Day Max
191 Spaces	Paved	30Width/60Length
Laundry	Heated Pool	Bike Rental

Water Wheel RV Park
Located in one of the best recreation areas of Oregon.

200 Williamson River Dr, Chiloquin, OR 97624	(541) 783-2738	March 1 to December 1
$38-$42	Good Sam	None
28 Spaces	Gravel	22Width/60Length
Metered LP Gas	Fishing Supplies	

Big Pines RV Park
Spacious lots among the trees ensure you have a comfortable trip.

135151 Highway 97 N, Crescent, OR 97733	(541) 433-2785 https://www.bigpinesrvpark.com/	April 1 to October 31
$40	Military/Good Sam	None
63 Spaces	Gravel	45Width/100Length
Restrooms and Showers	Self-Service RV Wash	Recreation Hall

Crescent Junction RV Park
Stay among a wonderfully wooded park.

20030 Crescent Lake Hwy	(541) 433-5300	May 1 to October 31

Crescent Lake, OR 97733	http://crescentjunctionrv.com/	
$25-$30	Military/Good Sam	None
30 Spaces	Paved	35Width/55Length
Restrooms and Showers	Laundry, Recreation Hall	Patios, Tables

Shelter Cove Resort
Unwind in comfortable accommodations.

27600 W Odell Lake Road, Crescent, OR 97733	(541) 433-2601 https://highwaywestvacations.com	All Year
$52-$75	Military/Good Sam	None
74 Spaces	Paved/Gravel	30Width/55Length
Firewood, Supplies	Restaurant, Fishing	Paddle Boats, Rentals

Diamond Lake RV Park
Stay just four miles from the north entrance to Crater Lake National Park.

3500 Diamond Lake Loop, Diamond Lake, OR 97731	(541) 793-3318 http://diamondlakervpark.com/	May 15 to October 15
$46-$49	Military/Good Sam	Pet Quantity
100 Spaces	Paved/Gravel	30Width/60Length
Bike Rentals	Cabin Rentals	Firewood

Steens Mountain Wilderness Resort
Located in the heart of the Oregon Outback.

35678 Resort Ln, Frenchglen, OR 97736	(541) 493-2415 https://steensmountainresort.com	March 1 to December 10
$33-$38	Good Sam	None
50 Spaces	Gravel	45Width/90Length
RV Supplies	Outdoor Games	Fishing Supplies

Rogue Valley Overniters
A clean and quiet park close to nature.

1806 NW 6th St, Grants Pass, OR 97526	(541) 479-2208 http://roguevalleyovernighters.com/	All year
$37	Good Sam	Pet Breed
93 Spaces	Paved	24Width/70Length
Recreation Hall	Game Room	Restrooms and Showers

Moon Mountain RV Resort

Centrally located to everything in the beautiful Rogue Valley.

3298 Pearce Park Rd, Grants Pass, OR 97526	(541) 479-1145 moonmountainrv.com/	All Year
$45	Military/Good Sam	RV Age, Pet Breed
51 Spaces	Paved	20Width/60Length
Internet	Cable	Laundry

Oregon Motel 8 & RV Park

Engage in lots of outdoor activities and points of interest around you.

5225 N Highway 97, Klamath Falls, OR 97601	(541) 883-3431 oregonmotel8rvpark.com/	All Year
$46-$49	Good Sam	Pet Quantity
33 Spaces	Gravel	18Width/60Length
Showers	Rentals	Heated Pool

Junipers Reservoir RV Resort

A full-service RV park at a working cattle ranch.

91029 Highway 140, Lakeview, OR 97630	(541) 947-2050 http://www.junipersrv.com/	May 1 to October 15
$39-$45	Military/Good Sam	None
40 Spaces	Gravel	30Width/80Length
Rentals	Showers	Horseshoes

Tri City RV Park

A pet-friendly park at rates most travelers can afford.

187 N Old Pacific Hwy, Myrtle Creek, OR 97457	(541) 860-5000 https://tricityrvpark.com/	All Year
$36	Good Sam	Pet Quantity
70 Spaces	Paved	24Width/50Length
RV Wash	Tables, Cable	RV Supplies

Lone Mountain RV Resort

Explore everything above and below ground when you visit the Oregon Caves.

169 Lone Mountain Rd, O Brien, OR 97534	(541) 596-2878 lonemountainrv.com/	All Year
$35-$50	Military/Good Sam	None
44 Spaces	Paved	24Width/75Length
Rentals	Outdoor Games	Firewood

Rice Hill RV Park

Easy access on and off the interstate.

1120 John Long Rd, Rice Hill, OR	(541) 849-2335 ricehill-rvpark.com/	All Year
$39	Good Sam	None
43 Spaces	Paved	30Width/70Length
Patios, Tables	RV Wash	Rec. Hall

Holiday RV Park

Located in the heart of the beautiful Rogue Valley.

201 N Phoenix Rd, Phoenix, OR 97535	(541) 535-2183 https://holidayrvpark.net/	All Year
$50	Military/Good Sam	RV Age
100 Spaces	Paved	22Width/70Length
RV Supplies	Outdoor Games	Heated Pool

Rising River RV Park

Located on the bank above the Umpqua River.

5579 Grange Rd, Roseburg, OR 97471	(541) 679-7256 https://www.risingriverrv.com/	All Year
$47	Military/Good Sam	Pet Breed
90 Spaces	Paved	30Width/60Length
Rec. Hall	Outdoor Games	Fishing Guides

Sunny Valley RV Park

A beautiful park-like setting conveniently located in southwest Oregon.

140 Old Stage Rd, Wolf Creek, OR 97497	(541) 479-0209 sunnyvalleyrvparkandcampground.com/	March 1 to November 1
$30-$35	Military/Good Sam	Pet Breed
38 Spaces	Paved/Gravel	30Width/40Length
Game Room	Pool, Firewood	Horseshoes

Hi-Way Haven RV Park

Built on the site of a classic drive-in movie theater. It still offers movies that you can view.

609 Fort Mckay Rd, Sutherlin, OR 97479	(541) 459-4557 https://www.hiwayhaven.com/	All Year
$35-$47	Military/Good Sam	None
100 Spaces	Paved	26Width/60Length
Movies, Rentals	Cable, Rec. Hall	Game Room, Pavilion

Oregon – East

Eastern Oregon is far from the coast, but still has its own natural beauty and rugged wilderness to explore. There are a handful of wonderful parks that can serve as your base camp while you explore the surrounding area or enjoy an outdoor adventure.

Mt View RV

A full-service resort with the rustic charm of the Oregon Trail.

2845 Hughes Ln, Baker City, OR 97814	(541) 523-4824 http://www.mtviewrv.com/	All Year
$40-$42	Military/Good Sam	None
97 Spaces	Paved	26Width/70Length
Heated Pool	Playground	Rec. Hall

Burns RV Park

Experience a quiet getaway in eastern Oregon in the high desert.

1273 Seneca Dr, Burns, OR 97720	(541) 573-7640 https://burnsrvpark.net/	All Year
$31-$44	Military/Good Sam	None
52 Spaces	Gravel	30Width/75Length
RV Supplies	Outdoor Games	Rentals

Wildhorse Resort

Your time here can be action-packed, relaxed, or somewhere in between.

46510 Wildhorse Blvd, Pendleton, OR 97801	(800) 654-9453 http://www.wildhorseresort.com/	All Year
$37-$65	Military/Good Sam	None
100 Spaces	Paved	30Width/60Length
Snack Bar	Golf, Driving Range	Exercise Room

Pilot RV Park

Your perfect base camp for sightseeing and recreation in eastern Oregon.

2125 S Highway 395, Stanfield, OR 97875	(541) 449-1189 https://www.pilotrvpark.com/	All Year
$42-$48	Military/Good Sam	None
48 Spaces	Paved	30Width/75Length
Showers	Horseshoes	Patios and Tables

Pennsylvania

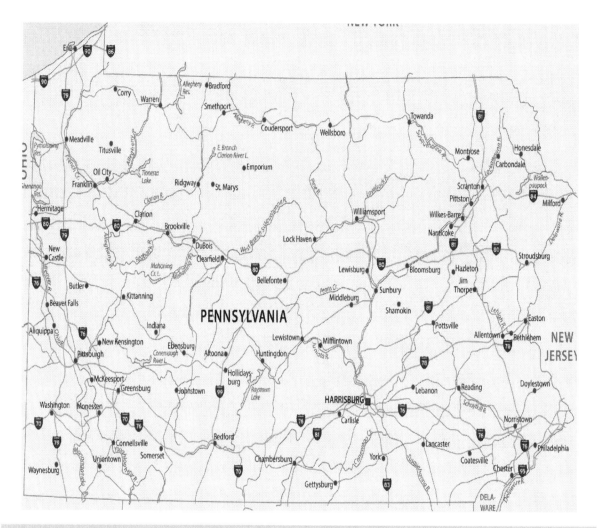

Pennsylvania – North

Northern Pennsylvania gives you a range of the most outdoor activities. There is no limit to what you can do in this area. There are mountains, valleys, and lakes, so you have no shortage of adventures to plan. Stay at any of the parks in this area for a long-term stay while you experience the surrounding area.

Silver Valley Campsites
Located in the middle of the beautiful Pocono Mountains.

| 101 Silver Valley Cir, Saylorsburg, PA 18353 | (570) 992-4824 http://www.silvervalleycamp.com/ | All Year |

$50-$55	Military/Good Sam	None
140 Spaces	Gravel	31Width/60Length
RV Supplies	Restaurant	Planned Activities

Tanglewood Camping
Stay in the Lake and Canyon Country of Pennsylvania.

787 Tanglewood Rd, Covington, PA 16917	(570) 549-8299 http://tanglewoodcamping.com/	May 1 to October 31
$46-$54	Military/Good Sam	Pet Size, Pet Quantity
144 Spaces	Gravel	30Width/60Length
Outdoor Games	Fishing Supplies	Cabin Rentals

Gaslight Campground
Just minutes from water activities on the Allegheny River.

6297 Emlenton Clintonville Rd, Emlenton, PA 16373	(724) 867-6981 https://gaslightcamping.com	April 1 to October 31
$37-$40	Military/Good Sam	None
128 Spaces	Gravel	25Width/60Length
Game Room	Heated Pool	Cabin Rentals

Presque Isle Passage RV Park
Just seven miles to Lake Erie.

6300 Sterrettania Rd, Fairview, PA 16415	(814) 833-3272 https://presqueislepassage.com/	All Year
$37-$58	Military/Good Sam	None
136 Spaces	Gravel	25Width/65Length
Fishing Supplies	Firewood, Rentals	Horseshoes

West Haven RV Park
Located on 50 acres of beautiful woods and meadows.

6601 Sterrettania Rd, Erie, PA 16415	(814) 403-3243 https://westhavenrvpark.com/	May 1 to October 23
$42-$62	Military/Good Sam	None
158 Spaces	Paved/Gravel	25Width/70Length
Firewood	Outdoor Games	Onsite RV Service

Pioneer Campground
Stay atop Sonestown Mountain at 2,300 feet.

307 Pioneer Trl, Muncy Valley, PA 17758	(570) 946-9971 https://pioneercampground.com	April 15 to December 15
$46-$56	Military/Good Sam	None

71 Spaces	Gravel	45Width/60Length
Guest Services	Planned Activities	Outdoor Games

Four Seasons Campgrounds
The best camping in the heart of the Poconos.

249 Babbling Brook Rd, Scotrun, PA 18355	(570) 629-2504 fourseasonscampgrounds.com/	April 28 to October 10
$54-$65	Good Sam	None
116 Spaces	Paved/Gravel	30Width/65Length
Recreation Hall	Swimming Pool	Fire Rings

Otter Lake Camp Resort
A great family camping destination in the Poconos.

1639 Marshalls Creek Rd, East Stroudsburg, PA 18302	(570) 223-0123 https://otterlake.com/	All Year
$48-$84	None	None
300 Spaces	Paved	30Width/60Length
RV Supplies	Paddle Boats	Outdoor Games

Mountain Vista Campground
You can enjoy endless fun in the Poconos Mountains.

415 Taylor Dr, East Stroudsburg, PA 18301	(570) 223-0111 mountainvistacampground.com/	May 1 to October 20
$47-$65	Good Sam	None
185 Spaces	Paved/Gravel	40Width/75Length
Pool, RV Wash	Cable, Firewood	Gym, Snack Bar

Hemlock Campground
A family fun camping experience in the heart of the Poconos.

559 Hemlock Dr, Tobyhanna, PA 18466	(570) 894-4388 http://hemlockcampground.com/	May 1 to October 31
$59	Military/Good Sam	None
74 Spaces	Paved/Gravel	28Width/65Length
Gated, Pool	Games, Fire Rings	Firewood

Cozy Creek Family Campground
The place to create family memories.

30 Vacation Ln, Tunkhannock, PA 18657	(570) 836-4122 northeastpacamping.com/	All Year
$40-$68	Military/Good Sam	Pet Quantity
110 Spaces	Gravel	40Width/60Length

Lehigh Gorge Campground

Located along the scenic Lehigh River.

4585 State Street White Haven, PA 18661	570-443-9191 lehighgorgecampground.com/	April 15 to November 30
$47-$53	Military/Good Sam	None
200 Spaces	Paved/Gravel	45Width/75Length
Gated, Grocery	Pool, Game Room	Rec. Hall, Pavilion

Woodland Campground

Here are many outdoor activities to enjoy, including a stocked fishing pond.

314 Egypt Rd, Woodland, PA 16881	(814) 857-5388 http://woodlandpa.com/	April 1 to November 15
$46	Military/Good Sam	Pet Quantity, Pet Breed
73 Spaces	Gravel	25Width/75Length
Fishing	Outdoor Games	Rentals

Pennsylvania – South

Southern Pennsylvania is home to Amish country and rugged natural beauty.

Shady Grove Campground
A great family camping experience.

65 Poplar Dr, Denver, PA 17517	(717) 484-4225 shadygrovecampground.com/	All Year
$59-$64	Military/Good Sam	None
112 Spaces	Gravel	30Width/60Length
Internet	Fishing Supplies	Cabin Rentals

Friendship Village Campground
There are plenty of nearby activities to enjoy.

348 Friendship Village Rd, Bedford, PA 15522	(814) 623-1677 https://www.fvofb.com/	All Year
$45-$61	Military	Pet Quantity
285 Spaces	Paved/Gravel	40Width/70Length
Pedal Carts	Pool, Rec.Hall	Firewood

Whispering Pines Camping Estates
Located in the scenic Red Rock Mountains.

1557 N Bendertown Rd, Stillwater, PA 17878	(570) 925-6810 http://www.wpce.com/	All Year
$47-$55	Military/Good Sam	Pet Quantity/Pet Breed
65 Spaces	Gravel	40Width/60Length
Model Rentals	Game Room	Paddle Boats

Sun Valley RV Resort
The facilities here make for a convenient and comfortable experience.

451 East Maple Grove Road, Narvon, PA 17555	(717) 445-6262	April 1 to November 1
$49-$60	Military/Good Sam	None
248 Spaces	Paved/Gravel	25Width/60Length
Gate Access	Onsite RV Service	Game Room

Mountain Creek Campground
Stay in the beautiful South Mountains of Pennsylvania.

349 Pine Grove Rd, Gardners, PA 17324	(717) 486-7681 mountaincreekcamping.com/	March 15 to November 20
$42-$66	Military/Good Sam	None

228 Spaces	Gravel	30Width/65Length
Gate Access	Pool, Golf Carts	Rec. Hall

Deer Run Camping Resort

The perfect place to enjoy the nature of Southern Pennsylvania.

111 Sheet Iron Roof Rd, Gardners, PA 17324	(717) 486-8168	April 1 to October 31
$40-$61	Military/Good Sam	Pet Quantity
170 Spaces	Gravel	25Width/70Length
Cabin Rentals	Planned Activities	Outdoor Games

Hickory Run Campground

Stay in the beautiful countryside.

285 Greenville Rd, Denver, PA 17517	(717) 336-5564 hickoryruncampground.com/	April 1 to November 1
$38-$47	Military	$38-$47
255 Spaces	Paved/Gravel	30Width/75Length
Outdoor Games	Rec. Hall	Gate Access

Hershey Road Campground

Just a few miles from Hershey Park.

1590 Hershey Rd, Elizabethtown, PA 17022	(717) 367-1179 hersheyconewago.com/	All Year
$69-$145	Military/Good Sam	None
192 Spaces	Paved	38Width/70Length
Cabin Rentals	Pool	Game Room

Artillery Ridge Camping Resort

Just a mile from town and offering a resort-style park.

610 Taneytown Rd, Gettysburg, PA 17325	(717) 334-1288 https://www.artilleryridge.com/	All Year
$69-$76	Military/Good Sam	None
180 Spaces	Gravel	40Width/60Length
Guest Services	Outdoor Games	Rec. Hall

Gettysburg Campground

A family campground along Marsh Creek.

2030 Fairfield Rd, Gettysburg, PA 17325	(717) 334-3304 gettysburgcampground.com/	April 3 to November 22
$45-$74	Military/Good Sam	None
240 Spaces	Gravel	25Width/70Length

Harrisburg East Campground

Centrally located between Hershey, Lancaster, and Gettysburg.

1134 Highspire Rd, Harrisburg, PA 17111	(717) 939-4331 http://hbgeastcampground.com/	All Year
$60-$105	Military/Good Sam	None
67 Spaces	Paved/Gravel	35Width/60Length
Lawn Bowling	Firewood, Cable	Heated Pool

Tucquan Park Family Campground

Located in the Susquehanna River hills.

917 River Rd, Holtwood, PA 17532	(717) 284-2156 https://camptucquanpark.com/	All Year
$47-$51	Military/Good Sam	None
155 Spaces	Gravel	30Width/60Length
Pool, Firewood, Ice	Cabin Rentals	Rec. Hall

Jonestown AOK Campground

A great central location, easily accessible by some of the most popular towns.

145 Old Rte 22, Jonestown, PA 17038	(717) 865-2526 jonestownaokcampground.com	All Year
$45	Military/Good Sam	None
179 Spaces	Paved/Gravel	24Width/60Length
Internet	Pavilion	Horseshoes

Flory's Cottages & Camping

Located in central Lancaster County.

99 N Ronks Rd, Ronks, PA 17572	(717) 687-6670 floryscamping.com/	All Year
$43-$63	Good Sam	None
71 Spaces	Gravel	30Width/100Length
Cabin Rentals	Game Room	Rec. Hall

Country Acres Campground

Clean, quiet camping in Lancaster County.

20 Leven Rd, Gordonville, PA 17529	(717) 687-8014 https://bird-in-hand.com	March 21 to November 30
$59-$68	Good Sam	14 Day Max Stay
95 Spaces	Gravel	36Width/60Length
Gated, Pool	Rec. Hall, Horseshoes	Playground, Fire Rings

Old Mill Stream Campground

Located along a stream and offering modern camping amenities.

2249 Lincoln Highway E, Lancaster, PA 17602	(717) 299-2314 oldmillstreamcampground.com/	All Year
$43-$68	Military	Pet Quantity, 14 Day Max
157 Spaces	Paved/Gravel	30Width/60Length
Guest Services	Activities	Cabin Rentals

Waterside Campground

A brief description.

475 Locust Rd, Lewistown, PA 17044	(717) 248-3974 watersidecampground.com/	All Year
$48-$61	Military/Good Sam	Pet Quantity
236 Spaces	Paved/Gravel	30Width/60Length
Gated	Boat Rental	Outdoor Games

Paradise Stream Family Campground

Great activities and spacious sites mean you'll have a great time.

693 Paradise Stream Rd, Loysville, PA 17047	(717) 789-2117 campparadisestream.com/	April 13 to October 28
$61-$71	Military/Good Sam	Pet Quantity
196 Spaces	Gravel	40Width/75Length
Gated, Pool	Rec. Hall, Cabins	Pedal Carts

Pinch Pond Family Campground

Located in the foothills, this park is the perfect blend of camping experience and touring fun.

3075 Pinch Rd, Manheim, PA 17545	(717) 665-7640 https://pinchpond.com/	All Year
$46-$50	Good Sam	None
190 Spaces	Paved/Gravel	35Width/60Length
Gated, Pool	Cabins, Cable	Guest Services

Yogi at Shangri-La

A beautiful wooded setting for you to enjoy your vacation.

670 Hidden Paradise Rd, Milton, PA 17847	(570) 524-4561 jellystoneshangri-la.com/	All Year
$50-$74	Military/Good Sam	Pet Quantity
175 Spaces	Gravel	30Width/60Length
Rec. Hall, Lodge Room	Game Room, Pool	Laundry

Spring Gulch Resort Campground
Full-amenity outdoor lifestyle is what you'll find here.

475 Lynch Rd, New Holland, PA 17557	(888) 416-6242	March 21 to December 1
$58-$92	Good Sam	Pet Breed
290 Spaces	Paved/Gravel	40Width/65Length
Cabins, Playground	Pool, Horseshoes, Gym	Cable, Laundry, Internet

Fox Den Acres Campground
Where you can have a pleasant stay and a wonderful camping experience.

390 Wilson Fox Rd, New Stanton, PA 15672	(724) 925-7054 http://www.foxdenacres.com/	May 1 to October 31
$36	None	None
160 Spaces	Gravel	30Width/75Length
RV Supplies	Pool	Playground

Twin Grove RV Resort
The best family resort in Pennsylvania right off the interstate.

1445 Suedberg Road, Pine Grove, PA 17963	(717) 865-4602 https://twingrove.com/	All Year
$44-$70	Military/Good Sam	Pet Quantity, Pet Breed
214 Spaces	Paved/Gravel	30Width/80Length
Pool, Gated	Playground	Gym, Bike Rentals

Bear Run Campground
Conveniently located to Pittsburgh by the interstate or public transportation.

184 Badger Hill Rd, Portersville, PA 16051	(724) 368-3564 bearruncampground.com/	April 15 to October 30
$39-$67	Military/Good Sam	Pet Quantity/Pet Breed
225 Spaces	Paved	35Width/60Length
Cabins, Fishing Guides	Boat Rentals	Game Room

Yogi Bear's Jellystone Park
You'll have no trouble keeping busy here.

340 Blackburn Rd, Quarryville, PA 17566	(717) 610-4505 https://jellystonepa.com/	April 18 to November 2
$47-$158	None	Pet Quantity
175 Spaces	Paved/Gravel	40Width/60Length
Planned Activities	Heated Pool	Guest Services

Pine Cove Beach Club & RV Resort
Offering everything you could want to enjoy your trip.

116 Beach Dr, Charleroi, PA 15022	(724) 239-2900 Website	April 1 to September 30
$50-$65	Military/Good Sam	None
57 Spaces	Paved/Gravel	38Width/60Length
Gated, Waterslide	Planned Activities	Playground, Rec. Hall

Rhode Island

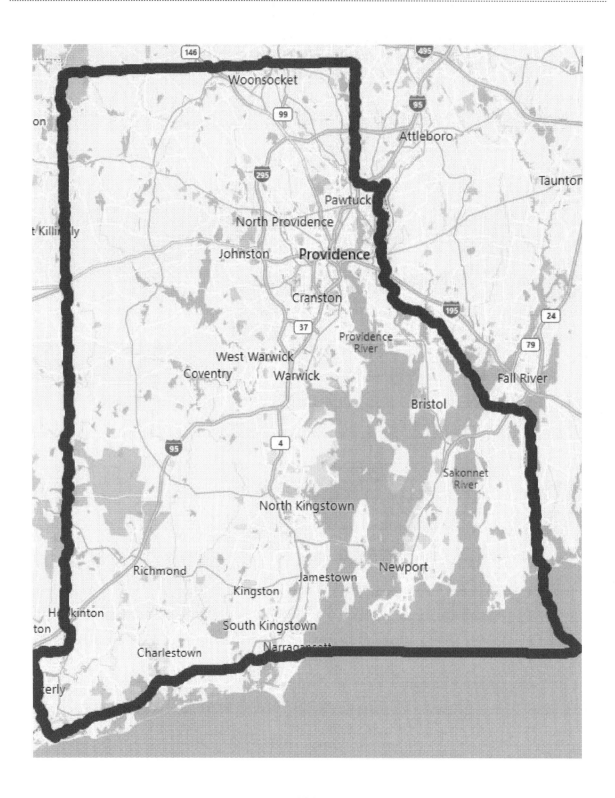

Rhode Island is a small state in New England. You can easily explore the best parts of this state from an RV park. There are two great options for a place to stay while enjoying outdoor activities or while visiting the quaint towns in this state.

Ashaway RV Resort
A park conveniently located near beaches, golf courses, rivers, and casinos.

235 Ashaway Rd, Bradford, RI 02808	(401) 377-8100 https://ashawayrvresort.com/	April 15 to October 15
$65-$75	Good Sam	Pet Breed
260 Spaces	Gravel	30Width/60Length
Shuffleboard, Pool	Gated, Playground	Tennis, Pedal Carts

Ginny-B Campground
A family camping experience in the woods outside of Foster.

7 Harrington Rd, Foster, RI 02825	(401) 397-9477 http://ginny-bcampground.com/main/	May 1 to September 30
$41	None	None
225 Spaces	Paved	30Width/60Length
Rec. Hall	Fishing Supplies	Outdoor Games

South Carolina

South Carolina is a varied state with towering mountain peaks, rolling plains, and beautiful seaside beaches. There is no shortage of outdoor adventures to be had in this state

Lake Hartwell Camping & Cabins
Nestled in the foothills of the Blue Ridge Mountains along beautiful Lake Hartwell.

200 Wham Rd, Anderson, SC 29625	(864) 287-3161 koa.com/campgrounds/anderson/	All Year
$29-$37	Military/Good Sam	Pet Quantity, Breed
128 Spaces	Paved/Gravel	25Width/55Length
Internet	RV Supplies, Fishing Guides	Rec. Hall, Pool

Oak Plantation Campground
You'll enjoy the picturesque setting and convenient location.

3540 Savannah Hwy, Johns Island, SC 29455	(843) 766-5936 http://oakplantationcampground.com/	All Year
$52-$66	Military/Good Sam	None
220 Spaces	Paved	35Width/80Length
Internet, Firewood	Cable, Pool, Ice	Playground, Games

Camp Pedro Campground
A wonderful park to stay at that gives you a southwest theme to enjoy.

3346 Highway 301 N, Hamer, SC 29547	(843) 774-2417 https://www.sobpedro.com/	All Year
$32-$48	Military/Good Sam	None
100 Spaces	Paved	40Width/100Length
Internet, Gated	Restaurant	Pool, Lounge

Crown Cove RV Park
Once you get here, you'll never want to leave.

8332 Regent Pkwy, Fort Mill, SC 29715	(803) 547-3500 crowncovervpark.com/	All Year
$53	Military/Good Sam	None
151 Spaces	Paved	28Width/70Length
Internet, Cable	Playground	Laundry

Camp Lake Jasper RV Resort
Just minutes off the interstate, this park puts you close to all the action.

44 Camp Lake Drive, Hardeeville, SC 29927	(843) 784-5200	All Year
$55-$65	Military/Good Sam	Pet Quantity
90 Spaces	Paved	38Width/90Length
Firewood, Internet	Planned Activities	Fire Rings, Boat Rental

Hilton Head Harbor RV Resort
A beautiful waterside resort with comfortable sites.

43A Jenkins Rd, Hilton Head Island, SC 29925	(843) 681-3256 https://www.hiltonheadharbor.com/	All Year
$79-$99	Military	None
200 Spaces	Paved	35Width/65Length
Restaurant, Gym	RV Wash, Fishing Supplies	Gym, Laundry

Lake Aire RV Park
A quality campground with a private fishing lake.

4375 Hwy 162, Hollywood, SC 29449	(843) 571-1271 https://www.lakeairerv.com/	All Year
$46-$52	Military/Good Sam	Pet Quantity
92 Spaces	Gravel	30Width/75Length
Fishing, Pool	Playground	Games

Magnolia RV Park
Easy access on and off the interstate.

567 Fairview Church Rd, Kinards, SC 29355	(864) 697-1214 http://magnoliarvparksc.com/	All Year
$30-$36	Military/Good Sam	None
41 Spaces	Gravel	32Width/60Length
Firewood, Pool	Rec. Hall, Games	Playground, Tables

Barnyard RV Park
Come here to relax and feel at home.

201 Oak Dr, Lexington, SC 29073	(803) 957-1238 http://www.barnyardrvpark.com	All Year
$38	Military/Good Sam	None
129 Spaces	Paved	30Width/85Length
Internet	RV Supplies	Pavilion

WillowTree RV Resort
Spacious sites with a wonderful outdoor atmosphere.

520 Southern Sights Dr, Longs, SC 29568	(843) 756-4334 https://willowtreervr.com/	All Year
$52-$74	None	Pet Breed
106 Spaces	Paved	50Width/100Length
Horseshoes	Rec. Hall, Pool	Cabin Rentals

Apache Family Campground
This oceanfront campground features a private pier.

9700 Kings Rd, Myrtle Beach, SC 29572	(843) 449-7323 https://apachefamilycampground.com/	All Year
$40-$81	Military	Pet Quantity, Pet Breed
997 Spaces	Paved/Gravel	25Width/60Length
Gated, Internet	Fishing, Game Room	Pool, Snack Bar

North Myrtle Beach RV Resort

This is a one of a kind luxury resort that offers something for everyone.

260 Old Crane Rd, Little River, SC 29566	(843) 390-4386 northmyrtlebeachrvresortanddrydock.com/	All Year
$45-$82	None	Pet Breed
133 Spaces	Paved	50Width/75Length
Gated, Firewood	Restaurant, Pool	Boat Rental, Cable

Cypress Camping Resort

The perfect place to vacation with family.

101 Cypress Rv Way, Myrtle Beach, SC 29588	(843) 293-0300 https://cypresscampingresort.com/	All Year
$40-$75	Military/Good Sam	None
107 Spaces	Gravel	35Width/65Length
Boat Rentals, Pool	Paddle Boats, Fishing	Cabin Rentals, Ice

Briarcliffe RV Resort

The first thing you'll notice about this resort is its beauty.

10495 N Kings Hwy, Myrtle Beach, SC 29572	(843) 272-2730 http://www.briarcliffervresort.com/	All Year
$52-$72	Good Sam	None
281 Spaces	Paved	30Width/60Length
Shuffleboard, Internet	Model Rentals	Game Room

Ocean Lakes Family Campground

An oceanfront camping resort with outstanding amenities and activities galore.

6001 S Kings Hwy, Myrtle Beach, SC 29575	(843) 238-5636 https://www.oceanlakes.com/	All Year
$38-$96	None	Pet Breed
3436 Spaces	Paved	35Width/53Length
Internet, Snack Bar	Game Room	Cabin Rentals

Lakewood Camping Resort

Considered one of the best campgrounds in South Carolina.

5901 S Kings Hwy, Myrtle Beach, SC 29575	(877) 525-3966 https://lakewoodcampground.com/	All Year
$32-$90	Military	Pet Quantity, Pet Breed
2000 Spaces	Paved	30Width/60Length
Internet, Snack Bar	Model Rentals	Gym, Shuffleboard

Pirateland Family Camping Resort
Here you'll enjoy the best in oceanfront camping.

5401 S Kings Hwy, Myrtle Beach, SC 29575	(843) 238-5155 https://www.pirateland.com/	All Year
$35-$90	None	Pet Breed
1390 Spaces	Paved	24Width/60Length
Fishing Supplies	Pool, Paddle Boats	Planned Activities

Myrtle Beach Travel Park
Here you'll enjoy oceanfront camping at its finest.

10108 Kings Rd, Myrtle Beach, SC 29572	(843) 449-3714 http://www.myrtlebeachtravelpark.com/	All Year
$44-$87	None	None
1150 Spaces	Paved/Gravel	30Width/55Length
Pool, Gated	Fishing Supplies	Guest Services

Clemson RV Park at the Grove
Just minutes from the interstate and historic Pendleton.

150 Dalton Dr, Pendleton, SC 29670	(864) 228-2858 https://clemsonrv.com/	All Year
$54	Military/Good Sam	None
300 Spaces	Gravel	24Width/60Length
RV Supplies	Fishing Guides	Outdoor Games

Palmetto Shores RV Resort
There are plenty of activities in the nearby area to keep you busy.

5215 Dingle Pond Rd, Summerton, SC 29148	(803) 478-6336 http://palmettoshoresrvresort.com/	All Year
$50	Military/Good Sam	RV Age
92 Spaces	Gravel	40Width/75Length
Cabin Rentals	Snack Bar, Gated	Fishing Guides

Jolly Acres RV Park
Take a relaxing break near St. George, just off the interstate.

289 Horne Taylor Rd, Saint George, SC 29477	(843) 563-8303 http://www.syrrrun.com/	All Year
$34-$37	Military/Good Sam	Pet Breed
38 Spaces	Gravel	35Width/78Length
Playground	Rec. Hall, Laundry	Games, RV Wash

River Bottom Farms Family Campground

Located in beautiful rolling farmland.

357 Cedar Creek Rd, Swansea, SC 29160	(803) 568-4182 http://www.riverbottomfarms.com/	All Year
$36-$42	Military/Good Sam	Pet Breed
62 Spaces	Gravel	33Width/63Length
Outdoor Games	Pool, Fishing Supplies	Internet

South Dakota

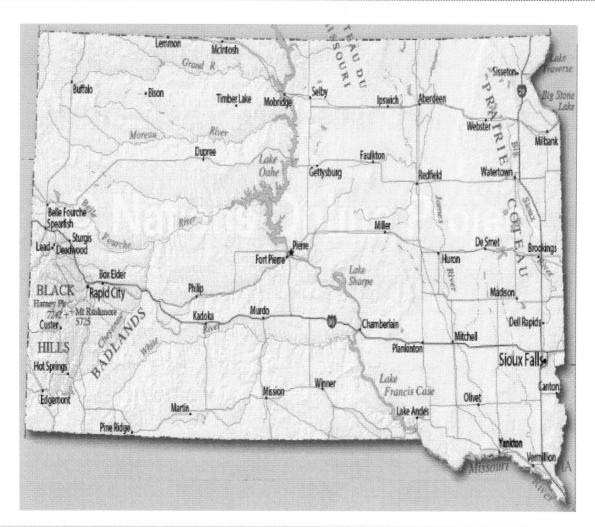

South Dakota – East

The eastern part of South Dakota is more than open farmland and prairie. There is a range of outdoor activities to enjoy and historic towns to see. There are several good parks to choose from in this area while exploring local attractions or planning an outdoor adventure.

Wylie Park Campground
This is a park inspired by children's nursery rhymes.

2301 24th Ave NW, Aberdeen, SD 57401	(605) 626-3512 http://www.aberdeen.sd.us/276/Wylie-Park-Campground	April 1 to November 1
$37	Good Sam	None
115 Spaces	Paved	34Width/60Length

Oasis Campground

Come and stay at this campground, one of the best in South Dakota.

600 E SD Highway 16, Oacoma, SD 57365	(605) 234-6959 http://www.alsoasis.com/	April 15 to November 1
$44	Military/Good Sam	Pet Breed
75 Spaces	Gravel	30Width/65Length
Internet, Cable	Game Room	Pool, Cabins

R & R Campground & RV Park

A simple and basic campground offering the standard amenities.

1700 S Burr St, Mitchell, SD 57301	(605) 996-8895 https://www.sdcampgrounds.com/	May 1 to September 30
$36-$40	Military/Good Sam	Pet Breed
40 Spaces	Paved/Gravel	30Width/70Length
Firewood	Pool, Lodge Room	Playground

Dakota Campground

Easy access on and off the interstate.

1800 W Spruce St, Mitchell, SD 57301	(605) 996-9432	April 1 to November 30
$28-$32	Military/Good Sam	None
54 Spaces	Gravel	30Width/70Length
Firewood	Cabin Rentals	Playground

New Frontier RV Park

Spend a night or more at a clean park under the open Prairie sky.

432 S Spruce St, Presho, SD 57568	(605) 895-2604 http://newfrontiercampground.com/	April 1 to November 1
$45	Military/Good Sam	None
60 Spaces	Gravel	24Width/60Length
Driving Range	Guest Services	Bike Rentals

Dakota Sunsets RV Park

Easy access to Sioux Falls and Mitchell.

25495 US Highway 81, Salem, SD 57058	(605) 425-9085 https://dakotasunsets.com/	April 15 to October 31
$32-$39	Military/Good Sam	None
54 Spaces	Paved/Gravel	28Width/78Length
Pool, Firewood	Pavilion	Playground

Sioux Falls Yogi Bear

Experience both quality and value at this park.

26014 478th Ave, Brandon, SD 57005	(605) 332-2233 jellystonesiouxfalls.com/	April 1 to November 30
$40-$69	Military/Good Sam	None
112 Spaces	Gravel	35Width/70Length
ATM, RV Supplies	Pool, Cabins	Outdoor Games

Tower RV Park

A campground within a few minutes of all the main local attractions.

4609 W 12th St, Sioux Falls, SD 57106	(605) 332-1173 towercampground.com/	All Year
$50-$55	Military/Good Sam	Pet Breed
119 Spaces	Paved/Gravel	50Width/60Length
Internet	Guest Services	Outdoor Games

South Dakota – West

Western South Dakota is home to major parks and monuments such as Mount Rushmore. Plus, you'll find towns like Deadwood, where you can experience real-life western shootouts and other historical sites. There are a great number of outdoor activities to enjoy in the surrounding area. Plus, there are plenty of great parks that can serve as your base camp while having a great vacation.

Buffalo Ridge Camp Resort
This is your best base camp when exploring the Black Hills.

245 Centennial Dr, Custer, SD 57730	(605) 673-4664 https://custerhospitality.com	May 25 to October 2
$36-$90	Good Sam	Pet Quantity
106 Spaces	Gravel	30Width/65Length
Internet	Pool, Cabins	Rec. Hall

Beaver Lake Campground
Relax in a tranquil park the way it should be.

12005 US Highway 16, Custer, SD 57730	(605) 673-2464 beaverlakecampground.net/	March 15 to November 10
$34-$60	Military/Good Sam	None
88 Spaces	Gravel	40Width/60Length
Firewood	Cable, Cabins	Outdoor Games

Custer's Gulch RV Park
Enjoy the quiet and relax by the campfire.

25112 Golden Valley Road Custer, SD 57730	(605) 673-4647 http://www.custersgulch.com/	May 15 to October 14
$34-$54	Military/Good Sam	Pet Quantity, Breed
70 Spaces	Gravel	45Width/75Length
Rec. Hall	Guest Services	Cabins

Fish'N Fry Campground
Stay among majestic pines near a mountain stream while exploring the Black Hills.

21390 Us Highway 385, Deadwood, SD 57732	(605) 578-2150 http://stay.fishnfrycampground.com/	May 15 to September 16
$36-$40	Military/Good Sam	None
59 Spaces	Gravel	16Width/60Length
RV Supplies	Model Rentals	Rec. Hall, Fishing

Whistler Gulch Campground

Stay just minutes from downtown Deadwood.

235 Cliff St Hwy 85 South, Deadwood, SD 57732	(605) 578-2092 https://www.whistlergulch.com/	May 1 to September 30
$47-$55	Military/Good Sam	None
123 Spaces	Paved	20Width/60Length
Tennis, Firewood	Internet, Lodge Room	Guest Services, Pool

Larsson's Crooked Creek Resort

The perfect place for history buffs, families, and those looking for an outdoor adventure.

24184 Hyw 16 & Us 385, Hill City, SD 57745	(605) 574-2418 crookedcreekresort.com/	May 15 to October 5
$61-$71	Military/Good Sam	Pet Breed
84 Spaces	Paved/Gravel	20Width/65Length
Firewood	Restaurant, Lodge Room	Gym, Pool, Cabins

Rafter J Bar Ranch Camping Resort

A premier camping resort in the Black Hills near Mount Rushmore.

12325 Rafter J Rd, Hill City, SD 57745	(605) 574-2527 https://www.rafterj.com/	May 1 to October 1
$46-$72	Good Sam	Pet Breed
180 Spaces	Paved/Gravel	40Width/60Length
Guest Services	Fishing Supplies	Cabins, Pool

Horse Thief Campground

Have a relaxing, fun, and memorable vacation here.

24391 Highway 87, Hill City, SD 57745	(800) 657-5802 https://www.horsethief.com/	May 15 to October 1
$53-$63	Military/Good Sam	Pet Breed
66 Spaces	Gravel	32Width/60Length
Horseshoes	Guest Services, Pool	Firewood, Internet

Rushmore Shadows Resort

Just 15 minutes to most cities and sites in the area.

23680 Busted Five Ct, Rapid City, SD 57702	(605) 343-4544 midwestoutdoorresorts.com	May 1 to October 15
$50-$85	Military/Good Sam	None
198 Spaces	Paved	30Width/60Length
Gated, Firewood	Pool, Games, Tennis	Playground

Lazy J RV Park & Campground

Offering panoramic views and wonderful amenities for an excellent stay.

4110 S Highway 16, Rapid City, SD 57701	(605) 342-2751 https://www.rcrvpark.com/	April 15 to October 15
$47-$55	Military/Good Sam	Pet Breed
72 Spaces	Paved	26Width/60Length
Playground, Pool	Laundry, Cabins	Lodge Room

Happy Holiday Resort

There are six national parks and monuments within easy travel distance of this resort.

8990 S Highway 16, Rapid City, SD 57702	(605) 342-8101 happyholidayrvresort.com/	All Year
$35-$49	Military/Good Sam	None
190 Spaces	Paved/Gravel	22Width/54Length
RV Supplies	Cabins, Game Room	Rec. Hall, Lodge Room

Heartland RV Park

A modern RV park just 20 minutes from Mount Rushmore.

24743 S Highway 79, Hermosa, SD 57744	(605) 255-5460 https://heartlandrvpark.com/	All Year
$30-$80	Military/Good Sam	None
215 Spaces	Gravel	30Width/80Length
Internet, Pool	Rec. Hall, Cabins	Guest Services

American Buffalo Resort

The best of the resorts in the Black Hills.

13752 S Highway 16, Rapid City, SD 57702	(605) 342-5368 https://americanbuffaloresort.com/	May 25 to September 30
$40-$85	Military/Good Sam	Pet Quantity
74 Spaces	Paved/Gravel	20Width/60Length
Cabins, Mini Golf	Guest Services	Firewood

Chris' Camp & RV Park

A full-service park with all the amenities.

701 Christensen Dr, Spearfish, SD 57783	(800) 350-2239 http://chriscampground.com/	April 15 to October 15
$39-$45	Military/Good Sam	None
135 Spaces	Paved/Gravel	20Width/75Length
Guest Services	Pool, Cabins	Activities

Elkhorn Ridge RV Resort

Rustic elegance at the Black Hills.

20189 US Highway 85, Spearfish, SD 57783	(605) 722-1800 https://elkhornridgeresort.com/	All Year
$40-$75	Military/Good Sam	Pet Quantity
186 Spaces	Paved	38Width/90Length
Guest Services	Putting Green	Playground

No Name City Luxury Cabins & RV Park

A full-service resort in the Black Hills area of South Dakota.

20899 Pleasant Valley Dr, Sturgis, SD 57785	(605) 347-8891 http://nonamecity.com/	May 1 to October 15
$35-$45	Military/Good Sam	Pet Breed
42 Spaces	Gravel	24Width/100Length
Rec. Hall, Lounge	Cabins, Pool	Playground

Rush No More RV Resort

Come stay among natural beauty.

21137 Brimstone Pl, Sturgis, SD 57785	(605) 347-2916 https://www.rushnomore.com/	All Year
$42-$55	Military/Good Sam	None
125 Spaces	Paved/Gravel	32Width/75Length
Internet, Guest Services	Game Room, Pool	Cabins, Yurts

Sleepy Hollow Campground

Your perfect base camp for exploring Badlands National Park.

118 W 4th Ave, Wall, SD 57790	(605) 279-2100 sleepyhollowcampgroundsd.com/	April 15 to October 31
$37-$50	Military/Good Sam	Pet Breed
59 Spaces	Gravel	24Width/65Length
Pool, Cabins	Playground	Firewood, Internet

Tennessee

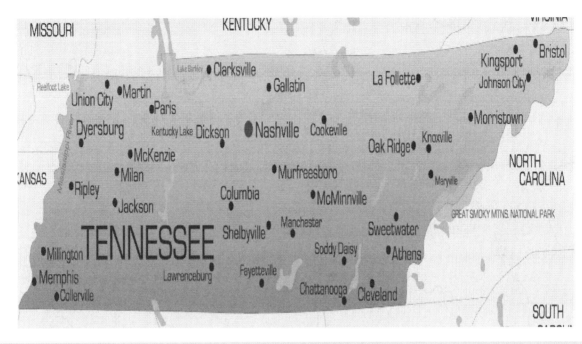

Tennessee – West

Western Tennessee offers plenty of things for all interests.

Chattanooga Holiday Travel Park
A park with plenty of amenities just off the interstate.

1709 S Mack Smith Rd, Chattanooga, TN 37412	(800) 693-2877 http://chattacamp.com/	All Year
$46-$49	Military/Good Sam	None
140 Spaces	Gravel	30Width/60Length
Cabins, Pool	Rec. Hall, Firewood	Laundry, Internet

Raccoon Mountain Campground
This campground is located at the highest-rated cave attraction in Tennessee.

319 W Hills Dr, Chattanooga, Chattanooga, TN 37419	(423) 821-9403 raccoonmountain.com/	All Year
$45-$70	Good Sam	RV Age, Pet Breed
60 Spaces	Gravel	25Width/65Length
Caving, Internet	Pool, Cabins	Rec. Hall, Gym

Clarksville RV Park

Close to restaurants and shopping.

1270 Tylertown Rd, Clarksville, TN 37040	(931) 648-8638 https://clarksvillervpark.com/	All Year
$39-$42	Military/Good Sam	None
67 Spaces	Gravel	30Width/65Length
Pool, Cabins	Rec. Hall	Playground

Deer Run RV Resort

Full-service park with a private lake.

3609 Peavine Firetower Rd, Crossville, TN 38571	(931) 484-3333 deerrunrvresort.com/	All Year
$41-$46	Military/Good Sam	None
346 Spaces	Gravel	40Width/80Length
Golf Carts, Fishing Supplies	Cabins, Snack Bar	Gated, Internet

Spring Lake RV Resort

Relax at this peaceful campground or fish in the private lake.

255 Fairview Dr, Crossville, TN 38571	(931) 707-1414 springlakervtn.com/	All Year
$37-$40	Military/Good Sam	None
60 Spaces	Gravel	45Width/75Length
Fishing	Rec. Hall	Firewood

Bean Pot Campground

Your spot for planning and starting your next adventure.

23 Bean Pot Campground Loop, Crossville, TN 38571	(877) 848-7958 beanpotcampground.com/	All Year
$28-$31	Military/Good Sam	None
54 Spaces	Gravel	25Width/65Length
Pool	Cabins	Firewood

Manchester KOA

Easy access on and off the interstate between Nashville and Chattanooga.

586 Campground Road, Manchester, TN 37355	(931) 728-9777 koa.com/campgrounds/manchester/	All Year
$46-$90	Military	None
39 Spaces	Gravel	37Width/65Length
Fishing Supplies	Activities	Rentals

Memphis Graceland RV Park

Located just off Elvis Presley Blvd, right across the street from Graceland.

3691 Elvis Presley Blvd, Memphis, TN 38116	(901) 396-7125 https://www.graceland.com	All Year
$40-$46	Military/Good Sam	None
77 Spaces	Paved/Gravel	25Width/60Length
Cabins	Pool	Gated

Two Rivers Campground

Known as Music City, here you can visit the Grand Ole Opry.

2616 Music Valley Dr, Nashville, TN 37214	(615) 883-8559 tworiverscampground.com/	All Year
$46-$60	Military/Good Sam	None
104 Spaces	Paved/Gravel	24Width/54Length
. Pool	Cable	Internet

Nashville Shores Lakeside Resort

A paradise for family camping vacations.

4001 Bell Rd, Hermitage, TN 37076	(615) 889-7050 https://www.nashvilleshores.com/	February 1 to December 1
$55-$80	MilitaryGood Sam	14 Day Max Stay
100 Spaces	Paved	30Width/60Length
Cabins	Gated	Shuffleboard

Green Acres RV Park

A large, friendly, and full-service RV park in Western Tennessee.

215 Ziffle Cir, Savannah, TN 38372	(731) 926-1928 greenacresrvparktn.com/	All Year
$50	None	Restrictions
49 Spaces	Paved/Gravel	30Width/120Length
Internet	Pool	Rec. Hall

Tennessee – East

East Tennessee is popular for the Great Smoky Mountains and offers a range of wonderful outdoor activities. There are small and large towns to visit with plenty of local attractions. Plus, there are quite a few wonderful parks where you can set up camp while taking all the time you need to explore the surrounding area.

Lakeview RV Park
A pet-friendly, full-service RV park.

4550 Highway 11 E Ste 1, Bluff City, TN 37618	(423) 538-5600 https://lakeviewrvpark.com/	All Year
$40-$44	Military/Good Sam	None
151 Spaces	Gravel	30Width/45Length
Pool, Cable	Playground	Rec.Hall

Smoky Mountain Premier
Located in Cosby, just 20 minutes from Gatlinburg.

4874 Hooper Hwy, Cosby, TN 37722	(423) 532-7183 https://smokymountainpremierrvresort.com/	All Year
$57-$82	Military	Pet Quantity
70 Spaces	Gravel	30Width/80Length
Rec. Hall, Gym	Cable, Pool, Cabins, Fire Rings	Firewood, Internet

Twin Creek RV Resort
Enjoy staying in peace and beauty while exploring the Great Smoky Mountains.

1202 E Pkwy, Gatlinburg, TN 37738	(800) 252-8077 https://twincreekrvresort.com/	March 29 to December 1
$76-$80	Military/Good Sam	Pet Quantity, Breed
85 Spaces	Paved	30Width/60Length
Cable, Pool	Rental, Ice	Internet, Showers

Greenbrier Campground
Located along the Little Pigeon River.

2353 E Pkwy, Gatlinburg, TN 37738	(865) 430-7415 smokymountaincamping.com/	March 1 to December 31
$45-$75	Military/Good Sam	None
119 Spaces	Gravel	28Width/60Length
Rentals	Horseshoes	Firewood

Smoky Bear Campground

Close to two entrances to the Great Smoky Mountains National Park.

Highway 321, Gatlinburg, TN 37738	(865) 436-8372	March 15 to November 30
$48-$58	Military/Good Sam	None
44 Spaces	Paved	30Width/80Length
Internet	Pool	Rec. Hall

Pigeon River Campground

Easy access on and off the interstate.

3375 Hartford Rd, Hartford, TN 37753	(844) 766-2267 campinginthesmokymountains.com/	March 1 to October 31
$45-$55	Military/Good Sam	None
12 Spaces	Gravel	30Width/50Length
Horseshoes	Fishing Supplies	Games

Riverpark Campground

Stay along the Nolichucky River and enjoy a range of outdoor activities.

3937 Highway 81 S, Jonesborough, TN 37659	(423) 753-5359 http://riverparkcampground.net/	All Year
$39-$51	Military/Good Sam	Pet Quantity
37 Spaces	Grael	30Width/60Length
RV Supplies	Gated	Rentals

Rocky Top Campground

A quiet and relaxing adult only park.

496 Pearl Ln, Blountville, TN 37617	(423) 323-2535 http://rockytopcampground.com/	All Year
$42	Military/Good Sam	21+
35 Spaces	Paved	25Width/65Length
Sauna, Showers	Rentals	Game Room

Volunteer Park Family Campground

Your closest option to the center of Knoxville.

9514 Diggs Gap Rd, Heiskell, TN 37754	(865) 938-6600 http://volparktn.com	All Year
$37-$42	Military/Good Sam	Pet Quantity
125 Spaces	Paved/Gravel	24Width/50Length
Pool	Horseshoes	Rec. Hall

Creekside RV Park
Just four miles from Dollywood and plenty of local attractions.

2475 Henderson Springs Rd, Pigeon Forge, TN 37863	(865) 428-4801 https://creeksidervpark.com/	March 1 to January 1
$38-$49	Military/Good Sam	None
115 Spaces	Paved	27Width/60Length
Firewood	Pool, Internet	RV Service

Pine Mountain RV Park
Enjoy the beauty of the Smoky Mountains.

411 Pine Mountain Rd, Pigeon Forge, TN 37863	(865) 453-9994 https://pinemountainrvpark.com/	All Year
$35-$65	Military/Good Sam	Pet Size, Breed
61 Spaces	Paved	35Width/60Length
Cabins	Pool	Gym

Camp RiversLanding
Stay in the seclusion of the Smoky Mountains.

304 Day Springs Rd, Pigeon Forge, TN 37863	(800) 848-9097 https://campriverslanding.com/	All Year
$45-$64	Military/Good Sam	None
114 Spaces	Paved	28Width/50Length
Pool	Rec. Hall	Game Room

Riveredge RV Park
Live a great outdoor life and make memories to last a lifetime.

4220 Huskey St, Pigeon Forge, TN 37863	(877) 881-7222 https://stayriveredge.com/	All Year
$40-$63	Military/Good Sam	None
171 Spaces	Paved	27Width/55Length
Pool, Cabins	Game Room	Firewood

King's Holly Haven RV Park
Located along Waldens Creek at the foot of Wears Mountain.

647 Wears Valley Rd, Pigeon Forge, TN 37863	(865) 453-5352 http://www.hollyhavenrvpark.com/	All Year
$28-$40	Good Sam	RV Age
162 Spaces	Paved	25Width/60Length
Pool, Playground	Pavilion	Laundry

Yogi Bear's Jellystone Park
This park puts you close to the attractions of Pigeon Forge.

3404 Whaley Dr, Pigeon Forge, TN 37863	(865) 453-8117 https://pigeonforgejellystone.com	All Year
$35-$69	Military/Good Sam	None
101 Spaces	Paved	28Width/50Length
Pool	Cable	Rentals

River Plantation RV Resort
Located in a peaceful valley bordered by the Little Pigeon River.

1004 Parkway, Sevierville, TN 37862	(800) 758-5267 riverplantationrv.com/	All Year
$31-$72	Military/Good Sam	None
299 Spaces	Gravel	30Width/75Length
Pool	Cable	Rentals

The Ridge Outdoor Resort
The newest park in the heart of the Smoky Mountains.

1250 Middle Creek Rd, Sevierville, TN 37862	(865) 505-3111 https://theridgeoutdoorresort.com/	All Year
$46-$80	Military/Good Sam	None
49 Spaces	Paved	40Width/70Length
Rentals	Firewood	Activities

Ripplin' Waters Campground
A quiet family campground with sites along the river.

1930 Winfield Dunn Pkwy, Sevierville, TN 37876	(865) 453-4169 https://www.ripplinwatersrv.com/	All Year
$38-$43	Good Sam	Pet Breed
156 Spaces	Paved/Gravel	24Width/100Length
Rentals	Pool	Firewood

Big Meadow Family Campground
Offering all the comforts you want and more.

8215 Cedar Creek Rd, Townsend, TN 37882	(865) 448-0625 bigmeadowcampground.com/	All Year
$62-$67	None	None
71 Spaces	Gravel	30Width/75Length
Gated	Internet	Cable

Texas

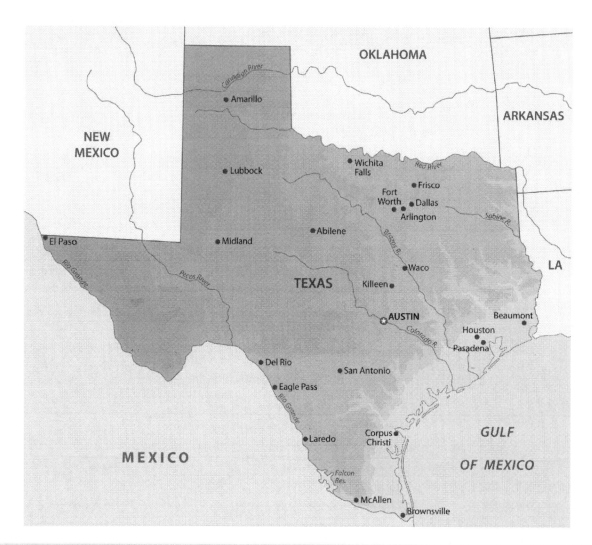

Texas – Panhandle

The Texas panhandle offers a few wonderful outdoor adventures.

Whistle Stop RV Resort

Visit Frontier Texas and the Abilene Zoo. This is your place to enjoy your vacation.

695 E Stamford St, Abilene, TX 79601	(325) 704-5252 http://whistlestoprvresort.com/	All Year
$40-$55	Military/Good Sam	RV Age, Pet Quantity, Breed
114 Spaces	Gravel	40Width/100Length
Pool, Cable	Rec. Hall	Playground

Abilene RV Park

Stay here and find out what fun in Texas is all about.

6195 E Interstate 20, Abilene, TX 79601	(325) 672-2212 https://abilenetexasrvpark.com	All Year
$39	Military/Good Sam	RV Age, Pet Quantity, Breed
66 Spaces	Gravel	20Width/56Length
Cabin	Guest Services	Rec. Hall, Pool

Fort Amarillo RV Resort

This park has a wonderful western setting.

10101 Business Interstate 40, Amarillo, TX 79124	(806) 331-1700 http://fortrvparks.com/	All Year
$45	Military/Good Sam	Pet Quantity, Pet Breed
105 Spaces	Paved/Gravel	30Width/75Length
Game Room	Tennis, Pool	Internet

Oasis RV Resort

The newest, finest, and largest RV park in Amarillo.

2715 Arnot Rd, Amarillo, TX 79124	(806) 356-8408 https://www.myrvoasis.com/	All Year
$56-$65	Military/Good Sam	None
179 Spaces	Paved	39Width/75Length
Internet	Pool, Cabins	Rec. Hall

Big Texan RV Ranch

Easy roads and comfortable RV sites await you.

1414 Sunrise Dr, Amarillo, TX 79104	(806) 373-4962 https://amarilloranch.com/	All Year
$40	Military/Good Sam	Pet Breed
156 Spaces	Paved	30Width/90Length
Rec. Hall	Playground	Internet

Lubbock RV Park

You can also choose to relax at your site and enjoy the wonderful amenities.

4811 N Interstate 27 27, Lubbock, TX 79403	(806) 747-2366 http://lubbockrvpark.com/	All Year
$40	Military/Good Sam	Pet Quantity
98 Spaces	Paved	25Width/70Length
Rec. Hall	Laundry	Outdoor Games

Midessa Oil Patch RV Park

A pet-friendly park that will serve as a base camp while you explore all the surrounding area.

4220 S County Road 1290, Odessa, TX 79765	(432) 563-2368 midessaoilpatchrvpark.com	All Year
$40	Military/Good Sam	Pet Quantity/Pet Breed
130 Spaces	Paved	25Width/60Length
Pool	Pavilion	Games

Coffee Creek RV Resort

The hospitality and amenities here are focused on giving you a relaxing and enjoyable stay.

13429 S Highway 281, Santo, TX 76472	(940) 769-2277	All Year
$40	Good Sam	None
115 Spaces	Gravel	35Width/90Length
Playground	Cabins, Pool	Rec.Hall

Twin Pine RV Park

Easy access to the highway and minutes from Lubbock.

1202 N Highway 84, Slaton, TX 79364	(806) 828-3311 http://www.twinpinervpark.com/	All Year
$38	Military/Good Sam	None
72 Spaces	Paved/Gravel	32Width/70Length
Internet	Showers	Laundry

Mesa Verde RV Park

Stay within minutes to a number of attractions in the area.

503 E Highway 62, Wolfforth, TX 79382	(806) 773-3135 https://rvlubbock.com/	All Year
$40	Military/Good Sam	Pet Quantity, Pet Breed
78 Spaces	Paved	35Width/70Length
Pool	RV Wash	Cable

Texas – Big Bend

The biggest attraction here is the Big Bend National Park. There are two great parks to stay while you explore all this area has to offer.

Mission RV Park
Stay in a quiet country setting while still being close to area attractions.

1420 Rv Dr, El Paso, TX 79928	(915) 859-1133 https://missionrvparklp.com/	All Year
$44	Military/Good Sam	Pet Breed
188 Spaces	Paved	24Width/70Length
Pavilion	RV Supplies	Pool, Cable

Fort Stockton RV Park
Enjoy activities or relax at your site.

3604 Koa Rd, Fort Stockton, TX 79735	(432) 395-2494 fortstocktonrvpark.com/	All Year
$40	Military/Good Sam	None
180 Spaces	Gravel	32Width/70Length
Pool, Ice	Laundry	Restaurant

Texas – Hill Country

The Hill Country region of Texas is full of great outdoor activities. It is also home to several great historic towns with wonderful attractions. There are plenty of parks to choose from in the area that will give you a great place to stay while exploring the surrounding area.

Oak Forest RV Resort
No matter why you need an RV park, this is your place to stay.

8207 Canoga Ave, Austin, TX 78724	(512) 697-4206 https://www.robertsresorts.com/	All Year
$55	Military/Good Sam	Pet Breed
289 Spaces	Paved	28Width/75Length
Internet	Playground	Cabins

Austin Lone Star RV Resort
Enjoy all the famous attractions of downtown Austin.

7009 S I-35, Austin, TX 78744	(512) 444-6322	All Year
$53-$80	Military/Good Sam	Pet Quantity, Breed
156 Spaces	Paved/Gravel	33Width/65Length
Gated	Internet	Rec. Hall

La Hacienda Sun RV Resort
This luxury RV resort is located near the metropolitan area of Austin.

5220 Hudson Bend Rd, Austin, TX 78734	(512) 266-8001	All Year
$52-$68	Military/Good Sam	Pet Breed
181 Spaces	Paved	40Width/90Length
Cabins	Pool	Cable

Summit Vacation & RV Resort
Located along the beautiful Guadalupe River.

13105 River Rd, New Braunfels, TX 78132	(830) 964-2531 summitresorttexas.com/	All Year
$34-$54	Military/Good Sam	Pet Breed
106 Spaces	Paved	45Width/80Length
Shuffleboard	Cabins	Tennis

Yogi Bear's Jellystone Park
A park designed for family fun and offering everything.

12915 Fm 306,	(830) 256-0088	All Year

Canyon Lake, TX 78133	https://jellystonehillcountry.com/	
$54-$83	Military	RV Age, Pet Breed
78 Spaces	Paved	15Width/50Length
Cabins, Firewood	Snack Bar, Pool	Guest Services

Alsatian RV Resort
A peaceful, scenic country setting.

1581 County Road 4516, Castroville, TX 78009	(830) 931-9190 http://www.alsatianresort.com/	All Year
$40-$95	Military/Good Sam	None
67 Spaces	Paved	41Width/110Length
Driving Range	Internet	Cabins

Parkview Riverside RV Park
A beautiful riverfront park in the heart of the Texas hill country.

2561 County Road 350, Concan, TX 78838	(830) 232-4006 parkviewriversiderv.com/	All Year
$48-$67	Military/Good Sam	None
99 Spaces	Paved	28Width/65Length
Firewood	Fishing Supplies	Game Room

Yogi Bear's Guadalupe River
A campground along the Guadalupe River.

2605 Junction Hwy 27, Kerrville, TX 78028	(830) 460-3262 https://jellystoneguadalupe.com/	All Year
$42-$140	Military	RV Age, Pet Quantity
160 Spaces	Paved	30Width/70Length
Lounge	Firewood	Rec. Hall

Buckhorn Lake Resort
This is the best place to choose as a base camp when exploring the Hill Country of Texas.

2885 Goat Creek Rd, Kerrville, TX 78028	(830) 895-0007 https://www.buckhornlake.com/	All Year
$46-$57	Military/Good Sam	Pet Quantity
132 Spaces	Paved	32Width/90Length
Pool	Playground	Internet

Sunset Point on Lake LBJ
A resort located on the constant level lake LBJ.

2322 Wirtz Dam Rd, Marble Falls, TX 78654	(830) 798-8199 http://sunsetpointlbj.com/	All Year

$55-$114	Military/Good Sam	RV Age, Pet Quantity, Breed
60 Spaces	Paved	30Width/70Length
Gated	Internet	Fishing Supplies

Hill Country Cottage and RV Resort
The perfect getaway for the winter months.

131 S Rueckle Rd, New Braunfels, TX 78130	(830) 625-1919	All Year
$56-$74	Military/Good Sam	Pet Quantity, Pet Breed
250 Spaces	Paved	30Width/80Length
Cabins	Snack Bar	Game Room

Pecan Park Riverside RV Park
Relax in a scenic, peaceful area along the San Marcos River.

50 Squirrel Run, San Marcos, TX 78666	(512) 396-0070 http://www.pecanpark.com/	All Year
$55-$69	Military/Good Sam	RV Age, Pet Breed
145 Spaces	Paved/Gravel	35Width/75Length
Playground	Pool	Rec. Hall

Texas – Prairies and Lakes

The prairie and lake region of Texas offers a range of options. You can view local attractions or enjoy outdoor activities. There are several great RV parks where you can stay and enjoy your vacation time.

Texas Ranch RV Resort
One of the newest and best destinations for your next Texas vacation.

9101 US-67, Alvarado, TX 76009	(817) 295-5594 https://txranchresort.com/	All Year
$60	Good Sam	Pet Breed
95 Spaces	Gravel	37Width/72Length
Internet	RV Supplies	Cable, Pool

Treetops RV Resort
The most beautiful place to stay in the Metroplex.

1901 W Arbrook Blvd, Arlington, TX 76015	(817) 467-7943	All Year
$55-$66	Military/Good Sam	Pet Size, Quantity, Breed
174 Spaces	Paved	25Width/70Length
Cable, Pool	Patios, Tables	Internet

Shady Creek RV Park
All the amenities you expect in a resort park.

1893 Fm 1385, Aubrey, TX 76227	(972) 347-5384 shadycreekrvpark.com/	All Year
$60	Military/Good Sam	Pet Breed
261 Spaces	Paved	35Width/65Length
Rec.Hall	Pool	RV Wash

Hwy 71 RV Park
This is an extraordinary area of Texas.

931 Union Chapel Rd, Cedar Creek, TX 78612	(512) 321-7275 https://hwy71rvpark.com/	All Year
$30-$50	Military/Good Sam	Pet Breed
129 Spaces	Paved	32Width/70Length
Gated	Internet	Cable

Hidden Creek RV Resort
Here you'll have a luxurious camping experience.

5780 E State Highway 21, Bryan, TX 77808	(979) 778-1200 http://www.hiddencreekrv.com/	All Year
$49-$68	Military /Good Sam	RV Age, Pet Quantity, Breed
98 Spaces	Paved	30Width/60Length
Playground	Pool	Internet

Canton Creek RV Park
Nightly, weekly, and monthly rates available.

32891 State Highway 64, Wills Point, TX 75169	(903) 865-6000 cantoncreekrvpark.com	All Year
$40-$45	Military/Good Sam	Pet Breed
50 Spaces	Gravel	30Width/65Length
Horseshoes	Rentals	Pool

Mill Creek Ranch Resort
Embrace nature with first-class amenities at this premier resort destination.

1880 N Trade Days Blvd, Canton, TX 75103	(903) 567-6020 https://millcreekranchresort.com/	All Year
$39-$69	Military/Good Sam	None
100 Spaces	Paved	32Width/100Length
Game Room, Firewood	Cable, Laundry	Paddle Boats, Rentals

Bennett's RV Ranch
Relax or plan a day of camping fun at this park.

3101 Old Granbury Rd, Granbury, TX 76049	(817) 279-7500 Website	All Year
$40	Military/Good Sam	Pet Quantity, Pet Breed
44 Spaces	Paved	30Width/68Length
Playground	Rec. Hall	Laundry

Traders Village RV Park
Conveniently located off the interstate.

2602 Mayfield Rd, Grand Prairie, TX 75052	(972) 647-8205	All Year
$42-$45	Military/Good Sam	Pet Size, Quantity, Breed
126 Spaces	Paved	21Width/60Length
Shuffleboard	Pool	ATM, RV Supplies

The Vineyards Campground

A nationally acclaimed park with a peaceful setting and lakefront views.

1501 N Dooley St, Grapevine, TX 76051	(888) 329-8993 vineyardscampground.com/	All Year
$49-$74	Military/Good Sam	None
93 Spaces	Paved	40Width/85Length
Bike Rentals	Frisbee Golf	Planned Activities

Colorado Landing RV Park

Stay in a peaceful setting along the Colorado River.

64 E Bluff Vw, La Grange, TX 78945	(979) 968-9465 https://www.coloradolanding.com/	All Year
$40	Military/Good Sam	Pet Breed
98 Spaces	Paved	30Width/90Length
Horseshoes	Internet	Pool

Bluebonnet Ridge RV Park

Stay in a relaxing country setting while enjoying Texan hospitality.

16543 FM 429, Terrell, TX 75161	(972) 524-9600 https://www.bluebonnetrv.com/	All Year
$45	Military/Good Sam	RV Age, Pet Quantity, Breed
150 Spaces	Paved	33Width/90Length
Gym, Tennis	Pavilion, Cable	Pool, Internet

I 35 RV Park

A convenient park with easy access off the interstate and accessible sites.

15131 North I-35, Elm Mott, TX 76640	(254) 829-0698 https://www.i35rvpark.com/	All Year
$43-$46	Military/Good Sam	None
249 Spaces	Paved	24Width/75Length
Rec. Hall	Internet	Breakfast

Oak Creek RV Park

Enjoy quality services and facilities at this top-rated park.

7652 W Interstate 20, Weatherford, TX 76088	(817) 594-0200 https://oakcreekrvpark.com/	All Year
$45	Good Sam	None
125 Spaces	Paved	30Width/70Length
Lodge Room	Cable	Internet

Texas – Piney Woods

This area of Texas is home to historical sites and lots of outdoor activity options. Whether you want to plan an adventure or simply sit back and enjoy the area for the winter months, you'll find something you like here.

Bushman's RV Park
A top-rated RV park with unique amenities.

51152 US Highway 69 N, Bullard, TX 75757	(903) 894-8221 bushmansrvpark.com/	All Year
$39	Military/Good Sam	None
97 Spaces	Paved	40Width/70Length

Leisure Lane RV Resort
A top-rated resort with many amenities.

15406 FM 3083, Conroe, TX 77302	(936) 231-2313 https://leisurelanervresort.com/	All Year
$55	Military/Good Sam	Pet Breed
90 Spaces	Paved	35Width/75Length
Gated	Internet	Pool, Cable

Summer Breeze USA Conroe
A family-friendly resort with beautiful grounds and amenities.

3043 Waukegan Rd, Conroe, TX 77306	(936) 264-2854 https://summerbreezeusa.com/	All Year
$50-$65	Military/Good Sam	Pet Quantity, Pet Breed
92 Spaces	Gravel	30Width/70Length
Gated, Internet	Cabins, Pool	Playground

Shallow Creek RV Resort
Located near Gladewater's Antique District.

5261 State Highway 135, Gladewater, TX 75647	(903) 984-4513 http://www.shallowcreek.com/	All Year
$40	Good Sam	RV Age, Pet Quantity, Breed
63 Spaces	Paved	31Width/90Length
Golf, Gym	Internet	Pool, Cable

Fernbrook Park
This is the best place to stay while you explore the Piney Woods area of East Texas.

2073 Fm 2011, Longview, TX 75603	(903) 643-8888 https://www.fernbrookpark.com/	All Year

$45-$50	Good Sam	Pet Quantity, Pet Breed
108 Spaces	Paved	34Width/77Length
Internet, Pool	Cable, Games	Pavilion

Tyler Oaks RV Resort
Visit the nearby American Freedom Museum.

10855 Highway 69 N, Tyler, TX 75706	(430) 235-2030 https://tyleroaksrvresort.com/	All Year
$38-$43	Military/Good Sam	Pet Quantity, Pet Breed
119 Spaces	Paved	35Width/72Length
Gated	Firewood	Games

Lake Conroe RV
Rent one of the many onsite boats or use your own.

11720 Thousand Trl, Willis, TX 77318	(855) 826-2336	All Year
$52-$55	Good Sam	Pet Quantity, 14 Day Max
363 Spaces	Paved/Gravel	30Width/70Length
Boat Rental	Playground	Rec. Hall

Texas – Southern Plains

A beautiful place to stay if you want to visit historical sites or plan an outdoor adventure. There are a number of parks where you can stage day activities. Some are closer to town attractions while others are closer to outdoor activities.

Winter Ranch RV Resort
Surround yourself with citrus trees in a subtropical setting.

600 State Highway 495, Alamo, TX 78516	(956) 781-1358 https://www.rvresorts.com/winter-ranch.html	All Year
$45	Military/Good Sam	None
688 Spaces	Paved	30Width/60Length
Gated	Internet	Pool

Trophy Gardens
South Texas is your place for a winter destination.

800 Fm 495, Alamo, TX 78516	(956) 787-7717 https://www.rvresorts.com/trophy-gardens.html	All Year
$45	Military/Good Sam	None
699 Spaces	Paved	35Width/60Length
Pool	Gated	Internet

Alamo Rose RV Resort
Just an hour from South Padre Island.

938 S Alamo Rd, Alamo, TX 78516	(956) 783-2600	All Year
$45	Military/Good Sam	None
435 Spaces	Paved	30Width/50Length
Pool	Rec. Hall	Shuffleboard

Casa Del Valle RV Resort
The perfect place to relax and enjoy the beauty of the Rio Grande Valley.

1048 N Alamo Rd, Alamo, TX 78516	(956) 783-5008	All Year
$20-$38	Military/Good Sam	None
368 Spaces	Paved	30Width/70Length
Internet	Gated	Rec. Hall

Kenwood RV Resort

The mild winter climate makes this a great vacation destination.

1201 N Main St Lot 1, La Feria, TX 78559	(956) 797-1851	All Year
$20-$39	Military/Good Sam	Pet Quantity, Pet Breed
278 Spaces	Paved	28Width/45Length
Gated	Horseshoes	Shuffleboard

VIP-La Feria RV Park

This 55+ community offers a unique experience.

300 E Expy 83, La Feria, TX 78559	(956) 797-1043 http://viplaferia.com/	All Year
$37-$40	Good Sam	55+, Pet Size, Quantity
360 Spaces	Paved	30Width/60Length
Activities	Rec. Hall	Game Room

Bentsen Palm Village RV Resort

One of the top RV resorts in the United States.

2500 S Bentsen Palm Dr. Ste 267B, Palmview, TX 78572	(956) 585-5568 https://www.bentsenpalm.com/	All Year
$49-$69	Good Sam	Pet Quantity
233 Spaces	Paved	41Width/80Length
Laundry	Internet	Rentals

Bluebonnet RV Resort

The goal of this park is outstanding customer service.

16543 FM 429, Terrell, TX 75161	(972) 524-9600 https://www.bluebonnetrv.com/	All Year
$38	Military/Good Sam	Pet Quantity
332 Spaces	Paved	25Width/50Length
Pool	Gated	Internet

Tropic Star RV Resort

Just an hour from Gulf Shore Beaches so you can relax or enjoy water sports.

1401 S Cage Blvd, Pharr, TX 78577	(956) 787-5957 https://www.rvresorts.com/tropic-star.html	All Year
$45	Military/Good Sam	Pet Quantity
1182 Spaces	Paved	30Width/60Length
Activities	Putting Green	Internet

Tip O Texas RV Resort
The best place to spend your winter and relax during your stay.

101 E Sioux Rd, Pharr, TX 78577	(956) 787-9959	All Year
$45	Military/Good Sam	Pet Quantity, Pet Breed
846 Spaces	Paved	25Width/55Length
Internet	Laundry	Rentals

Texas Trails RV Resort
Pharr is a great place to shop with lots of dining options.

501 W Owassa Rd, Pharr, TX 78577	(956) 787-6538	All Year
$45	Military/Good Sam	Pet Quantity
866 Spaces	Paved	30Width/60Length
Pool	Gated	Rentals

Travelers World RV Resort
The closest RV resort to the River Walk and the Alamo.

2617 Roosevelt Ave, San Antonio, TX 78214	(210) 532-8310	All Year
$53-$58	Military/Good Sam	Pet Quantity, Pet Breed
165 Spaces	Paved	30Width/70Length
Rentals	Gym, Cable	Playground

Admiralty RV Resort
Close to Sea World with a free shuttle to take you there.

1485 N Ellison Dr, San Antonio, TX 78251	(210) 647-7878 admiraltyrvresort.com	All Year
$55-$75	Military/Good Sam	Pet Quantity, Pet Breed
198 Spaces	Paved	22Width/60Length
Rec.Hall	Activities	Rentals

Blazing Star Luxury RV Resort
Relax or enjoy a planned activity.

1120 West Loop # 1604 N., San Antonio, TX 78251	(210) 680-7827	All Year
$52-$83	Military, Good Sam	None
229 Spaces	Paved	30Width/55Length
Planned Activities	Outdoor Games	Pool, Rentals

Tejas Valley RV Park

Close to everything in a quiet setting.

13080 Potranco Rd, San Antonio, TX 78245	(210) 679-7715 https://www.tejasvalleyrvpark.com/	All Year
$30-$45	Military/Good Sam	Pet Quantity, Pet Breed
117 Spaces	Paved	35Width/60Length
Pool	Internet	Rentals

Greenlake RV Resort

A five star RV resort and a fine RV vacation destination.

10842 Green Lake St, San Antonio, TX 78223	(210) 467-9178 https://www.qualityrvresorts.com	All Year
$38-$60	Good Sam	None
237 Spaces	Paved	30Width/65Length
Internet	Pool	Rec. Hall

Stone Creek RV Park

Offering a western theme with a taste of the Old West.

18905 Interstate 35 N, Schertz, TX 78154	(830) 609-7759 http://www.stonecreekrvpark.com/	All Year
$46-$49	Military/Good Sam	Pet Breed
231 Spaces	Paved	33Width/60Length
Pool	Rec. Hall	Pavilion

Alamo City RV Park

Offering the closest and easiest access to the San Antonio Rodeo Grounds.

1011 Gembler Rd, San Antonio, TX 78219	(210) 337-6501 https://www.alamocityrv.com	All Year
$45-$60	Military/Good Sam	Pet Breed
162 Spaces	Paved	30Width/60Length
Pool	Guest Services	Games

Snow to Sun RV Resort

A relaxed setting with exceptional convenience.

1701 N International Blvd, Weslaco, TX 78599	(956) 968-0322	All Year
$22-$37	Military/Good Sam	Pet Quantity, Pet Breed
489 Spaces	Paved	25Width/50Length
Shuffleboard	Pool	Model Rentals

Texas – Gulf Coast

Mont Belvieu RV Resort
The finest RV destination in Baytown.

6103 S FM 565, Baytown, TX 77523	(832) 900-2227 http://www.montbelvieurvresort.com/	All Year
$44-$78	Good Sam	None
242 Spaces	Paved	30Width/65Length
Rentals	Pool	Cable, Gated

Houston East RV Resort
Conveniently located on the interstate.

11810 I-10 E, Baytown, TX 77523	(281) 383-3618 https://houstoneastrvresort.com/	All Year
$44-$54	Military/Good Sam	Pet Quantity, Pet Breed
146 Spaces	Paved	30Width/70Length
Lodge Room	Cabins	Gated, Internet

Brazoria Lakes RV Resort
A beautiful RV destination.

109 Stephen F. Austin Trail, Brazoria, TX 77422	(979) 798-1000 https://www.qualityrvresorts.com/	All Year
$50-$77	Good Sam	None
266 Spaces	Paved	30Width/70Length
Outdoor Games	Golf Carts	Rec. Hall, Gated

Houston West RV Park
Located near the Typhoon Texas Water Park and Katy Mills Mall.

35303 Cooper Rd, Brookshire, TX 77423	(281) 375-5678 https://www.hwrvpark.com/	All Year
$40-$42	Military/Good Sam	Pet Quantity, Pet Breed
179 Spaces	Gravel	30Width/70Length
Internet	Pool	Game Room

Colonia Del Rey RV Park
The highest-rated park in Corpus Christi.

1717 Waldron Rd, Corpus Christi, TX 78418	(361) 937-2435 https://www.ccrvresorts.com/	All Year
$40-$48	Good Sam	Pet Breed
208 Spaces	Paved	25Width/70Length
Planned Activities	Pool, Cable	Horseshoes

El Campo Lost Lagoon RV Resort

Featuring the world's largest residential pool.

665 County Road 451, El Campo, TX 77437	(979) 275-1600 http://eclostlagoon.com/	All Year
$55-$80	Military/Good Sam	Pet Quantity, Pet Breed
227 Spaces	Paved	42Width/82Length
Pool	Snack Bar	Playground

Stella Mare RV Resort

The best place to immerse yourself in your vacation on Galveston Island.

3418 Stella Mare Ln, Galveston, TX 77554	(409) 632-7017 stellamarervresort.com/	All Year
$69-$91	Military/Good Sam	Pet Quantity, Pet Breed
195 Spaces	Paved	27Width/90Length
Rec. Hall	Pool	Internet

Jamaica Beach RV Resort

Enjoy a Jamaican style resort.

17200 Termini San Luis Pass Rd, Galveston, TX 77554	(409) 632-0200 https://www.jbrv.net/	All Year
$48-$62	Military/Good Sam	Pet Quantity, Pet Breed
181 Spaces	Paved	31Width/65Length
Fishing Supplies	Pool	Playground

Dellanera RV Park

Experience beautiful ocean views while walking along 1,000 feet of sandy beaches.

10901 San Luis Pass Rd, Galveston, TX 77554	(409) 797-5102 https://www.galveston.com/dellanera/	All Year
$41-$59	None	None
65 Spaces	Paved	20Width/55Length
Internet	Fishing Guides	Rec. Hall

Galveston Island RV Resort

Large, spacious sites and beautiful sunsets await you here.

23700 Termini San Luis Pass Rd, Galveston, TX 77554	(409) 200-2745 https://galvestonrv.com/	All Year
$43-$74	Military/Good Sam	RV Age, Pet Breed
116 Spaces	Paved	35Width/70Length

Tropic Winds RV Resort
Located in the heart of Rio Grande Valley.

1501 N. Loop 499, Harlingen, TX 78550	(888) 586-6356	All Year
$46	Military/Good Sam	Pet Quantity
535 Spaces	Paved	40Width/50Length
Shuffleboard	Gym	Pavilion

Park Place Estates
Relax or take part in the many planned activities.

5401 W Bus 83, Harlingen, TX 78552	(956) 412-4414 https://www.rvresorts.com/park-place-estates.html	All Year
$45	Military/Good Sam	None
847 Spaces	Paved	38Width/45Length
Tennis, Cable	Rec. Hall	Activities

Fig Tree RV Resort
There is plenty to do here while you enjoy the sunny winter months.

15257 W Frontage Rd, Harlingen, TX 78552	(956) 423-6699 http://figtreervresort.com	All Year
$33	Good Sam	Pet Size, Breed
197 Spaces	Paved	35Width/50Length
Rec. Hall	Shuffleboard	Internet

San Jacinto Riverfront RV Park
Enjoy a peaceful, laidback riverfront atmosphere.

540 S Main St, Highlands, TX 77562	(281) 426-6919 http://www.sjriverfrontrvresort.com/	All Year
$55-$89	Good Sam	None
310 Spaces	Paved	30Width/70Length
Activities	Gated	Internet

Hitchcock RV Park
Conveniently located off the interstate.

8330 Hwy 6, Hitchcock, TX 77563	(409) 986-5090 http://www.hitchcockrv.com/	All Year
$50	Military/Good Sam	RV Age, Pet Breed
60 Spaces	Paved	30Width/75Length
Internet	Gated	Guest Services

Allstar RV Resort
Located less than a mile off the highway.

10650 SW Plaza Ct, Houston, TX 77074	(713) 981-6814 https://www.qualityrvresorts.com/	All Year
$47-$65	Good Sam	None
126 Spaces	Paved	27Width/60Length
RV Supplies	Pool	Rec. Hall

Advanced RV Resort
Just minutes from Houston area attractions.

2850 S Sam Houston Pkwy E, Houston, TX 77047	(713) 433-6950 https://advancedrvpark.com/	All Year
$64-$69	Military/Good Sam	RV Age, Pet Breed
230 Spaces	Paved	30Width/65Length
Gated	Rec. Hall	Game Room

Traders Village RV Park
Here is your opportunity to shop for anything and get the best bargains.

7979 N Eldridge Pkwy, Houston, TX 77041	(281) 890-5500 http://tradersvillagervpark.com	All Year
$36	Good Sam	Pet Quantity, Pet Breed
284 Spaces	Paved	20Width/68Length
Shopping	Pool	Gated

Lakeview RV Resort
A five-star resort park with everything you could ever want.

11991 Main St, Houston, TX 77035	(713) 723-0973 https://www.qualityrvresorts.com	All Year
$56-$70	Good Sam	None
281 Spaces	Paved	13Width/66Length
Gated, Internet	Model Rentals, Pool	Rec. Hall, Patios

Southlake RV Resort
A five-star resort offering great amenities.

13701 Hycohen Rd, Houston, TX 77047	(832) 804-8088 https://www.qualityrvresorts.com	All Year
$56-$60	Good Sam	None
121 Spaces	Paved	31Width/60Length
Internet	Pavilion	Gated

Island RV Resort

Enjoy an island getaway with lots of recreation and entertainment.

700 6th St, Port Aransas, TX 78373	(361) 749-5600 https://www.islandrvresort.com/	All Year
$57	Good Sam	Pet Quantity, Pet Breed
200 Spaces	Paved	24Width/60Length
Pool	Internet	Rec. Hall

Texas Lakeside RV Resort

Stay a day, a week, or longer at this beautiful RV resort.

2499 W Austin St, Port Lavaca, TX 77979	(361) 551-2267 http://www.texaslakesidervresort.com/	All Year
$50-$65	Military/Good Sam	RV Age, Pet Breed
178 Spaces	Paved	32Width/85Length
Activities	Fishing Supplies	Rec. Hall

Sea Breeze RV Community Resort

A great location near Corpus Christi.

1026 Sea Breeze Ln, Portland, TX 78374	(361) 643-0744 http://seabreezerv.com/	All Year
$55-$59	Military/Good Sam	Pet Quantity, Pet Breed
164 Spaces	Gravel	22Width/60Length
Pool	Activities	Fishing Guides

Ancient Oaks RV Park

Enjoy beautiful grounds in a family-friendly park.

1222 Highway 35 S, Rockport, TX 78382	(361) 729-5051 http://properties.camping.com/	All Year
$35-$45	Good Sam	RV Age, Pet Breed
165 Spaces	Paved	24Width/60Length
Activities	Firewood	Game Room

Lagoons RV Resort

The premier resort in the coastal bend area.

600 Enterprise Blvd, Rockport, TX 78382	(361) 729-7834 https://www.lagoonsrv.com/	All Year
$50	Military/Good Sam	RV Age, Pet Breed
360 Spaces	Paved	26Width/70Length
Activities	Cable	Cabins, Pool

Lone Star Jellystone Park
A friendly, clean, and active atmosphere.

34843 Betka Rd, Waller, TX 77484	(979) 826-4111 https://lonestarjellystone.com/	All Year
$49-$78	Military/Good Sam	Pet Quantity, Pet Breed
154 Spaces	Paved	23Width/55Length
Snack Bar	Cable	Firewood

Utah

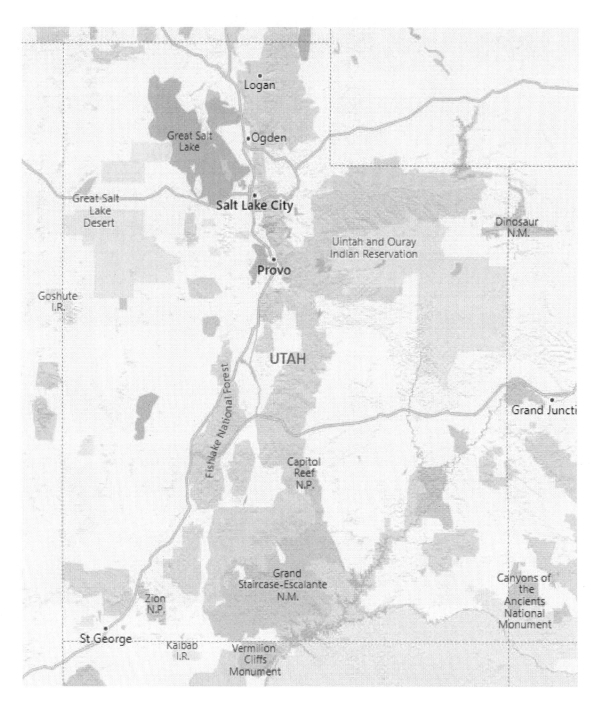

Utah is a state of rugged wilderness and bustling cities. There are plenty of outdoor activities and day trips to enjoy when staying at any of the parks in this state.

Mountain Valley RV Resort

Located in the beautiful Heber Valley.

2120 S Highway 40, Heber City, UT 84032	(435) 657-6100 https://mountainvalleyrv.com/	All Year
$40-$79	Military/Good Sam	None
150 Spaces	Paved	30Width/75Length
Rec. Hall	Activities	Rentals

WillowWind RV Park

A great place to stay while exploring all the National Parks in the area.

80 S 1150 W, Hurricane, UT 84737	(435) 635-4154 http://www.willowwindrvpark.com/	All Year
$45-$55	Military/Good Sam	Pet Breed
176 Spaces	Paved	25Width/66Length

Moab Valley RV Resort

Excellent camping near Arches National Park.

1773 N Highway 191, Moab, UT 84532	(435) 259-4469	All Year
$44-$84	Military/Good Sam	None
69 Spaces	Paved/Gravel	24Width/58Length
Pool	Rentals	Cable

Goulding's Monument Valley Campground

Take a tour guided by local Navajos.

2000 S Main St, Monument Valley, UT 84536	(435) 727-3235	All Year
$39-$62	Military/Good Sam	None
66 Spaces	Paved	32Width/60Length
Pool	Lodge Room	Firewood

Lakeside RV Campground

A beautiful country setting located close to everything.

4000 W Center St, Provo, UT 84601	(801) 373-5267 http://lakesidervcampground.com/	All Year
$39-$42	Military/Good Sam	None
125 Spaces	Paved/Gravel	22Width/65Length
Playground	Firewood	Pool

Salt Lake City KOA
Enjoy miles of riverside trails.

1400 West North Temple, Salt Lake City, UT 84116	(801)328-0224 https://koa.com/campgrounds/salt-lake-city/	All Year
$50-$79	Military	None
183 Spaces	Paved	26Width/60Length
Playground	Rentals	Pool

McArthur's Temple View RV Resort
Located in the heart of St George.

975 S Main St, Saint George, UT 84770	(435) 673-6400 https://www.templeviewrv.com/	All Year
$42	Military/Good Sam	Pet Breed
270 Spaces	Paved	30Width/60Length
Activities	Shuffleboard	Game Room

Zion River Resort RV Park
Minutes from Zion National Park.

730 E Sr 9, Virgin, UT 84779	(435) 635-8594 https://www.zionriverresort.com/	All Year
$37-$74	Military/Good Sam	Pet Quantity, Pet Breed
112 Spaces	Paved	30Width/65Length
Firewood	Rentals	Pool

Vermont

Vermont is a small state packed with things to do. Whether you want to spend your days antique shopping, relaxing, or taking part in an outdoor adventure, you'll find it here. There are two excellent RV parks where you can stay while you explore this wonderful state.

Lone Pine Campsites
The focus here is to make your stay as enjoyable as possible.

52 Sunset View Rd, Colchester, VT 05446	(802) 878-5447 lonepinecampsites.com/	May 1 to October 15
$48-$90	Military/Good Sam	Pet Quantity
280 Spaces	Paved	30Width/66Length
Internet	Pool	Tennis

Limehurst Lake Campground
Camp along the beautiful shores of Limehurst Lake.

4104 VT Rt 14, Williamstown, VT 05679	(802) 433-6662 https://www.limehurstlake.com/	May 1 to October 15
$45-$50	Good Sam	Pet Breed
57 Spaces	Gravel	20Width/70Length
Internet, Snack Bar	Boat Rentals	Snack Bar

Virginia

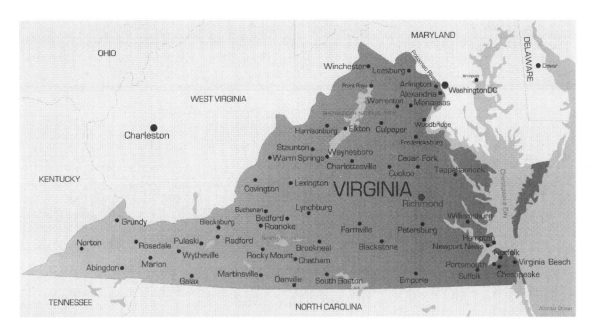

Virginia is a state full of wonderful outdoor activities. There are mountains, valleys, and even sandy beaches. There are also historic towns and sports activities. There is no shortage of things to enjoy during your stay here. There are several parks to choose from that will put you near the activities you want to enjoy.

Americamps RV Resort
Easy access on and off the interstate.

11322 Air Park Rd, Ashland, VA 23005	(804) 798-5298	All Year
$47-$96	Military/Good Sam	14 Day Max Stay
200 Spaces	Paved	30Width/68Length
Internet	Pool	Rec.Hall

Chesapeake Campgrounds
Enjoy a range of wonderful outdoor activities.

693 George Washington Chesapeake, VA 23323	(757) 485-0149 https://chesapeakecampgroundva.com	All Year
$24-$43	None	None
140 Spaces	Paved	30Width/50Length
Mini Golf	Tennis	Driving Range

Misty Mountain Camp Resort
Enjoy a relaxing time at the foothills of the Blue Ridge Mountains.

56 Misty Mountain Rd, Greenwood, VA 22943	(888) 647-8900 mistymountaincampresort.com/	All Year
$38-$62	Military/Good Sam	Pet Quantity
127 Spaces	Paved/Gravel	30Width/100Length
Playground	Firewood	Fishing

Cozy Acres Campground
Thirty minutes from the capital city of Richmond.

2177 Ridge Rd, Powhatan, VA 23139	(804) 598-2470 http://cozyacres.com/	April 1 to November 15
$46-$77	Military/Good Sam	None
116 Spaces	Paved/Gravel	35Width/70Length
Pool	Cabins	Game Room

Grey's Point Camp
Enjoy a range of water activities and fishing in the Chesapeake Bay.

3601 Grey's Point Road, Topping, VA 23169	(877) 570-2267	April 1 to November 15
$40-$90	Military/Good Sam	None
700 Spaces	Paved	30Width/62Length
Paddle Boats	Fishing Supplies	Playground

Bethpage Camp-Resort
Stay somewhere great along the Chesapeake Bay.

679 Browns Ln, Urbanna, VA 23175	(877) 570-2267	All Year
$45-$95	Military/Good Sam	None
894Spaces	Paved	30Width/70Length
Activities	Restaurant	Internet

North Landing Beach RV Resort
During your stay, enjoy access to a private sandy beach.

161 Princess Anne Rd, Virginia Beach, VA 23457	(757) 426-6241 https://northlandingbeach.com/	All Year
$51-$89	Military/Good Sam	None
160 Spaces	Paved/Gravel	45Width/70Length
Beach Access	Gated	Playground

American Heritage RV Park
Enjoy a relaxing stay among green meadows and woodlands.

146 Maxton Ln, Williamsburg, VA 23188	(757) 566-2133 http://americanheritagervpark.com/	All Year
$50-$85	Military/Good Sam	None
145 Spaces	Paved	30Width/60Length
Cable	Rentals	Pool

Washington

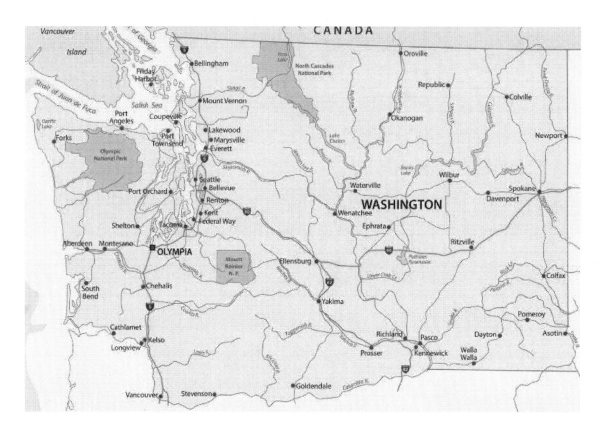

Washington is a beautiful state full of natural wonders and breathtaking scenery.

Northern Quest RV Resort
Stay in high-end luxury on your next vacation to Washington.

100 N Hayford Rd, Airway Heights, WA 99001	(877) 871-6772 https://www.northernquest.com/	All Year
$60-$75	Military/Good Sam	Pet Quantity, 14 Day Max
67 Spaces	Paved	50Width/80Length
Casino, Gated	Internet, Restaurant	Gym, Cabins

Toutle River RV Resort
One of the largest and best-equipped resorts in the Northwest.

150 Happy Trails Rd, Castle Rock, WA 98611	(360) 274-8373 http://www.greatrvresort.com/	All Year
$49	Good Sam	Pet Breed
306 Spaces	Paved	35Width/100Length
Internet, RV supplies	Game Room	Activities

Midway RV Park

Located at the midpoint between Seattle and Portland.

3200 Galvin Rd, Centralia, WA 98531	(800) 600-3204 http://www.midwayrvparkwa.com/	All Year
$46-$54	Military/Good Sam	Pet Size, Pet Breed
62 Spaces	Paved	27Width/66Length
Laundry	Internet	Games

Granite Lake Premier RV Resort

Lakefront sites at the confluence of the Snake and Clearwater Rivers.

306 Granite Lake Dr, Clarkston, WA 99403	(509) 751-1635 http://www.premierrvresorts.com	All Year
$53-$60	Military/Good Sam	None
75 Spaces	Paved	28Width/60Length
Activities	Guest Services	Gym, Cabins

Columbia Sun RV Resort

A new resort designed for the largest of RV rigs.

103907 Wiser Pkwy, Kennewick, WA 99338	(509) 420-4880 https://www.columbiasunrvresort.com/	All Year
$45-$60	Military/Good Sam	Pet Quantity, Pet Breed
145 Spaces	Paved	38Width/115Length
Model Rentals	Game Room	Internet

Liberty Lake RV Campground

Within walking distance to shopping, entertainment, and dining.

22751 E Appleway Ave, Liberty Lake, WA 99019	(509) 868-0567 libertylakervcampground.com/	All Year
$55-$78	Good Sam	Pet Quantity, Pet Breed
120 Spaces	Paved	32Width/90Length
Internet	Playground	Pool

Wine Country RV Park

Located in the center of wine country.

330 Merlot Dr, Prosser, WA 99350	(509) 786-5192 http://www.winecountryrvpark.com/	All Year
$38-$66	Military/Good Sam	None
125 Spaces	Paved	29Width/70Length
Internet	Firewood	Rec. Hall

Horn Rapids RV Resort
This is the best place to stay when in the area.

2640 Kingsgate Way, Richland, WA 99354	(509) 375-9913 http://hornrapidsrvresort.com/	All Year
$47	Military/Good Sam	Pet Breed
225 Spaces	Paved	24Width/70Length
Cable	Internet	Pool, Hot Tub

North Spokane RV Campground
Enjoy playing or relaxing.

10904 N Newport Hwy, Spokane, WA 99218	(509) 315-5561 northspokanervcampground.com/	All Year
$55-$78	Military/Good Sam	Pet Quantity/Pet Breed
87 Spaces	Paved	32Width/70Length
Playground	Cable	Internet

Columbia Riverfront RV Park
A quiet park along the beach of the Columbia River.

1881 Dike Rd, Woodland, WA 98674	(360) 225-2227 http://columbiariverfrontrvpark.com/	All Year
$46-$54	Military/Good Sam	Pet Quantity, Pet Breed
76 Spaces	Paved	28Width/80Length
Playground	Internet	Horseshoes, Pool

West Virginia

West Virginia offers you plenty of opportunities to explore history or the great outdoors. There is one park that stands out above the rest for a great vacation experience.

Huntington KOA Holiday
Camp in the wild and wonderful area of West Virginia.

290 Fox Fire Road, Milton, WV 25541	(304) 743-5622 https://koa.com/campgrounds/huntington/	All Year
$39-$80	None	None
110 Spaces	Paved	30Width/65Length
Lodge Room	Internet, Cabins	Fishing Supplies

Wisconsin

Wisconsin offers more than just cheese. There are wonderful towns to visit and outdoor adventures to plan. Come stay at one of the top parks in Wisconsin.

Baileys Grove Campground
Offering a peaceful park-like setting.

2552 County Road F, Baileys Harbor, WI 54202	(920) 839-2559 baileysgrovecampground.com/	May 1 to October 18
$41-$57	Military/Good Sam	Pet Breed
117 Spaces	Gravel	30Width/60Length
Internet	Pool	Game Room

Hayward KOA
A family fun destination in the Wisconsin North Woods.

11544 N US Highway 63, Hayward, WI 54843	(715) 634-2331 koa.com/campgrounds/hayward/	May 1 to October 6
$45-$69	None	None
200 Spaces	Gravel	35Width/50Length
Firewood	Snack Bar	Rentals

Milton KOA
A clean, modern facility with activities every weekend.

872 E State Rd 59, Milton, WI 53563	(608) 868-4141 https://koa.com/campgrounds/milton-wi/	April 25 to October 20
$42-$87	None	None
264 Spaces	Gravel	34Width/90Length
Planned Activities	Cabin Rentals	Internet

Wyoming

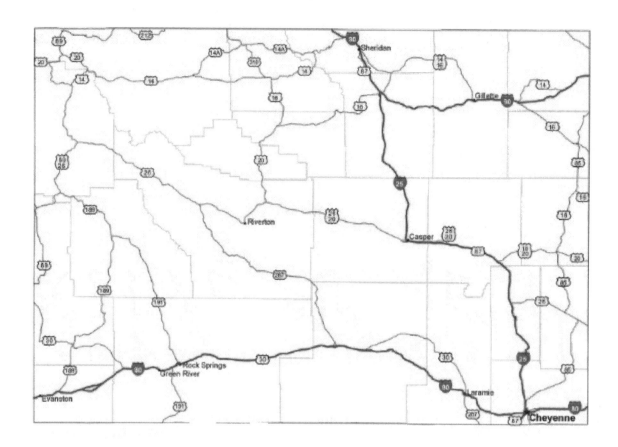

Wyoming is located on the Great Plains. There are many outdoor activities you can enjoy here. Plus, there are towns of all sizes to explore. Stay at one of the top three parks in Wyoming to enjoy your stay.

Deer Park
Located between Mt. Rushmore and Yellowstone.

146 US Highway 16 E, Buffalo, WY 82834	(307) 684-5722 http://deerparkrv.com/	May 1 to September 30
$39-$50	Military/Good Sam	None
67 Spaces	Gravel	25Width/65Length
Cabin Rentals	Internet	Firewood

Rivers Edge RV Resort
A large, upscale facility that is available year-round.

6820 Santa Fe Circle, Evansville, WY 82636	(307) 234-0042 http://www.riversedgervresort.net/	All Year

$41-$47	Military/Good Sam	None
73 Spaces	Gravel	35Width/65Length
Internet	Cabin Rentals	Playground

Mountain View RV Park
Located near the interstate for easy access to local attractions.

117 Government Valley Rd, Sundance, WY 82729	(307) 283-2270 mtnviewcampground.com/	April 1 to November 15
$39-$65	Military/Good Sam	None
56 Spaces	Gravel	26Width/60Length
Internet	Snack Bar	Cabin Rentals

Special Thanks

I would like to impart my sincere, heartfelt thanks to you, the reader of this guidebook. Thank you so much for taking an interest in what has become my life's work. I do hope you have gotten something positive out of your purchase.

I would also like to thank my friend Fred Bevins. He has been an amazing resource for curating the information in this book. As he has been traveling around the United States for nearly the past 20 years, his knowledge has been immense. Thanks, Fred.

I would also like to thank Sarah Edwards for proofreading this book for me. She came up with the idea of formating this book into tables to make it easier to read. Thank you, Sarah!

Countless others contributed their ideas and suggestions to me via social media. There are too many to name here, but I appreciate all of them. Thank you, Facebook and Twitter friends!

Conclusion

The years I have spent traveling the United States have been the most challenging, rewarding, and amazing years of my life. I wish I had started it sooner!

It's not always the cheapest way to travel, but when you're looking for some creature comforts and amenities during your travels, staying at an RV resort can be the answer.

Hopefully, this listing of privately owned campgrounds, RV parks, and resorts has been beneficial to you in your RV adventures.

Please don't forget to leave me a review wherever you purchased this book. Reviews really help me, not only for rankings, but I also take your suggestions to heart.

I will continue to make notes and keep track of the wonderful places to stay while living in an RV. I would have continued to update this book had it not been for my friends asking me to publish what I had compiled already.

Stay safe, and have fun on your RV trips!

Made in the USA
Columbia, SC
31 May 2020

98770142R00248